Chicago

"All you've got to do is decide to go
and the hardest part is over.

So go!"

TONY WHEELER, COFOUNDER – LONELY PLANET

THIS EDITION WRITTEN AND RESEARCHED BY
Karla Zimmerman,
Sara Benson

Contents

CLAYTON HAUCK FOR LONGMAN & EAGLE ©

BRUCE LEIGHTY / GETTY IMAGES ©

CHARLES COOK / GETTY IMAGES ©

(left) **Longman & Eagle p160** Savor a meal at this Michelin-starred tavern.
....
(above) **Navy Pier p69** Stroll around Chicago's most visited attraction.
....
(right) **Ron Santo statue p113** Pay tribute at Wrigley Field.
....

Andersonville & Uptown p126

Lake View & Wrigleyville p110

Logan Square & Humboldt Park p153

Lincoln Park & Old Town p96

Wicker Park, Bucktown & Ukrainian Village p137

Gold Coast p82

Near North & Navy Pier p67

Near West Side & Pilsen p164

The Loop p44

South Loop & Near South Side p178

Hyde Park & South Side p192

Welcome to Chicago

Steely skyscrapers, top chefs, rocking festivals – the Windy City will blow you away with its low-key cultured awesomeness.

Art & Architecture

It's hard to know what to gawk at first. High-flying architecture is everywhere, from the stratospheric, glass-floored Willis Tower to Frank Gehry's swooping silver Pritzer Pavilion to Frank Lloyd Wright's stained-glass Robie House. Whimsical public art studs the streets. So you're walking along and wham, there's an abstract Picasso statue that's not only cool to look at, you're allowed to go right up and climb on it. For art museums, take your pick: impressionist masterpieces at the massive Art Institute, psychedelic paintings at the mid-sized Museum of Mexican Art or outsider drawings at the small Intuit gallery.

Chowhounds' Delight

Loosen the belt. You've got a lot of eating to do. On the menu: peanut butter and banana-topped waffles for breakfast (at Stephanie Izard's Little Goat), a fig and goat-cheese-slathered elk sausage for lunch (at Hot Doug's hot-dog shop), and 20 courses of centrifuged, encapsulated molecular gastronomy for dinner (at Grant Achatz's Alinea).

You can also chow on a superb range of ethnic eats from Vietnamese pho to Mexican carnitas, Polish pierogi and Swedish almond tarts. Still hungry? Order a late-night deep-dish pizza.

Sports Fanatics

Chicago is a maniacal sports town, with a pro team for every season (two teams, in baseball's case). Watching a game is a local rite of passage, whether you slather on the blue and orange body paint for a Bears football game, join the raucous baseball crowd in Wrigley Field's bleachers, or plop down on a bar stool at the neighborhood tavern for whatever match is on TV. Count on making lots of spirited new friends. Should the excitement rub off and inspire you to get active yourself, the city's 24 beaches and 580 parks offer a huge array of play.

Rollicking Festivals

Chicago knows how to rock a festival. Between March and September it throws around 200 shindigs. The specialty is music. Blues Fest brings half a million people to Grant Park to hear guitar notes slide and bass lines roll, all for free. During Lollapalooza's three-day mega-party, rock bands thrash while the audience dances in an arm-flailing frenzy. Smaller, barbecue-scented street fests take place in the neighborhoods each weekend – though some rival downtown for star power on their stages (oh, hey, Olivia Newton-John at Northalsted Market Days).

Why I Love Chicago

By Karla Zimmerman, Author

I've lived in the city for 25 years, and I never get bored. There's something groovy going on any night of the week. Like tonight: should I see the Grant Park Orchestra playing Shostakovich's 5th Symphony in Millennium Park, or a guitar-drum duo called Earring at Empty Bottle? I love that Tibetan dumplings, Mexican carnitas and crème brûlée doughnuts are all equally, easily accessible from local eateries. I love how total strangers sitting next to each other in a bar watching a Blackhawks game become high-fiving pals by evening's end. Chicago really is my kind of town.

For more about our authors, see p320.

Top: Chicago's lakefront

Chicago's
Top 10

Art Institute of Chicago (p19)

1 The second-largest art museum in the country, the Art Institute houses a treasure trove from around the globe. The collection of impressionist and post-impressionist paintings is second only to those in France, and the number of surrealist works is tremendous. Wander the endless marble and glass corridors, and you'll find rooms stuffed with Japanese prints, Grecian urns, suits of armor, Grant Wood's *American Gothic*, Edward Hopper's *Nighthawks* and one very big, dotted Seurat. The Modern Wing dazzles with Picassos and Miros.

👁 *The Loop*

Millennium Park (p46)

2 It's the playful heart of the city, shining with whimsical public art. Go head, walk under Anish Kapoor's Cloud Gate – aka 'The Bean' – and touch its silvery smoothness. Let the human gargoyles of Jaume Plensa's Crown Fountain gush water on you to cool down in summer. Unfurl a blanket by Frank Gehry's swooping silver band shell as the sun dips, wine corks pop and gorgeous music fills the twilight air. Or try to find the secret garden abloom with prairie flowers and a wee, gurgling river.

BELOW: FRANK GEHRY'S JAY PRITZKER PAVILION

👁 *The Loop*

EDUCATION IMAGES / JIG / GETTY IMAGES ©

Sky-High Views
(p51)

3 For superlative seekers, Willis Tower is it: the city's tallest building (and one of the world's loftiest). Breathe deeply during the ear-popping, 70-second elevator ride to the 103rd floor Skydeck, then stride to one of the glass-enclosed ledges that juts out in mid-air. Look down 1450ft. Crikey. The lakeside John Hancock Center also rises high in the sky. Ascend to the 96th-floor lounge, order a cocktail and watch the city sparkle out around you. It's especially lovely at night.

TOP LEFT: VIEW FROM WILLIS TOWER (P51)

⊙ *The Loop*

Wrigley Field *(p112)*

4 A tangible sense of history comes alive at the 100-year-old baseball park, thanks to the hand turned scoreboard, iconic neon entrance sign, legendary curses and time-honored traditions that infuse games played here. No matter that the hapless Cubbies haven't won a championship since 1908 – shoveling down hot dogs and drinking Old Style beer in the raucous bleachers makes for an unforgettable afternoon. No tickets? No worries. Peep in the 'knot-hole,' a garage door–sized opening on Sheffield Ave, to watch the action for free.

🏃 *Lake View & Wrigleyville*

Architecture Cruises *(p265)*

5 Who cares if all the backward neck-bending causes a little ache? There's no better way to feel Chicago's steely power than from low on the water looking up while cloud-poking towers glide by and Iron bridges arch open to lead the way. The skyline takes on a surreal majesty as you float through its shadows on a river tour, and landmark after eye-popping landmark flashes by. Guides' architecture lessons carry on the breeze, so you'll know your Beaux Arts from International Style by day's end.

🏃 *Transport*

Public Art (p55)

6 You can't walk two blocks downtown without bumping into an extraordinary sculpture. The granddaddy is Picasso's *Untitled* (what the heck is it – an Afghan hound?), set smack in Daley Plaza. Jean Dubuffet's abstract creation is officially titled *Monument with Standing Beast* but everyone calls it 'Snoopy in a Blender.' Marc Chagall's grand mosaic *Four Seasons* is more recognizable, depicting Chicago scenes. And Alexander Calder's hulking, red-pink *Flamingo* does indeed look like the namesake bird, but only after you've had a few beers.

BELOW: *MONUMENT WITH STANDING BEAST* SCULPTURE (P55)

👁 **The Loop**

Comedy & Theater (p107)

7 A group of jokesters began performing intentionally unstructured skits in a Chicago bar a half-century ago, and voilà – improv comedy was born. Second City still nurtures the best in the biz, though several other improv theaters also work from booze-fueled suggestions that the audience hollers up. Among the city's 200 theaters are powerhouse drama troupes such as Hollywood-star-laden Steppen-wolf, and heaps of fringey, provocative 'off-Loop' companies. The coolest ones base admission cost on a dice roll, or let you pay what you can.

RIGHT: SECOND CITY (P107)

☆ **Lincoln Park & Old Town**

MELISSA FARLOW / NATIONAL GEOGRAPHIC SOCIETY / CORBIS ©

CHARLES COOK / GETTY IMAGES ©

Blues & Rock *(p189)*

8 In Chicago no genre is as iconic as the blues – the electric blues, to be exact. When Muddy Waters and friends plugged in their amps circa 1950, guitar grooves reached new decibel levels. Hear it in clubs around town, such as Buddy Guy's Legends, where the icon himself still takes the stage, or Rosa's Lounge, where it's a bit more down and dirty. The blues paved the way for rock 'n' roll, so it's no surprise that cool little clubs hosting edgy indie bands slouch on many a street corner.

LEFT: BUDDY GUY'S LEGENDS (P189)

☆ *South Loop & Near South Side*

Global Eats *(p252)*

9 During the last decade chefs such as Grant Achatz, Rick Bayless, Graham Elliot and many others put Chicago on the culinary map. They won a heap of James Beard awards, and suddenly international critics were dubbing Chicago one of the globe's top eating destinations. The beauty here is even the buzziest restaurants are accessible: they're visionary yet traditional, pubby at the core and decently priced. You can also dive into a superb range of ethnic eats in Chicago's neighborhoods, from Vietnamese pho to Mexican carnitas to Swedish almond tarts.

RIGHT: FRONTERA GRILL (P76)

✕ *Chicago Dining*

CHARLES COOK / GETTY IMAGES ©

PETER PEARSON / GETTY IMAGES ©

Navy Pier *(p69)*

10 Stretching away from the skyline and into the blue of Lake Michigan, half-mile long Navy Pier is Chicago's most-visited attraction. Its charms revolve around the cool breezes and sweet views, especially from the stomach-turning, 150ft Ferris wheel. High-tech rides, splash fountains, big boats and greasy snacks blow the minds of young ones. Live music, Shakespearean theater and whopping fireworks displays entertain everyone else. And by all means seek out the stained-glass museum and its pièce de résistance: stained-glass Michael Jordan.

◉ *Near North & Navy Pier*

What's New

Hostel Boom

Several independent, boutique-like hostels have opened recently. Most are set in lofty old buildings with hardwood floors, and they offer amenities such as rooftop decks for barbecues and common rooms with huge flat-screen TVs and video games. The best part is they're located in neighborhoods with great nightlife. So far three new hostels have popped up in Wicker Park and Bucktown, one in Wrigleyville and one in the Gold Coast.

Virgin Hotel

If it's not open yet it will be very soon: Virgin Hotel, the first of billionaire Richard Branson's empire, in the 27-story, art deco Dearborn Bank Building. (p222)

Little Goat

Complete with twirly stools and all-day breakfast such as the bacon syrup-sauced Fat Elvis waffles, Top Chef–winner Stephanie Izard's Little Goat is a diner for the foodie masses. (p171)

Constellation

The taste-making producer of Pitchfork Music Festival opened Constellation, an intimate club where progressive jazz and improvised music fill the air. (p122)

Logan Square

More and more pie shops, coffee roasters, craft distilleries and *Bon Appetit*-recommended restaurants keep opening in hep-cat Logan Square. (p153)

Laugh Factory

Chicago's Laugh Factory is an offshoot of the famed parent club in LA, bringing veteran stand-up comedians and quite a few rising stars to the mic. (p122)

Great Chicago Fire Festival

The inaugural Great Chicago Fire Festival pays homage to the 1871 city-torching conflagration in October, with funky illuminated sculptures by Redmoon Theater. (p176)

Hot Tix

Hot Tix, the half-price theater ticket broker, opened an outlet in the Block 37 shops downtown. It's open daily, as opposed to the other two locations that close on Monday. (p65)

Divvy

The city's bike-sharing program, called Divvy, makes it easy to wheel around thanks to a network of 4000 bicycles at 400-odd stations scattered around town. (p265)

Half Acre Tap Room

Half Acre was one of the first local craft brewers, and it's one of the first to open a no-frills tap room pouring just its own beers. Many more Chicago microbrewers are following its lead... (p116)

For more recommendations and reviews, see **lonelyplanet. com/chicago**

Need to Know

For more information, see Survival Guide (p261)

Currency
US dollar ($)

Language
English

Visas
Visitors from Canada, the UK, Australia, New Zealand, Japan and many EU countries do not need visas for stays of less than 90 days. Other nationals might (see http://travel.state.gov).

Money
ATMs widely available. Credit cards accepted at most hotels, restaurants and shops.

Cell Phones
Europe and Asia's GSM 900/1800 standard does not work in the USA. Consider buying a cheap local phone with a pay-as-you-go plan.

Time
Central Standard Time (GMT/UTC minus six hours).

Tourist Information
See www.choosechicago.com or visit the Chicago Cultural Center Visitors Center (Map p290; www.choosechicago.com; 77 E Randolph St; ☺9am-7pm Mon-Thu, 9am-6pm Fri & Sat, 10am-6pm Sun; 🛜; ⓜBrown, Orange, Green, Purple, Pink Line to Randolph).

Daily Costs

Budget:
Less than $100
➡ Dorm bed: $35–40
➡ Lunchtime specials: $10–15
➡ Transit day pass: $10
➡ Discount theater or blues club ticket: $10–25

Midrange:
$100–250
➡ Hotel or B&B double room: $100–200
➡ Dinner in a casual restaurant: $20–30
➡ Architecture boat tour: $40
➡ Cubs bleacher seat: $40–60

Top end:
Over $250
➡ Luxury hotel double room: $400
➡ Dinner at Alinea: $265
➡ Lyric Opera ticket: $200

Advance Planning

Three months before Book your hotel. Reserve at restaurants such as Alinea, Next, Topolobampo and Girl and the Goat.

One month before Browse www.goldstar.com for half-price tickets to theater, sports events and concerts.

One week before Check www.hottix.org for half-price theater tickets. Go online to buy discount cards (www.gochicago card.com or www.citypass.com) or tickets for Shedd Aquarium. Check www.chicagoreader.com to see entertainment options and make bookings.

Useful Websites

Lonely Planet (www.lonely planet.com/chicago) Destination information, hotel bookings and more.

Choose Chicago (www.choose chicago.com) Official tourism site with sightseeing and event info.

Chicagoist (www.chicagoist. com) Quirky take on food, arts and events.

Gapers Block (www.gapers block.com) News and events site with Chicago attitude.

WHEN TO GO

Peak season is June through August when it's warm and festivals rock. It's freezing between November and March, so bargains abound. December is festive.

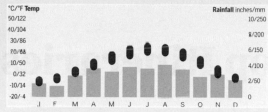

Arriving in Chicago

O'Hare International Airport The Blue Line El train ($5) runs 24/7. Trains depart every 10 minutes or so; they reach the city center in 40 minutes. Shuttle vans cost $32, taxis around $50.

Chicago Midway Airport The Orange Line El train ($3) runs between 4am and 1am. Trains depart every 10 minutes or so; they reach downtown in 30 minutes. Shuttle vans cost $27, taxis cost $30 to $40.

Union Station All trains arrive here, and Megabus arrives a block away. For transportation onward, the Blue Line Clinton stop is a few blocks south. The Brown, Orange, Purple and Pink Line station at Quincy is about a half-mile east. Taxis queue along Canal St outside the station entrance.

For much more on **arrival** see p262

Getting Around

The El (a system of elevated/subway trains) is the main way to move around the city. Buses are also useful for certain routes. Buy a day pass for $10 at El stations.

➡ **Train** El trains are fast, frequent and ubiquitous. Some lines operate 24/7; others between 4am and 1am.

➡ **Bus** Buses cover areas that the El misses. Most run at least from early morning until 10pm, some go later. Some don't run on weekends.

➡ **Taxi** Easy to find downtown, north to Andersonville and west to Wicker Park/Bucktown. But costly.

➡ **Boat** Water taxis travel along the river and lakefront and offer a fun way to reach the Museum Campus or Chinatown.

➡ **Bicycle** Abundant rental shops and the Divvy bike-share program make cycling a doable option.

For much more on **getting around** see p263

Sleeping

Accommodation will likely be your biggest expense in Chicago. The best digs are groovy, wired-up boutique hotels, especially those set in architectural landmarks. Several independent hostels have popped up over the past few years in fun, outlying neighborhoods such as Wicker Park and Wrigleyville. Enormous business hotels cater to conventioneers in the Loop and Near North. Low-key B&Bs are scattered in the Gold Coast, Wicker Park and Lake View and are often cheaper than hotels.

Useful Websites

➡ Chicago Bed & Breakfast Association (www.chicago -bed-breakfast.com) Represents 18 properties, with links to book.

➡ Choose Chicago (www. choosechicago.com) Options from the city's official website.

➡ Hotel Tonight (www. hoteltonight.com) National discounter with last-minute deals at funky boutique hotels; book via the free app.

For much more on **sleeping** see p215

Top Itineraries

Day One

The Loop (p44)

 You might as well dive right in with the big stuff. Take a boat or walking tour with the **Chicago Architecture Foundation** and ogle the most sky-scraping collection of buildings the US has to offer. Saunter over to **Millennium Park** to see 'the Bean' reflect the skyline and to splash under Crown Fountain's human gargoyles.

> **Lunch** The Gage (p61) dishes up Irish-tinged grub with a fanciful twist.

The Loop (p44)

Explore the **Art Institute of Chicago**, the nation's second-largest art museum. It holds masterpieces aplenty, especially impressionist and post-impressionist paintings (and paperweights). Then head over to **Willis Tower**, zip up to the 103rd floor and step out onto the glass-floored ledge. Yes, it is a long way down.

> **Dinner** Taxi or El to the West Loop to Little Goat (p171).

Near West Side & Pilsen (p164)

 The West Loop parties in the evening. Cocktail fans will want to try odd-but-delicious concoctions such as 'buttered popcorn' at the **Aviary**, recent Beard Award winner for best drinks in the nation. **Haymarket Pub & Brewery** pours great beers and has the Drinking and Writing Theater inside.

Day Two

Near North & Navy Pier (p67)

 Take a stroll on Michigan Ave – aka the **Magnificent Mile** – where big-name department stores ka-ching in a glittering row. Mosey over to **Navy Pier**. Take a spin on the Ferris wheel and seek out the cooler-than-you-think **Smith Museum of Stained Glass Windows**.

> **Lunch** Grab a bite on the pier at Harry Caray's Tavern (p78).

South Loop & Near South Side (p178)

Spend the afternoon at the Museum Campus (the water taxi from Navy Pier is a fine way to get there). Miles of aisles of dinosaurs and gemstones stuff the **Field Museum**. Whales, sharks and dolphins swim in the kiddie-mobbed **Shedd Aquarium**. Meteorites and supernovas are on view at the **Adler Planetarium**.

> **Dinner** Hop the Blue Line to Damen for bike-themed Handlebar (p144).

Wicker Park, Bucktown & Ukrainian Village (p137)

 Wander along Milwaukee Ave and take your pick of booming bars, indie rock clubs and and hipster shops. **Quimby's** shows the local spirit; the bookstore stocks zines and graphic novels, and is a linchpin of Chicago's underground culture. The **Double Door** and **Hideout** are sweet spots to catch a bad-ass band.

Osaka Garden (p197)

Day Three

Lincoln Park & Old Town (p96)

 Dip your toes in Lake Michigan at **North Avenue Beach**. Amble northward through the sprawling greenery of **Lincoln Park**. Stop at **Lincoln Park Zoo** to see lions and tigers and bears (the polar kind). Pop into **Lincoln Park Conservatory** to smell exotic blooms.

> **Lunch** Munch a char-dog and cheddar fries at Wiener's Circle (p104).

Lake View & Wrigleyville (p110)

Make your way north to **Wrigley Field** for an afternoon baseball game. The atmospheric, century-old ballpark hosts the woefully cursed Cubs. Afterward practice your home-run swing (and beer drinking) at **Sluggers**, one of many high-fiving bars that circle the stadium.

> **Dinner** Mmm, mussels and *frites* at Hopleaf (p132).

Andersonville & Uptown (p126)

Andersonville has several fine taverns to hang out at and sink a pint, like **Simon's**. Or see what's on at the **Neo-Futurists** theater. Jazz hounds can venture to the **Green Mill**, a timeless venue to hear jazz, watch a poetry slam or swill a martini. Al Capone used to groove on it.

Day Four

Hyde Park & South Side (p192)

 The **Museum of Science & Industry** isn't kidding around with its acres of exhibits. There's a German U-boat, mock tornado and exquisite doll house for starters. **Osaka Garden** floats nearby. Groovy university bookstores such as **57th Street Books** and **Powell's** offer shelves of weighty tomes.

> **Lunch** Colorful cafe Medici (p203) makes a mean thin-crust pizza.

Hyde Park & South Side (p192)

Linger in Hyde Park, as there's more to do. Architecture buffs can tour **Robie House**, Frank Lloyd Wright's Prairie-style masterpiece. Check out the **Nuclear Energy sculpture**, where the atomic age began. Make your way north to the Kenwood neighborhood to see **Obama's house** and Muhammad Ali's former pad.

> **Dinner** Sip whiskey while waiting for a table at Longman & Eagle (p160).

Logan Square & Humboldt Park (p153)

Nightlife options abound in Logan Square. Knock back slurpable beers at **Revolution Brewing**. See what arty band is playing for free at wee **Whistler**. Or imbibe at **Scofflaw**, a true gin joint where juniper is treated with reverence.

If You Like...

Famous Museums

Field Museum of Natural History Explore collections of dinosaurs, gems, mummies and enormous taxidermied lions. (p180)

Shedd Aquarium Commune with whales, dolphins, sharks and other fascinating creatures from the deep. (p181)

Art Institute of Chicago Gawk at Monets, modern works, paperweights and much more at the nation's second-largest art museum. (p49)

Adler Planetarium Journey to the nether regions of outer space at this lakeside gem. (p182)

Museum of Science & Industry Geek out at the largest science museum in the western hemisphere. (p195)

Offbeat Museums

International Museum of Surgical Science Amputation saws, iron lungs, antique hemorrhoid surgery toolkits and a roomful of cadaver murals cram a creepy old mansion. (p87)

Smith Museum of Stained Glass Windows Just when you've had your fill of Victorian curlicues and Tiffany Jesuses, you see it: stained-glass Michael Jordan. (p74)

Money Museum You'll emerge richer than when you entered, thanks to a take-home bag of shredded currency and a photo with the million-dollar briefcase. (p57)

Frank Lloyd Wright's atrium in the Rookery (p56)

Busy Beaver Button Museum
Thousands upon thousands of groovy pin-back buttons. (p155)

Leather Archives & Museum
Scholarly displays about leather, fetish and S&M subcultures, including relics such as the Red Spanking Bench. (p128)

Chicago Sports Museum The Cubs' infamous Bartman ball and Sammy Sosa's corked bat are among the displays inside Harry Caray's Tavern. (p78)

Contemporary Art

Museum of Contemporary Art
Consider it the Art Institute's brash, rebellious sibling: a collection that always pushes boundaries. (p85)

Millennium Park Jaume Plensa's video-screen, glass-block Crown Fountain leads the pack of whimsical artworks throughout the park. (p46)

The Picasso Baboon, dog, woman? You decide what Pablo's public artwork is. And feel free to slide down the sloping base. (p55)

Museum of Contemporary Photography Tidy and engaging (and free), it's a great stop in the South Loop. (p186)

Pilsen Mural Tours A local artist leads you through the neighborhood's trove of art-splashed buildings (p177)

Mars Gallery It's pop art presided over by a kitty cat (he's the assistant manager). (p170)

Frank Lloyd Wright

Robie House The low eaves and graceful lines of Wright's Hyde Park masterpiece were emulated around the world. (p194)

Rookery Wright gave the atrium a light-filled, Prairie-style renovation that features 'floating' staircases. (p56)

Frank Lloyd Wright Home & Studio See where the master lived and worked for the first 20 years of his career. (p208)

Charnley-Persky House Only 19 years old when he designed it, Wright declared the 11-room abode the 'first modern building.' (p86)

Photo Ops

Chicago Theatre sign What's more perfect than a six-story-high neon sign spelling out the city's name? (p57)

Cloud Gate The awesomely mirrored sculpture lets you take a self-portrait with a skyline background. (p46)

Art Institute lions These iconic beasts guard the front entrance and reach their full glory wearing Blackhawks helmets after a Stanley Cup win. (p50)

Wrigley Field entrance The red, art deco–style marquee makes an especially fine backdrop when neon-lit at night. (p112)

Mr Beef sign It's a ritual to snap a photo under the dumpy sign before indulging in the city's best Italian beef sammie. (p75)

Harpo Studios sign Oprah is long gone, but fans still stop by to get a photo beside her famous emblem. (p166)

Skyscrapers

Willis Tower Chicago's tallest building lets you ascend 103 floors, then peer straight down from a glass-floored ledge. (p51)

Aqua Tower Jeanne Gang's wavy, 82-story beauty is the world's tallest building designed by a woman. (p58)

For more top Chicago spots, see the following:
➡ Eating (p26)
➡ Drinking & Nightlife (p29)
➡ Entertainment (p31)
➡ Shopping (p33)
➡ Sports & Activities (p35)
➡ Gay & Lesbian (p37)

PLAN YOUR TRIP IF YOU LIKE...

John Hancock Center Get high in Chicago's third-tallest tower at the 94th-floor observatory or 96th floor lounge. (p84)

Trump Tower The Donald built Chicago's second-tallest building and made it into a glassy, uber-luxe hotel. (p224)

Tribune Tower This neo-Gothic cloud-poker is inlaid with stones from the Taj Mahal, Parthenon, Lincoln's Tomb and more. (p72)

Marina City The groovy corn-cob towers look like something from a *Jetsons* cartoon. (p73)

Chicago Federal Center Ludwig Mies van der Rohe launched the modern skyscraper look with this boxy, metal-and-glass structure. (p248)

Gangster Sites

Green Mill Al Capone's favorite speakeasy; the tunnels where he hid the booze are still underneath the bar. (p134)

Biograph Theater Where the 'lady in red' betrayed 'public enemy number one' John Dillinger, whom the FBI shot in the alley. (p103)

Union Station Fans of *The Untouchables* film can see where the baby carriage bounced down the stairs during the Ness–Capone gang shootout. (p57)

St Valentine's Day Massacre Site Where Capone's men, dressed as cops, killed seven members of Bugs Moran's gang. (p103)

Untouchable Gangster Tour Hokey but fun bus ride taking in famous mob sites around town. (p266)

Parks & Gardens

Lincoln Park Chicago's largest green space is where the city comes out to play. (p98)

Lurie Garden Find Millennium Park's secret garden and you're treated to a prairie's worth of wildflowers. (p48)

Garfield Park Conservatory Pretty plants under glass, plus the Monet Garden recreates the impressionist painter's French flower patch. (p167)

Humboldt Park Zigzagging paths, an iris-edged lagoon, flowery gardens, a makeshift beach and food trucks selling Puerto Rican snacks comprise the 207 acres. (p155)

Northerly Island The prairie-grassed nature park offers a tranquil escape from the nearby Museum Campus. (p183)

Palmisano Park It's carved from an old rock quarry and reveals sweet skyline views from walkways made of recycled debris. (p197)

Lincoln Park Conservatory The small but potent dose of tropical blooms is especially welcome during winter. (p99)

Pop Culture

Daley Plaza Site of the *Blues Brothers* epic car-crashing chase scene. (p57)

Marina City The strangely charming, corn cob–shaped towers show up everywhere from *Ferris Bueller's Day Off* to Wilco album covers. (p73)

Original Playboy Mansion Hugh Hefner launched the magazine and began wearing his all-day pajamas here. (p87)

Route 66 sign The famous Mother Road starts downtown by the Art Institute. (p54)

Hyde Park Hair Salon The barber chair that President Obama sat in is now enshrined in bulletproof glass. (p197)

Hilton Chicago Ground zero for the 1968 Democratic Convention riots, where police threw protesters through the plate-glass windows. (p231)

Buckingham Fountain The water spout featured in the opening credits of the classic TV comedy *Married... with Children*. (p54)

Windy City Icons

Billy Goat Tavern Subterranean dive where newspaper reporters have long boozed; also famous for spawning the Curse of the Cubs. (p74)

Buddy Guy's Legends The top spot in town to hear the blues, especially when Mr Guy himself takes the stage. (p189)

Wrigley Field One hundred years old and still going strong with its hand-turned scoreboard, ivy-covered walls, raucous bleacher seats and legendarily hexed team. (p112)

Pizzeria Uno Deep-dish pizza was invented here in 1943, although the claim to fame is hotly debated. (p76)

Second City It launched the improv comedy genre and the careers of funny folk such as Bill Murray, Tina Fey, Steve Carell and Stephen Colbert. (p107)

Ethnic Neighborhoods

Pilsen Chicago's Mexican community clusters here, where the salsas scald, the fruit drinks soothe and the tortillas are fresh from the neighborhood factory. (p164)

Chinatown Small but bustling, its charms are nibbling chestnut cakes, sipping tea, slurping noodles and shopping for Hello Kitty trinkets. (p186)

Argyle Street It's the fishy-smelling heart of 'Little Saigon,' good for bubble tea, pho, banh mi sandwiches and exotic Asian wares. (p128)

Paseo Boricua The 'Puerto Rican Passage' is a mile-long stretch of Division St in Humboldt Park, stuffed with island-food cafes and shops. (p155)

Devon Ave It's mostly a mash-up of Indian and Pakistani businesses, but Russian and Orthodox Jewish shops mix in, too. It's all a delicious browse. (p132)

Wicker Park Division St was once a polka-bar-lined thoroughfare known as 'Polish Broadway'; a few lingering eateries still serve pierogi and borscht. (p137)

Andersonville The Swedish American Museum and Swedish Bakery give a feel for what life was once like in this northern 'hood. (p126)

Greektown On Halsted St west of the loop, the culture is still going strong in baklava-wafting bakeries and wine-pouring tavernas. (p172)

Month by Month

January

It's the coldest month, with temperatures hovering around 22°F (−6°C), and the snowiest month, with around 10in total. Everyone stays inside and drinks.

Chinese New Year Parade

Crowds amass on Wentworth Ave in Chinatown to watch dragons dance, firecrackers burst and marching bands bang their gongs. The exact date varies according to the lunar calendar, but it's typically in late January or early to mid-February. (www.chicago chinatown.org)

March

Will the sun ever shine again? Windy City-zens fret during the grayest and windiest month, when temperatures linger at 37°F (3°C). Some fun events take the edge off.

Chiditarod

This crazy-costume, Burning Man–esque version of the Iditarod (the famed Alaskan sled-dog race) swaps humans for huskies and shopping carts for sleds. Teams haul canned food for local pantries along the Near West Side route. Held on the first Saturday in March. (www.chiditarod.org)

St Patrick's Day Parade

It's a city institution: after the parade along S Columbus Dr, the local plumbers union dyes the Chicago River shamrock green (pouring in the secret, biodegradable coloring near the N Columbus Dr bridge). Held the Saturday before March 17. (www.chicago stpatsparade.com)

May

Finally, the weather warms and everyone dashes for the parks, lakefront trails, baseball stadiums and beer gardens. Beaches open over Memorial Day weekend. Hotels get busy.

Cinco de Mayo Festival & Parade

The three-day, family-friendly bash draws thousands to Douglas Park near Pilsen with food, music and carnival rides the first weekend in May. Sunday's colorful parade along Cermak Ave (beginning at Damen Ave) marks the finale.

Bike the Drive

On the last Sunday in May cars are banned from Lake Shore Dr, and 20,000 cyclists take to the road. Riding 15 miles along the lakefront as the sun bursts out is a thrill. Pancakes and live music follow in Grant Park. (www.bikethedrive.org)

June

Schools let out. Beaches get busy. Festival season ramps up. The temperature hangs at an ideal 69°F (21°C). Alas, it rains a third of the days.

Chicago Blues Festival

It's the globe's biggest free blues fest, with four days of the electrified music that made Chicago famous. More than 500,000 people unfurl blankets by the multiple stages that take over Grant Park in early June. (www.chicagobluesfestival.us)

✪✪ Printers Row Lit Fest

This popular free event, sponsored by the *Chicago Tribune,* features thousands of rare and not-so-rare books for sale, plus author readings. The browsable booths line the 500 to 700 blocks of S Dearborn St in early June. (www.printersrowlitfest.org)

☆ Just for Laughs Chicago

Montreal's famous comedy festival exports to Chicago, and for six days mid-month more than 100 funny people – including some Very Big Names – make 'em laugh at theaters around town. (www.justforlaughs chicago.com)

✪✪ Grant Park Music Festival

The Grant Park Orchestra, composed of top musicians from symphonies around the globe, plays free concerts in Millennium Park's Pritzker Pavilion on Wednesday, Friday and Saturday evenings from mid-June through mid-August. It's a summer ritual to bring wine and a picnic. (www.grantparkmusic festival.com)

✪✪ Pride Parade

On the last Sunday in June, colorful floats and risqué revelers pack Halsted St in Boystown. It's the GLBT community's main event, and more than 800,000 people come to the party. (chicagopride.gopride.com)

July

The month Chicagoans wait for all year. Festivals rock the neighborhoods every weekend. Millennium Park has concerts downtown nightly. Fireflies glow everywhere. It can be hot and humid, but who cares?

✕ Taste of Chicago

The mid-month, five-day food festival in Grant Park draws hordes for a smorgasbord of ethnic, meaty, sweet and other local edibles – much of it served on a stick. Several stages host free live music, including big-name bands. (www.tasteofchicago.us)

✪✪ Pitchfork Music Festival

It's sort of Lollapalooza Jr, for bespectacled indie-rock fans. Sonic Youth, the Flaming Lips and other indie heroes shake up Union Park for three days in mid-July. A day pass costs $50. (www.pitchforkmusic festival.com)

August

Ah, more awesome summer: warm weather, concerts, festivals, baseball games, beach frolicking. Tourists are still here en masse, so lodging prices are high and lines can be long.

✪✪ Lollapalooza

This mega rock festival once traveled city to city; now its permanent home is Chicago. It's a raucous event, with 130 bands – including many A-listers – spilling off eight stages in Grant Park the first Friday–Sunday in August. A day pass costs $95. (www.lollapalooza.com)

☆ Chicago Air & Water Show

The third weekend in August, windows rattle as the latest military planes buzz the lakefront from Fullerton Ave south to Oak St. North Ave Beach is the epicenter. Two million people attend the free event. (www.chicagoairand watershow.us)

✪✪ Chicago Jazz Fest

Chicago's longest-running free music fest, now in its fourth decade, attracts top names on the national jazz scene. The brassy notes bebop over Labor Day weekend on multiple stages in Millennium Park and the Chicago Cultural Center. (www.chicagojazzfestival.us)

September

Kids go back to school and beaches close after Labor Day weekend. Peak season begins to wind down.

✪✪ EXPO Chicago

Top galleries from around the globe show off their contemporary and modern art on Navy Pier during a long weekend in mid-September. Local galleries get in on the action by offering special tours and programs concurrently. (www.expochicago.com)

October

Temperatures drop, to an average of 53°F (12°C). Baseball is over, but

(Top) Pride Parade
(Bottom) Crowd at Lollapalooza

JIANG XINTONG / XINHUA PRESS / CORBIS ©

STEVEN C. MITCHELL / EPA / CORBIS ©

basketball and hockey begin at month's end. The Bears and tailgate parties are in full swing.

🎆 Great Chicago Fire Festival

It's a newbie on the calendar, a theatrical homage to the 1871 conflagration and the city's rebirth afterward. It includes acrobats, bands and a parade of illuminated sculptures floating down the Chicago River. Redmoon Theater puts it all together. Held in mid-October. (www.redmoon.org)

🏃 Chicago Marathon

More than 45,000 runners compete on the 26-mile course through the city's heart, cheered on by a million spectators. Held on a Sunday in October (when the weather can be pleasant or freezing), it's considered one of the world's top five marathons. (www.chicago marathon.com)

December

'Tis the holiday season, and the city twinkles with good cheer. Michigan Ave bustles with shoppers and shines with a million lights. The ice rinks open. Hotel bargains abound.

🔒 Christkindlmarket

A traditional German holiday market takes over Daley Plaza all month, wafting sausages, roasted nuts and spiced wine along with Old World handicrafts. It starts around Thanksgiving and goes until Christmas Eve. (www. christkindlmarket.com)

With Kids

Ferocious dinosaurs at the Field Museum, an ark's worth of beasts at Lincoln Park Zoo, lakefront boat rides and sandy beaches are among the top choices for toddlin' times. Add in a groovy dance party and festivals of spring kites and winter lights, and it's clear Chicago is a kid's kind of town.

PANORAMIC IMAGES / GETTY IMAGES ©

Shedd Aquarium (p181)

Outdoor Activities

Parks

Millennium Park is a hot favorite. Kids love to run underneath and touch The Bean sculpture, while Crown Fountain serves as a de facto water park to splash in. **Lincoln Park** has the free zoo where lions roar and apes swing. At the southern end, kids can get up close to goats, ponies, cows and chickens at the Farm-in-the-Zoo, and see ducks along the Nature Boardwalk. The train ride and the carousel (each around $3 per ride) – with its wood-carved pandas, cheetahs and tigers – bring squeals of delight.

Beaches

Sand and swimming! Lifeguards patrol the city's 24 lakefront beaches throughout the summer. Waves are typically pint-sized – perfect for pint-sized swimmers. **North Ave Beach** is the most crowded (and you do have to share it with skimpy-suited 20-somethings), but the selling point is the location near both downtown and Lincoln Park Zoo. The steamboat-shaped beach house is totally kid-friendly, serving ice cream and burgers, and it has bathrooms and lockers. **Montrose Beach** is farther flung, but it also has bathrooms and a snack bar. It's less crowded and more dune-packed and nature-filled. Remember to check the beach website (www.cpd beaches.com) before you head out to make sure the water isn't off limits due to high winds or bacteria levels.

Navy Pier

Amusements abound on the half-mile-long wharf. A giant whirling swing, the sky-high Ferris wheel, a musical, hand-painted carousel, 18 holes of miniature golf, remote-control boats, a funhouse maze – all here, and then some. Popcorn, ice cream, burgers and other treats add to the carnival atmosphere.

Cycling

Bobby's Bike Hike and Bike Chicago rent children's bikes and bikes with child seats. Both also offer child-friendly tours. Try Bobby's 'Tike Hike,' which rolls by Lincoln Park Zoo and a statue of Abe Lincoln. Kids aged 10 and under are welcome on the

4.5-mile route, Bike Chicago's 'Lincoln Park Adventure' is also suitable for kids.

Boat Rides

The schooner *Windy* departs from Navy Pier and offers a pirate-themed cruise on most days, plus kids can help sail the boat. Water taxis offer another wind-in-your-hair experience. The boats that toddle along the lakefront between Navy Pier and the Museum Campus are popular with families.

Kid-Friendly Museums

The reigning favorite is the **Chicago Children's Museum**, geared to kids aged 10 and under, with a slew of hands-on building, climbing and inventing exhibits. The **Field Museum** brings on the dinosaurs; the Crown Family PlayLab, on the ground floor, lets kids excavate bones and make loads of other discoveries. It's open Thursday to Monday from 10am to 3pm.

Almost all exhibits at the **Shedd Aquarium** are aimed at children. Head to the Polar Play Zone to climb in a faux submarine, explore an ice cave and press your nose against the glass as whales and dolphins swim by. In the **Art Institute**, the Ryan Education Center provides interactive games (such as puzzles of famous works) and art-making activities. And families could spend a week in the **Museum of Science & Industry** and not see it all. Staff conduct 'experiments' in various galleries throughout the day, such as dropping things off the balcony and creating mini explosions.

Theater & TV

Yeah, baby. **Chic-A-Go-Go** (www.roctober. com/chicagogo) is a cable-access TV show that's like a kiddie version of *Soul Train*. Check the website for taping dates and locations to join the groovy dance party.

The **Chicago Children's Theatre** (☑773-227-0180; www.chicagochildrenstheatre.org) is dedicated exclusively to putting on quality productions for young audiences. Most plays are adapted from children's books, so you might see *The Very Hungry Caterpillar* or the world premiere of *Mr Chickee's Funny Money* set to music. Performances take place at venues around town.

Emerald City (Map p298; ☑773-935-6100; www.emeraldcitytheatre.com; 2540 N Lincoln Ave; Ⓜ Red, Brown, Purple Line to Fullerton) is another kid-focused troupe. It presents everything from blockbusters such as *High School Musical* to fairy tales like *Rapunzel*. Performances are at the Apollo Theater.

Festivals

Chicago Kids and Kites Festival

On a Saturday in early May, hundreds of colorful kites soar and dip around Montrose Beach. The city supplies free kite-making kits, and professional flyers demonstrate how to harness the wind. Face painting and balloon artists round out the fun.

Kidzapalooza

Lollapalooza isn't just for arm-flailing, mosh-pit-thrashing adults. Kidzapalooza is a festival within the giant rock festival. In addition to the stellar line-up of kid-favorite bands, budding rock stars can bang sticks in the Drum Zone and get a Mohawk in the kids' area.

Magnificent Mile Lights Festival

During the free **Magnificent Mile Lights Festival** (www.magnificentmilelightsfestival. com), held the Saturday before Thanksgiving, Mickey Mouse and a posse of family-friendly musicians kick off the holiday season by turning on the Mag Mile's one million lights.

Chicago Diner (p118)

 # Eating

Deep-dish pizza grabs the glory, but Chicago's culinary scene goes well beyond. Inventive chefs have flocked in, thanks to lower costs than other big cities and the abundance of Midwestern farm fare. Gastronomes, see Chicago Dining (p252) for a run-down of city specialties and the bountiful ethnic neighborhoods that stir in Polish pierogi, Indian samosas and soul vegetarian food.

Eat Streets

Randolph Street, West Loop Chicago's best and brightest chefs cook at downtown's edge.

Clark Street, Andersonville Nouveau Korean, home-style Japanese, traditional Belgian and sweet Swedish.

Division Street, Wicker Park Copious sidewalk seating spills out of hip bistros and cafes.

Argyle Street, Uptown Thai and Vietnamese noodle houses steam up this little corridor.

18th Street, Pilsen Mexican bakeries and *taquerias* mix with hipster cafes and barbecue joints.

Tours

Chicago Food Planet Tours (☎212-209-3370; www.chicagofoodplanet.com; 3hr tours $47-60) Go on a guided walkabout where you'll graze through seven neighborhood eateries.

Fork & the Road (www.forkandtheroad.com; tours per person $50; ⏰late-May–Sep) Local foodies lead bike rides (around 16 miles) to various restaurants and markets to chat with chefs and, of course, eat their wares.

Chicago Chocolate Tours (☎312-929-2939; www.chicagochocolatetours.com; 2½hr tours per person $40) A guided walk to candy makers, bakeries and sweet shops.

A Foodie's Perfect Day

Start the morning at a farmers market. Green City Market, the city's largest, has cooking demos by top chefs. Next go on a graze with Chicago Food Planet Tours. Late afternoon, munch an epicurean weenie at Hot Doug's. For dinner, go upscale in West Loop or laid back at Logan Square.

Food Trucks

Until 2012 it was illegal to cook on a food truck in Chicago. Food had to be prepared elsewhere, and then just served from the truck. But now food trucks are cooking and rolling en masse. They generally prowl office worker–rich hot spots such as the Loop and Near North around lunchtime, and then Wicker Park and Lake View toward evening. Most trucks tweet their location; @Chicago-Mag/chicago-food-trucks amalgamates them.

Eating by Neighborhood

➡ **The Loop** Lunch spots for office workers, not much late night. (p58)

➡ **Near North & Navy Pier** Huge variety, from deep-dish pizza to ritzy seafood. (p74)

➡ **Gold Coast** Epicenter of sceney steakhouses and swanky eateries. (p87)

➡ **Lincoln Park & Old Town** A smorgasbord, from elite Alinea to cute French bistros to student bites. (p103)

➡ **Lake View & Wrigleyville** Good midrange places for vegetarians and global food lovers. (p116)

➡ **Andersonville & Uptown** Cozy, International array in Andersonville; noodle houses in Uptown's Little Saigon. (p129)

➡ **Wicker Park, Bucktown & Ukrainian Village** Dense with comfort food and cafes. (p142)

➡ **Logan Square & Humboldt Park** Inventive foodie mecca, sans reservations. (p155)

➡ **Near West Side & Pilsen** West Loop for Chicago's hottest chefs; Greektown, Little Italy and Pilsen for ethnic fare. (p171)

➡ **South Loop & Near South Side** Cheap eats for students give way to Chinatown flavors. (p188)

➡ **Hyde Park & South Side** Far flung hipster chow in Bridgeport, earthy cafes in Hyde Park. (p201)

NEED TO KNOW

Price Ranges

In our listings we've used the following price codes to represent the cost of a main dish at dinner.

$	under $10
$$	$10 to $20
$$$	more than $20

Opening Hours

Most restaurants: breakfast 7am or 8am to 11am, lunch 11:30am to 2.30pm, dinner 5pm or 6pm to 10pm Sunday to Thursday, to 11pm or midnight Friday and Saturday.

Reservations

➡ It's a good idea to make a reservation for eateries in the midrange and top-end price brackets, especially on weekends. A phone call that afternoon or the day before is usually sufficient.

➡ There are exceptions, ie mega-hot restaurants that require serious pre-planning or places that don't take reservations at all. We've indicated this within reviews.

➡ Many restaurants let you book online through **OpenTable** (www.opentable.com).

BYO

Many restaurants are BYO, so it's fine to bring your own wine or beer (occasionally there's a corkage fee of a few dollars).

Tipping

Tipping 15% of the total bill is the accepted minimum. If service is good, 20% is the norm.

Credit Cards

Almost all restaurants accept credit cards, aside from a smattering of budget places.

Websites

➡ **LTH Forum** (www.lthforum.com) Local chow hounds rant and rave.

➡ **Happy Cow** (www.happycow.net) Vegetarian options.

➡ **Chicago Farmers Markets** (www.chicagofarmersmarkets.us) Where to find them.

Lonely Planet's Top Choices

Hot Doug's (p155) Beloved joint that elevated the hot dog to 'haute' dog.

Hopleaf (p132) Locals pile in for the mussels, *frites* and 200-strong beer list.

Longman & Eagle (p160) Michelin-starred, shabby-chic tavern for breakfast, lunch or dinner.

Little Goat (p171) Top Chef Stephanie Izard's delicious comfort-food diner.

Ruxbin (p146) Teeny spot where passionate chefs cook artful dinners.

Hoosier Mama Pie Company (p145) Supreme flaky goodness.

Best by Budget

$
Cafecito (p58) Fat Cuban sandwiches.

French Market (p60) Foodie stalls sprawl through the train station.

Podhalanka (p142) Pierogi and other Polish comfort food.

Big Star Taqueria (p142) Tacos for Wicker Park foodies.

$$
Reno (p156) Logan Square gathering spot for wood-fired pizzas.

Kuma's Corner (p156) Hulking burgers with a side of heavy metal.

Publican Quality Meats (p171) Beefy sandwiches straight from the butcher's block.

Xoco (p75) Celeb chef Rick Bayless' Mexican street-food hut.

$$$
Girl and the Goat (p172) Rockin' ambience and dishes starring the titular animal.

Alinea (p104) Molecular gastronomy from one of the world's best restaurants.

Nightwood (p174) Dinner made from whatever local farms deliver that day.

Graham Elliot (p77) Twelve to 15 whimsical courses from the tattooed TV chef.

Best by Cuisine

Latin
Topolobampo/Frontera Grill (p76) Rick Bayless' flavor-packed signature restaurants, an Obama favorite.

Irazu (p143) Chicago's lone Costa Rican eatery whips up distinctive, peppery fare.

Borinquen (p160) Birthplace of the garlic-and-fried-plantain jibarito sandwich.

Flo (p145) Hungover hipsters crave the breakfast burritos.

Asian
Le Colonial (p90) Banana-leaf-wrapped fish that'll transport you to Saigon.

Andy's Thai Kitchen (p118) Real-deal, hot-spiced fare from a Thai master.

Tank Noodle (p133) The city's best pho wafts from this Uptown stalwart.

Yusho (p161) Grilled Japanese street food and colorful cocktails.

Vegetarian
Chicago Diner (p118) The local scene's long-standing all-veg linchpin.

Green Zebra (p146) Chicago's highfalutin' veg-out spot.

Karyn's on Green (p173) Making vegan sexy.

Victory's Banner (p116) New Age, meat-free bliss (and a great brunch).

Pizzerias
Giordano's (p75) Perfectly tangy tomato sauce.

Pizano's (p61) Makes a great thin crust to supplement the deep dish.

Pequod's (p104) Sweet sauce and caramelized cheese.

Hot Dogs
Hot Doug's (p155) Goes beyond gourmet weenies with a killer Chicago-style dog, too.

Vienna Beef Factory Store & Cafe (p143) Franks at the factory with the folks who made 'em.

Wiener's Circle (p104) Char-dogs, cheddar fries and lots of unruly swearing.

Best Brunch
Sweet Maple Cafe (p173) Fresh-baked biscuits and banana pancakes.

Meli Cafe (p173) Goat cheese and fig omelets in Greektown.

Big Jones (p133) Dishes from New Orleans and the Carolina Lowcountry.

Best for Kids
RJ Grunt's (p104) Burgers and milkshakes by the zoo.

Gino's East (p75) Write on the walls while you wait for your pizza.

Margie's (p143) Gigantic hot fudge sundaes.

Drinking & Nightlife

Chicagoans love to hang out in drinking establishments. Blame it on the long winter, when folks need to huddle together somewhere warm. Blame it on summer, when sunny days make beer gardens and sidewalk patios so splendid. Whatever the reason, drinking in the city is a widely cherished civic pastime.

Beer

Chicago has long been a beer-drinking town. You can get a bottle of rank-and-file favorites Pabst and Old Style. But an explosion of craft brewers means you can drink much better. Watch the taps for Half Acre, Revolution, 5 Rabbit, Metropolitan, Two Brothers and Three Floyds, all brewed locally.

Cocktails

The craft cocktail craze is in full swing. Mixologists do their thing using small-batch liqueurs and fresh-squeezed juices. It may sound pretentious, but most of the bars are actually pretty cool.

How to Find a Real Chicago Bar

To discover classic, character-filled bars on your own, look for the following: an 'Old Style' beer sign swinging out front; a well-worn dart board and/or pool table inside; patrons wearing Cubs, White Sox or Bears ball caps; and sports on TV.

Clubs

Clubs cluster in three main areas: River North/West Loop, where the venues tend to be huge and luxurious (with dress codes); Wicker Park/Ukie Village, where they're typically more casual; and Wrigleyville/Boystown, where they fall somewhere in between. Most clubs use social media to provide discounts on admission, so check before heading out.

Drinking by Neighborhood

→ **The Loop** Hotel bars but not much else, especially after 10pm. (p61)

➜ **Near North & Navy Pier** Scores of options from dives to champagne bars; also a club hub. (p78)

➜ **Gold Coast** Martini lounges for folks on the prowl. (p91)

➜ **Lincoln Park & Old Town** Student saloons around Lincoln and Halsted Sts; quirky gems in Old Town. (p106)

➜ **Lake View & Wrigleyville** Sports bars around Wrigley Field, dance clubs in Boystown. (p119)

➜ **Andersonville & Uptown** Awesome beer bars and low-key GLBT drinkeries. (p134)

➜ **Wicker Park, Bucktown & Ukrainian Village** Cocktail lounges and wine bars, peppered with mom-and-pop joints. (p146)

➜ **Logan Square & Humboldt Park** Hipster dive bars, microbreweries, gin lounges. (p161)

➜ **Near West Side & Pilsen** USA's best cocktails in West Loop, artist hangouts in Pilsen. (p175)

➜ **South Loop & Near South Side** Slim pickings. (p189)

➜ **Hyde Park & South Side** Sip alongside locals in Bridgeport. (p203)

NEED TO KNOW

Opening Hours

➡ Bars and pubs: 11am to 2am (3am on Saturday), some bars until 4am (5am on Saturday)

➡ Nightclubs: 9pm to 2am (3am on Saturday), some clubs until 4am (5am on Saturday)

How Much?

➡ Bottle of Old Style beer $3

➡ Pint of local microbrew $6

➡ Glass of wine $8

➡ Craft cocktail $11

➡ Cup of coffee $2

Tipping

Per round 10–15%, minimum per drink $1

Credit Cards

Most bars and clubs will run a tab on your credit card, though small neighborhood taverns can be cash only.

Door Policies

➡ Some clubs don't allow blue jeans, tennis shoes or baseball caps. In most of the places we've reviewed you can come as you are.

➡ The drinking age is 21. Take your driver's license or passport out at night: you will be asked for ID.

Websites

➡ **Chicago Reader** (www. chicagoreader.com) Bar and club listings.

➡ **ClubZone** (www.club zone.com) Covers the nightclub scene, guest lists for events.

Lonely Planet's Top Choices

Old Town Ale House (p106) Trendy tipplers and grizzled regulars sip under bawdy paintings.

Maria's Packaged Goods and Community Bar (p203) Artsy neighborhood gathering spot with excellent microbrews.

Revolution Brewing (p161) Industrial-chic brewpub pouring righteous ales.

Gingerman Tavern (p119) Tattooed rockers play pool and sip fine beers.

Simon's (p134) Neighborhood stalwart with a ballsy jukebox and Swedish spiced wine in winter.

Best Beer

Delilah's (p106) Spirited punk bar with all kinds of odd ales (whiskeys too).

Map Room (p146) Globe-laden tavern with 200 brews from around the world.

Half Acre Tap Room (p116) Local craft brewer that cooks up fine suds.

Best Cocktails

Aviary (p175) Molecular gastronomy applied to booze.

Matchbox (p148) Teensy space with big gimlets.

Billy Sunday (p161) Impeccable libations and Things in Jars.

Best Wine

Bar Pastoral (p119) Sample widely via half glasses and supplement with cheese.

Lush Wine and Spirits (p147) Buy a bottle in the shop, drink it in the hip bar.

Best Views

Signature Lounge (p91) Ascend to the Hancock Center's 96th floor and gawp.

J Parker (p106) The lake and skyline look sweet from this Lincoln Park rooftop.

Best Local Scene

Happy Village (p148) Festive boozing and camaraderie playing table tennis.

Skylark (p175) Where Pilsen's underground goes for cheap drinks and tater tots.

Clark Street Ale House (p78) Join post-shift workers over pretzels and microbrews in the back beer garden.

Best Dance Clubs

Smart Bar (p120) Intimate club that's serious about its DJs.

Late Bar (p162) Groovy, new-wave club that draws an uber-mixed crowd.

Best Sports Bars

Sluggers (p120) Sidestep the Cubs revelers and head for the batting cages.

Murphy's Bleachers (p120) Traditional watering hole steps from Wrigley Field's bleacher seats.

Johnny's Ice House East (p175) Knock back Labatt's with hockey fans.

Best Coffee

Intelligentsia (p62) Local roaster known for strong java.

Dollop (p78) Baristas do caffeinated wonders in the sunny space.

Entertainment

*Finding something to do in Chicago on any given night is effortless, and
the spectrum of entertainment that's available in every price range is
overwhelming. Just flip through the city's newsweekly, the* Reader, *with its
pages of theater openings and concert announcements, and Chicagoans'
insatiable appetite for nocturnal amusement becomes apparent.*

Music

Blues and jazz have deep roots in Chicago,
and indie rock clubs slouch on almost every
corner – for more details, see Music & the
Arts, p255. Besides mega-bashes such as
Blues Fest, Lollapalooza and Pitchfork, the
following are a must for any music fan's
calendar:

Riot Fest (www.riotfest.org) Big-name punk
bands scream in Humboldt Park for three days in
mid-September.

Wavefront Music Festival (www.wavefrontmu-
sicfestival.com) Montrose Beach transforms into an
electronic dance party for three days in early July.

Hideout Block Party (www.hideoutchicago.
com) The taste-making indie rock club hosts a
two-day party in early September with the hippest
of bands.

World Music Festival (www.worldmusicfestival.
org) Musicians from around the globe descend
for 10 days of free performances, anchored by the
Chicago Cultural Center. Held in mid-September.

Theater

Beyond the flashy Theater District in the Loop,
Chicago has many adventurous small stages
known as 'off-Loop' theaters. Keep an eye out
for troupes such as **Theater Oobleck** (www.
theateroobleck.com) and House Theatre (p149).

Film

Movies in the Parks is a summer tradition.
The **Chicago Park District** (www.chicago
parkdistrict.com) has the nightly schedule.
The **Chicago International Film Festival**
(312-683-0121; www.chicagofilmfestival.com) is
the star event; it rolls in October.

Entertainment by Neighborhood

➡ **The Loop** The neon-lit Theater District,
everything classical and Millennium Park free
concerts. (p62)

➡ **Near North & Navy Pier** Shakespeare, jazz and
blues. (p78)

➡ **Gold Coast** Smattering of theater, jazz. (p93)

➡ **Lincoln Park & Old Town** Second City, blues,
outdoor theaters, indoor theaters. (p107)

➡ **Lake View & Wrigleyville** Heaps of rock, improv
and little jazzy clubs. (p121)

➡ **Andersonville & Uptown** Historic venues
including the Green Mill cluster in Uptown. (p134)

➡ **Wicker Park, Bucktown & Ukrainian Village**
Best area for cool-cat rock clubs. (p148)

➡ **Logan Square & Humboldt Park** Artsy, far-
reaching music and theater venues. (p162)

➡ **Near West Side & Pilsen** A few far-flung
theaters. (p176)

➡ **South Loop & Near South Side** Big for blues,
jazz and dance. (p189)

➡ **Hyde Park & South Side** Remote theater and
blues. (p204)

NEED TO KNOW

Ticket Shops

➔ **Hot Tix** (www.hottix.org) sells same-week drama, comedy and performing-arts tickets for half-price (plus a $4 service charge). The selection is best early in the week.

➔ Book online or at the three Hot Tix outlets: 72 E Randolph St, N State St (p65) and E Pearson St (p91).

Websites

➔ **Chicago Reader** (www.chicagoreader.com) Great listings for music, arts, film.

➔ **Chicago Music** (www.chicagomusic.org) Tuneful listings across genres.

➔ **Broadway in Chicago** (www.broadwayinchicago.com) Touring show info.

➔ **See Chicago Dance** (www.seechicagodance.com) Covers all things dance-related.

➔ **Goldstar** (www.goldstar.com) Half-price offers from national ticket broker.

Lonely Planet's Top Choices

Green Mill (p134) Listen to jazz or a poetry slam while sipping martinis with Al Capone's ghost.

Second City (p107) The improv bastion that launched many a jokester's career.

Hideout (p148) Feels like your grandma's basement but with alt-country bands and literary readings.

Buddy Guy's Legends (p189) The icon's club puts the best blues bands on stage.

Grant Park Orchestra (p62) Everyone's favorite group to picnic with at Pritzker Pavilion.

Best Blues & Jazz

Green Mill (p134) Big names in jazz bebop in this timeless tavern.

Buddy Guy's Legends (p189) Sick licks fill the air day and night.

BLUES (p107) Small, crackling club with seasoned local players.

Rosa's Lounge (p162) Unvarnished joint where dedicated fans feel the blues.

Best Rock

Empty Bottle (p149) Go-to club for edgy indie rock.

Double Door (p148) Cool buzz bands smash through sets.

Metro (p121) Bands on the way up thrash here first.

Best Classical & Opera

Chicago Symphony Orchestra (p63) World-renowned, with a smokin' brass section.

Lyric Opera (p63) High Cs in a chandeliered venue.

Best Theater

Steppenwolf Theatre (p107) Drama club of Malkovich, Sinise and other Hollywood stars.

Goodman Theatre (p62) Excellent new and classic American plays.

Neo-Futurists (p135) Original works make you laugh and ponder.

Best Comedy

Second City (p107) The group that invented improv is still the best in the biz.

iO Theater (p121) Another improv house that's sent many on to stardom.

ComedySportz (p121) Two teams compete for your laughs.

Best for Free

Whistler (p162) Artsy little club where indie bands and jazz trios brood.

International Screenings Program (p64) Foreign films play at the Cultural Center.

Best Dance

Hubbard Street Dance Chicago (p63) Foremost modern troupe in town.

Joffrey Ballet (p63) Famed dancers leap through the classical repertoire.

Best Cinema

Music Box (p122) Art-house palace with a sense of humor.

Facets Multimedia (p108) Offbeat stuff you won't see anywhere else.

Shopping

From the glossy stores of the Magnificent Mile to the countercultural shops of Lake View to the indie designers of Wicker Park, Chicago is a shopper's destination. It has been that way from the get-go. After all, this is the city that birthed the department store and traditions such as the money-back guarantee, bridal registry and bargain basement.

Specialties

Music is big. Independent record stores flood Chicago's neighborhoods, supported by the thriving live-music scene in town. Vinyl geeks will find heaps of stacks to flip through. Vintage and thrift fashions are another claim to fame. Folks here don't throw out their old bowling shirts, pillbox hats, faux-fur coats and costume jewelry. Instead, they deposit used duds at vintage or secondhand stores, of which there are hundreds. Art- and architecture-related items are another Chicago specialty.

Locally Made Wares

Several stores proffer handbags, pendants, dresses and journals that city artisans have stitched, sewn and glue-gunned themselves. You're pretty much guaranteed a one-of-a-kind item to take home. The Indie Designer Market (inside the massive Randolph Street Market) is the epicenter of such craftiness.

Chicago-Style Fashions

It's difficult to find 'Chicago-style' fashions to take home, mostly because there isn't a distinct Chicago style. If anything, it's casual, comfortable and defined by cold weather. That's not to say there aren't trendsetters. Thanks to the Art Institute and its fashion program, a lot of budding designers do their own thing. The shops along Damen Ave in Bucktown are a good place to seek out their wares.

Shopping by Neighborhood

➡ **The Loop** National chains, plus souvenir and arts-and-crafts winners. (p64)

➡ **Near North & Navy Pier** Home to the Magnificent Mile, lined with sleek big-name retailers. (p79)

➡ **Gold Coast** Oak St offers luxury brand boutiques, while malls rise on Michigan Ave. (p93)

➡ **Lincoln Park & Old Town** Urban living chains throng Halsted and Clybourn Sts; posh shops around Armitage Ave. (p108)

➡ **Lake View & Wrigleyville** Shops for punks and kitschy hipsters around Clark and Belmont Sts; naughty stuff in Boystown. (p123)

➡ **Andersonville & Uptown** Quality antiques, fashion and locally made wares along Clark St. (p135)

➡ **Wicker Park, Bucktown & Ukrainian Village** Oddball and vintage on Milwaukee Ave, local designers on Damen Ave, crafters on Division St. (p149)

➡ **Logan Square & Humboldt Park** Far-flung indie shops with stylish goods for hipsters. (p163)

➡ **Near West Side & Pilsen** Where the markets are, plus funky vintage shops in Pilsen. (p176)

➡ **South Loop & South Side** Crafty in the South Loop; inexpensive homewares and trinkets in Chinatown. (p190)

➡ **Hyde Park & South Side** Bookstores galore. (p204)

NEED TO KNOW

Opening Hours

➡ Shops: 11am to 7pm Monday to Saturday, noon to 6pm Sunday.

➡ Malls: 10am to 8pm or 9pm, 11am to 6pm Sunday.

Taxes

Sales tax on goods (excluding food) is 9.25%.

Websites

➡ **Chicago Magazine Sales Check** (www.chicagomag.com/Radar/Sales-Check/) Publishes a round-up of sales and new store openings on a week-by-week basis.

➡ **Daily Candy** (www.dailycandy.com/chicago) Local style and trends.

➡ **Refinery 29** (www.refinery29.com/chicago) Fashion news, events and sales.

Lonely Planet's Top Choices

Chicago Architecture Foundation Shop (p64) Pick up a mini Willis Tower model or skyline poster.

Jazz Record Mart (p79) One-stop shop for Chicago jazz and blues tunes.

Strange Cargo (p123) A huge array of iconic T-shirt iron-ons, from Coach Ditka to a Chicago-style hot-dog diagram.

Quimby's (p149) Ground zero for comics, zines and underground culture.

Logan Hardware (p163) Awesome vinyl plus vintage arcade games to get your Donkey Kong on.

Best Markets

Randolph Street Market (p176) Scads of antiques and indie designer wares in a festival ambience.

Maxwell Street Market (p176) Historic market for socks and hubcaps, now known for Mexican food stalls.

Handmade Market (p152) Monthly DIY crafters' fair held at a bar.

Best Music

Dusty Groove (p150) Killer stacks of vinyl hold rare soul and funk beats.

Reckless Records (p150) Great place to get the scoop on local indie rock bands.

Groove Distribution (p176) Browse the warehouse for club music alongside DJs.

Best Fashion

Wolfbait & B-girls (p163) Local designers sew wares on-site.

Akira (p151) Of-the-moment jeans and other garb.

Ms Catwalk (p151) Fun, well-curated clothes and accessories.

Best for Kids

American Girl Place (p94) Have tea and get a new hair style with your doll.

Hershey's (p94) Chocolate, chocolate and more chocolate.

Boring Store (p150) Super-cool gear for junior spies.

Best Souvenirs

Art Institute of Chicago (p49) Posters and notecards of the collection's masterpieces.

Garrett Popcorn (p79) The sweet and salty Chicago mix will haunt your dreams.

Sports World (p124) Heavy on Cubs gear, but other Chicago teams get their due, too.

Best Books

Open Books (p93) Welcoming used bookstore with a whopping selection.

57th Street Books (p204) Lose yourself in the labyrinth.

Seminary Cooperative Bookstore (p204) Brainy store beloved by Nobel Prize winners.

Best Vintage

Una Mae's Freak Boutique (p150) Emerge looking all Jackie O in your new old hat.

US #1 (p150) Bowling and western-wear shirts plus racks of jeans.

Belmont Army Surplus (p124) Peacoats and other vintage military fashions.

Best Arts & Crafts

ShopColumbia (p190) Goods from Columbia College's arty students.

Andersonville Galleria (p135) Three floors of craftiness from local indie vendors.

Illinois Artisans Shop (p65) The best creations from craftsfolk throughout the state.

Sports & Activities

Chicago is a rabid sports town, and fans of the pro teams are mythically die-hard. It's not all about passively watching sports, though. Chicago offers plenty of places to get active via its city-spanning shoreline, 24 beaches and 580 parks. After a long, cold winter, everyone goes outside to play.

Spectator Sports

The football-playing Bears ignite the most fervor. They're followed by baseball's heated, perpetually losing Cubs; basketball's try-hard Bulls; hockey's young, Stanley Cup–winning Blackhawks; the up-and-down White Sox, the second baseball team in town; and the soccer-playing Fire. For more details see the Understand chapter Sports (p249).

Watersports

Visitors often don't realize Chicago is a beach town, thanks to mammoth Lake Michigan lapping its side. There are 24 official strands of sand patrolled by lifeguards in summer. Swimming is popular, though the water is pretty freaking cold. Beaches at Montrose and North Ave rent kayaks and paddleboards. Other kayak companies have set up along the Chicago River.

Cycling

The 18-mile lakefront trail is a beautiful ride along the water, though on nice days it's packed. It starts at Hollywood Ave and rolls down to 71st St. The **Active Transportation Alliance** (www.activetrans.org) publishes a bike trail map, lists cycling events and is an all-round resource gold mine. **Chicago Critical Mass** (www.chicagocriticalmass.org) sponsors popular, traffic-disrupting rides in several neighborhoods.

Running

Tons of runners use the lakefront trail and paths in Lincoln Park. The **Chicago Area Runners Association** (www.cararuns.org) has the lowdown on races and free daily fun runs around town.

Sports & Activities by Neighborhood

➡ **The Loop** Cycling, ice skating and kayaking options; free workouts in Millennium Park. (p65)

➡ **Near North & Navy Pier** Bike rentals near Navy Pier. (p80)

➡ **Gold Coast** Busy Oak St Beach fringes the skyscrapers; kayaking at the neighborhood's western edge. (p95)

➡ **Lincoln Park & Old Town** The masses play in Lincoln Park and at North Ave Beach. (p109)

➡ **Lake View & Wrigleyville** Pro baseball at Wrigley Field, plus bowling and golfing. (p125)

➡ **Andersonville & Uptown** Montrose Beach is the surfing and skateboarding hot spot. (p136)

➡ **Logan Square & Humboldt Park** Walking paths in Humboldt Park. (p155)

➡ **Near West Side & Pilsen** Pro basketball and hockey at United Center. (p177)

➡ **South Loop & Near South Side** Pro football and sledding at Soldier Field, walking paths on Northerly Island. (p191)

➡ **Hyde Park & South Side** Pro baseball at US Cellular Field, beaches and lagoon-filled Jackson Park. (p204)

NEED TO KNOW

Opening Hours

➡ Parks: 6am to 11pm

➡ Beaches: 11am to 7pm late May to early September for swimming; same hours as parks otherwise

Best Websites

➡ **Chicago Beaches** (www.cpdbeaches.com) Info on swim advisories due to currents or water pollution.

➡ **Chicago Park District** (www.chicagopark district.com) Lowdown on all the parks and their facilities and events.

➡ **Chicago Park District Golf** (www.cpdgolf. com) Book tee times.

Tickets

You can try to buy tickets to games direct from team websites or stadiums, or from scalpers outside the venues. Or you can try online providers. Most charge an inconvenient 'convenience' fee.

➡ **Ticketmaster** (www. ticketmaster.com)

➡ **TicketExchange by Ticketmaster** (www. ticketexchangebyticket master.com)

➡ **StubHub** (www.stub hub.com)

➡ **Goldstar** (www.gold star.com)

➡ **Craigslist** (www. chicago.craigslist.org) No fee; online scalping service.

Lonely Planet's Top Choices

Wrigley Field (p125) It's hard to beat a day at the Cubs' home ballpark, beer in hand in the sun-splashed bleachers.

McCormick Tribune Ice Rink (p46) Sublime skating set between the Bean and Michigan Ave.

Bobby's Bike Hike (p80) Friendly guides lead the way on South Side and hot-dog-eating rides.

Montrose Beach (p136) Lovely stretch of sand, surf, dunes and a beach bar.

Wateriders (p95) Slither past downtown's skyscrapers on a river kayaking tour.

Best Pro Teams

Chicago Bears (NFL; www. chicagobears.com)

Chicago Blackhawks (NHL; www.chicagoblackhawks.com)

Chicago Bulls (NBA; ww.nba. com/bulls)

Chicago Cubs (MLB; www. cubs.com)

Chicago Fire (MLS; www. chicago-fire.com)

Chicago White Sox (MLB; www. whitesox.com)

Best Bike Rides

Bobby's Bike Hike (p80) Groovy tours for children, and pizza and beer lovers, and those interested in gangster sites.

Bike Chicago (p65) More excellent tours from Lincoln Park to Obama's house.

Bike the Drive (p21) A glorious ride on Lake Shore Drive the one day a year when cars are banned.

Best Paddling

Wateriders (p95) Glide along for the cool 'Ghost and Gangster' tour.

Kayak Chicago (p136) Learn to paddleboard at Montrose Beach.

Urban Kayaks (p66) Rentals and fireworks tours launch right downtown from the Riverwalk.

Best Beaches

Montrose Beach (p136) Birdwatching and kitesurfing add to the usual beachy sports.

North Avenue Beach (p109) Party time at the boathouse and on the volleyball courts.

63rd St Beach (p205) Regal beach house and fun fountains for kids.

Oak St Beach (p95) Sand box in the shadow of skyscrapers.

Best Golf

Diversey Driving Range (p109) Hit buckets of balls in Lincoln Park.

Sydney R Marovitz Golf Course (p125) Nine-hole course with killer skyline views.

Jackson Park Golf Course (p205) The only city-run course with 18 holes.

Best Winter Activities

McCormick Tribune Ice Rink (p46) The city's most popular and atmospheric rink.

Maggie Daley Park (p66) The new ice ribbon makes for fine skating.

Sledding Hill (p191) Big slope by Soldier Field with snow-making machine.

Rainbow flag, Boystown (p116)

☆ Gay & Lesbian

Exploring kinky artifacts in the Leather Archives & Museum, or playing a game of naughty Twister at a rollicking street fair? Shopping for fur-lined handcuffs, or clubbing alongside male go-go dancers? Chicago's flourishing GLBT scene in party-hearty Boystown and easygoing Andersonville offers plenty of choices.

Festivals

The main event on the calendar is the **Pride Parade** (http://chicagopride.gopride.com; ☺late Jun), held the last Sunday in June. It winds through Boystown and attracts more than 800,000 risqué revelers. **North Halsted Street Market Days** (www.northalsted.com; ☺early Aug) is another wild time in Boystown. It's a steamy two-day street fair in mid-August. Crafty, incense-wafting vendors line Halsted Street, but most folks come for the drag queens in feather boas, Twister games played in the street and disco divas (Gloria Gaynor!) on the main stage. The **International Mr Leather** (www.imrl.com) contest brings out lots of men in, well, leather in late May. Speakers, workshops and parties take place around town, with the main event happening at a downtown hotel or theater.

Museums & Tours

The Leather Archives & Museum (p128) holds all sorts of fetish and S&M artifacts,

NEED TO KNOW

Business Hours

➜ Bars: 11am to 2am (3am on Saturday), some bars until 4am (5am on Saturday).

➜ Clubs: 9pm to 2am (3am on Saturday), some clubs until 4am (5am on Saturday).

Websites

➜ **Windy City Times** (www.windy citymediagroup.com) GLBT newspaper, published weekly. Website is the main source for events and entertainment.

➜ **Chicago Area Gay & Lesbian Chamber of Commerce** (www.glchamber. org) Has an online tourism directory.

➜ **Purple Roofs** (www.purpleroofs.com) Website listing queer accommodations, travel agencies and tours.

➜ **Pink magazine** (www.pinkmag.com) Covers the scene for gay visitors.

➜ **Chances Dances** (www.chances dances.org) Organizes queer dance parties at clubs around town.

from the Red Spanking Bench to the painting *Last Supper in a Leather Bar with Judas Giving Christ the Finger*. It's inside a repurposed synagogue north of Ander-sonville. Chicago Greeter (p266) offers free, guided sightseeing trips through the city's gay neighborhoods. You must reserve at least 10 days in advance.

Theater

Keep an eye out for **About Face Theatre** (Map p302; ☎773-784-8565; www.aboutface theatre.com), an itinerant ensemble that stages plays dealing with gay and lesbian themes at theaters around Chicago. They're well-regarded and have recently won the Jeff Award (sort of like the local Tony Award) for best new play.

Community Center

The mod, glassy **Center on Halsted** (www.centeronhalsted.org; 3656 N Halsted St) is the Midwest's largest GLBT community center. It's mostly a social service organization for locals, but visitors can use the free wi-fi and reading library, plus there's a Whole Foods grocery store inside.

Gay & Lesbian by Neighborhood

➜ **Lake View & Wrigleyville** Home to Boystown, dense with bars and clubs on N Halsted St between Belmont Ave and Grace St. (p119)

➜ **Andersonville & Uptown** Chicago's other main area of GLBT bars, but in a more relaxed, less party-oriented scene. (p134)

Lonely Planet's Top Choices

Big Chicks (p134) Super-friendly, all-inclusive bar with cheap drinks, a beer garden and rockin' weekend DJs.

Sidetrack (p120) Thumping dance music, show-tune singalongs and prime people-watching.

Hamburger Mary's (p134) Cabaret, karaoke, burgers and a booze-soaked outdoor patio for good times.

Unabridged Bookstore (p123) Shelves of gay fiction and queer spirituality.

Spyner's (p120) A lady-heavy dive bar that shines during karaoke nights.

Best Bars

Big Chicks (p134) It's often called the friendliest gay bar in Chicago.

Hamburger Mary's (p134) Swill the housemade brews and watch the action from the patio.

Crew (p134) One of the few sports bars that also hosts underwear contests for guys.

Atmosphere (p134) Scrabble games, go-go dancers and drag revues – there's something for everyone.

Best Dance Clubs

Sidetrack (p120) It's massive and packed with frisky boys in tight jeans.

Berlin (p120) Thirty-year-old institution where party people dance till the sun comes up.

Hydrate (p121) Guys, just take off your shirt and boogie.

Spin (p121) Serious dancers, chatty cruisers and a Friday shower contest.

Best for Lesbians

Spyner's (p120) Get ready to belt out that Alanis Morissette tune after a few brews.

Closet (p121) A small, laid-back bar for ladies until the boys crash late night.

Best Shops

Unabridged Bookstore (p123) Well-curated stacks on hard-to-find GLBT topics; good sci-fi, too.

Women & Children First (p135) Feminist-focused tomes, children's books and big-name author readings.

Gay Mart (p124) Novelties such as a 'homo depot' button.

Egoist Underwear (p124) Naughty knickers including a sublime selection of G-strings.

Best Restaurants

HB (p119) Fork into delicious comfort food while Boystown buzzes outside the windows.

Tweet (p133) Decadent organic breakfasts next door to Big Chicks bar.

Best Gay Stays

Villa Tosca (p228) Silky B&B on Halsted St, smack in Boystown's midst.

Flemish House (p226) Gold Coast B&B with gay-friendly owners.

Best Western Hawthorne Terrace (p228) Reasonably priced hotel, steps from Boystown's main vein.

Explore Chicago

CHICAGO'S
TOP SIGHTS

Neighborhoods at a Glance

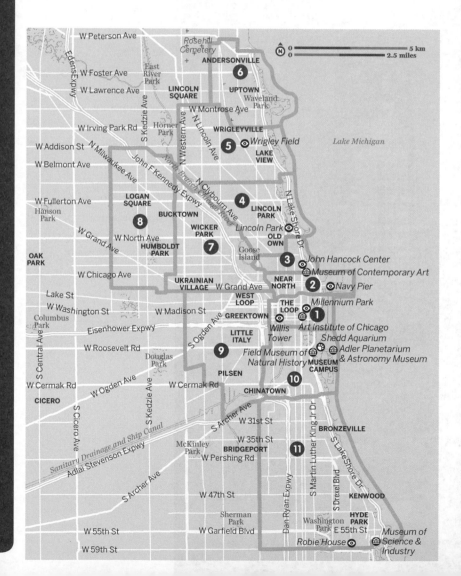

W Peterson Ave

Rosehill Cemetery

Edens Expwy

W Foster Ave

East River Park

ANDERSONVILLE
6

W Lawrence Ave

LINCOLN SQUARE

UPTOWN

S Kedzie Ave

W Montrose Ave

Waveland Park

N Western Ave

N Lincoln Ave

WRIGLEYVILLE

W Irving Park Rd

Horner Park

5 ◉ Wrigley Field

Lake Michigan

W Addison St

N Milwaukee Ave

LAKE VIEW

W Belmont Ave

John F Kennedy Expwy

North Branch Chicago River

N Clybourn Ave

N Lake Shore Dr

W Fullerton Ave

LOGAN SQUARE

4

LINCOLN PARK

Hanson Park

BUCKTOWN
8

W North Ave

WICKER PARK

Lincoln Park

N Lake Shore Dr

W Grand Ave

HUMBOLDT PARK
7

OLD TOWN ◉

OAK PARK

Goose Island

3 ◉ John Hancock Center
🏛 Museum of Contemporary Art

W Chicago Ave

UKRAINIAN VILLAGE

W Grand Ave

NEAR NORTH

2 ◉ Navy Pier

Lake St

WEST LOOP

THE LOOP

Millennium Park

W Washington St

W Madison St

GREEKTOWN

1

Columbus Park

S Central Ave

Eisenhower Expwy

S Ogden Ave

LITTLE ITALY

Willis Tower

Art Institute of Chicago

W Roosevelt Rd

Douglas Park

9

Field Museum of 🏛
Natural History

Shedd Aquarium

🏛 Adler Planetarium
& Astronomy Museum

MUSEUM CAMPUS

W Cermak Rd

W Ogden Ave

S Kedzie Ave

PILSEN

CICERO

S Cicero Ave

W Cermak Rd

CHINATOWN
10

S Archer Ave

W 31st St

S Martin Luther King Jr Dr

BRONZEVILLE

Sanitary Drainage and Ship Canal

Adlai Stevenson Expwy

S Archer Ave

McKinley Park

W 35th St
BRIDGEPORT
W Pershing Rd

11

S Lake Shore Dr

S Drexel Blvd

Dan Ryan Expwy

W 47th St

KENWOOD

Sherman Park

W Garfield Blvd

HYDE PARK

Washington Park

E 55th St

Museum of Science & Industry

W 55th St

Robie House ◉

W 59th St

N 0 ___ 5 km
0 ___ 2.5 miles

❶ The Loop p44

The Loop is Chicago's center of action, named for the elevated train tracks that lasso its streets. The Art Institute, Willis Tower, Theater District and Millennium Park are top draws among the skyscrapers.

❷ Near North & Navy Pier p67

The Near North packs in hotels, deep-dish pizza parlors, art galleries and so many upscale stores that its main vein - Michigan Ave - has been dubbed the 'Magnificent Mile.' Navy Pier unfurls a half-mile-long wharf of tour boats and carnival rides.

❸ Gold Coast p82

Furs and Rolls Royces are de rigueur in the Gold Coast. By day the cloud-poking Hancock Center and provocative Museum of Contemporary Art beckon. At night, Rush Street entertains with swanky steakhouses and piano lounges.

❹ Lincoln Park & Old Town p96

Lincoln Park is a sprawling lakefront oasis of ponds, paths, beaches and zoo animals. Next door, stylish Old Town hangs on to its free-spirited past with artsy bars and improv comedy bastion Second City.

❺ Lake View & Wrigleyville p110

Wrigley Field, both cursed and hallowed, draws baseball pilgrims. The bar-filled neighborhood around it parties hard and collides with the rainbow banners of Boystown, the nearby gay district. Kicky eateries and shops cater to the masses.

❻ Andersonville & Uptown p126

Vestiges of Andersonville's Swedish past remain, but today the area is about foodie taverns, funky boutiques and gay and lesbian bars. Uptown offers historic jazz houses, such

as the Green Mill (Al Capone's fave), along with the thriving cateries of 'Little Saigon.'

❼ Wicker Park, Bucktown & Ukrainian Village p137

These three neighborhoods are hot property. Hipster record stores, thrift shops and cocktail lounges have shot up, though vintage Eastern European dive bars linger on many street corners. The restaurant and rock club scene is unparalleled.

❽ Logan Square & Humboldt Park p153

Weenie-maker Hot Doug's, heavy-metal burger bar Kuma's and Michelin-starred Longman & Eagle bring gastronomes to Logan Square. Puerto Rican stronghold Humboldt Park is the place to sample a *jibarito*, the local sandwich specialty.

❾ Near West Side & Pilsen p164

The meat-packing West Loop buzzes with hot-chef restaurants and the hippest art galleries. Greektown and Little Italy serve ethnic fare nearby. In Pilsen, Mexican culture mixes with Chicago's bohemian underground, and colorful murals, taquerias and cafes result.

❿ South Loop & Near South Side p178

In the South Loop, the Field Museum, Shedd Aquarium and Adler Planetarium huddle at the Museum Campus. Historic buildings dot the area, including Chess Records, the seminal blues label. Chinatown bustles with noodle shops and exotic wares.

⓫ Hyde Park & South Side p192

Brainy Hyde Park holds bookstores galore and sights such as Frank Lloyd Wright's Robie House and the Museum of Science & Industry. Irish enclave Bridgeport has blossomed with bars and galleries, while Bronzeville has architecture and jazzy black-history shrines.

NEIGHBOURHOODS AT A GLANCE

The Loop

Neighborhood Top Five

1 Exploring arty **Millennium Park** (p46), where freebies beckon all day long, from morning yoga classes to afternoon splashes in Crown Fountain and evening concerts at Frank Gehry's swooping silver band shell.

2 Admiring color-swirled Monets, Renoirs and one very big Seurat at the **Art Institute of Chicago** (p49).

3 Gaping at sky-high ingenuity on a **Chicago Architecture Foundation** (p54) tour.

4 Stepping onto the glass-floored ledge and peering 1454ft straight down from **Willis Tower** (p51).

5 Chowing huge omelets and chatting with 80-year-old waitresses at Route 66 remnant **Lou Mitchell's** (p58).

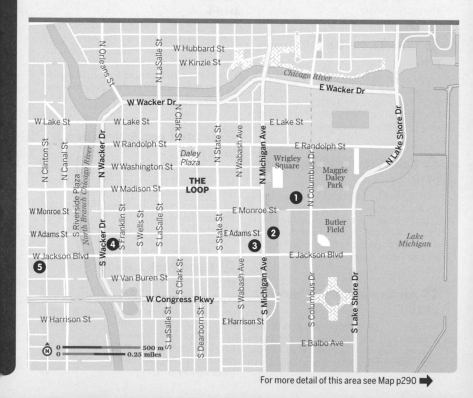

For more detail of this area see Map p290 ➡

Explore The Loop

The Loop is Chicago's center of action – its financial and historic heart – and it pulses with energy. Tumultuous tides of pinstriped businessfolk rush the sidewalks, while clattering El trains roar overhead. Above the melee, a towering forest of steel and stone soaks in the sun (or snow, as the case may be).

But it's not all work, work, work here. The Loop is also Chicago's favorite playground. Grant Park unfurls as a sprawling green buffer between the skyscrapers and Lake Michigan. Millennium Park is Grant's crown jewel, sparkling in the northwest corner. Both host bashes galore, especially in summer when everything from Blues Fest and Lollapalooza to the Grant Park Orchestra makes sweet music for the masses.

The Loop is home to big-ticket attractions such as the Art Institute, the Theater District and the city's world-famous architecture and public art. So count on spending significant time in the neighborhood. Take in the parks, art and cloud-scraping towers by day, then see a theater show or free Millennium Park concert at night. Despite the evening entertainment, the Loop clears out by 9pm or so.

Local Life

→ **Amish Donuts** Downtown workers throng the Thursday farmers market at Daley Plaza (p57). Keep an eye out for the Amish ladies who tempt passersby to their baked-goods stand with offers of free donuts.

→ **German Fests** It's tradition to visit the Berghoff (p61) in December when it's festooned with old-world Christmas decorations. It's also a ritual to *prost* beers during Berghoff's Oktoberfest, which takes over the plaza at Adams and Dearborn Sts in mid-September.

→ **Happy Hour** College students and off-duty office workers head to Miller's Pub (p61) when the day is done.

Getting There & Away

→ **El** All lines converge in the Loop. Clark/Lake and State/Lake are useful transfer stations.

→ **Bus** Number 56 runs along Milwaukee Ave from Wicker Park into the Loop; bus 151 comes down Michigan Ave from the lakefront in the north.

→ **Metra** Trains going south to Hyde Park and on into Indiana depart from Millennium Station; most other regional trains depart from Ogilvie or Union stations.

→ **Car** It'll cost you more to park in the Loop than anywhere else in the city. Meters cost $6.50 per hour (maybe more by the time you're reading this). Parking lots cost about $38 per day. **Millennium Park Garage** (www.millenniumgarages.com; 5 S Columbus Dr; per 3/24hr $23/30) is one of the cheapest.

Lonely Planet's Top Tip

Pack a picnic and meander over to Millennium Park to hear a free concert. Indie rock, jazz or classical performers take the stage nightly, including many big-name musicians. **Pastoral** (p60) and **Toni Patisserie** (p62) can set you up with deli goods and wine.

Best Places to Eat

→ Lou Mitchell's (p58)
→ Gage (p61)
→ Cafecito (p58)
→ Pizano's (p61)
→ French Market (p60)

For reviews, see p58 →

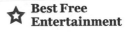

Best Places to Drink

→ Berghoff (p61)
→ Cyrano's Cafe & Wine Bar (p61)
→ Miller's Pub (p61)
→ Toni Patisserie & Cafe (p62)
→ Intelligentsia Coffee (p62)

For reviews, see p61 →

Best Free Entertainment

→ Grant Park Orchestra (p62)
→ Civic Orchestra of Chicago (p63)
→ International Screenings Program (p64)
→ Chicago Chamber Musicians (p64)

For reviews, see p62 →

TOP SIGHT
MILLENNIUM PARK

Chicago's showpiece shines with whimsical public art. Where to start amid the mod designs? Pritzker Pavilion, Frank Gehry's swooping silver band shell? Jaume Plensa's *Crown Fountain*, with its human gargoyles? Anish Kapoor's silvery sculpture *Cloud Gate* (aka 'the Bean')? Or maybe someplace away from the crowds, such as the veiled Lurie Garden abloom with prairie flowers. Summer concerts and winter ice-skating add to the fun.

The Park That Almost Wasn't

Millennium Park originally was slated to open in 2000 to coincide with the millennium (hence the name), but construction delays and escalating costs pushed it back. The whole thing seemed headed for disaster, since the original budget was $150 million, yet costs were rising far in excess of that. The final bill came to $475 million. Private donors – families such as the Pritzkers and Crowns, and corporate donors such as Boeing – ended up paying $200 million to complete the project.

The Magic Bean

The park's biggest draw is 'the Bean' – officially titled *Cloud Gate* – Anish Kapoor's 110-ton, silver-drop sculpture. It reflects both the sky and the skyline, and everyone clamors around to take a picture and to touch its silvery smoothness. Good vantage points for photos are at the sculpture's north and south ends. For great people-watching, go up the stairs on Washington St, on the Park Grill's north side, where there are shady benches.

DON'T MISS...

➜ Skyline photo with the Bean
➜ Getting wet in Crown Fountain
➜ Concert and picnic at Pritzker Pavilion
➜ Lurie Garden tour
➜ Winter ice-skating

PRACTICALITIES

➜ Map p290
➜ ☎312-742-1168
➜ www.millennium park.org
➜ 201 E Randolph St
➜ ⏰6am-11pm
➜ 🚻
➜ Ⓜ Brown, Orange, Green, Purple or Pink Line to Randolph

The Bean wasn't always so well loved. Kapoor was still polishing and grinding the 168 stainless steel plates that comprise the sculpture when the city first showed it to the public in 2004. The surface was supposed to be seamless – and it is now. But it wasn't then, and soon after its debut it went back under wraps. It didn't re-emerge until 2006.

Splashy Crown Fountain

Jaume Plensa's Crown Fountain is another crowd-pleaser. Its two, 50ft-high, glass-block towers contain video displays that flash a thousand different faces. The people shown are all native Chicagoans and they all agreed to strap into Plensa's special dental chair, where he immobilized their heads for filming. Each mug puckers up and spurts water, just like the gargoyles atop Notre Dame Cathedral. A fresh set of nonpuckering faces appears in winter, when the fountain is dry.

On hot days the fountain crowds with locals splashing in the streams to cool off. Kids especially love it. Bring a towel to dry off.

Pritzker Pavilion & Great Lawn Freebies

Pritzker Pavilion is Millennium Park's acousti-cally awesome band shell. Architect Frank Gehry designed it and gave it his trademark swooping sil-ver exterior. Supposedly it's inspired by gefilte fish, a classic Jewish dish that, as a child, Gehry watched his grandma make every week; he was struck by the fish's shape and movement before she hacked it to death. The pipes that criss-cross over the lawn are threaded with speakers, so that's where the sound comes from.

The pavilion hosts free concerts at 6:30pm most nights June to August. There's indie rock and new music on Monday, world music and jazz on Thurs-day, and classical music on Wednesday, Friday and Saturday. On Tuesday there's usually a movie beamed onto the huge screen on stage. Seats are available up close in the pavilion, or you can sit in the grassy Great Lawn that unfurls behind.

For all shows – but especially the classical ones, which the top-notch Grant Park Orchestra performs – folks bring blankets, picnics, wine and beer. There is nothing quite like sitting on the lawn, looking up through Gehry's wild grid and seeing all the skyscraping architecture that forms the backdrop *while* hearing the music. If you want a seat up close, arrive early.

The pavilion hosts daytime action, too. Concert rehearsals take place Tuesday to Friday, usually from 11am to 1:30pm, offering a taste of music if you

TOURS

The Millennium Park Greeter Service offers free walking tours of the grounds daily at 11:30am and 1pm, from late May to mid-October. Departure is from the Chicago Cultural Center Visitors Center, across the street at 77 E Randolph St. Space is limited to 10 people on a first-come, first-served basis.

Millennium Park is actually a rooftop garden – the world's largest, they say. A busy parking garage and Metra rail's Millennium Station lie underneath.

FAMILY FUN

Those with little ones in tow should make a bee-line for the Family Fun Tent in the park's north-west corner. Every day in summer it offers free arts, crafts and games for kids between 10am and 3pm. There's usu-ally a music sing-along (10am) and a reading circle (11am) as part of the mix.

Concessions, bath-rooms and a gift shop are available at McCormick Tribune Plaza (where the ice rink is in winter) on Michigan Ave.

can't catch the evening show. Each Saturday free exercise classes turn the Great Lawn into a groovy fitness center. Instructors backed by live music-makers lead tai chi at 7am, yoga at 8am, Pilates at 9am and dance at 10am.

The Secret Garden

If the crowds at the Bean, Crown Fountain and Pritzker Pavilion are too much, seek out the peaceful Lurie Garden, which uses native plants to form a botanical tribute to Illinois' tall-grass prairie. Visitors often miss the area, because it's hidden behind a big hedge. Yellow coneflowers, poet's daffodils, bluebells and other gorgeous blooms carpet the 5-acre oasis; everything is raised sustainably and without chemicals. A little river runs through it, where folks kick off their shoes and dangle their feet.

From May to September, volunteers lead free tours through the garden on Fridays between 11am and 1:30pm, and on Sundays between 10am and 1:30pm. They last 20 minutes and depart every 15 to 20 minutes. No reservations required, just show up at the south end of the boardwalk. Staff also offer free workshops on topics such as how to make lip balm using herbs from the garden. These require advance registration; sign up at www.luriegarden.org. The garden is at the Millennium Park's southeast end.

BP Bridge & Nichols Bridgeway

In addition to Pritzker Pavilion, Frank Gehry also designed the snaking BP Bridge that spans Columbus Dr. The luminous sheet-metal walkway connects Millennium Park (from the back of the Great Lawn) to the new Maggie Daley Park, which has ice-skating and rock climbing among its activity arsenal. The bridge offers great skyline views, too.

The Nichols Bridgeway is another pedestrian-only span. Renzo Piano designed this silver beauty. It arches from the park over Monroe St to the Art Institute's 3rd-floor contemporary sculpture garden (which is free to view). Piano, incidentally, also designed the museum's Modern Wing, which is where the sculpture garden is located.

Cycling & Ice-Skating

The McDonald's Cycle Center, in the park's northeast corner near the intersection of Randolph St and Columbus Dr, is the city's main facility for bike commuters, with 300 bike storage spaces plus showers. It's also a convenient place to pick up rental bikes from Bike Chicago (p65), including road, hybrid, tandem and children's bikes.

Tucked between the Bean sculpture and the twinkling lights of Michigan Ave, the McCormick Tribune Rink fills with skaters in winter. It operates from late November to late February and it's hands down the city's most scenic rink. Admission is free; skate rental costs $10. In summer the rink morphs into the Park Grill's alfresco cafe.

Harris Theater & Boeing Galleries

The Harris Theater for Music and Dance anchors the park's north side on Randolph St. More than 35 cutting-edge troupes from the Chicago Opera Theater to Hubbard Street Dance Chicago call it home. This is ground zero for the city's dance scene.

The two Boeing Galleries flank the park on the north and south sides. The outdoor spaces display changing exhibits of contemporary sculpture and photomurals.

◉ TOP SIGHT
ART INSTITUTE OF CHICAGO

The second-largest art museum in the country, the Art Institute of Chicago has the kind of celebrity-heavy collection that routinely draws gasps from patrons. Grant Wood's *American Gothic*? Check. Edward Hopper's lonely *Nighthawks*? Yep. Georges Seurat's *A Sunday Afternoon on the Island of La Grande Jatte*? Here. The museum's collection of impressionist and postimpressionist paintings is second only to those in France, and the number of surrealist works is tremendous.

Tips for Visitors

The vast museum unfurls through 1 million sq ft. There are two entrances: the Modern Wing on Monroe St and the Main Wing on Michigan Ave. The Modern Wing is the newer addition. Dazzling with natural light, it allows works by Picasso, Miró, Brancusi and the like to shine, and provides gallery space for new, cutting-edge multimedia work. The Main Wing houses the bulk of the collection, spanning genres throughout the ages.

Allow two hours to browse the museum's highlights; art buffs should allocate much longer. Ask at the information desk about free talks and tours once you're inside.

Advance tickets are available, but unless there's a blockbuster exhibit going on they're usually not necessary. The entrance queue moves fast.

The museum offers a full slate of children's programming Stop by the Ryan Education Center (on Level 1 in the Modern Wing) to see what hands-on activities staff are conducting.

DON'T MISS...

➡ Free app with tour suggestions
➡ *American Gothic*
➡ *Nighthawks*
➡ Lions guarding the entrance
➡ *A Sunday Afternoon on the Island of La Grande Jatte*

PRACTICALITIES

➡ Map p290
➡ ☏312-443-3600
➡ www.artic.edu
➡ 111 S Michigan Ave
➡ adult/child $23/free
➡ ⊙10:30am-5pm, to 8pm Thu
➡ 🚻

APP TOURS

Download the Art Institute's free app, either at home or using the museum's wi-fi. It offers more than 50 tours through the collection, including a Half Day Tour, an Impressionist Tour and the Birthday Suit Tour of naked works. Routes are divided by collection, theme or time available. It works off an internal GPS that isn't the world's most accurate, so expect to walk a lot.

The beloved lions guarding the entrance may seem identical, but they actually have different stances, expressions and measurements. Their creator, Edward Kemeys, described the south lion as closely watching something in the distance, while the north lion has his back up and is ready to spring. They remain regal and dignified, even when the museum plops fiberglass Blackhawks helmets on their heads when the team is in the Stanley Cup (or Bears helmets when the team is in the Super Bowl, etc).

Outdoor Freebies

You can see a fair bit of art without even entering the museum. The north garden (enter from Michigan Ave) has Alexander Calder's *Flying Dragon*, a little buddy to his *Flamingo* in the Loop. The Stock Exchange Arch, a revered architectural relic, rises up on the museum's northeast side. The 3rd-floor contemporary sculpture garden provides cool city views and connects to Millennium Park via the modern, pedestrian-only Nichols Bridgeway.

Must-See Works: Floor 2

This is where the majority of highlights hang.
➡ *A Sunday Afternoon on the Island of La Grande Jatte* by Georges Seurat (Gallery 240) – Get close enough for the painting to break down into its component dots and you'll see why it took Seurat two long years to complete his pointillist masterpiece.

➡ *The Bedroom* by Vincent van Gogh (Gallery 241) – It depicts the sleeping quarters of the artist's house in Arles. It's the second of three versions of the painting, executed during Van Gogh's 1889 stay at an asylum.

➡ *Stacks of Wheat* by Claude Monet (Gallery 243) – Paintings of the 15ft-tall stacks located by the artist's farmhouse in Giverny were part of a series that effectively launched Monet's career when they sold like hotcakes at a show he organized in 1891.

➡ *Nighthawks* by Edward Hopper (Gallery 262) – His lonely, poignant snapshot of four solitary souls at a neon-lit diner was inspired by a Greenwich Ave restaurant in Manhattan.

➡ *American Gothic* by Grant Wood (Gallery 263) – The artist, a lifelong resident of Iowa, used his sister and his dentist as models for the two stern-faced farmers.

Must-See Works: Other Floors

➡ *America Windows* by Marc Chagall (Gallery 144) – Chagall created the huge, blue stained-glass pieces to celebrate the USA's bicentennial.

➡ *The Old Guitarist* by Pablo Picasso (Gallery 391A) – The elongated figure is from the artist's Blue Period, reflecting not only Picasso's color scheme but his mindset as a poor, lonely artist in Paris in the early years.

➡ *Inventions of the Monsters* by Salvador Dalí (Gallery 396) – He painted it in Austria immediately before the Nazi annexation. The title refers to a Nostradamus prediction that the apparition of monsters presages the outbreak of war. The artist's profile is visible in the lower left corner, along with that of his wife, Gala.

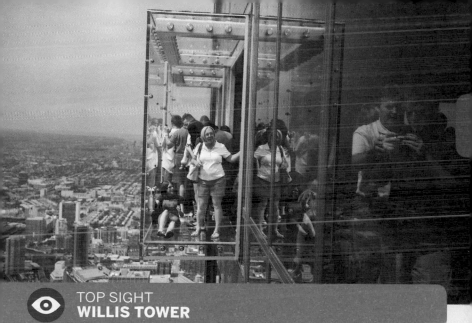

TOP SIGHT
WILLIS TOWER

Poor Willis Tower. First it had a confusing name change (it was the Sears Tower until insurance broker Willis Group Holdings bought the naming rights). Then it lost its 'tallest building in the USA' designation when New York's One World Trade Center shot past it. No matter. The 103rd-floor Skydeck still puts you 1454ft up in the clouds. Glass-floored ledges jut out in midair and give a knee-buckling perspective straight down. And the view sweeps over four states.

Enter via Jackson Blvd, then take the elevator down to the waiting area, where you go through security and pay admission. Queues can be up to an hour on busy days (peak times are in summer, between 11am and 4pm Friday to Sunday). Buying tickets online saves some time, but there's a $2.50 surcharge per ticket (and you must be able to print them).

Once you're in, there's a factoid-filled film to watch. You'll learn about the 43,000 miles of phone cable used, the 2232 steps to the roof, and how the tower height is the equivalent of 313 Oprahs (or 262 Michael Jordans). And then the ear-popping, 70-second elevator ride to the top. From here, the entire city stretches below and you can see exactly how Chicago is laid out. On good days you can see for 40 to 50 miles, as far as Indiana, Michigan and Wisconsin. On hazy or stormy days you won't see much at all, so don't bother.

The four ledges are on the deck's west side. They're like glass-encased boxes hanging out from the building's frame. If crowds are light, you can sprawl out on one for the ultimate photo op.

For those who prefer a drink with their vista, the Gold Coast's John Hancock Center is a better choice.

DON'T MISS...
→ The ledges
→ Sunset views
→ Skyscraper trivia during the elevator ride
→ Feeling the tower sway

PRACTICALITIES
→ Map p290
→ ☏312-875-9696
→ www.the-sky deck.com
→ 233 S Wacker Dr
→ adult/child $18/12
→ ⊙9am-10pm Apr-Sep, 10am-8pm Oct-Mar
→ Ⓜ Brown, Orange, Purple or Pink Line to Quincy

The Loop – Architecture

When the Great Fire of 1871 burned down the city, it created the blank canvas that allowed Chicago's mighty architecture to flourish. The city presented the world with the first skyscraper soon after, and it has been home to big ideas in modern design ever since. The Loop is ground zero for gawking.

1. Reliance Building (p56)
This glass-paneled beauty set the precedent for modern skyscraper design.

2. Marquette Building (p56)
Mosaics in the entrance illustrate the adventures of explorer Jacques Marquette.

3. Staircase, Monadnock Building (p56)
Architectural innovations of the 1890s are showcased in this landmark building.

4. Sullivan Center (p56)
Ornate metalwork adorns the entrance to this building, designed in 1899.

 # SIGHTS

MILLENNIUM PARK   PARK
See p46.

ART INSTITUTE OF CHICAGO   MUSEUM
See p49.

WILLIS TOWER   TOWER
See p51.

**CHICAGO CULTURAL
CENTER**   CULTURAL BUILDING
Map p290 (☏312-744-6630; www.chicagocul-turalcenter.org; 78 E Washington St; ⊗8am-7pm Mon-Thu, 8am-6pm Fri, 9am-6pm Sat, 10am-6pm Sun; ⓂBrown, Orange, Green, Purple, Pink Line to Randolph) FREE This block-long build-ing houses ongoing art exhibitions and foreign films, as well as jazz, classical and electronic dance music concerts at lunch-time (12:15pm weekdays). It also contains the world's largest Tiffany stained-glass dome, Chicago's main Visitors Center and StoryCorps' recording studio (where folks tell their tale, get a CD of it and have it pre-served in the Library of Congress). All free!

Foreign films screen on Wednesday at 6:30pm from May to September. Story-Corps operates on Thursday (2pm to 7pm) and Saturday (10am to 5pm). Check the daily schedule posted at the entrances (at both Randolph and Washington Sts) to see what else is going on.

The exquisite, beaux-arts building be-gan its life as the Chicago Public Library in 1897. The Gilded Age interior mixes white Carrara and green Connemara marble throughout. The gorgeous Tiffany dome is on the 3rd floor, where the library circula-tion desk used to be. The building's splen-dor was meant to inspire the rabble to-ward loftier goals. You can explore on your own, or take a free building tour (1:15pm Wednesday, Friday and Saturday), which departs from the Randolph St lobby. There's also free wi-fi and seating areas throughout the building.

**CHICAGO ARCHITECTURE
FOUNDATION**   GALLERY
Map p290 (CAF; ☏312-922-3432; www.architec-ture.org; 224 S Michigan Ave; ⊗9am-5:30pm; ⓂBrown, Orange, Green, Purple, Pink Line to Ad-ams) FREE CAF is the premier keeper of Chi-cago's architectural flame. Dip in to check out the galleries in the atrium (behind the shop). The 'Chicago Model City' display pro-vides a cool 3D overview of local skyscrap-ers. You can also get the lowdown on CAF's extensive roster of boat and walking tours and make bookings here.

The foundation's shop sells stacks of books about local buildings and architects if you prefer to do it yourself.

ROUTE 66 SIGN   HISTORIC SITE
Map p290 (E Adams St btwn S Michigan & Wa-bash Aves; ⓂBrown, Orange, Green, Purple, Pink Line to Adams) Attention Route 66 buffs: the Mother Road's starting point is here. Look for the sign that marks the spot on Adams St's south side as you head west toward Wa-bash Ave. From Chicago the route moseys 2400 miles onward to Los Angeles past neon signs, mom-and-pop motels and pie-filled diners.

BUCKINGHAM FOUNTAIN   FOUNTAIN
Map p290 (cnr E Congress Pkwy & S Columbus Dr; ⓂRed Line to Harrison) Grant Park's center-piece is one of the world's largest squirters,

---

LOCAL KNOWLEDGE

THE PEDWAY

Come wintertime, when the going gets tough and icy sleet knifes your face, head down to the Pedway. Chicago has a 40-block labyrinth of underground walkways, built in conjunction with the subway trains. The system isn't entirely connected (ie it would be difficult to walk from one end of the Loop to the other underground), and you'll find that you rise to the surface in the oddest places – say, an apartment building, a hotel lobby or Macy's. The walkways are also hit-or-miss for amenities: some have coffee shops and fast-food outlets tucked along the way, some have urine smells, but they're an interesting place to soak up local life. The city posts 'Pedway' signs above ground at points of entry. City Hall is a good place to dive under. **Chicago Detours** (☏312-350-1131; www.chicagodetours.com; tours from $26) provides a free map to download from its website for DIY jaunts. The company also offers guided excur-sions that include the passageways.

PUBLIC ART TO PONDER

Several mind-blowing public artworks have popped up in the Loop over the decades.

Untitled (Map p290; 50 W Washington St; ⓂBlue Line to Washington) – Pablo Picasso's work, which everyone just calls 'the Picasso', is the granddaddy of Chicago's public art. The artist was 82 when the work was commissioned. The US Steel Works in Gary, Indiana, made it to Picasso's specifications and erected it in 1967 in Daley Plaza. When Chicago tried to pay Picasso for the work, he refused, saying the sculpture was meant as a gift to the city. At the time, many locals thought the abstract piece was hideous and should be torn down and replaced with a statue of Cubs legend Ernie Banks.

Miró's Chicago (Map p290; 69 W Washington St; ⓂBlue Line to Washington) – Originally called *The Sun, The Moon and One Star*, Joan Miró's monument sits across the street from Daley Plaza. Miró hoped to evoke the 'mystical force of a great earth mother' with the 40ft sculpture, made of various metals, cement and tile in 1981.

Monument with Standing Beast (Map p290; 100 W Randolph St; ⓂBrown, Orange, Green, Purple, Pink, Blue Line to Clark/Lake) – French sculptor Jean Dubuffet created the piece, which some call 'Snoopy in a Blender'. The 1984 white fiberglass work looks a little like inflated puzzle pieces and has a definite Keith Haring–esque feel to it. As you can see by the large number of kids crawling around inside, it's a hands-on piece of art.

Four Seasons (Map p290; 10 S Dearborn St; ⓂBlue Line to Monroe) – Russian-born artist Marc Chagall loved Chicago and in 1974 he donated this grand mosaic to the city. Using thousands of bits of glass and stone, the artist portrayed six scenes of the city in hues reminiscent of the Mediterranean coast of France, where he kept his studio. Chagall continued to make adjustments, such as updating the skyline, after the work arrived in Chicago.

Flamingo (Map p290; 50 W Adams St; ⓂBlue Line to Jackson) – Alexander Calder's soaring red-pink sculpture provides some much-needed relief from the stark facades of the federal buildings around it. Calder dedicated the sculpture in October 1974 by riding into the Loop on a bandwagon pulled by 40 horses, accompanied by a circus parade.

For the locations of more public artworks stashed around the city, pick up a copy of the useful *Chicago Public Art Guide* at any visitors center, or check the website www.cityofchicago.org/publicart. And don't forget to visit the Bean (p46), the reigning Loop fave.

with a 1.5-million-gallon capacity and a 15-story-high spray. It lets loose on the hour from 9am to 11pm mid-April to mid-October, accompanied at night by multicolored lights and music.

Wealthy widow Kate Sturges Buckingham gave the magnificent structure to the city in 1927 in memory of her brother, Clarence. She also wisely left an endowment to maintain and operate it. The central fountain symbolizes Lake Michigan, with the four water-spouting sea creatures representing the surrounding states.

HAROLD WASHINGTON LIBRARY CENTER LIBRARY
Map p290 (☑312-747-4300; www.chipublib.org; 400 S State St; ⊘9am-9pm Mon-Thu, to 5pm Fri

& Sat, 1-5pm Sun; ⓂBrown, Orange, Purple, Pink Line to Library) This grand, art-filled building with free internet terminals and wi-fi is Chicago's whopping main library. Major authors give readings here and exhibits are constantly shown in the galleries. The light-drenched, 9th-floor Winter Garden is a sweet hideaway for reading, writing or just taking a load off, though it's a bit of a hike to get there.

Take the escalators to the 3rd floor (home of the browsable newspapers and computer commons), then transfer to the elevator to go up six more floors. And those green-copper creatures staring down from the exterior roof? They're wise old owls.

FAMOUS LOOP ARCHITECTURE

Ever since Chicago presented the world with the first skyscraper in 1885, it has thought big with its architecture and pushed the envelope of modern design. The Loop is ground zero for gawking.

Monadnock Building (Map p290; www.monadnockbuilding.com; 53 W Jackson Blvd; Ⓜ Blue Line to Jackson) Architecture buffs on a pilgrimage bow down first to Monadnock, two buildings in one that depict a crucial juncture in skyscraper development. The north half is the older, traditional design from 1891 (with thick, load-bearing walls), while the south is the newer, more modern half (with a metal frame that allows for jazzier-looking walls and bigger windows).

Rookery (Map p290; www.gowright.org/rookery; 209 S LaSalle St; ⊙9:30am-5:30pm Mon-Fri; Ⓜ Brown, Orange, Purple, Pink Line to Quincy) The 1888 Rookery looks hulking and fortresslike outside, but it's light and airy inside thanks to Frank Lloyd Wright's atrium overhaul. Step inside and have a look. Tours ($5 to $10) are available at noon on weekdays. Pigeons used to roost here, hence the name.

Marshall Field Building (Map p290; 111 N State St; ⊙10am-8pm Mon-Thu, to 9pm Sat, 11am-7pm Sun; Ⓜ Brown, Orange, Green, Purple, Pink Line to Randolph) Weep all you want over the old Marshall Field's becoming Macy's; the building remains a classic no matter who's in it. The iconic bronze corner clocks on the outside have given busy Loop workers the time for more than 100 years now. Inside, a 6000-sq-ft dome designed by Louis Comfort Tiffany caps the northside atrium; 50 artists toiled for 18 months to make it.

Sullivan Center (Map p290; www.thesullivancenter.com; 1 S State St; Ⓜ Red Line to Monroe) Louis Sullivan designed this ornate building in 1899. For a century it was home to the Carson Pirie Scott & Co department store. Check out the superb metalwork around the main entrance at State and Madison Sts, and try to find Sullivan's initials amid the flowing botanical and geometric forms. Target took over the building's main space in 2012.

Marquette Building (Map p290; www.marquette.macfound.org; 140 S Dearborn St; ⊙7am-10pm; Ⓜ Blue Line to Monroe) The architects behind the Marquette Building made natural light and ventilation vital components. While that's nice, the most impressive features are the sculptured panels and mosaics that recall the exploits of French explorer Jacques Marquette; look for them above the entrance and in the lobby.

Reliance Building (Map p290; 1 W Washington St; Ⓜ Blue Line to Washington) With its 16 stories of shimmering glass, framed by brilliant white terra-cotta details, the Reliance Building is a breath of fresh air. The structure's lightweight internal metal frame supports a glass facade that gives it a feeling of lightness, a style that didn't become universal until after WWII. Today the Reliance houses the chic Hotel Burnham (p218). Added historical bonus: Al Capone's dentist drilled teeth in what's now room 809.

Santa Fe Building (Map p290; 224 S Michigan Ave; Ⓜ Brown, Orange, Green, Purple, Pink Line to Adams) Architect Daniel Burnham kept his offices in this 1904 terra-cotta beauty. Enter the lobby and look up at the vast light well Burnham placed in the center – he gave this same feature to the Rookery. Appropriately enough, the Santa Fe Building now houses the Chicago Architecture Foundation.

Kluczynski Building (Map p290; 230 S Dearborn St; Ⓜ Blue Line to Jackson) Last, but certainly not least, no discussion of famed Loop architecture is complete without mentioning the boxy, metal-and-glass International style of Ludwig Mies van der Rohe. His Kluczynski Building, part of the Chicago Federal Center, is a prime example; he designed many more buildings at the Illinois Institute of Technology.

CHICAGO BOARD OF TRADE
ARCHITECTURE

Map p290 (141 W Jackson Blvd; Ⓜ Brown, Orange, Purple, Pink Line to LaSalle) This building is a 1930 art-deco gem. Inside, manic traders swap futures and options – a mysterious process that has something to do with corn. Or maybe it's wheat. From outside gaze up at the giant statue of Ceres, the Roman goddess of agriculture, that tops the building. You can walk around the public areas, but security is tight beyond that.

The only way to see the trading floor in action is via the Chicago Architecture Foundation's (p54) occasional tours ($10).

MONEY MUSEUM
MUSEUM

Map p290 (☏312-322-2400; www.chicagofed. org; 230 S LaSalle St; ☺8:30am-5pm Mon-Fri; Ⓜ Brown, Orange, Purple, Pink Line to Quincy) **FREE** This small museum in the Federal Reserve Bank of Chicago is fun for a quick browse. The best exhibits include a giant glass cube stuffed with one million $1 bills (they weigh 2000lb) and a counterfeit display differentiating real bills from fakes. Learn why we call $1000 a 'grand', and snap a sweet photo clutching the million-dollar-stuffed briefcase.

You'll also get a free bag of shredded currency to take home. The museum is a school-group favorite. At 1pm there's a 45-minute guided tour. When you enter the building, look for the 'visitors center' sign (it doesn't say 'Money Museum'), and note you'll have to go through a metal detector.

UNION STATION
ARCHITECTURE

Map p290 (☏312-655-2385; www.chicagounion-station.com; 225 S Canal St; Ⓜ Brown, Orange, Purple, Pink Line to Quincy) The wonderfully restored 1925 building looks like it stepped right out of a gangster movie. In fact, it's been used to great effect in exactly this way. Remember director Brian De Palma's classic *The Untouchables*, when Eliott Ness loses his grip on the baby carriage during the shoot-out with Al Capone's henchmen? And the carriage bounces down the stairs in slow motion? Those steps are here.

They're the north ones from Canal St to the waiting room. Come during the day when Amtrak and Metra riders stride through the space, which is dappled with bright shafts of sunlight from the banks of windows.

DALEY PLAZA
PLAZA

Map p290 (www.thedaleycenter.com; 50 W Washington St; Ⓜ Blue Line to Washington) The Picasso sculpture marks the heart of Daley Plaza, which is the place to be come lunchtime, particularly when the weather warms. You never know what will be going on – dance performances, bands, ethnic festivals, holiday celebrations, a farmers market (7am to 3pm Thursdays) – but you do know it'll be free. City Hall rises to the plaza's west over Clark St.

Daley Plaza remains a pilgrimage site to many as the film location where the Blues Brothers drove through and crashed into the Daley Center's plate-glass windows.

CHICAGO THEATRE
THEATER

Map p290 (☏312-462-6363; www.thechicago theatre.com; 175 N State St; Ⓜ Brown, Orange, Green, Purple, Pink Line to State/Lake) Take a gander at the six-story sign out front. It's an official landmark (and an excellent photo op). Everyone from Duke Ellington to Frank Sinatra to Prince has taken the stage here over the years (and left their signature on the famous backstage walls). The real show-stopper, though, is the opulent French baroque architecture, including the lobby modeled on the Palace of Versailles.

Opened in 1921 the theater originally screened silent movies with a full orchestra and white-gloved ushers leading patrons to their seats. Tickets cost just 50 cents, so rich and poor alike could revel in the splendor. Today it's a concert venue. Tours ($12) are available daily in summer, less often the rest of the year.

RIVERWALK
WATERFRONT

Map p290 (Chicago River waterfront along Wacker Dr, btwn N Lake Shore Dr & N State St; Ⓜ Brown, Orange, Green, Purple, Pink, Blue Line to State/Lake) Clasping the Chicago River's south side along Wacker Dr, this mile-long promenade provides a peaceful spot to take a break from downtown's hullabaloo. Access it from the stairs at any bridge. Outdoor cafes and bike and kayak rental shops dot the way and there's also a Vietnam veteran's memorial (near N Wabash Ave), a small river history museum (at N Michigan Ave) and sightseeing boats sprinkled in.

To the east, between Columbus and Lake Shore Drs on the river's north side, Centennial Fountain shoots a massive arc of water across the river. It spurts for 10 minutes straight every hour on the hour, from 10am to 2pm and again from 5pm to midnight. The exercise is meant to commemorate the labor-intensive reversal of the Chicago River in 1900, which tidily began sending all of the city's wastes downriver rather than into the lake. (Chicago's neighbors downstate, as you can imagine, do not go out of their way to celebrate this feat of civil engineering). The Riverwalk is slated to expand west to Lake St over the next few years.

AQUA TOWER ARCHITECTURE

Map p290 (225 N Columbus Dr; MBrown, Orange, Green, Purple, Pink Line to State/Lake) Renowned local architect Jeanne Gang designed the spectacularly undulating building, which was completed in 2010 to much acclaim. The 82-story tower is the world's tallest building designed by a woman. The Radisson Blu Aqua Hotel (p219) takes up floors 1 to 18; the remaining floors hold apartments and offices.

✖ EATING

★LOU MITCHELL'S BREAKFAST $

Map p312 (www.loumitchellsrestaurant.com; 565 W Jackson Blvd; mains $6-11; ⊘5:30am-3pm Mon-Sat, 7am-3pm Sun; ✚; MBlue Line to Clinton) A relic of Route 66, Lou's brings in elbow-to-elbow locals and tourists for breakfast. The old-school waitresses deliver fluffy omelets that hang off the plate and thick-cut French toast with a jug of syrup. They call you 'honey' and fill your coffee cup endlessly. There's often a queue to get in, but free donut holes and Milk Duds help ease the wait.

CAFECITO CUBAN $

Map p290 (www.cafecitochicago.com; 26 E Congress Pkwy; sandwiches $5-7; ⊘7am-9pm Mon-Fri, 10am-6pm Sat & Sun; ⬚; MBrown, Orange, Purple, Pink Line to Library) Attached to the HI-Chicago (p218) hostel and perfect for the hungry, thrifty traveler, Cafecito serves killer Cuban sandwiches layered with citrus-garlic-marinated roasted pork and ham. Strong coffee and hearty egg sandwiches make a fine breakfast. Ask at the counter for the free wi-fi password.

NATIVE FOODS CAFE VEGETARIAN $

Map p290 (www.nativefoods.com; 218 S Clark St; mains $8-10; ⊘10:30am-9pm Mon-Sat, 11am-7pm Sun; ⬚; MBrown, Orange, Purple, Pink Line to

🏃 Neighborhood Walk
A Postcard Perspective

START PICASSO SCULPTURE
END WILLIS TOWER
LENGTH 2.25 MILES, FOUR HOURS

Why buy postcards when you can make your own? A camera, comfortable shoes, a day spent clicking away at Loop sights and you'll have your own picture-postcard perspective of the city.

Begin at Daley Plaza, scratching your head over Picasso's **❶Untitled** (p55) sculpture. The artist never would say what the 1967 iron work represents. Most people believe it's the head of a woman. But Picasso also drew pictures of his dog that look similar. Then there's the baboon theory... Whatever it is, it has become a well-known Chicago symbol. The most intriguing perspective may just be laying faceup, camera angled, looking at the nose of the beast.

For more landmark public art, cross the street to **❷Miró's Chicago** (p55). Spanish artist Joan Miró unveiled his robot/pagan fertility-goddesslike sculpture in 1981, on his 88th birthday. He originally titled it *The Sun, the Moon and One Star*. The star is the fork projecting off the top. The moon is the sphere at the center. The sun is... Oh, never mind. Just snap.

What could be more postcard perfect than a six-story-high sign spelling the town's name? Any time is fine to capture the marquee for the **❸Chicago Theatre** (p57), but if your tour falls on a cloudy day, that would eliminate harsh shadows.

'Meeting under the clock' has been a Chicago tradition since 1897, when retailer Marshall Field installed the **❹Old Marshall Field's Clock** at Washington and State Sts outside his department store. The timepiece weighs more than 7.5 tons. A photo beneath the clock is a must.

The 38ft-diameter Tiffany dome at the **❺Chicago Cultural Center** (p54), the world's largest, is well worth photographing (as is the 1897 building's hodgepodge of Greek, Roman and European architectural styles). But you're really here to get inspiration from the architectural photos in the Landmark Chicago Gallery.

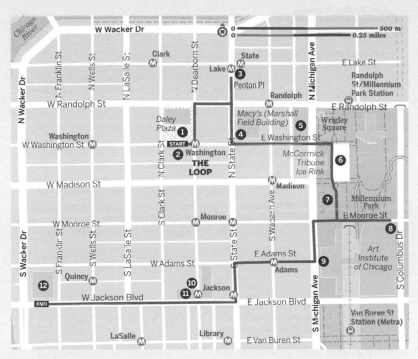

THE LOOP

The ongoing exhibition shows 72 black-and-white images of prominent structures by well-known local shutterbugs such as Richard Nickel (more on him to come...).

Plenty of Kodak moments happen at 24-acre Millennium Park. Your first stop is the sculpture Chicagoans call 'the Bean', officially known as **6 Cloud Gate** (p46). Stand on the west side of the giant mirrored blob, hold the camera at waist level and you can take a self-portrait with a skyline background.

Mosey onward to the human gargoyles puckering up at **7 Crown Fountain** (p47). Geysers spout from the ground in front of two 50ft LED screens projecting images of peoples' faces. When an open-mouthed guy or gal appears, the fountain spews water so it looks like they're spitting. Use a fast shutter speed and stick to a side view unless you've got a waterproof camera.

Many of renowned architect Louis Sullivan's buildings have been demolished. But you can get up close to his exquisite terracotta ornamentation at the **8 Chicago Stock Exchange Arch**, which was rescued and placed outside the Art Institute (on the northeast side). A telephoto lens can

isolate the detail. Your arch pictures will be considerably less risky than those Richard Nickel took. While the Stock Exchange was abandoned and awaiting demolition in 1972, the famed photographer entered to document the scene. The building collapsed, taking his life.

Around the front of the Art Institute stand two 1894 bronze **9 lions** – city mascots of sorts. They wore helmets when the Blackhawks won the 2010 Stanley Cup and White Sox caps during the 2005 pennant. They wear wreathes around their necks at Christmastime. Zoom in for a striking profile shot silhouetted against city buildings.

Alexander Calder's **10 Flamingo** (p55) is another easily recognized piece of monumental public art in Chicago. That bright red paint job should photograph well, especially if you frame it against Mies van der Rohe's groundbreaking 1974 glass-and-steel **11 Kluczynski Building** (p56) in the Chicago Federal Center. Aligning the building's edge on a slight diagonal will add dynamism to a shot of the 1454ft-tall **12 Willis Tower** (p51). A final photo from the 103rd-floor Skydeck sums it up: high-rises galore, lake beyond – that's the Loop.

FRENCH MARKET

The **French Market** (Map p290; www.frenchmarketchicago.com; 131 N Clinton St; ⊘10am-7pm Mon-Fri, to 4pm Sat; MGreen Line to Clinton), located in the Ogilvie train station, is a favorite of local chow hounds. They equate it to a food-truck pod, with eclectic vendors specializing in a couple of high-quality dishes each. The Euro-style hall with tables is not particularly atmospheric, but no one seems to mind when everything costs less than $10. Sniff around the aisles and see what appeals. Our favorites:

➡ Saigon Sisters – They are indeed two sisters and they ladle out Vietnamese *pho* (noodle soup) and *banh mi* (baguette sandwiches). Try the Sun Tanned Cow, with coconut-milk-braised beef ribs, lime leaves and ginger.

➡ Fumare Meats – Revered for its Montreal-style smoked-meat sandwiches.

➡ Pastoral – A branch of the artisan deli chain (p60) wafts its wares.

➡ Lillie's Q – The chef has won several national prizes for his family barbecue recipes. Southern-style boiled peanuts, grits (ground corn cooked to a cereal-like consistency) and collard greens accompany the meaty goodness.

➡ Beaver's Donuts – The small but mighty dough bombs drip with chocolate, caramel and peanut-butter toppings.

➡ Frietkoten – Belgian fries arrive in a paper cone slathered in one of 20 sauces. The stall sells European and craft brews to help wash the *frites* down.

Quincy) 🍴 This national chain of vegan fast-casual food makes life easy for folks who don't eat animals. The meatball sandwich rocks the seitan, while the scorpion burger fires up hot-spiced tempeh. Local beers and organic wines accompany the wide-ranging menu of Greek, Asian, Mexican and Italian-inspired dishes. Soy-free, gluten-free and nut-free menus are available for allergy sufferers.

WESTMINSTER HOT DOG   AMERICAN $

Map p290 (www.westminsterhotdog.com; 11 N Wells St; hot dogs $3-8; ⊘10:30am-3pm Mon-Fri; MBrown, Orange, Purple, Pink Line to Washington) While Westminster is no Hot Doug's (p155), it's darn delectable and a helluva lot easier to get to than Doug's. The no-frills hot-dog-stand ambience is a front for fancy-pants sausages made on-site daily – say, a wild elk beer brat with Guinness blueberry sauce and crinkle-cut fries. Items start disappearing from the menu board by 1pm.

PASTORAL   DELI $

Map p290 (www.pastoralartisan.com; 53 E Lake St; sandwiches $8-10; ⊘10:30am-8pm Mon-Fri, 11am-6pm Sat & Sun; MBrown, Orange, Green, Purple, Pink Line to Randolph or State/Lake) Pastoral makes a mean sandwich with artisan cheeses and meats. Fresh-shaved serrano ham, Basque salami and other carnivorous fixings meet smoky mozzarella, Gruyere and piquant spreads on crusty breads. Vege-

tarians get a smattering of cheese and veggie options to choose from. There's limited seating, as most folks take away (especially for picnics in nearby Millennium Park).

The shop sells bottles of beer and wine, too. Pastoral has another branch in the Loop's French Market, as well as one in Lakeview.

DO-RITE DONUTS   BAKERY $

Map p290 (www.doritedonuts.com; 50 W Randolph St; donuts $2.50-3.50; ⊘6:30am-2pm Mon-Fri, from 7am Sat & Sun; MBlue Line to Washington) The line snakes out the door at Do-Rite's shoebox-size shop. Office workers clamor for peanut butter banana, coffee cream and chocolate-ganache-dripping Boston cream donuts to jump-start their day. They're typically served warm (small fryers mean frequent, hot-off-the press batches). A gluten-free option is always on the menu.

OASIS   MIDDLE EASTERN $

Map p290 (☎312-443-9534; 21 N Wabash Ave; mains $5-8; ⊘10am-5pm Mon-Fri, 11am-3pm Sat; MBrown, Orange, Green, Purple, Pink Line to Madison) Walk past diamonds, gold and other bling in the jewelers' mall before striking it rich in this cafe at the back. Creamy hummus, crisp falafel and other Middle Eastern favorites fill plates at bargain prices. Eat in or carry out to nearby Millennium Park.

FALAFILL
MIDDLE EASTERN $

Map p290 (www.eatfalafill.com; 72 E Adams St; mains $6-9; ☺11am-5:30pm Mon-Fri; ⓂBrown, Orange, Green, Purple, Pink Line to Adams) A student favorite located steps from the Art Institute, this outpost of the local mini-chain has just a few tables. Order at the counter and choose a filling of falafel, steak, chicken or Lebanese beef sausage, then choose a sandwich or salad base. Afterward customize it at the topping bar with cilantro chutney, Moroccan olives, pickled ginger and 15 other garnishes.

PIZANO'S
PIZZERIA $$

Map p290 (✆312-236-1777; www.pizanoschicago. com; 61 E Madison St; 10-inch pizzas from $14; ☺11am-2am Sun-Fri, to 3am Sat; ☎; ⓂBrown, Orange, Green, Purple, Pink Line to Madison) Pizano's is a good recommendation for deep dish newbies, since it's not jaw-breakingly thick. The thin-crust pies that hit the checker-clothed tables are good too, winning rave reviews for crispness. Some of the waitstaff are characters who've been around forever, which adds to the convivial ambience. It's open late (with a full bar), which is a Loop rarity.

GAGE
PUB $$$

Map p290 (✆312-372-4243; www.thegagechicago. com; 24 S Michigan Ave; mains $17-36; ☺11am-11pm, to midnight Fri; ⓂBrown, Orange, Green, Purple, Pink Line to Madison) It's clear from the formidable Scotch egg – a sausage-encased, deep-fried, hard-boiled beast with the girth of a softball – that this elegant, Irish-tinged gastropub is serious about its menu. Standards include the Camembert-topped Gage burger and Guinness-battered fish and chips, while more exotic options include roast saddle of elk and barbecued bison short ribs.

The booze rocks, too, including a solid whiskey list and small-batch beers that pair with the food. Ask the knowledgeable servers about what will work best with your meal. Note the bar stays open later, usually until 2am.

TRATTORIA NO 10
ITALIAN $$$

Map p290 (✆312-984-1718; www.trattoriaten. com; 10 N Dearborn St; mains $18-29; ☺11:30am-9pm Mon-Thu, to 10pm Fri, 5-10pm Sat; ⓂBlue Line to Washington) This clubby bistro is just steps from the Loop theater district and fills up fast with ticket-holders. The straightforward menu provides exception-ally flavorful takes on familiar items such as ravioli (try the one filled with asparagus tip, *bufala* cheese and sun-dried tomatoes) and risotto with pesto and chicken. Gluten-free pasta is available. Reservations are a good idea.

DRINKING & NIGHTLIFE

Choices are relatively limited at night. Move a few blocks onward to the Near North and the boozer bounty increases

BERGHOFF
BAR

Map p290 (www.theberghoff.com; 17 W Adams St; ☺11am-9pm Mon-Sat; ⓂBlue, Red Line to Jackson) The Berghoff dates from 1898 and goes down in the annals of history as the first spot in Chicago to serve a legal drink after Prohibition (ask to see the liquor license stamped '#1'). Little has changed around the antique wood bar since then. Belly up for frosty mugs of the house brand beer; five-brew flights are a fine way to determine your favorite.

You can also order sauerbraten (seasoned, oven-roasted beef), schnitzel and other old-world classics from the adjoining restaurant next door.

CYRANO'S CAFE & WINE BAR
CAFE

Map p290 (www.cyranoscafeontheriver.com; Riverwalk, 233 E Wacker Dr; ☺11am-10pm early May-Oct; ⓂBrown, Orange, Green, Purple, Pink Line to State/Lake) Cyrano's casual tables sit amid a jumble of bright-hued flowers along the Riverwalk (p57). Swirl a glass of beer, Champagne, Beaujolais, Riesling or Cotés de Gascogne from the French owner's list while watching the boats drift by. Sandwiches, cheese plates and ice cream supplement the drinks.

MILLER'S PUB
PUB

Map p290 (www.millerspub.com; 134 S Wabash Ave; ☺10am-4am; ⓂBrown, Orange, Green, Purple, Pink Line to Adams) The beauty of Miller's isn't so much literal, though it's attractive enough with dark-wood furnishings, stained glass and lots of nostalgic sports photos and oil paintings adorning the walls. The real beauty comes from the late-night hours in an area where most places close by 10pm. Even better: Miller's pours a whopping selection of craft and Belgian brews and serves a big, meaty menu.

TONI PATISSERIE & CAFE CAFE

Map p290 (www.tonipatisserie.com; 65 E Washington St; ⊙8am-8pm Mon-Sat, to 5pm Sun; ⓂBrown, Orange, Green, Purple, Pink Line to Randolph or Madison) Toni's provides a cute refuge for a glass of wine. The Parisian-style cafe has a small list of French reds, whites and sparkling wines to sip at the close-set tables while you try to resist the eclairs, macaroons and tiered cakes tempting from the glass case. It also sells bottles for takeaway (handy for park picnics).

INTELLIGENTSIA COFFEE CAFE

Map p290 (www.intelligentsiacoffee.com; 53 E Randolph St; ⊙6:30am-8pm Mon-Fri, 7am-9pm Sat, 7am-7pm Sun; ⓂBrown, Orange, Green, Purple, Pink Line to Randolph) Intelligentsia is a local chain that roasts its own beans and percolates good strong stuff. Staff know their wares: they recently won the US Barista Championship. The modern, industrial coffee-bar makes a good pre- or post-Millennium Park fuel up. There's another Loop outlet in the Monadnock Building (p56).

PLAZA AT PARK GRILL CAFE

Map p290 (www.parkgrillchicago.com/plaza; 11 N Michigan Ave; ⊙from 11am mid-May–early Oct; ⓂBrown, Orange, Green, Purple, Pink Line to Madison) If you want lively people-watching in the thick of it all, hit the Plaza. Set in Millennium Park between the Bean sculpture and Michigan Ave, the summer-only bar sprawls where the ice-skating rink is during colder months. It can be pricey and cheesy (cover bands!), but it's the neighborhood's hot spot for alfresco boozing.

☆ ENTERTAINMENT

GOODMAN THEATRE THEATER

Map p290 (☑312-443-3800; www.goodman theatre.org; 170 N Dearborn St; ⓂBrown, Orange, Green, Purple, Pink, Blue Line to Clark/Lake) The Goodman reigns alongside the Steppenwolf Theatre (p107) as Chicago's top drama house and its Theater District facility is gorgeous. It specializes in new and classic American productions and has been cited several times as one of the best regional theaters in the USA. Its annual production of *A Christmas Carol* has become a local family tradition.

At 10am, Goodman puts unsold tickets for the current day's performance on sale for half-price online. They're also available at the box office starting at noon.

GRANT PARK ORCHESTRA CLASSICAL MUSIC

Map p290 (☑312-742-7638; www.grantparkmusic festival.com; Pritzker Pavilion, Millennium Park; ⊙6:30pm Wed & Fri, 7:30pm Sat mid-Jun–mid-Aug; ⓂBrown, Orange, Green, Purple, Pink Line to Randolph) FREE It's a summertime must-do. The Grant Park Orchestra and Grant Park Chorus – composed of top-notch musi-

---

THEATER DISTRICT PALACES

Chicago boasts several dreamboat old theaters that have been renovated and reopened in recent years as part of the Loop's Theater District. Signs are posted in front of each palatial property, detailing the zaniness that went on during its 1920s heyday. The theaters now host touring shows, everything from Cuban ballet companies to Disney musicals. **Broadway in Chicago** (www.broadwayinchicago.com) handles tickets for most of them. The venues cluster at State and Randolph Sts; try to walk by at night when they're at their festive, neon-lit best.

Auditorium Theatre (Map p290; http://auditoriumtheatre.org; 50 E Congress Pkwy; ⓂBrown, Orange, Purple, Pink Line to Library)

Bank of America Theatre (Map p290; 18 W Monroe St; ⓂBlue, Red Line to Monroe)

Cadillac Palace Theatre (Map p290; 151 W Randolph St; ⓂBrown, Orange, Purple, Pink Line to Washington)

Chicago Theatre (Map p290; www.thechicagotheatre.com; 175 N State St; ⓂBrown, Orange, Green, Purple, Pink Line to State/Lake)

Ford Center/Oriental Theatre (Map p290; 24 W Randolph St; ⓂBrown, Orange, Green, Purple, Pink Line to State/Lake)

cians from symphonies worldwide – put on free classical concerts at Millennium Park's Pritzker Pavilion. Patrons bring lawn chairs, blankets, wine and picnic fixings to set the scene as the sun dips, the skyscraper lights flicker on and glorious music fills the night air.

If you can't catch the evening show, rehearsals take place Tuesday to Friday, usually from 11am to 1:30pm. The orchestra played in Grant Park in the early days, hence the misleading name.

CHICAGO SYMPHONY ORCHESTRA
CLASSICAL MUSIC

Map p290 (312-294-3000; www.cso.org; 220 S Michigan Ave; MBrown, Orange, Green, Purple, Pink Line to Adams) Riccardo Muti leads the CSO, one of America's best symphonies, known for fervent subscribers and an untouchable brass section. Cellist Yo-Yo Ma is the group's creative consultant and a frequent soloist. The season runs from September to May at Symphony Center; Daniel Burnham designed the Orchestra Hall. The group also plays summer shows at the outdoor Ravinia Festival in suburban Highland Park.

LYRIC OPERA OF CHICAGO
OPERA

Map p290 (312-332-2244; www.lyricopera.org; 20 N Wacker Dr; MBrown, Orange, Purple, Pink Line to Washington) Tickets are hard to come by for this top-notch modern opera company, which fills the ornate Civic Opera House with a shrewd mix of common classics and daring premieres from September to March. If your Italian isn't up to much, don't be put off; much to the horror of purists, the company projects English 'supertitles' above the proscenium.

CIVIC ORCHESTRA OF CHICAGO
CLASSICAL MUSIC

Map p290 (312-294-3420; www.cso.org; 220 S Michigan Ave; MBrown, Orange, Green, Purple, Pink Line to Adams) **FREE** Founded in 1919, this orchestra is something of the kid sibling to the Chicago Symphony Orchestra, made up of young players who often graduate to the big-time professional symphonic institutions around the world. It's the only training orchestra of its kind in the world and tickets to performances at Symphony Center are free (or $2 per ticket if you reserve in advance).

HUBBARD STREET DANCE CHICAGO
DANCE

Map p290 (312-850-9744; www.hubbardstreetdance.com; 205 E Randolph St; MBrown, Orange, Green, Purple, Pink Line to Randolph) Hubbard St is the preeminent dance group in the city, with a well-deserved international reputation to match. The group is known for energetic and technically virtuoso performances under the direction of some of the best choreographers in the world. They leap at the Harris Theater (p63) in Millennium Park.

JOFFREY BALLET
DANCE

Map p290 (312-386-8905; www.joffrey.com; 10 E Randolph St; MBrown, Orange, Green, Purple, Pink Line to Randolph) The famed Joffrey has flourished since it relocated from New York in 1995. Noted for its energetic work, the company frequently travels the world and boasts an impressive storehouse of regularly performed repertoire. Joffrey practices and instructs in the swanky new Joffrey Tower on Randolph St in the Theater District, though it typically performs at the Auditorium Theatre.

The annual run of *The Nutcracker* draws big crowds.

GENE SISKEL FILM CENTER
CINEMA

Map p290 (312-846-2600; www.siskelfilmcenter.org; 164 N State St; MBrown, Orange, Green, Purple, Pink Line to State/Lake) The former Film Center of the School of the Art Institute was renamed for the late *Chicago Tribune* film critic Gene Siskel. It shows everything from amateurish stuff by students to wonderful but unsung gems by Estonian directors. The monthly schedule includes theme nights of forgotten American classics.

CHICAGO OPERA THEATER
OPERA

Map p290 (312-704-8414; www.chicagooperatheater.org; 205 E Randolph St; MBrown, Green, Orange, Purple, Pink Line to Randolph) Duke Ellington's *Queenie Pie* and Ernest Bloch's *Macbeth* are the 2014 schedule headliners – indications of this innovative group's broad range. Performances usually take place at the Harris Theater to great critical acclaim.

HARRIS THEATER FOR MUSIC AND DANCE
THEATER

Map p290 (www.harristheaterchicago.org; 205 E Randolph St; MBrown, Orange, Green, Purple, Pink

ℹ️ DISCOUNT TICKETS

Swing by Hot Tix (p32), which sells same-week theater tickets for half-price (plus a service charge of $4 or so). Drama, comedy and performing arts venues citywide have seats on offer. You can also look and book on-line. The earlier in the week you visit, the better the selection.

Line to Randolph) This avant-garde theater in Millennium Park hosts a huge slate of performing arts groups, including Hubbard Street Dance Chicago, Music of the Baroque, Chicago Opera Theater and 35 others.

CHICAGO CHAMBER MUSICIANS
CLASSICAL MUSIC

Map p290 (📞312-819-5800; www.chicagochambermusic.org; 78 E Washington St; Ⓜ Brown, Orange, Green, Purple, Pink Line to Randolph) This 15-member ensemble is comprised of world-class soloists and Chicago Symphony Orchestra section leaders and is revered for its two affiliated groups – the Chicago String Quartet and CCM Brass. The best place to hear them is at the Chicago Cultural Center during free shows the first Monday of each month, from 12:15pm to 1pm in Preston Bradley Hall.

They also play at halls and theaters around town.

INTERNATIONAL SCREENINGS PROGRAM
CINEMA

Map p290 (📞312-744-6630; www.cinemachicago.org; 78 E Washington St; Ⓜ Brown, Orange, Green, Purple, Pink Line to Randolph) FREE The same group that puts on the Chicago International Film Festival hosts a free program from May to September showing foreign films in the Chicago Cultural Center's Claudia Cassidy Theater (2nd floor). Each movie screens on Wednesdays at 6:30pm. Seating is first come, first served.

MUSIC OF THE BAROQUE
CLASSICAL MUSIC

Map p290 (📞312-551-1415; www.baroque.org; 205 E Randolph St; Ⓜ Brown, Orange, Green, Purple, Pink Line to Randolph) One of the largest choral and orchestral groups of its kind in the USA, Music of the Baroque (MoB) brings the music of the Middle Ages and the Renaissance to vibrant life. Its Christmas brass and choral concerts are huge successes. It

performs at the Harris Theater (p63), as well as various churches around town.

CHICAGO SINFONIETTA
CLASSICAL MUSIC

Map p290 (📞312-236-3681; www.chicagosinfonietta.org; 220 S Michigan Ave; Ⓜ Brown, Orange, Green, Purple, Pink Line to Adams) This beloved organization is all about knocking down the cultural walls that surround traditional classical ensembles. Expect broad-minded premieres and wide-ranging guest artists, including jazz luminaries and ethnic folk musicians. Many of its concerts are at the Chicago Symphony Orchestra's center.

GIORDANO DANCE CHICAGO
DANCE

(www.giordanodance.org) This Chicago company was founded by one of the most important people in the history of American dance, Gus Giordano. Now headed by his daughter Nan, the company is out on the road for much of the year but still comes back for occasional performances in its hometown, often at the Harris Theater (p63).

🛍️ SHOPPING

CHICAGO ARCHITECTURE FOUNDATION SHOP
SOUVENIRS

Map p290 (www.architecture.org/shop; 224 S Michigan Ave; ⊙9:30am-6pm; Ⓜ Brown, Orange, Green, Purple, Pink Line to Adams) Skyline posters, Frank Lloyd Wright note cards, skyscraper models and heaps of books celebrate local architecture at this haven for anyone with an edifice complex. The items make excellent only-in-Chicago-type souvenirs.

POSTER PLUS
FINE ARTS

Map p290 (📞312-461-9277; www.posterplus.com; Ste 1150, 30 E Adams St; ⊙10am-6pm Mon-Fri; Ⓜ Brown, Orange, Green, Purple, Pink Line to Adams) Located a block and a half from the Art Institute, this superlative poster store carries loads of fun, Chicago-specific designs. Everything from vintage prints dating from the late 19th century to decades-old Blues Fest images to modern renderings of the skyline can be found among the stock.

AFTER SCHOOL MATTERS STORE
ARTS & CRAFTS

Map p290 (📞312-744-7274; 66 E Randolph St; ⊙10am-7pm Mon-Fri, 11am-5pm Sat; Ⓜ Brown, Orange, Green, Purple, Pink Line to Randolph)

It's a win-win proposition at this nonprofit entity: painters, sculptors and other artists get paid for creating their wares while teaching inner-city teens – who serve as apprentices – to do the same. Their artworks, including paintings, mosaic tables, puppets and carved-wood walking sticks, are sold in the gallery here. Profits return to the organization.

ILLINOIS ARTISANS SHOP ARTS & CRAFTS

Map p290 (312-814-5321; 2nd level, James R Thompson Center, 100 W Randolph St; ☺9am-5pm Mon-Fri; MBrown, Orange, Green, Purple, Pink, Blue Line to Clark/Lake) The best work of artisans from throughout the state is sold here, including ceramics, wine jugs, glassware, mobiles, toys, and glass and wood coaxed into jewelry. The enthusiastic staff will tell you all about the people who created the various pieces. The Illinois Art Gallery next door sells paintings and sculptures under the same arrangement.

AKIRA FOOTWEAR SHOES

Map p290 (312-346-3034; www.akirachicago com, 122 3 State St; ☺11am-9pm Mon-Sat, to 7pm Sun; MRed Line to Monroe) The Loop outpost of the trendy local chain offers fun footwear in the most recent styles. Fancy Chuck Taylors, cute silver sandals, colorful rain boots – whatever the look *du jour* is, you'll probably find it on the racks. There's lots of seating to try on your selections and most items are moderately priced.

BLOCK 37 MALL

Map p290 (www.block37.com; 108 N State St; ☺10am-8pm Mon-Sat, 11am-6pm Sun; MBlue Line to Washington) The stretch of State St between W Randolph and W Washington Sts is known as Block 37, a retail corridor that has been a city boondoggle for years. National retailers such as Puma, the Disney Store, Zara and Steve Madden shoes are there now and more shops supposedly are coming, but much of the space remains eerily empty. There is a Hot Tix desk on the 1st floor at the guest services area.

TARGET DEPARTMENT STORE

Map p290 (www.target.com; 1 S State St; ☺7am-10pm Mon-Fri, 9am-6pm Sat & Sun; MBrown, Orange, Green, Purple, Pink Line to Madison) The big-box retailer's downtown store sits in the landmark Sullivan Center building. It's a bit more upscale than the usual Target and it's a prime place to pick up picnicking

ARCHITECTURE BOOKS

For DIY explorations of Chicago's steely structures, staff at the Chicago Architecture Foundation Shop (p64) recommend using the *Pocket Guide to Chicago Architecture* by Judith Paine McBrien, or *A View from the River*, the foundation's book that highlights buildings along its popular tour-boat routes. The shop sells both paperbacks.

items (basket, blanket, paper plates, drinks, snacks) and other Chicago necessities (umbrella, warm hat). Upscale organic sandwich chain Pret A Manger is inside, too.

5 S WABASH AVE JEWELRY

Map p290 (www.jewelerscenter.com; 5 S Wabash Ave; ☺9am-5pm Mon-Sat; MBrown, Orange, Green, Purple, Pink Line to Madison) This historic building, on a block commonly referred to as 'Jewelers Row', is the center of Chicago's family jeweler trade. Hundreds of shops in here sell every kind of watch, ring, gemstone and bauble imaginable. Most are quick to promise, 'I can get it for you wholesale!'

CENTRAL CAMERA ELECTRONICS

Map p290 (312-427-5580; www.centralcamera. com; 230 S Wabash Ave; ☺8:30am-5pm Mon-Sat; MBrown, Orange, Green, Purple, Pink Line to Adams) Whatever your photo needs, Central Camera has the answer. Once shutterbugs step inside the long, narrow store, it will be days before they surface again.

🏃 SPORTS & ACTIVITIES

BIKE CHICAGO CYCLING

Map p290 (312-729-1000; www.bikechicago. com; 239 E Randolph St; bikes per hr/day from $10/35, tour adult/child from $39/25; ☺6:30am-8pm Mon-Fri, from 8am Sat & Sun, closed Sat & Sun Nov-Mar; MBrown, Orange, Green, Purple, Pink Line to Randolph) Rent a bike to explore DIY style, or go on a guided tour. The latter cover themes such as lakefront parks and attractions, pizza and hot-dog munching, or downtown's sights and fireworks at night (highly recommended). Prices include lock, helmet and map. This main branch is in

Millennium Park; there's a smaller branch on the Riverwalk.

MILLENNIUM PARK WORKOUTS   YOGA

Map p290 (www.millenniumpark.org; 201 E Randolph St; ⊙7-10am Sat early Jun-early Sep; MBrown, Orange, Pink, Purple, Pink Line to Randolph) FREE Each Saturday in summer, Millennium Park offers free exercise classes with instructors and live music on the Great Lawn. The lineup: tai chi at 7am, yoga at 8am, Pilates at 9am and Zumba dance at 10am.

URBAN KAYAKS   KAYAKING

Map p290 (☎312-965-0035; www.urbankayaks. com; 270 E Riverwalk South; per hr single/tandem $30/50, guided tour single/tandem from $50/90; ⊙10am-6pm; MBrown, Orange, Green, Purple, Pink Line to State/Lake) Located on the Riverwalk, this outfitter rents kayaks for explorations on the Chicago River. Beginners are welcome and a quick training session gets everyone situated before paddling off. The company also offers guided tours that glide past downtown's skyscrapers and historic sites. The nighttime fireworks jaunt is a sweet one.

MAGGIE DALEY PARK   SKATING

Map p290 (www.chicagoparkdistrict.com; 337 E Randolph St; MBrown, Orange, Green, Purple, Pink Line to Randolph) At press time, the old Daley Bicentennial Plaza (east over the bridge from Millennium Park) was being remade into Maggie Daley Park, with an ice-skating ribbon, rock-climbing sculptures and gardens to be completed in winter 2014.

Near North & Navy Pier

Neighborhood Top Five

1 Walking on boat-bedecked **Navy Pier** (p69) and taking in the views – especially from the stomach-churning 150ft Ferris wheel.

2 Hefting a gooey slice of deep-dish pizza at **Giordano's** (p75).

3 Shopping with the frenzied masses on the **Magnificent Mile** (p72).

4 Gawping at glassy Michael Jordan in the **Smith Museum of Stained Glass Windows** (p74).

5 Submerging beneath Michigan Ave to knock back burgers and Schlitz beer at the **Billy Goat Tavern** (p74).

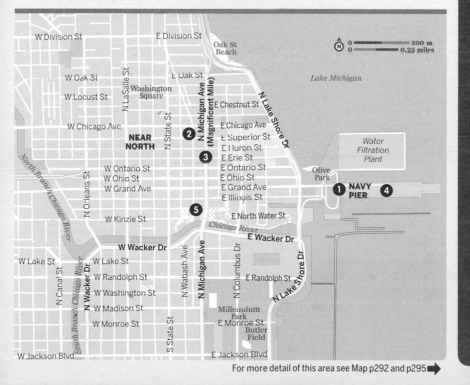

For more detail of this area see Map p292 and p295 ➡

Lonely Planet's Top Tip

Navy Pier is about a mile from the El station and the pier itself is a half-mile long. Prepare for lots of walking. The free trolley can help in summer. It picks up at the Red Line Grand station, then makes several stops along Illinois St heading east toward the pier. It then runs the length of the pier, before looping back along Grand Ave to the El station.

Best Places to Eat

➡ Xoco (p75)

➡ Giordano's (p75)

➡ Graham Elliot (p77)

➡ Billy Goat Tavern (p74)

➡ Mr Beef (p75)

For reviews, see p74 ➡

Best Places to Drink

➡ Clark Street Ale House (p78)

➡ Harry Caray's Tavern (p78)

➡ Brehon Pub (p78)

➡ Watershed (p78)

➡ Dollop (p78)

For reviews, see p78 ➡

Best Places to Shop

➡ Jazz Record Mart (p79)

➡ Abraham Lincoln Book Shop (p79)

➡ Garrett Popcorn (p79)

➡ Nike Chicago (p80)

➡ AllSaints (p80)

For reviews, see p79 ➡

Explore Near North & Navy Pier

The Loop may be where Chicago fortunes are made, but the Near North is where those fortunes are spent. Shops, restaurants and amusements abound. This is also where the majority of hotels roll out their welcome mats.

The epicenter is the upscale shopping haven of N Michigan Ave, aka the Magnificent Mile (Mag Mile). Stretching north from the Chicago River to Oak St, the road is silly with multistory malls, high-end department stores and outlets of big-name national chains. More than 450 shops ka-ching in the tidy span.

In the River North area, west of State St, art is the big business. What was formerly a grimy, noisy assortment of warehouses and factories has become Chicago's most prestigious gallery district.

Jutting off Near North's eastern end is Navy Pier, which attracts more visitors than any other sight in Chicago. It's a cavalcade of kid-oriented shops, rides, attractions and a big freakin' Ferris wheel, though adults will appreciate the criminally overlooked Smith Museum of Stained Glass Windows and the many opportunities for romantic, windswept strolling.

The Mag Mile and Navy Pier are busy day and night. Most visitors spend quite a bit of time in the neighborhood eating, if nothing else. A multitude of pizza parlors, Italian beef shacks and eclectic bistros ensures no one goes hungry during their visit.

Local Life

➡ **Art Crawl** Brave New Art World (p72) brings local artists and art appreciators together the first Thursday of the month to scope out River North's galleries.

➡ **Happy Hour** Clark Street Ale House (p78) is a neighborhood favorite for kicking back after work with a Midwest microbrew.

➡ **Big Swim** The city's triathletes dive in for swim practice in the shallow water at Ohio St Beach (p81).

Getting There & Away

➡ **El** Red Line to Grand for the Magnificent Mile's south end; Red Line to Chicago for the Mag Mile's north end; Brown, Purple Line to Chicago for River North.

➡ **Trolley** A free trolley runs from the Red Line Grand stop to Navy Pier from late May to early September.

➡ **Bus** Number 151 runs along N Michigan Ave; 65 heads to Navy Pier.

➡ **Car** The further you get away from the Mag Mile, the more common the metered parking ($4 per hour). Parking at Navy Pier's garage costs around $25 per day.

TOP SIGHT
NAVY PIER

Navy Pier was once the city's municipal wharf. Today it's Chicago's most visited attraction, with eight million people per year flooding its half-mile length. Locals may groan about its commercialization, but even they can't refute the brilliant lakefront views, cool breezes and whopping fireworks displays on Wednesdays (9:30pm) and Saturdays (10:15pm) in summer. Kids go gaga over the rides, fast-food restaurants and trinket vendors.

For the child-free, Navy Pier's charms revolve around the views and the ride on the gigantic, 150ft **Ferris wheel** (Map p295; per ride $6). It's much more exciting than any Ferris wheel has a right to be, mostly because of its dizzying height. The **carousel** (Map p295; per ride $5) is another classic, with bobbing carved horses and organ music. There's also a mini-golf course ($5) that weaves around the rides. A flotilla of competing tour boats departs from the pier's southern side.

A variety of acts appear throughout the summer at the **Skyline Stage**, a 1500-seat rooftop venue with a glistening white canopy. An **IMAX Theater** (Map p295; ☎312-595-5629; www.imax.com/chicago; tickets $12-16) and the Chicago Shakespeare Theater (p78) also call the pier home.

In summer **Shoreline Water Taxi** (www.shorelinesightseeing.com; one way adult/child $8/5; ☺10am-6:30pm late May-early Sep) runs from the docks to the Willis Tower and Shedd Aquarium. The boats are a fun, wind-in-your-hair alternative to land-based transportation.

Eating or drinking in a quality, noncheesy place is tough on the pier. The best bet is the **Beer Garden** (Map p295; www.chicagosbestbeergarden.com; ☺from 11am daily late May-Sep, Fri-Sun only Oct) or Harry Caray's (p78), the latter particularly if you're a Chicago sports fan (there's a mini museum inside). The city recently announced the pier will undergo a renovation to step up the dining options and add an ice rink.

DON'T MISS...

- ➡ Fireworks
- ➡ Ferris wheel
- ➡ Lakefront views
- ➡ Boat rides
- ➡ Beer garden

PRACTICALITIES

- ➡ Map p295
- ➡ ☎312-595-7437
- ➡ www.navypier.com
- ➡ 600 E Grand Ave
- ➡ ☺10am-10pm Sun-Thu, to midnight Fri & Sat
- ➡ ♿
- ➡ Ⓜ Red Line to Grand, then trolley

Near North & Navy Pier – on the Waterfront

Chicago has a nautical side, and Navy Pier is the place to experience it. Boats galore still tie up at the old municipal wharf, from powerboats to tall-masted schooners to water taxis that ply green-glinting Lake Michigan. The Chicago River slices through the neighborhood, too, adding more tour boats to the mix.

CHUCK ECKERT / ALAMY ©

BRUCE LEIGHTY / GETTY IMAGES ©

1. Marina City (p73)
Flash back to *The Jetsons* at these mod 'corn cob' towers.

2. Ohio St Beach (p81)
A conveniently located beach for a dip.

3. Navy Pier (p69)
This half-mile long pier is Chicago's most-visited attraction.

4. Riverwalk (p57)
Take in the Chicago skyline on this riverside promenade.

CHRISTOPHER F PHOTOGRAPHY / GETTY IMAGES ©

◉ SIGHTS

◉ Near North

MAGNIFICENT MILE   STREET

Map p292 (www.themagnificentmile.com; N Michigan Ave) Spanning Michigan Ave between the river and Oak St, the Mag Mile is Chicago's much-touted upscale shopping strip, where Bloomingdale's, Neiman Marcus and Saks will lighten your wallet. The city likes to claim that it's one of the top five shopping streets in the world. But that's a bit of a boast, because the retailers are mostly high-end chains that have stores throughout the country.

Granted, they're more slicked-up than usual and their vacuum-packed proximity on Michigan Ave is handy. Probably what's most magnificent is the millions of dollars they ring up annually. The road goes all out in December with a festive spread of tree lights and holiday adornments.

TRIBUNE TOWER   ARCHITECTURE

Map p292 (435 N Michigan Ave; MRed Line to Grand) Colonel Robert McCormick, eccentric owner of the *Chicago Tribune* in the early 1900s, collected – and asked his reporters to send – rocks from famous buildings and monuments around the world. He stockpiled pieces of the Taj Mahal, Westminster Abbey, the Great Pyramid and 140 or so others, which are now embedded around the tower's base.

The unusual 'bricks' are all marked and viewable from street level. And the tradition continues: a twisted piece from the World Trade Center wreckage is one of the more recent additions.

WRIGLEY BUILDING   ARCHITECTURE

Map p292 (400 N Michigan Ave; MRed Line to Grand) The Wrigley Building glows as white as the Doublemint Twins' teeth, day or night. Chewing-gum guy William Wrigley built it that way on purpose, because he wanted it to be attention-grabbing like a billboard. More than 250,000 glazed terracotta tiles make up the facade; a computer database tracks each one and indicates when each needs to be cleaned and polished.

Banks of megawatt lamps on the river's south side light up the tiles each night.

HOLY NAME CATHEDRAL   CHURCH

Map p292 (www.holynamecathedral.org; 735 N State St; ⊗8:30am-8:30pm Mon-Sat, to 7pm Sun; MRed Line to Chicago) Holy Name Cathedral is the seat of Chicago's Catholic Church and where its powerful cardinals do their preaching. It provides a quiet place for contemplation, unless the excellent choirs are practicing, in which case it's an entertain-

---

LOCAL KNOWLEDGE

RIVER NORTH GALLERIES

The River North district is the most established of Chicago's five gallery-rich zones (West Loop, Pilsen, Bridgeport and Wicker Park/Bucktown are the others), with art from top international names and price tags to match. It's also the most densely concentrated with galleries, so you can see a lot within a few-block radius. Franklin and Superior Sts are the bulls-eye. Most galleries have a map you can take covering the scene. **Brave New Art World** (www.bravenewartworld.com) hosts a free 'art crawl for the mainstream' on the first Thursday of each month, with beer from local brewers and talks by artists.

Local favorites include the following:

Richard Norton Gallery (Map p292; www.richardnortongallery.com; 222 Merchandise Mart Plaza; ⊗9am-5pm Mon-Fri; MBrown, Purple Line to Merchandise Mart) Specializes in impressionist and modernist works, as well as historic Chicago-focused art. Check out the early beach and street scenes of the city.

Project Room (Map p292; www.theprojectroompb.com; 217 W Huron St ; ⊗11am-6pm Wed-Sat; MBrown, Purple Line to Chicago) Organizes globe-spanning exhibits such as Tibetan photos, Cuban prints and Chilean paintings.

Judy A Saslow Gallery (Map p292; www.jsaslowgallery.com; 300 W Superior St; ⊗11am-6pm Tue-Fri, to 5pm Sat; MBrown, Purple Line to Chicago) Displays eye-popping outsider art plus tribal and ethnographic artifacts.

THE DOWNWARD SPIRE

Remember the **Chicago Spire** (Map p292; 400 N Lake Shore Dr), uberarchitect Santiago Calatrava's new building that was set to become the nation's tallest? At 2000ft, it would've dwarfed the Willis Tower. Excitement was high (pun!) and nicknames for the twisting design abounded – The Twizzler, The Drill Bit, The Vibrator among them. Developers broke ground in 2007, but construction came screeching to a halt in late 2008 when the economy went limp and funds dried up. Now there's a dormant 76ft-deep, 110ft-wide hole in the ground at downtown's pricey edge. The developers still vow they'll get the money and finish the Spire. If not, it might live up to its less savory nickname: 'The Big Screw'.

ing respite. Check out the sanctuary's ceiling while you're inside. The hanging red hats are for Holy Name's deceased cardinals; the hats remain until they turn to dust.

Built in 1875 to a design by the unheralded Patrick Keely, the cathedral has been remodeled several times, most recently after a fire in 2009. Thus the bullet holes from a Capone-era hit outside the church are no longer visible. Actually, a couple of gangland killings took place near here. In 1924, North Side boss Dion O'Banion was gunned down in his florist shop (738 N State St) after he crossed Al Capone. In 1926, his successor, Hymie Weiss, died en route to the cathedral in a hail of bullets that came from the window at 740 N State St.

The cathedral is open most of the day and holds frequent services.

MERCHANDISE MART
BUILDING

Map p292 (800-677-6278; www.mmart.com; 222 Merchandise Mart Plaza; ⊙9am-6pm Mon-Fri, 10am-3pm Sat; Ⓜ Brown, Purple Line to Merchandise Mart) The Merchandise Mart is the world's largest commercial building and largest LEED-certified building (Leadership in Energy and Environmental Design; silver status, thanks in part to a hefty thermal storage facility). Spanning two city blocks, the 1931 behemoth has its own zip code and gives most of its copious space to wholesale showrooms for home furnishing and design professionals. The first two floors are mall-like and open to the public.

To go beyond these you must be escorted by an interior designer, architect or other industry professional. The Mart also hosts occasional design shows that are open to the public; check the 'events' section of the website for details.

Outdoors on the Mart's river side, a collection of heads on poles rises up like giant Pez dispensers. This is the Merchant's Hall of Fame; the creepy busts depict famous local retailers such as Marshall Field and Frank Woolworth.

DRIEHAUS MUSEUM
MUSEUM

Map p292 (312-482-8933; www.driehaus museum.org; 40 E Erie St; adult/child $20/10; ⊙10am-5pm Tue-Sat, noon-5pm Sun; Ⓜ Red Line to Chicago) Set in the exquisite Nickerson Mansion, the Driehaus Museum immerses visitors in Gilded Age decorative arts and architecture. You'll feel like a *Great Gatsby* character as you wander the three floors stuffed with sumptuous *objets* and stained glass. Guided tours ($5 extra) are available at 11am and 2pm (1:30pm and 3pm on Sundays). No need to book; just show up 15 minutes beforehand.

MARINA CITY
ARCHITECTURE

Map p292 (300 N State St; Ⓜ Brown, Orange, Green, Purple, Pink Line to State/Lake) For some postmodern fun, check out the twin 'corncob' towers of the 1962 mixed-use Marina City. Designed by Bertrand Goldberg, it has become an iconic part of the Chicago skyline, showing up on the cover of the Wilco CD *Yankee Hotel Foxtrot*. The condos that top the spiraling parking garages are especially picturesque at Christmas, when owners decorate the balconies with lights.

POETRY FOUNDATION
LIBRARY

Map p292 (www.poetryfoundation.org; 61 W Superior St; ⊙11am-4pm Mon-Fri; Ⓜ Red Line to Chicago) FREE This odd, mod building is where *Poetry* magazine is published. The reading room makes a nice refuge from inclement weather. Pop in and grab a book or journal to read on the smattering of couches. Well-known poets do readings here. The website offers a free downloadable audio tour of iconic city sites matched with the poetry they inspired.

NEAR NORTH & NAVY PIER SIGHTS

FAMILY-FRIENDLY SIGHTS & ACTIVITIES

Near North and Navy Pier have a lot for families to do.

➡ Chicago Children's Museum (p74) – tots can climb, dig and splash their way through the educational playground.

➡ Navy Pier (p69) – the carnival-like wharf spins a Ferris wheel, carousel and other rides.

➡ Bobby's Bike Hike (p80) – the cycling company offers a guided two-hour, four-mile 'tike hike' for families.

➡ Gino's East (p75) – everyone gets to scribble on the walls while waiting for their deep-dish pizza.

MUSEUM OF BROADCAST COMMUNICATIONS MUSEUM
Map p292 (www.museum.tv; 360 N State St; adult/child $12/6; ☉10am-5pm Tue-Sat; ⓜRed Line to Grand) This museum of radio and TV nostalgia opened in 2012. It's pretty sparsely populated considering the admission price. But if you have a hankering to see old Bozo the Clown clips, or the camera that taped the famous Nixon-Kennedy debate, or the salvaged door from Oprah's studio, it might be for you.

◉ Navy Pier

NAVY PIER WATERFRONT
See p69.

SMITH MUSEUM OF STAINED GLASS WINDOWS MUSEUM
Map p295 (☎312-595-5024; 600 E Grand Ave; ☉10am-10pm Sun-Thu, to midnight Fri & Sat; ⓜRed Line to Grand, then trolley) FREE Navy Pier doesn't promote this impressive attraction very well, but hiding along the lower-level terraces of Festival Hall is the country's first museum dedicated entirely to stained glass. Many of the 150 pieces on display were made in Chicago (a stained-glass hub in the late 1800s, thanks to the influx of European immigrants), and most hung at one point in Chicago churches, homes or office buildings.

Even if you think stained glass is something for blue-haired grandmas, you should make a point of coming by. The articulately explained collection ranges from typical Victorian religious themes to far-out designs; the rendition of basketball great Michael Jordan is especially noteworthy. Stained glass Ben Franklin glows nearby on a printer's window. And who knew stained glass helped spark feminism? It did, according to women-forged windows from the 1893 World's Fair. Fans of Louis Comfort Tiffany will rejoice to find 13 of his works hanging here.

CHICAGO CHILDREN'S MUSEUM MUSEUM
Map p295 (☎312-527-1000; www.chicagochildrensmuseum.org; 700 E Grand Ave; admission $14; ☉10am-6pm Sun-Wed, to 8pm Thu-Sat; ⚫; ⓜRed Line to Grand, then trolley) Designed to challenge the imaginations of toddlers through to 10-year-olds, this colorful museum near Navy Pier's main entrance gives its young visitors enough hands-on exhibits to keep them climbing and creating for hours. Among the favorites, Dinosaur Expedition explores the world of paleontology and lets kids excavate 'bones.' They can also climb a ropey schooner and bowl in a faux alley.

Waterways lets them get wet (and learn about hydroelectric power). And they can use real tools to build things in the Invention Lab. The museum is free for all ages on Thursdays from 5pm to 8pm; it's free for kids aged 15 and under on the first Sunday of the month.

✗ EATING

★**BILLY GOAT TAVERN** BURGERS $
Map p292 (www.billygoattavern.com; lower level, 430 N Michigan Ave; burgers $4-6; ☉6am-2am Mon-Fri, 10am-2am Sat & Sun; ⓜRed Line to Grand) *Tribune* and *Sun-Times* reporters have guzzled in the subterranean Billy Goat for decades. Order a 'cheezborger' and Schlitz beer, then look around at the newspapered walls to get the scoop on infamous local stories, such as the Cubs Curse (involving the tavern owner and his slighted pet goat). The place is a tourist magnet, but it's a deserving one.

If the cantankerous Greeks manning the grill sound familiar, it's because they enjoyed the fame of John Belushi's *Saturday Night Live* skit ('Cheezborger! Cheezborger! No fries! Cheeps!'). The Billy Goat is also a fine spot for cheap, late-night boozing. Follow the tavern signs that lead below Michigan Ave to get here. And ignore the other outlets around town; this is the original and the one with the most personality.

MR BEEF
SANDWICHES $

Map p292 (www.mrbeefonorleans.com; 666 N Orleans St; sandwiches $4-7; ⊘9am-5pm Mon Fri, 10am-3pm Sat, plus 10:30pm-4am Fri & Sat; MBrown, Purple Line to Chicago) At this local classic the Italian beef sandwiches come with long, spongy white buns that begin dribbling (that's a good thing!) after a load of the spicy meat and cooking juices has been ladled on. In a recent episode of the Travel Channel's *Food Wars*, Mr Beef won as Chicago's best beef hands down over its main competitor, Al's.

Don't be afraid of the dumpy decor. Eaters from Jerry Springer to Jay Leno have devoured at the picnic-style tables. Cash only.

PORTILLO'S
AMERICAN $

Map p292 (☑312-587-8910; www.portillos.com; 100 W Ontario St; mains $4-7; ⊘10am-11pm Sun-Thu, to midnight Fri & Sat; MRed Line to Grand) Die-hard hot-dog purists might bemoan the lack of true Chicago dogs in the vicinity of tourist hot spots, but this outpost of the local Portillo's chain – gussied up in a *nearly* corny 1930s gangster theme – is the place to get one. Try one of its famous dogs and a slice of the heavenly chocolate cake: far and away the best inexpensive meal in the neighborhood.

EGGSPERIENCE
AMERICAN $

Map p292 (☑312-870-6773; www.eggsperience cafe.com; 35 W Ontario St; mains $6-10; ⊘6am-4pm Sun-Thu, 24hr Fri & Sat; MRed Line to Grand) It's 4am and you're starving? This bright, clean, sprawling diner – open 24 hours during the weekend – will fix the problem with its big portions of pancakes, omelets, club sandwiches and other staples, plus your very own pot of coffee.

XOCO
MEXICAN $$

Map p292 (www.rickbayless.com; 449 N Clark St; mains $9-13; ⊘8am-9pm Tue-Thu, to 10pm Fri & Sat; MRed Line to Grand) ✐ At Rick Bayless' Mexican street-food restaurant (pronounced 'SHOW-co') everything is sourced from local small farms. Crunch into warm *churros* (spiraled dough fritters) with chili-spiked hot chocolate for breakfast, crusty *tortas* (sandwiches, like the succulent ham and Wisconsin cheddar) for lunch and *caldos* (meal-in-a-bowl soups) for dinner. Queues can be long; breakfast is the least crowded time.

GIORDANO'S
PIZZERIA $$

Map p292 (www.giordanos.com; 730 N Rush St; small pizzas from $15; ⊘11am-10:30pm Sun-Thu, to 11:30pm Fri & Sat; MRed Line to Chicago) The founders of Giordano's, Efren and Joseph Boglio, claim that they got their winning recipe for stuffed pizza from – aww – their mother back in Italy. If you want a slice of heaven, order the 'special,' a stuffed pie containing sausage, mushroom, green pepper and onions. We think it vies for best deep-dish pizza in Chicago.

PURPLE PIG
MEDITERRANEAN $$

Map p292 (☑312-464-1744; www.thepurple pigchicago.com; 500 N Michigan Ave, small plates $8-16; ⊘11:30am-midnight Sun-Thu, to 1am Fri & Sat; ✐; MRed Line to Grand) Here you'll find 'cheese, swine and wine,' as the tagline says, but also veggie antipasti and Mediterranean seafood. The milk-braised pork shoulder is the hamtastic specialty. Dishes are meant to be shared and the long list of affordable vinos gets the good times rolling at communal tables both indoors and out. It's a great place for a late-night bite.

PARIS CLUB
FRENCH $$

Map p292 (☑312-595-0800; www.parisclub chicago.com; 59 W Hubbard St; mains $13-25; ⊘4pm-late Mon-Fri, from 10am Sat & Sun; MRed Line to Grand) Paris Club is a go-to spot for celebrity sightings. The cafe has won crowds for its breezy take on French fare, from 50 affordable wines to bite-size *croque monsieur* to *escargot* sold by the piece. The retractable-roofed upstairs lounge pulls in big-name DJs Wednesday to Saturday.

GINO'S EAST
PIZZERIA $$

Map p292 (www.ginoseast.com; 162 E Superior St; small pizzas from $15; ⊘11am-9:30pm Mon-Sat, from noon Sun; MRed Line to Chicago) In the great deep-dish pizza wars, Gino's is easily one of the top-five heavies. And it encourages customers to do something other pizzerias would never allow: cover every available surface (except for the actual food) with

THE DEEP-DISH DEBATE

Everyone agrees the Near North neighborhood is where deep-dish pizza originated. But as to who invented it? That's where the consensus ends.

What we do know is that pizza first bulked up in 1943. That's when a chef who thought big arrived on the scene. He rolled out the mighty dough that cradled the first deep-dish pie – with a full inch of red sauce, chopped plum tomatoes and shredded American-style mozzarella cheese – and the city went gaga.

So who is this genius? The nod usually goes to Ike Sewell, who owned a restaurant called Pizzeria Uno. But Ike's cook Rudy Malnati (father of Lou) claimed he created the gooey-cheesed behemoth. The war over who's first, and best, continues today.

graffiti. The pizza is something you'll write home about: the classic stuffed cheese and sausage pie oozes countless pounds of cheese over its crispy cornmeal crust.

PIZZERIA UNO
PIZZERIA **$$**

Map p292 (www.unos.com; 29 E Ohio St; small pizzas from $13; ⊘11am-1am Mon-Fri, to 2am Sat, to 11pm Sun; Ⓜ Red Line to Grand) Ike Sewell supposedly invented Chicago-style pizza here on December 3, 1943, although his claim to fame is hotly contested. A light, flaky crust holds piles of cheese and a herb-laced tomato sauce. The pizzas take a while, but stick to the pitchers of beer and cheap red wine to kill time and avoid the salad and other distractions to save room for the main event.

Sister outlet Pizzeria Due is one block north; it's marginally less packed than Uno. If mobs aren't your thing, nearby Giordano's is a swell option.

LOU MALNATI'S
PIZZERIA **$$**

Map p292 (www.loumalnatis.com; 439 N Wells St; small pizzas from $7; ⊘11am-11pm Mon-Thu, 11am-midnight Fri & Sat, noon-11pm Sun; Ⓜ Brown, Purple Line to Merchandise Mart) It's a matter of dispute, but some say Malnati is the innovator of Chicago's deep-dish pizza (Lou's father Rudy was a cook at Pizzeria Uno, which also lays claim to the title). Malnati's certainly concocted the unique 'buttercrust' and the 'sausage crust' (it's literally just meat, no dough) to cradle its tangy toppings.

GREEN DOOR TAVERN
PUB **$$**

Map p292 (⌂312-664-5496; www.greendoor chicago.com; 678 N Orleans St; mains $9-14; ⊘11:30am-late Mon-Sat, noon-9pm Sun; Ⓜ Brown, Purple Line to Chicago) The Green Door, tucked in an 1872 building, is your place to mingle with locals over a beer and well-made burgers amid old photos and memorabilia. During Prohibition years, a door painted green

meant there was a speakeasy in the basement. It's still there and now holds a small comedy theater. Daily specials provide substantial savings that can be parlayed into additional microbrews.

CAFE IBERICO
SPANISH **$$**

Map p292 (⌂312-573-1510; www.cafeiberico.com; 739 N LaSalle St; tapas $6-13; ⊘11am-11:30pm Sun-Thu, to 1am Fri & Sat; Ⓜ Brown, Purple Line to Chicago) Iberico's creative tapas burst with flavor. Among the standouts: *salpicon de marisco* (seafood salad with shrimp, octopus and squid), *croquetas de pollo* (chicken and ham puffs with garlic sauce) and *vieiras a la plancha* (grilled scallops with saffron). The cafe's heady sangria draws wearied Loop workers by the dozen in the summer.

★TOPOLOBAMPO/FRONTERA GRILL
MEXICAN **$$$**

Map p292 (⌂312-661-1434; www.rickbayless. com; 445 N Clark St; Topolo mains $35-49, Frontera mains $23-29; ⊘11:30am-9:30pm Tue-Thu, to 10:30pm Fri, 5:30-10:30pm Sat; Ⓜ Red Line to Grand) Perhaps you've seen chef-owner Rick Bayless on TV, stirring up pepper sauces and other jump-off-the-tongue Mexican creations. His isn't your typical taco menu: Bayless uses seasonal, sustainable ingredients for his wood-grilled meats, flavor-packed mole sauces, chili-thickened braises and signature margaritas. Though they share space, Topolobampo and Frontera Grill are actually two separate restaurants: Topolo is sleeker and pricier, while Frontera is more informal.

Both places are always packed. Frontera takes some reservations but mostly seats on a first-come basis. Reserve in advance for Topolobampo (six to eight weeks beforehand is recommended). Note the restaurants close between 2:30pm and 5:30pm (in which case you might want to try Bayless' lower-priced Xoco (p75) eatery next door). Frontera also serves brunch on Saturday, starting at 10:30am.

Who knows – you might see President Obama forking in next to you. Topolobampo is his favorite restaurant. He and Michelle prefer table 65.

GRAHAM ELLIOT   MODERN AMERICAN $$$

Map p292 (☑312 624 9975; www.grahamel liot.com; 217 W Huron St; 12-/15 course menu $125/165; ⊙5-10pm Tue-Sat; ⓂBrown, Purple Line to Chicago) Each meal starts with insanely addictive truffle-oil-and-Parmesan popcorn. Chef Graham Elliot, one of Chicago's young-buck gastro luminaries (and a TV star), then takes whimsy to new levels in such dishes as his foie gras lollypop coated in Pop Rocks. Set menus (modifiable for vegetarians) come in 12 or 15 courses. Adventurous eaters who appreciate trendy food in an industrial, rock-and-roll atmosphere will like it most.

Reservations are essential Elliot also runs **Graham Elliot Bistro** (Map p312; www. gebistro.com; 841 W Randolph St) in the West Loop, where more traditional, à la carte dishes are available.

TRU   FRENCH $$$

Map p292 (☑312-202-0001; www.trurestaurant. com; 676 N St Clair St; set menus $115-158; ⊙6-10pm Mon-Thu, to 11pm Fri, 5-11pm Sat; ⓂRed Line to Chicago) Considered one of the city's best, Tru's *prix fixe* menu (from seven to 13 courses) is artful and capricious, with highly seasonal offerings, a renowned cheese course and brilliant desserts. As you might expect by the price, the service is ace and a jacket is required for men.

Getting a nibble doesn't have to break the bank, though; all *prix fixe* items are available à la carte in the adjoining lounge.

SHAW'S CRAB HOUSE   SEAFOOD $$$

Map p292 (☑312-527-2722; www.shawscrab house.com; 21 E Hubbard St; mains $23-39; ⊙11:30am-10pm Mon-Thu, to 11pm Fri, 4:30-11pm Sat, 10am-10pm Sun; ⓂRed Line to Grand) Shaw's beautiful old dining room and adjoining lounge have an elegant, historic feel, complemented by dark woods and sea-worn nautical decor. The efficient servers can tell you what menu selections are freshest, as well as provide a sustainable seafood menu. A crab cake appetizer

and key lime pie dessert make faultless bookends to any meal.

CHICAGO CHOP HOUSE   STEAKHOUSE $$$

Map p292 (☑312-787-7100; www.chicagochop house.com; 60 W Ontario St; mains $50-75; ⊙5-11pm; ⓂRed Line to Grand) This comfortable, upscale steakhouse does Chicago proud. Expect perfectly cured meats hand cut onsite and an atmosphere befitting the city's famous politicos and mob bosses – many of whom look down from framed portraits lining the walls. If you're not up for a slab of meat, you can always pop in to the piano bar and sample the 600-strong wine list.

BANDERA   AMERICAN $$$

Map p292 (☑312-644-3524; 535 N Michigan Ave; mains $17-30; ⊙11:30am-10pm Sun-Thu, to 11pm Fri & Sat; ⓂRed Line to Grand) Looking up at the entry to this 2nd-story restaurant on Michigan Ave, you'd have no idea of the gem that waits inside. The red-bedecked Bandera has the comfortable retro feel of an expensive supper club, without the snooty waiters (and at half the price). American classics – grilled fish, rotisserie chicken and banana cream pie – predominate here.

When you've shopped till you've dropped, this is the place to come pick yourself back up again.

NOMI   FUSION $$$

Map p292 (☑312-239 4030; www.nomirestau rant.com; 800 N Michigan Ave; mains $28-39; ⊙7am-10pm; ⓂRed Line to Chicago) NoMi is perched on the 7th floor of the Park Hyatt hotel, offering a sleek, art-filled interior and spectacular views over the Magnificent Mile. Dishes combining French fare with Asian flair range from Chesapeake Bay crab to sushi to chicken roulade. Reserve a window table around sunset – it's one of the most romantic experiences that Chicago has to offer. Reservations are required.

GENE & GEORGETTI   STEAKHOUSE $$$

Map p292 (☑312-527-3718; www.geneand georgetti.com; 500 N Franklin St; mains $27-45; ⊙11am-11pm Mon-Thu, to midnight Fri & Sat; ⓂBrown, Purple Line to Merchandise Mart) For once, a place touting itself as one of Frank Sinatra's favorite restaurants can back it up – a fact evidenced in the framed pic of Ol' Blue Eyes by the door. Old-timers, politicos and crusty regulars are seated downstairs. New-timers, conventioneers and tourists are seated upstairs. The steaks are the same on both levels: thick, well aged and well priced.

SUNDA
ASIAN $$$

Map p292 (✆312-644-0500; www.sundachicago. com; 110 W Illinois St; mains $25-34; ⊙11:30am-11pm Mon-Wed, to midnight Thu-Sat, 10am-11pm Sun; Ⓜ Red Line to Grand) When celebrities and star athletes come to town, they make a beeline for Sunda. Nicole Richie, A-Rod, Jamie Foxx and other scenesters glam it up while swirling specialty cocktails and forking into pan-Asian dishes and sushi, set against a backdrop of black-lacquered wood and travertine marble. Make reservations a few weeks in advance for prime-time weekend dinner.

🍷 DRINKING & NIGHTLIFE

★CLARK STREET ALE HOUSE
BAR

Map p292 (www.clarkstreetalehouse.com; 742 N Clark St; ⊙from 4pm; Ⓜ Red Line to Chicago) Do as the retro sign advises and 'Stop & Drink Liquor.' The Ale House has a rotating assortment featuring several Midwestern microbreweries. Work up a thirst on the free pretzels, order a three-beer sampler for $6 and cool off in the beer garden out back. This place is tops in the neighborhood.

HARRY CARAY'S TAVERN
BAR

Map p295 (www.harrycaraystavern.com; 700 E Grand Ave; ⊙11am-10pm Sun-Thu, to midnight Fri & Sat; Ⓜ Red Line to Grand, then trolley) Order a brewski at this bar named after the Cubs' famed announcer, then sip while perusing the memorabilia-filled cases that comprise the Chicago Sports Museum. Shake your head in sadness at the last-out ball from 1945 World Series (the last time the Cubs were in the championship) and Sammy Sosa's corked bat. Harry's also enshrines relics for Da Bears, Bulls, Blackhawks and White Sox. It's located on Navy Pier, near the entrance.

BREHON PUB
PUB

Map p292 (✆312-642-1071; www.brehonpub. com; 731 N Wells St; ⊙from 11am Mon-Fri, from noon Sat & Sun; Ⓜ Brown, Purple Line to Chicago) This Irish stalwart is a fine example of the corner saloons that once dotted the city. The ample selection of draft beer in frosted glasses is served to neighborhood crowds perched on the high stools.

WATERSHED
BAR

Map p292 (www.watershedbar.com; 601 N State St; ⊙from 5pm Mon-Sat; Ⓜ Red Line to Grand) This cozy basement bar has a speakeasy-meets-ski-lodge vibe. All of the beer and spirits hail from the Great Lakes region (hence the name) and staff procure several hard-to-find gems. Watershed sits beneath Pop's for Champagne, the long-standing wine bar where a mature crowd sips from a list of nearly 200 sparkling vintages.

SOUND-BAR
CLUB

Map p292 (✆312-787-4480; www.sound-bar. com; 226 W Ontario St; ⊙10pm-4am Thu & Fri, to 5am Sat; Ⓜ Brown, Purple Line to Chicago) This 4000 sq ft nightspot rises above the city's other sprawling megaclubs by way of superstar trance and house DJs (John Digweed, Dimitri from Paris etc). There's an amazing sound system and a dramatic setting of futuristic neon and steely, minimalist decor.

DOLLOP
CAFE

Map p292 (www.dollopstreeterville.com; 345 E Ohio St; ⊙6am-9pm; 🛜; Ⓜ Red Line to Grand) Modern, sunny coffee-slinger Dollop fires up a mean espresso among its caffeinated arsenal. Local baked treats such as Hoosier Mama pies provide the sugar.

TERRACE AT TRUMP TOWER
LOUNGE

Map p292 (✆312-588-8600; 401 N Wabash Ave; ⊙from 2pm; Ⓜ Brown, Orange, Green, Purple, Pink to State/Lake) Trump's small, view-a-riffic, 16th-floor alfresco lounge is for when you want to live large, with a glass of sparkling wine in hand, looking at the Wrigley Building and the river from a bird's-eye vantage point.

☆ ENTERTAINMENT

CHICAGO SHAKESPEARE THEATER
THEATER

Map p295 (✆312-595-5600; www.chicago shakes.com; 800 E Grand Ave; Ⓜ Red Line to Grand, then trolley) Snuggled into a beautiful, highly visible home on Navy Pier, this company is at the top of its game, presenting works from the Bard that are fresh, inventive and timeless. In summer the group puts on Shakespeare in the Parks – free performances of one of Will's classics that travel to 18 neighborhoods.

ANDY'S
JAZZ

Map p292 (www.andysjazzclub.com; 11 E Hubbard St; cover charge $5-15; ⊘from 4pm; MRed Line to Grand) This comfy jazz club programs a far-ranging lineup of local traditional, swing, bop, Latin, fusion and Afro-pop acts, along with the occasional big-name performer. It has been on the scene for several years and its downtown location makes it a popular spot for postwork boppers.

BLUE CHICAGO
BLUES

Map p292 (⊘312-661-0100; www.bluechicago. com; 536 N Clark St; cover charge $8-10; ⊘from 8pm; MRed Line to Grand) If you're staying in the neighborhood and don't feel like hitting the road, you won't go wrong at this mainstream blues club. Commanding local acts such as Big Time Sarah wither the mics nightly.

HOUSE OF BLUES
LIVE MUSIC

Map p292 (www.houseofblues.com; 320 N Dearborn St; MBrown, Orange, Green, Purple, Pink Line to State/Lake) House of Blues has multiple stages and, despite the name, not all play in the minor key groove. The one that does is the Back Porch Stage, with live blues nightly. The bands aren't necessarily big names, but they're always high quality.

Shows from Sunday to Wednesday start at 8pm, when a $10 cover charge kicks in. If you come early and dine in the restaurant, you avoid the fee. From Thursday to Saturday, shows start at 6:30pm and 9pm. Arrive before 9pm to avoid the cover charge.

UNDERGROUND WONDER BAR
LIVE MUSIC

Map p292 (⊘312-266-7761; www.underground wonderbar.com; 710 N Clark St; cover charge $5-15; ⊘from 5pm; MRed Line to Chicago) This live-music venue run by musician Lonie Walker features little-known jazz and blues performers, along with the occasional rock or reggae player. The club is tiny and Lonie herself takes the stage with her 'big bad-ass company band' several nights a week.

HOWL AT THE MOON
LIVE MUSIC

Map p292 (⊘312-863-7427; www.howlatthe moon.com; 26 W Hubbard St; ⊘from 5pm Mon-Sat, from 7pm Sun; MRed Line to Grand) The Guns 'n' Roses covers, happy-hour specials and flirty singles scene here could make nearly anyone into a piano bar convert.

FREE BLUES

In addition to being a great restaurant, Shaw's Crab House (p77) is a great blues venue. The restaurant's Oyster Bar has local blues bands rocking it Sunday through Thursday from 7pm to 10pm. And it's free. Drinks and Shaw's top-notch seafood are available, of course. Locals are clued in to the scene and the bar usually packs a crowd.

Billy Joel? Sorry, how about AC/DC? Lots of bachelorette parties sing along at Howl (which is part of a national chain).

 SHOPPING

JAZZ RECORD MART
MUSIC

Map p292 (www.jazzmart.com; 27 E Illinois St; ⊘10am-8pm Mon-Sat, noon-5pm Sun; MRed Line to Grand) You have to hunt for this place, but jazzheads, blues aficionados and vintage vinyl collectors seek it out, as it makes the short list of best record stores in the nation. You can spend hours fingering through the rows of dusty LPs or chatting with owner Bob Koester and his dedicated staff about local blues and jazz.

Fans of Chicago blues will find heaps of aural souvenirs, especially from the shop's boutique label, Delmark.

ABRAHAM LINCOLN BOOK SHOP
BOOKS

Map p292 (⊘312-944-3085; www.alincolnbook shop.com; 357 W Chicago Ave; ⊘9am-5pm Tue, Wed & Fri, to 7pm Thu, 10am-4pm Sat; MBrown, Purple Line to Chicago) This hushed, museum-like shop carries new, used and antiquarian books about Honest Abe, the Civil War and the presidency in general. If you want a real, Lincoln-signed White House memo – and have $30,000 to drop on it – you'll walk out of here a satisfied customer. At the other end of the spectrum are used books for $5. Ring the doorbell for entry.

The knowledgeable staff regularly hold open round-table discussions with Civil War scholars.

GARRETT POPCORN
FOOD

Map p292 (⊘312-944-2630; www.garrettpop corn.com; 625 N Michigan Ave; ⊘10am-9pm Mon-Thu, 9am-10pm Fri & Sat, to 8pm Sun; MRed Line to Grand) Like lemmings drawn to a cliff, people form long lines outside this store on the Mag Mile. Granted, the caramel corn is heavenly and the cheese popcorn decadent, but is it worth waiting in the whipping snow for a chance to buy some? Actually, it is. Buy the Chicago Mix, which combines the two flavors.

One estimate says Chicagoans wolf down a collective 480,000lb per year. The entrance is on Ontario St.

NIKE CHICAGO
SPORTS

Map p292 (☑312-642-6363; twitter.com/nikechicago; 669 N Michigan Ave; ⊙10am-9pm Mon-Sat, to 7pm Sun; MRed Line to Chicago) This flashy Nike outpost is a cool place to meander. The 1st floor is a temple to Chicago Bulls legend Michael Jordan; there's more Jordan-brand merchandise here than in any store worldwide. The 2nd floor is loaded with football and soccer gear. The 3rd floor has treadmills where runners can try out shoes. And the 4th floor has an area to design your own swooshed kicks.

A free running club takes off from the store every Thursday at 6:30pm.

ALLSAINTS
CLOTHING, ACCESSORIES

Map p292 (us.allsaints.com; 700 N Michigan Ave; ⊙10am-9pm Mon-Sat, 11am-8pm Sun; MRed Line to Chicago) The British brand lays out its vintage-inspired men's and women's styles in a sprawling store decorated with 1800 antique sewing machines. Most of the wares come in Euro-cool black or gray.

BURBERRY
FASHION

Map p292 (www.burberry.com; 633 N Michigan Ave; ⊙10am-8pm Mon-Fri, to 7pm Sat, noon-6pm Sun; MRed Line to Grand) What is the bizarre, five-story building on Michigan Ave that has an exterior covered in plaid? It's the British luxury fashion house Burberry, of course. The iconic company is known for its plaid designs and its trench coats, all of which are here in abundance. The plaid lights up at night, by the way.

CRATE & BARREL
HOMEWARES

Map p292 (☑312-787-5900; www.crateandbarrel.com; 646 N Michigan Ave; ⊙10am-8pm Mon-Sat, 11am-6pm Sun; MRed Line to Grand) The handsome housewares purveyor started right here in Chicago and this glassy, sassy uberstore is the flagship. Inside, suburban soccer moms fill their carts with hip but functional lamps, wine goblets, casserole dishes and brass beds, same as the downtown loft nesters shopping beside them.

APPLE STORE
ELECTRONICS

Map p292 (☑312-981-4104; www.apple.com; 679 N Michigan Ave; ⊙10am-9pm Mon-Thu, to 8pm Fri & Sat, 11am-7pm Sun; 🛜; MRed Line to Chicago) This bright, airy store offers iPads, iPods and everything else for Mac enthusiasts splayed across butcher-block tables. The user-friendly setup comes with plenty of clued-up staff to answer product questions, a 'genius bar' on the 2nd floor to sort out equipment issues and free internet access on machines throughout the store.

ZARA
CLOTHING, ACCESSORIES

Map p292 (☑312-750-0780; www.zara.com; 700 N Michigan Ave; ⊙10am-8pm Mon-Sat, 11am-7pm Sun; MRed Line to Chicago) New products arrive weekly and inventory changes biweekly at Spanish fashion house Zara. It's sort of Gap meets H&M, with youthful, off-the-runway styles at low prices in women's, men's and kids' clothing. The three-story building is Zara's biggest US store.

SHOPS AT NORTH BRIDGE
MALL

Map p292 (☑312-327-2300; www.theshopsatnorthbridge.com; 520 N Michigan Ave; ⊙10am-9pm Mon-Sat, 11am-7pm Sun; MRed Line to Grand) Shops at North Bridge appeals to a less aggressively froufrou demographic than some of the other Mag Mile malls, with stores such as Swatch and Harley Davidson. The multilevel mall connects anchor department store Nordstrom to Michigan Ave via a gracefully curving, shop-lined atrium.

🏃 SPORTS & ACTIVITIES

BOBBY'S BIKE HIKE
CYCLING

Map p292 (☑312-915-0995; www.bobbysbikehike.com; 465 N McClurg Ct; half-/full day from $23/32; ⊙8am-8pm Jun-Aug, 8:30am-7pm Sep-Nov & Mar-May, closed Dec-Feb; MRed Line to Grand) Locally based Bobby's earns rave reviews from riders. It rents bikes and has easy access to the Lakefront Trail. It also offers cool tours ($35 to $59) of South Side gangster sites, the lakefront, nighttime vistas and venues to indulge in beer and hot dogs. It's located at the River East Docks' Ogden Slip.

BIKE CHICAGO NAVY PIER   CYCLING
Map p295 (www.bikechicago.com; 600 E Grand Ave; bikes per hr/day from $10/35; ⊘8am-10pm Jun-Aug, 9am-7pm spring & fall, closed Nov-Mar; ⓂRed Line to Grand, then trolley) It rents bikes (and offers tours) from a seasonal booth on Dock St. Bike Chicago's main, year-round shop is in Millennium Park.

OHIO ST BEACH   BEACH
Map p295 (www.cpdbeaches.com; ⓂRed Line to Grand, then trolley) Just a few minutes' walk from Navy Pier, this small beach is convenient for those who want a quick dip. The water's shallowness makes it the preferred spot for triathletes practicing open-water swims. A cafe pours beer and wine and serves sandwiches.

Gold Coast

Neighborhood Top Five

1 Getting high at the **John Hancock Center** (p84) by taking the 20mph elevator to the 96th-floor lounge for a tall drink and sparkling views.

2 Perusing the avant-garde paintings, sculptures and videos at the **Museum of Contemporary Art** (p85).

3 Ogling the genteel mansions on **Astor St**.

4 Examining the eerie gallstones and cadaver murals at the **International Museum of Surgical Science** (p87).

5 Wandering along **Rush St** during the see-and-be-seen weekend nights (p87).

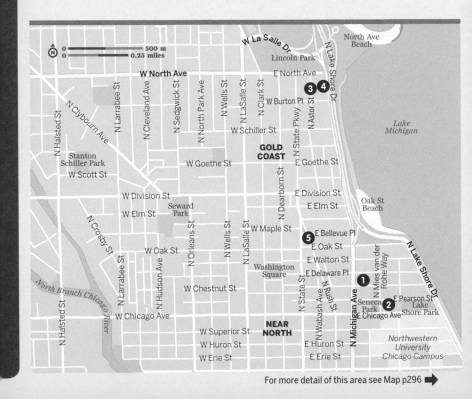

For more detail of this area see Map p296 ➡

Explore The Gold Coast

The Gold Coast has been the address of Chicago's crème de la crème for more than 125 years. When you stroll through the neighborhood, especially the Astor St area, you'll take in some of the most beautiful old mansions in Chicago. One of them belonged to Hugh Hefner and was the original Playboy Mansion.

Beyond the sky-high John Hancock Center and the underappreciated Museum of Contemporoary Art, there aren't many sights in the Gold Coast. The best way to get a feel for the neighborhood's moneyed present is to spend an afternoon browsing luxuriant designer wares around Oak and Rush Sts, or an evening among the glittering high heels and good cheekbones of the neighborhood's nightlife. On Friday evening, see-and-be-seen crowds glide through bars and restaurants at Rush and State Sts, where businessmen carve porterhouses while downing martinis and ogling the action – no wonder locals call the area the 'Viagra Triangle.' For window-shopping and people-watching, Chicago offers no finer spectacle.

East along Michigan Ave the shopping gives way to high-rise malls that will be likely destinations for anyone with kids. American Girl Place, Hershey's and the Lego Store send out their siren call from here. Oak St Beach is a stone's throw away, offering a bit of breathing room from the high-rise jungle and a fine place to dip your toes in the lake.

Local Life

→ **Hidden Treats** Only neighborhood folks know that Hendrickx Belgian Bread Crafter (p87), purveyor of top-notch chocolate croissants, hides inside the bland apartment building on Walton St.

→ **Low-Key Drinks** Locals looking for a well-made cocktail without the usual Gold Coast sceney vibe head upstairs to the relaxed bar at Le Colonial (p90).

→ **Late-Night Munchies** When the bars and clubs close, everyone heads to Tempo Cafe (p90), open 24/7 for skillet-fried replenishment.

Getting There & Away

→ **El** Red Line to Clark/Division for the northern reaches; Red Line to Chicago for the southern areas.

→ **Bus** Number 151 runs along Michigan Ave; 70 runs along Division St before swooping south to the Newberry Library.

→ **Car** Resident-only streets stymie street parking. Try LaSalle St, much of which is unmetered.

Lonely Planet's Top Tip

The Gold Coast may be one of Chicago's most moneyed neighborhoods, but it offers several freebies to take advantage of: the **International Museum of Surgical Science** (p87) and **Charnley-Persky House** (p86) are free on Tuesday and Wednesday respectively, while the **Newberry Library** (p87) and City Gallery at the **Water Tower** (p86) are always free.

✕ Best Places to Eat

→ Le Colonial (p90)

→ Francesca's on Chestnut (p90)

→ Hendrickx Belgian Bread Crafter (p87)

→ Pizano's (p90)

→ Tempo Cafe (p90)

For reviews, see p87

🍸 Best Places to Drink

→ Signature Lounge (p91)

→ Coq d'Or (p91)

→ Pump Room (p91)

→ Lodge (p91)

For reviews, see p91

🔒 Best Places to Shop

→ Open Books (p93)

→ Flight 001 (p93)

→ Burton Snowboards (p94)

→ American Girl Place (p94)

→ Hershey's (p94)

For reviews, see p93

JUAN SILVA / GETTY IMAGES ©

TOP SIGHT
JOHN HANCOCK CENTER

Chicago's third-tallest skyscraper (at 1127ft) is our favorite place to get high. In many ways the view here surpasses the one at Willis Tower, as the Hancock is closer to the lake and a little further north. Plus, you have a couple of options for taking in the view – one of which saves money *and* provides liquid refreshment.

So here's the deal: you can pay the admission price and ascend to the 94th-floor observatory. It offers informative displays that tell you the names of the surrounding buildings. There's the 'skywalk,' a sort of screened-in porch that lets you feel the wind and hear the city sounds. There's a sweet photo op where you get to 'clean' the skyscraper's windows. And there's a wee ice-skating rink from January to early April (for an extra $7). The observatory is probably your place if you have kids or if you're a newbie and want to beef up your Chicago knowledge.

Otherwise, head up to the 96th-floor lounge, where the view is free if you buy a drink ($6 to $16). That's right, here you'll get a glass of wine and a comfy seat while staring out at almost identical views from a few floors *higher*. The elevators for the lounge (and its companion restaurant on the 95th floor) are separate from the observatory. Look for signs that say 'Signature 95th/96th' one floor up from the observatory entrance.

The nighttime views from either floor are awesome, with city lights sparkling to the north, south and west. Navy Pier is east and in summer you can time your visit with the Pier's fireworks on Wednesdays (9:30pm) and Saturdays (10:15pm).

DON'T MISS...

➜ 20mph elevator ride

➜ Skywalk

➜ Window washer photo op

➜ Nighttime views, including Wednesday and Saturday fireworks in summer

PRACTICALITIES

➜ Map p296

➜ ☎888-875-8439

➜ www.jhochicago.com

➜ 875 N Michigan Ave

➜ adult/child $18/12

➜ ⊙9am-11pm

➜ Ⓜ Red Line to Chicago

TOP SIGHT
MUSEUM OF CONTEMPORARY ART (MCA)

Consider it the Art Institute's rebellious sibling, with especially strong minimalist, surrealist and book arts collections, as well as permanent works by Franz Kline, René Magritte, Cindy Sherman and Andy Warhol. Covering art from 1945 onwards, the MCA's collection spans the gamut, with displays arranged to blur the boundaries between painting, photography, sculpture, video and other media. Exhibits change regularly so you never know what you'll see, but count on it being provocative.

The MCA mounts themed exhibitions that typically focus on underappreciated or up-and-coming artists that curators are introducing to American audiences. For example, you might see a three-decade retrospective of German artist Isa Genzken's sculpture, or Turner Prize winner Simon Starling's mixed media works made of recycled materials.

Docents lead free, 45-minute tours through the galleries daily at 1pm, as well as Tuesdays at 2pm and 6pm, and weekends at 2pm and 3pm. Meet in the 2nd-floor lobby. You can also pick up a free audio tour from the front desk.

Don't forget to wander through the sculpture garden at the back. And check to see what's on in MCA's theater, which regularly hosts dance, film and speaking events by contemporary A-listers.

In summer a jazz band plays in the sculpture garden every Tuesday at 5:30pm. Patrons bring blankets and sip drinks from the bar. An art-making workshop for families takes place in the garden simultaneously. On Tuesday mornings a farmers market with veggies, cheeses and baked goods sets up on the front plaza from 7am to 3pm. Illinois residents have the added bonus of museum admission being free on Tuesdays.

The museum's shop wins big points for its jewelry pieces and colorful children's toys.

DON'T MISS...

➡ Free tours at 1pm
➡ Free audio tour
➡ Groovy shop
➡ Sculpture garden
➡ Terrace with lake views

PRACTICALITIES

➡ Map p296
➡ ☎312-280-2660
➡ www.mca chicago.org
➡ 220 E Chicago Ave
➡ adult/student $12/7
➡ ⏰10am-8pm Tue, to 5pm Wed-Sun
➡ Ⓜ Red Line to Chicago

◉ SIGHTS

JOHN HANCOCK CENTER ARCHITECTURE
See p84.

MUSEUM OF CONTEMPORARY ART MUSEUM
See p85.

WATER TOWER LANDMARK
Map p296 (cnr Chicago & Michigan Aves; MRed Line to Chicago) The 154ft-tall, turreted tower is a defining city icon: it was the sole downtown survivor of the 1871 Great Chicago Fire, along with the Pumping Station (aka Water Works), its associated building across the street. Today the tower houses the **City Gallery** (Map p296; ☑312-742-0808; ⊙10am-6:30pm Mon-Sat, to 5pm Sun) FREE, showcasing Chicago-themed works by local photographers.

Built in 1869, the tower and pumping station were constructed with local yellow limestone in a Gothic style popular at the time. It's this stone and lack of flammable interiors that saved them when the fire roared through town.

The Water Tower was the great hope of Chicago when it first opened, one part of a great technological breakthrough that was going to provide fresh, clean water for the city from intake cribs set far out in Lake Michigan. Before then, the city's drinking water had come from shore-side collection basins that sucked in sewage-laden water and industrial runoff from the Chicago River. Garnished with the occasional school of small fish, it all ended up in the sinks and bathtubs of unhappy Chicago residents.

Though the fish problem was solved by the new system, the plan was ultimately a failure. Sewage from the river, propelled by spring rains, made its way out to the new intake bins. The whole smelly situation didn't abate until the Chicago River was reversed in the 1890s (when engineers used canals and locks to send sewage away from Lake Michigan). By 1906 the Water Tower was obsolete and only public outcry saved it from demolition three times. Whether Oscar Wilde would have joined the preser-

---

LOCAL KNOWLEDGE

ASTOR STREET

In 1882, Bertha and Potter Palmer were the power couple of Chicago. Potter's web of businesses included the city's best hotel and a huge general merchandise store that he later sold to a clerk named Marshall Field. When the Palmers decided to move north from Prairie Ave to a manor at what is now 1350 N Lake Shore Dr, they set off a lemminglike rush of Chicago's wealthy to the neighborhood around them. The mansions sitting along Astor St, especially the 1300 to 1500 blocks, reflect the grandeur of that heady period. Here are the highlights, from south to north:

Charnley-Persky House (Map p296; ☑312-573-1365; www.charnleyhouse.org; 1365 N Astor St; tours Wed free, Sat $10; ⊙noon Wed, 10am & noon Sat Apr-Nov) While he was still working for Louis Sullivan, Frank Lloyd Wright (who was 19 at the time) designed the 11-room Charnley-Persky House and proclaimed with his soon-to-be-trademarked bombast that it was the 'first modern building.' Why? Because it did away with Victorian gaudiness in favor of plain, abstract forms that went on to become the modern style. It was completed in 1892 and now houses the Society of Architectural Historians. Guided tours are offered Wednesdays and Saturdays; they're first come, first served, up to 15 people.

Cyrus McCormick Mansion (Map p296; 1500 N Astor St) The industrialist's 1893 neoclassical home, designed by New York architect Stanford White, is one of the neighborhood standouts. McCormick and his family had the whole place to themselves, but it's now divided up into condos. It's still the high-rent district – a three-bedroom, three-bathroom unit goes for $1.75 million (washer and dryer included).

Archbishop's Residence (Map p296; 1555 N State St) The 1885 mansion that serves as the archbishop's abode spans an entire block between State and Astor Sts. The sweet crib, complete with 19 chimneys, is one of the perks that comes with leading the Chicago Catholic Archdiocese. Seven archbishops have lived here and world leaders from Franklin D Roosevelt to Pope John Paul II have crashed at the residence while in town.

vationists is debatable: when he visited Chicago in 1881 he called the Water Tower 'a castellated monstrosity with salt and pepper boxes stuck all over it.' Restoration in 1962 ensured the tower's survival.

INTERNATIONAL MUSEUM OF SURGICAL SCIENCE
MUSEUM

Map p296 (☎312-642-6502; www.imss.org; 1524 N Lake Shore Dr; adult/child $15/7, free Tue; ◷10am-4pm Tue-Fri, to 5pm Sat & Sun; 🚌151) This place verges on creepy with its amputation saws, iron lungs and other early tools of the trade strewn throughout a creaky, Gold Coast mansion. The ancient Roman vaginal speculum leaves a lasting impression, while the pointy-ended hemorrhoid surgery instruments serve as a reminder to eat lots of fiber. The collection of 'stones' (as in 'kidney' and 'gall-') and bloodletting displays look equally painful.

Medical art gets its due here, too, from a life-size, toga-clad sculpture of Hippocrates to a roomful of cadaver murals (available as postcards in the gift shop).

NEWBERRY LIBRARY
LIBRARY

Map p296 (☎312-943-9090; www.newberry. org; 60 W Walton St; ◷9am-5pm Tue-Sat; Ⓜ Red Line to Chicago) FREE The Newberry's public galleries are for bibliophiles: those who swoon over original Thomas Paine pamphlets about the French Revolution, or get weak-kneed seeing Thomas Jefferson's copy of the *History of the Expedition under Captains Lewis and Clark* (with margin notes!). Exhibits rotate yellowed manuscripts and tattered first editions from the library's extensive collection.

The library itself, stacked with books, maps, photographs and other humanities-related materials, is on the upper floors. Those trying to research far-flung branches of their family tree will have a field day here. Entry requires a library card, but one day passes are available for curious browsers. Once inside, you can pester the patient librarians with requests for help in tracking down all manner of historical ephemera. (The collection is noncirculating, though, so don't expect to take that 1st edition of the King James Bible home with you.) Free tours of the impressive building take place at 3pm Thursday and 10:30am Saturday.

ORIGINAL PLAYBOY MANSION
BUILDING

Map p296 (1340 N State Pkwy; Ⓜ Red Line to Clark/Division) The sexual revolution pretty much started in the basement 'grotto' of this 1899 mansion. Chicago magazine impresario Hugh Hefner bought it in 1959 and dubbed it the first Playboy Mansion, even hanging a brass plate over the door warning 'If You Don't Swing, Don't Ring.' Alas, Chicago became too square for Hef by the mid '70s, so he split and built a new Playboy Mansion in LA.

And that's where he remains today, in his pajamas. After he left, he donated the State St building to the School of the Art Institute for a dorm (imagine the pick-up lines!). It was gutted in 1993 and turned into four very respectable, very expensive condos. Hef's company, Playboy Enterprises, stayed headquartered in Chicago until 2012, and then it too moved west. The last vestige is 'Honorary Hugh M Hefner Way,' which is what the city renamed Walton St (at Michigan Ave) in an official tip of the hat to Hef.

WASHINGTON SQUARE
PARK

Map p296 (901 N Clark St; Ⓜ Red Line to Chicago) This plain-looking park across from the Newberry Library has quite a history. In the 1920s it was known as 'Bughouse Sq' because of the communists, socialists, anarchists and other -ists who gave soapbox orations here. Clarence Darrow and Carl Sandburg are among the respected speakers who climbed up and shouted.

In the 1970s, when it was a gathering place for young male prostitutes, it gained tragic infamy as the preferred pick-up spot of mass murderer John Wayne Gacy. Gacy took his victims back to his suburban home, where he killed them and buried their bodies in the basement. Convicted on 33 counts of murder (although the actual tally may be higher), he was executed in 1994.

Today the square bears little trace of its past lives – except for one weekend a year in late July. That's when the **Bughouse Debates** occur and orators return to holler at each other.

✗ EATING

HENDRICKX BELGIAN BREAD CRAFTER
BAKERY $

Map p296 (100 E Walton St; snacks $3-9; ◷8am-7pm Tue-Sat, 9am-3pm Sun; Ⓜ Red Line to Chicago) Hiding in a nondescript apartment building, Hendrickx is a local secret. Push open the bright-orange door and behold

Gold Coast – Magnificent Mansions

Astor St has been the address of Chicago's elite for more than 125 years. Several spectacular pieces of real estate went up back then, with well-heeled families trying to outdo each other in grandeur. Everyone from Frank Lloyd Wright to Hugh Hefner has passed through the neighborhood's distinguished doors.

1. Archbishop's Residence (p86)
The archbishop's abode spans an entire block and contains 19 chimneys.

2. Cyrus McCormick Mansion (p86)
This handsome 1893 mansion, built in neoclassical style, now houses condos.

3. Original Playboy Mansion (p87)
In 1959, Hugh Hefner and his sexual revolution rolled into the neighborhood.

4. Charnley-Persky House (p86)
Frank Lloyd Wright proclaimed this as the 'first modern building.'

LOCAL KNOWLEDGE

CUPCAKE ATM

The cupcake craze may be losing its pizzazz, but the novelty of getting a thick-icing'ed chocolate marshmallow or triple cinnamon confection at 2am from an automated teller machine is hard to resist. The Cupcake ATM dispenses 24 hours a day in front of **Sprinkles Cupcakes** (Map p296; www.sprinkles.com; 50 E Walton St; cupcakes $3.50; MRed Line to Chicago). The machine even stocks one for dogs (sugar-free, of course).

the waffles, white chocolate bread and dark chocolate croissants among the flaky, buttery, Belgian treats. The place is tiny, with just a few indoor seats, but in warm weather it sets up tables on the sidewalk. Soups and sandwiches are also available.

FOODLIFE INTERNATIONAL $

Map p296 (312-787-7100; www.foodlifechicago.com; 835 N Michigan Ave; mains $6-11; 8am-8pm Mon-Thu, to 8:30pm Fri & Sat, to 7pm Sun; MRed Line to Chicago) 'Call it a restaurant. Call it an eatery. Just don't call it a food court!' demands the mantra of Foodlife – a place with a dozen different globally themed kitchens featuring gourmet à la carte options in a sleek atmosphere. Sushi, stir-fries, pizza, pasta, burritos and barbecue are among the offerings. It's situated inside Water Tower Place mall.

FRANCESCA'S ON CHESTNUT ITALIAN $$

Map p296 (312-482-8800; www.miafrancesca.com; 200 E Chestnut St; mains $13-25; 11am-10pm Mon-Thu, to 11pm Fri & Sat, to 9pm Sun; MRed Line to Chicago) Part of a well-loved local chain, Francesca's buzzes with regulars who come for the trattoria's rustic standards, such as seafood linguine, spinach ravioli and mushroom-sauced veal medallions, all prepared with simple flair. A jazz band sets the mood on weekends. The restaurant is located in the Seneca building.

PIZANO'S PIZZERIA $$

Map p296 (www.pizanoschicago.com; 864 N State St; 10-inch pizzas from $14; 11am-2am Sun-Fri, to 3am Sat; MRed Line to Chicago) Congenial Pizano's gets lost amid Chicago's pizza places, which is a shame since it's one of the best and has an illustrious pedigree (founded by Rudi Malnati Jr, whose dad created

the deep-dish pizza, so the legend goes). The buttery crust impresses, even more so in its thin-crust incarnation. There's another Pizano's in the Loop.

TEMPO CAFE AMERICAN $$

Map p296 (312-943-3929; 6 E Chestnut St; mains $8-15; 24hr; MRed Line to Chicago) Bright and cheery, this upscale diner brings most of its meals to the table the way they're meant to be served – in a skillet. Its omelet-centric menu includes all manner of fresh veggies and meat, as well as sandwiches, soups and salads. After the bars close the scene here is chaotic and fun. Cash only.

PJ CLARKE'S AMERICAN $$

Map p296 (312-664-1650; www.pjclarkes-chicago.com; 1204 N State St; mains $11-20; 11:30am-2am Mon-Fri, from 10am Sat & Sun; MRed Line to Clark/Division) Chicago's straight, 30-something singles come to eyeball one another at this upscale restaurant-pub. Classy and cozy, PJ Clarke's specializes in comfort foods with high-end twists, like the gourmet burger with bordelaise sauce and the teriyaki skirt-steak sandwich.

LE COLONIAL FRENCH VIETNAMESE $$$

Map p296 (312-255-0088; www.lecolonialchicago.com; 937 N Rush St; mains $20-28; 11:30am-11pm Mon-Wed, to midnight Thu-Sat, to 10pm Sun; ; MRed Line to Chicago) Step into the dark-wood, candlelit room, where ceiling fans swirl lazily and big-leafed palms sway in the breeze, and you'd swear you were in 1920s Saigon. Staff can arrange loads of vegetarian and gluten-free substitutions among the curries and banana-leaf-wrapped fish dishes. If you want spicy, be specific; everything typically comes out mild. Le Colonial is perfect for a romantic date. You'll need reservations for a table, though walk-ins can head upstairs to the bar and eat there.

GIBSON'S STEAKHOUSE $$$

Map p296 (312-266-8999; www.gibsonssteakhouse.com; 1028 N Rush St; mains $30-55; 11am-midnight; MRed Line to Clark/Division) There is a scene nightly at this local original. Politicians, movers, shakers and the shaken-down swirl the famed martinis and compete for prime table space in the buzzing dining room. The bar is a prime stalking place for available millionaires. As for the meat on the plates, the steaks are as good as they come and ditto for the ginormous lobsters.

MORTON'S
STEAKHOUSE $$$

Map p296 (312-266-4820; www.mortons.com/statestreet; 1050 N State St; mains $30-75; 5-11pm Mon-Sat, to 10pm Sun; Red Line to Clark/Division) Morton's is a chain now, but Chicago is where it all began. The meat here is aged to perfection and displayed tableside before cooking. See that half a cow? It's the 48oz double porterhouse. Smaller – but still quite dangerous if dropped on your toe – are the fillets, strip steaks and other cuts. The immense baked potatoes could prop up church foundations. Or you could try the hash browns, a superb version of a side dish all too often ignored. Expensive reds anchor the wine list.

SIGNATURE ROOM AT THE 95TH
AMERICAN $$$

Map p296 (312-787-9596; www.signatureroom.com; 875 N Michigan Ave; mains $30-50; 11am-10pm Mon-Thu, to 11pm Fri & Sat, 10am-10pm Sun; Red Line to Chicago) Given that diners spend most of the meal view-gaping, you'd think the kitchen atop the Hancock wouldn't trouble itself over the food, but the chef does a fine job with the fish, steak and pasta dishes. The lunch buffet ($20, served Monday to Saturday) is the best deal, since the price isn't much more than a foodless ticket to the observation deck. Cheapskates should note they can get the same vista for the price of a (costly) beer, one floor up in the Signature Lounge (p91).

MIKE DITKA'S RESTAURANT
AMERICAN $$$

Map p296 (312-587-8989; www.ditkasrestaurants.com; 100 E Chestnut St; mains $20-45; 11am-10pm Mon-Thu, to 11pm Fri & Sat, 10am-10pm Sun; Red Line to Chicago) When it's too cold for a tailgate party, come to this spot in the Tremont Hotel owned by the famously cantankerous former coach of the Chicago Bears. The menu is as meaty as you'd expect (the Fridge burger could feed a family for weeks) and fans will love the memorabilia-filled display cases.

🍷⚓ DRINKING & NIGHTLIFE

★ SIGNATURE LOUNGE
LOUNGE

Map p296 (www.signatureroom.com; 875 N Michigan Ave; drinks $6-16; from 11am; Red Line to Chicago) Have the Hancock Observatory view without the Hancock Observatory admission price. Shoot straight up to the 96th floor and order a beverage while looking out over the city. It's particularly gape-worthy at night. Ladies: don't miss the bathroom view. Note that the lounge and restaurant have a separate elevator from the observatory. Look for signs that say 'Signature 95th/96th.'

COQ D'OR
LOUNGE

Map p296 (312-787-2200; 140 E Walton St; from 11am; Red Line to Chicago) This classy joint in the Drake Hotel opened the day after Prohibition was repealed. It offers a taste of old Chicago – burgundy-colored leather booths, a tuxedoed bartender and bejeweled women in furs sipping Manhattans. A piano player starts tinkling the ivories around 7pm.

PUMP ROOM
BAR

Map p296 (www.pumproom.com; 1301 N State Pkwy; from 5pm; Red Line to Clark/Division) Frank Sinatra and Bette Davis were among the movie stars who used to swirl martinis in the old Pump Room. It recently got a makeover that recaptures the glamor of yesteryear, and once again pretty people are drinking under the romantic paper-globe lights. Be sure to head downstairs by the bathrooms and check out the photos of the famous people who've dined here.

LODGE
BAR

Map p296 (312-642-4406; 21 W Division St; 2pm-4am Mon-Thu, from noon Fri-Sun; Red Line to Clark/Division) Dressed up like a misplaced hunting cabin, the Lodge has a bit more polish than most of its neighbors on Division St. A Wurlitzer jukebox spins oldies and the bowls of salty peanuts complement the abundance of beers on tap. The crowd of mostly 40-somethings drink like they mean it, sometimes until dawn.

ℹ DISCOUNT TICKETS

One of the city's three **Hot Tix** (163 E Pearson St; 10am-6pm Tue-Sat, 11am-4pm Sun) booths is in the Water Works building. Stop by to purchase half-price theater tickets. Drama, comedy and performing arts venues citywide have seats on offer for shows throughout the week. The earlier in the week you visit, the better the selection.

GOLD COAST DRINKING & NIGHTLIFE

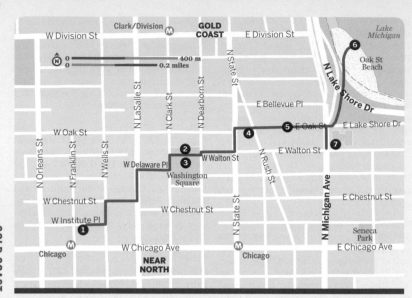

🏃 Local Life
Gold Coast Saunter

The Gold Coast has been the address of Chicago's wealthiest residents for more than 125 years. Bejeweled women glide in and out of the neighborhood's stylish boutiques. The occasional Rolls Royce wheels along the leafy streets. But it's not all so chichi. Plenty of, er, less gilded locals live here and have their hot spots, too.

❶ Do-Good Books

Thrifty hipsters in need of a good read browse the gently used stacks at Open Books (p93). Hours slip by as they scan shelves that hold *Little House on the Prairie* next to Gwyneth Paltrow's latest cookbook next to a 1987 guidebook to Alaska. All proceeds go toward the nonprofit shop's literacy programs for local kids.

❷ Scholarly Pursuits

Let's say you need a prehistoric map of Kentucky's Cumberland River Valley. Or a map of Saxon Britain circa 1000 AD. The Newberry Library (p87) has it! You don't need to be a research egghead to stop by, though. The on-site bookstore is known as one of the best places to find Chicago-themed tomes, such as a photo-filled treatise on local hot dogs.

❸ Bughouse Square

The park across from Newberry is officially called Washington Sq (p87), famed for its

history of soapbox orators. Many of them supposedly lived in nearby 'bughouses' (cheap hotels), hence the nickname. Today residents walking their dogs, workers eating lunch and crusty old-timers arguing with one another hang out around the flowing fountain. The park was added to the National Register of Historic Places in 1991.

❹ Barneys and Fred's

The neighborhood society ladies know where to go to have it all: Barneys New York (p94). The luxe department store offers six floors of high-fashion clothing and accessories. When they tire of shopping, the ladies then ascend to the penthouse restaurant – Fred's – for lobster bisque and a soothing glass of Chardonnay (best sipped on the terrace overlooking the lake).

❺ Boutique Bonanza

Oak Street is where moneyed locals come to find that hand-folded Hermès tie, a Harry Winston diamond or the perfect

Oak St Beach (p95)

ENTERTAINMENT

LOOKINGGLASS THEATRE
COMPANY
THEATER

Map p296 (312-337-0665; www.looking-glasstheatre.org; 821 N Michigan Ave; MRed Line to Chicago) This well-regarded troupe works in a nifty theater hewn from the old Water Works building. The ensemble cast – which includes cofounder David Schwimmer of TV's *Friends* – often uses physical stunts and acrobatics to enhance its dreamy, magical, literary productions.

BACK ROOM
JAZZ

Map p296 (312-751-2433; www.backroomchicago.com; 937 N Rush St; from 9pm; MRed Line to Chicago) After decades in its cozy shoebox of a space, the venerated jazz club moved in 2012 to this larger room underneath Le Colonial restaurant. Enter via the alleyway just north (you should see the sign). Bop purists, be warned: the tunes here can get more than a little smooth. There's a $20 cover charge and two-drink minimum.

ZEBRA LOUNGE
LIVE MUSIC

Map p296 (312-642-5140; 1220 N State St; from 5pm Mon-Fri, from 6pm Sat & Sun; MRed Line to Clark/Division) The piano in this tiny, dark and mirrored room can get as scratchy as the voices of the crowd, which consists mainly of older folks who like to sing along. The ivory strokers here are veterans who know their stuff.

☐ SHOPPING

OPEN BOOKS
BOOKS

Map p296 (312-475-1355; www.open-books.org; 213 W Institute Pl; 10am-7pm Mon-Sat, noon-6pm Sun; ☀; MBrown, Purple Line to Chicago) Buy a used book here and you're helping to fund this volunteer-based literacy group's programs, which range from in-school reading help for grade-schoolers to book publishing courses for teens. The jam-packed store has good-quality tomes and plenty of cushy sofas where you can sit and peruse your finds. Kids have their own castle-shaped reading nook. Books average around $5.

FLIGHT 001
ACCESSORIES

Map p296 (312-944-1001; www.flight001.com; 1133 N State St; 11am-7pm Mon-Sat, to 6pm Sun; MRed Line to Clark/Division) The brightly

---

pair of Jimmy Choo pumps. The designer boutiques line up in a pretty row along the street, between Michigan Ave and Rush St. Nonmoneyed locals window shop and sigh.

⑥ Rich in Sand

Oak St Beach (p95) has been the lay-out spot for downtowners for more than a century. Records show that area mansion owners were making complaints as early as 1910 that too many bathers were recreating on the prized stretch of sand. On sunny summer days the beach still fills with families and body-beautiful types vying for a place to unfurl a towel.

⑦ Classy Drinks

The Coq d'Or (p91) is in the Drake Hotel, which means plenty of out-of-towners are sitting at the bar. But residents from the neighborhood high-rises are the regulars. See the dapper older gentleman carving into a steak? Or the fur-coat-clad woman clutching her martini? They're here more nights than not, enjoying dinner, drinks and the jazzy crooners who entertain on weekends.

colored, hard-shelled luggage and the stock of travel gadgets will get a rise out of any would-be jet-setter. The sleek store resembles the interior of an airplane; the cash register area is even a retro airline ticket counter.

BURTON SNOWBOARDS
SPORTS

Map p296 (☑312-202-7900; www.burton.com; 56 E Walton St; ⊙11am-8pm Mon-Sat, to 6pm Sun; MRed Line to Chicago) Hey, Midwesterners shred the slopes too and this is where air dogs come to get their gear. Burton, of course, is the biggest brand in the business. Its multistory Chicago shop carries a sweet selection of boards, jackets, watches and other accessories. There's a chill-out lounge on the top floor where you can check email and watch snowboarding films.

AMERICAN GIRL PLACE
CHILDREN

Map p296 (www.americangirl.com; 835 N Michigan Ave; ⊙10am-8pm Mon-Thu, 9am-9pm Fri & Sat, 9am-6pm Sun; ⊛; MRed Line to Chicago) This is not your mother's doll shop; it's an *experience*. Here, dolls are treated as real people: the 'hospital' carts them away in wheelchairs for repairs; the cafe seats the dolls as part of the family during tea service; and the dolls' owners – usually outfitted in matching threads, naturally – take classes with their little pals.

Creepy? Maybe a little, but the fact that the average shopper's visit lasts three hours is a testament to the immersive environment. There are outlets in many cities now, but this flagship remains the largest and busiest.

HERSHEY'S
FOOD

Map p296 (www.thehersheycompany.com; 822 N Michigan Ave; ⊙10am-10pm; ⊛⊛; MRed Line to Chicago) How about a personalized chocolate bar with your photo on the wrapper? Hershey's has a handful of flashy retail stores around the globe and one is right here on the Mag Mile. Seasonal sweets and hard-to-find flavors of Kisses and other chocolates stock the shelves and there are usually samples to be scoffed.

LEGO STORE
CHILDREN

Map p296 (www.lego.com; 835 N Michigan Ave; ⊙10am-9pm Mon-Sat, 11am-6pm Sun; ⊛; MRed Line to Chicago) After oohing and aahhing at the cool models of rockets, castles and dinosaurs scattered throughout the store, kids can build their own designs at pint-sized

tables equipped with bins of the signature little bricks. It's located in Water Tower Place on the 2nd floor.

H&M
CLOTHING

Map p296 (☑312-640-0060; www.hm.com/us; 840 N Michigan Ave; ⊙9am-9:30pm Mon-Sat, 10am-8pm Sun; MRed Line to Chicago) This Swedish-based purveyor of trendy togs is usually packed with customers clawing the racks for high fashion at low prices. Men and women will find a variety of European-cut styles ranging from business suits to bathing suits. There's another outlet at 22 N State St, but this one is bigger.

ALTERNATIVES
SHOES

Map p296 (☑312-266-1545; www.altshoes.com; 5th fl, 900 N Michigan Ave; ⊙10am-7pm Mon-Sat, noon-6pm Sun; MRed Line to Chicago) The kinds of shoes that delight the eye and appall the feet are the specialty at this store, located in the 900 N Michigan mall. Featuring one of the most cutting-edge collections in town, its prices will gladden the hearts of budding Imelda Marcoses everywhere. Another outlet is located in Block 37 (p65) in the Loop.

BARNEYS NEW YORK
CLOTHING

Map p296 (☑312-587-1700; 15 E Oak St; ⊙10am-7pm Mon-Sat, 11am-6pm Sun; MRed Line to Chicago) Barneys provides the quintessential Gold Coast shopping experience. Its six floors sparkle with mega-high-end designer goods, while the penthouse holds a posh restaurant with a toasty fireplace. The on-site concierge books theater tickets for customers.

JIMMY CHOO
SHOES

Map p296 (☑312-255-1170; www.jimmychoo.com; 63 E Oak St; ⊙10am-6pm Mon-Sat, noon-5pm Sun; MRed Line to Chicago) The prices are almost as high as the stiletto heels at Jimmy Choo, revered foot stylist to the rich and famous. Oh, go ahead – be like J Lo and Beyoncé. All it takes is a toss of the head, the willingness to drop $800 on a pair of shoes and the attitude that footwear doesn't make the outfit – it is the outfit.

JIL SANDER
CLOTHING

Map p296 (☑312-335-0006; www.jilsander.com; 48 E Oak St; ⊙10am-6pm Mon-Sat; MRed Line to Chicago) Jil Sander's minimalist colors and simple designs somehow manage to remain fashionable long after other trendsetters have disappeared from the scene.

TOPSHOP
CLOTHING

Map p296 (us.topshop.com; 830 N Michigan Ave; ⊙10am-8pm Mon-Wed, to 9pm Thu-Sat, 11am-8pm Sun; MRed Line to Chicago) The popular British purveyor of youthful, urban-cool style recently opened this big store on the Magnificent Mile.

WATER TOWER PLACE
MALL

Map p296 (www.shopwatertower.com; 835 N Michigan Ave; ⊙10am-9pm Mon-Sat, 11am-6pm Sun; MRed Line to Chicago) Water Tower Place launched the city's love affair with vertical shopping centers. Many locals swear this first one remains the best. The mall houses 100 stores on seven levels, including Abercrombie & Fitch, Macy's, Aritzia (the mod Canadian chain), Akira (the hip local clothing vendor), Lego and American Girl Place.

900 N MICHIGAN
MALL

Map p296 (⌨312-915-3916; www.shop900.com; 900 N Michigan Ave; ⊙10am-7pm Mon-Sat, noon-6pm Sun; MRed Line to Chicago) This huge mall is home to an upscale collection of stores including Diesel, Gucci and J Crew, among many others. Water Tower Place is under the same management and they simply placed all the really expensive stores over here.

BEST BUY
ELECTRONICS

Map p296 (⌨312-397-2146; www.bestbuy.com; 875 N Michigan Ave; ⊙10am-9pm Mon-Sat, to 7pm Sun; MRed Line to Chicago) A convenient superstore for those looking to pick up laptop or cell phone supplies, Best Buy offers good prices on things like SIM cards, flash drives, hand-held computing devices and more. Come with a clear idea of what you want, as it can be difficult to flag down staff for help. The store is in the Hancock Center.

🏃 SPORTS & ACTIVITIES

OAK ST BEACH
BEACH

Map p296 (www.cpdbeaches.com; 1000 N Lake Shore Dr; MRed Line to Chicago) There aren't many cities outside of Florida that offer such an abundance of sand and (miniaturized) surf this close to their major business districts. Oak St Beach makes for a wonderful respite and offers a lower-key experience than certain beaches further north, where you're likely to get a volleyball spiked on your head if you're not paying attention. The 'beachstro' provides nourishment.

You can also rent umbrellas and lounge chairs. Lifeguards are on duty from 11am to 7pm in summer. The bulking Lake Shore Dr condos cast shadows in the afternoon, but the beach remains busy.

WATERIDERS
KAYAKING

(⌨312-953-9287; www.wateriders.com; 950 N Kingsbury St; per hr single/double $20/30; MBrown, Purple Line to Chicago) Wateriders rents out kayaks for paddles on the Chicago River. It also offers excellent tours, including the daily 2½-hour 'Ghost and Gangster' trip ($65) that glides by notorious downtown sites. The dock is at Kingsbury Yacht Club, where Oak St meets the river. It's about a half-mile northwest of the Brown/Purple Line El station at Chicago.

Lincoln Park & Old Town

Neighborhood Top Five

1 Meandering through **Lincoln Park** (p98) and hearing lions roar in the zoo, smelling exotic flowers in the conservatory and finding the calm of the hidden lily pool.

2 Laughing and drinking during an improv show at **Second City** (p107).

3 Digging into space-age, Jetsonslike cuisine at **Alinea** (p104).

4 Joining the fun in the sun at **North Ave Beach** (p109).

5 Seeing a provocative play at **Steppenwolf Theatre** (p107).

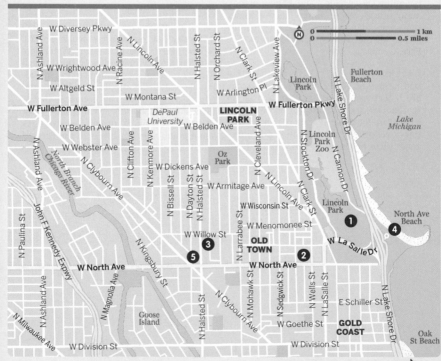

For more detail of this area see Map p298 ➡

Explore: Lincoln Park & Old Town

Lincoln Park – the green space – is the city's premier playground. Almost 50% larger than Central Park in New York, Lincoln Park is where Chicagoans flock when the weather warms to savor the lakefront oasis of ponds, paths and exotic creatures in the free zoo.

Lincoln Park is also the name for the abutting neighborhood, which is home to the city's yuppie population mixed with DePaul University's large student body. The area is alive day and night with people walking dogs, riding bikes, pushing strollers and looking for a place to park so they can shop in the swanky boutiques and eat in the excellent restaurants. Add in several theaters (led by world-renowned Steppenwolf) and lively blues and rock clubs, and you've got a day's worth of action here.

Old Town was the epicenter of Chicago's hippie culture in the 1960s. A few trippy holdovers from the old days remain, but now stylish stores and eateries stuff the neighborhood, which joins Lincoln Park to the south. Wells St is in the main vein and most visitors make a pilgrimage here at some point – it's the home of the comedy club and improv bastion, Second City.

Local Life

➡ **Funny Bar** Performers from Second City often duck into the Old Town Ale House (p106) for a beverage after the show.

➡ **Blues Jam** Musicians aged 17 to 70 tune up for the free blues jam at Kingston Mines (p107) every Sunday.

➡ **Farmers Market** Chicagoans flock to the park to stock up on farm fare at Green City Market (p103) on Wednesday and Saturday mornings.

Getting There & Away

➡ **El** Brown, Purple or Red Line to Fullerton or Brown, Purple Line to Armitage for Lincoln Park; Brown, Purple Line to Sedgwick, or Red Line to Clark/Division for Old Town.

➡ **Bus** Number 151 runs north from downtown via Michigan Ave and Lake Shore Dr and is good for reaching all the sites in the park itself; number 22 connects the Loop to Lincoln Park (the neighborhood) and runs along Clark St.

➡ **Car** Parking is difficult. In Lincoln Park, try the meters along Diversey Harbor. In Old Town, try the pay garage at Piper's Alley, at North Ave and Wells St.

Lonely Planet's Top Tip

While you have to pay admission to see shows at **Second City** (p107), there's free improv afterward. You heard right: show up at the Mainstage or etc stage after the last show of the evening (Friday excluded) and you can watch the performers riff through a half-hour of improv. The freebie begins at 10pm Monday to Thursday, 1am Saturday and 9pm Sunday. Arrive 15 minutes prior.

 Best Places to Eat

➡ La Fournette (p105)
➡ Twin Anchors (p105)
➡ Pequod's Pizza (p104)
➡ Alinea (p104)
➡ Balena (p105)

For reviews, see p103

Best Places to Drink

➡ Old Town Ale House (p106)
➡ Delilah's (p106)
➡ Goose Island Brewery (p106)
➡ Weeds (p106)
➡ J Parker (p106)

For reviews, see p106 ➡

⭐ **Best Places for Entertainment**

➡ Steppenwolf Theatre (p107)
➡ Second City (p107)
➡ BLUES (p107)
➡ Kingston Mines (p107)
➡ Lincoln Hall (p107)

For reviews, see p107

LINCOLN PARK & OLD TOWN

JOSE LUIS STEPHENS / GETTY IMAGES ©

TOP SIGHT
LINCOLN PARK

The neighborhood gets its name from this park, Chicago's largest. Its 1200 acres stretch for 6 miles, from North Ave north to Diversey Pkwy, where it narrows along the lake and continues until the end of Lake Shore Dr. The park's many lakes, trails and paths make it an excellent place for recreation. Cross-country skiing in the winter and sunbathing in warmer months are just two of the activities Chicagoans enjoy in the vast green space.

The park has a slew of free attractions within its leafy confines: the famed zoo, a toasty conservatory, an open-air theater and busy beaches. Be sure to seek out sculptor Augustus Saint-Gaudens' **Standing Lincoln** (Map p298), which shows the 16th president deep in contemplation right before he delivers a great speech. Saint-Gaudens based the work on casts made of Lincoln's face and hands while Lincoln was alive. The statue stands in its own garden east of the Chicago History Museum.

While you're in the museum area, walk over to the southeast corner of LaSalle Dr and Clark St and take a gander at the **Couch Mausoleum** (Map p298). It's the sole reminder of the land's pre-1864 use, when the entire area was a municipal cemetery. Many of the graves contained hundreds of dead prisoners from Camp Douglas, a horrific prisoner-of-war stockade on the city's South Side during the Civil War. Removing the bodies from the designated park area proved a greater undertaking than the city could stomach and, today, if you were to start digging at the south end of the park, you'd be liable to make some ghoulish discoveries.

Several markets and takeaway joints pop up along Clark St and Diversey Pkwy that are prime for picnic provisions.

DON'T MISS...
→ Zoo
→ Conservatory
→ Theater on the Lake
→ Standing Lincoln statue
→ Couch Mausoleum

PRACTICALITIES
→ Map p298
→ ⊙6am-11pm
→ ⊛
→ ▣151

◉ SIGHTS

◉ Lincoln Park

LINCOLN PARK   PARK
See p98.

LINCOLN PARK ZOO   ZOO
Map p298 (☏312-742-2000; www.lpzoo.org; 2200 N Cannon Dr; ⊙10am-4:30pm Nov-Mar, to 5pm Apr-Oct, to 6:30pm Sat & Sun Jun-Aug; ⊕; ▣151) **FREE** The abiding Lincoln Park Zoo opened in 1868 and remains a local freebie favorite, filled with gorillas, lions, tigers and other exotic creatures in the shadow of downtown. Check out the Regenstein African Journey, Ape House and dragonfly-dappled Nature Boardwalk for the cream of the crop.

Families swarm the zoo grounds, which are smack in the park's midst. Kids beeline for the Regenstein African exhibit, which puts them close to pygmy hippos, dwarf crocodiles and hissing cockroaches. The Ape House pleases with its swingin' gorillas and chimps. **Farm-in-the-Zoo** (Map p298) features a full range of barnyard animals in a faux farm setting at the zoo's south end and offers frequent demonstrations of cow milking, horse grooming and other chores. The half-mile-long Nature Boardwalk circles the adjacent South Pond and teaches about wetlands ecology; keep an eye out for endangered birds such as the black-crowned night heron.

The rest of the zoo is fairly typical. The exhibits for the lions and other big cats and for the sea lions are fine but unremarkable. Still, free is a good price, and if you come during the colder months you'll have many of the animals to yourself.

The zoo has multiple entrances around its perimeter. The Gateway Pavilion (on Cannon Dr) is the main one, where you can rent strollers, pick up a free map and see the schedule for the day's feedings, training demonstrations and zookeeper talks. Drivers, be warned: parking here is among the city's worst. If you do find a spot in the Cannon Dr lot, it can cost up to $35 for four hours.

LINCOLN PARK CONSERVATORY   GARDENS
Map p298 (☏312-742-7736; www.lincolnparkconservancy.org; 2391 N Stockton Dr; ⊙9am-5pm; ▣151) **FREE** Walking through the conservatory's three acres of desert palms, jungle

---

VIEW-WORTHY RIDE

One of Chicago's essential experiences is riding the El, and taking the Brown Line into the Loop is the optimal way to do it. Get on in Lincoln Park at either the Fullerton or Armitage stops, take a seat by the window and watch as the train clatters downtown, swinging past skyscrapers so close you can almost touch them. Stay aboard as the El loops the Loop and get off at the Clark stop if you want to remain downtown.

---

ferns and tropical orchids is like taking a trip around the world in 30 minutes. The glass-bedecked hothouse remains a sultry, 75-degree escape even in winter.

ALFRED CALDWELL LILY POOL   GARDENS
Map p298 (www.lincolnparkconservancy.org; 2391 N Stockton Dr; ⊙7:30am-dusk mid-Apr–Nov; ▣151) **FREE** The enchanting Lily Pool hides in a plot northeast of the Lincoln Park Conservatory, at the corner of Fullerton and Cannon Drs. Built in 1938 by landscape architect Jens Jenson, the garden is designated a National Historic Landmark for its Prairie style, native plant use and stonework that resembles the stratified canyons of the Wisconsin Dells.

The pool has become an important stopover for migrating birds and also welcomes turtles and dragonflies. It's a lovely escape from the Lincoln Park crowds. Docents lead free, half-hour tours on various weekends.

**PEGGY NOTEBAERT
NATURE MUSEUM**   MUSEUM
Map p298 (☏773-755-5100; www.naturemuseum.org; 2430 N Cannon Dr; adult/child $9/6; ⊙9am-5pm Mon-Fri, 10am-5pm Sat & Sun; ⊕; ▣151) Located across the street from the Caldwell Lily Pool, this hands-on museum has turtles and croaking frogs in its 1st-floor marsh, fluttering insects in its 2nd-floor butterfly haven and a bird boardwalk meandering through its rooftop garden. It's geared mostly for kids. Check the schedule for daily creature feedings. In winter, the Green City Market (p103) sets up inside on Saturdays.

Lincoln Park – Park Life

Chicago's largest park is where locals come out to play. They swim and spike volleyballs at North Ave Beach. They ogle the lions, tigers and other creatures in the zoo and nature museum. They browse for veggies and homemade pie at the Green City farmers market. But mostly they just hang out, kick a soccer ball or jog the leafy pathways.

YAN-CHUN TUNG / GETTY IMAGES ©

5

PETER PTSCHELINZEW / GETTY IMAGES ©

1. North Ave Beach (p109)
Enjoy sun and sports at Chicago's most popular beach.

2. Green City Market (p103)
In winter, Chicago's biggest farmers market moves indoors to the Peggy Notebaert Nature Museum.

3. Polar bear, Lincoln Park Zoo (p99)
Talk to the animals for free at this family-favorite zoo.

4. Peggy Notebaert Nature Museum (p99)
Keep your eyes peeled in the butterfly room on the 2nd floor of this museum.

5. Lincoln Park (p98)
The 1200-acre park offers many lakes, trails and paths.

4

LONELY PLANET / GETTY IMAGES ©

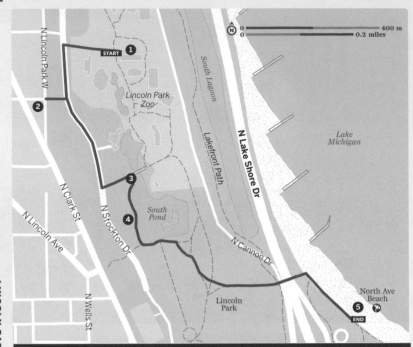

🏃 Neighborhood Walk
Zoo Touring with Tots

START LINCOLN PARK ZOO
END NORTH AVE BEACH
LENGTH 2 MILES, FOUR TO FIVE HOURS

Looking to entertain the little ones? A day in Lincoln Park will keep you busy without breaking the bank. Generations of Chicagoans have been coming here, to what's now one of the last free zoos in the country.

Stroll through recreated regions in the African Journey and watch Ape House monkeys play at the two best exhibits at the ❶ **Lincoln Park Zoo** (p99). Can your kids identify the smallest member of the bear family? The big beast prized for its horns? The panda of a different color?

Moving fast, you can hit the highlights of the zoo in two hours or so, before heading to ❷ **RJ Grunts** (p104) for lunch. The hostess will store your stroller while you order a chocolate-peanut-butter-banana milkshake and burgers. The menu, and the hubbub, are entirely kid-friendly.

Head back into the park and hop on the ❸ **Nature Boardwalk**, a half-mile path around the South Pond's wetlands ecosystem. Placards explain about the marshy environment and the critters that live there. The mod-looking arch you pass on the east side is the Education Pavilion. Local starchitect Jeanne Gang (of Aqua Tower fame) designed it and it's meant to resemble a turtle shell.

Next it's the big ol' barn and the ❹ **Farm-in-the-Zoo**. Little ones seem to love petting sheep, watching chicks hatch and learning how to milk a cow. Parents like that this, too, is free. By now you've spent more than four hours in the park. If you have enough energy to continue...

Walk south along the pond and turn east past ball fields before you cross the bridge to ❺ **North Avenue Beach** (p109). Grab a refreshment, rent a beach chair and watch the kids construct castles in the sand. Walk out on the curving breakwater for one of the city's best skyline views. It's the ideal background for a keepsake family photo.

BIOGRAPH THEATER
HISTORIC SITE

Map p298 (2433 N Lincoln Ave; MBrown, Purple, Red Line to Fullerton) In 1934, the 'lady in red' betrayed gangster John Dillinger at this theater, which used to show movies. FBI agents shot him in the alley beside the building. The whole thing started out as a date – Dillinger took new girlfriend Polly Hamilton to the show and Polly's roommate Anna Sage tagged along, wearing a red dress. Alas, Dillinger was a notorious bank robber and the FBI's very first 'Public Enemy Number One.' Sage also had troubles with the law and was about to be deported. To avoid it, she agreed to set up Dillinger. The venue now hosts plays by the Victory Gardens Theater.

ST VALENTINE'S DAY MASSACRE SITE
HISTORIC SITE

Map p298 (2122 N Clark St; ☐22) In perhaps the most infamous event of the Capone era, the mobster's henchmen, dressed as cops, lined up seven members of Bugs Moran's gang against the garage wall that used to stand here and sprayed them with bullets. After that, Moran cut his losses and Al Capone gained control of Chicago's North Side vice. The garage was torn down in 1967 to make way for a retirement home.

The facility's landscaped parking lot now lies at the site. A house (2119 N Clark St) used as a lookout by the killers stands across the street.

DEPAUL ART MUSEUM
MUSEUM

Map p298 (www.depaul.edu/museum; 935 W Fullerton Ave; ⊙11am-5pm Mon-Thu, to 7pm Fri, noon-5pm Sat & Sun; MBrown, Purple, Red Line to Fullerton) FREE DePaul University's compact new art museum hosts changing exhibits of 20th century works. Pieces from the permanent collection – by sculptor Claes Oldenburg, cartoonist Chris Ware, architect Daniel Burnham and more – hang on the 2nd floor. It's definitely worth swinging through if you're in the neighborhood; you can see everything in less than 30 minutes.

⊙ Old Town

CHICAGO HISTORY MUSEUM
MUSEUM

Map p298 (☐312-642-4600; www.chicagohistory.org; 1601 N Clark St; adult/child $14/free; ⊙9:30am-4:30pm Mon-Sat, noon-5pm Sun; ♦; ☐22) Curious about Chicago's storied past? Multimedia displays at this museum

cover it all, from the Great Fire to the 1968 Democratic Convention. President Lincoln's deathbed is here; the bell from Mrs O'Leary's cow is here. So is the chance to 'become' a Chicago hot dog covered in condiments (in the kids' area, but adults are welcome for the photo op).

The Diorama Hall is nifty, especially the model that shows the 1893 World's Fair set up. When you pay your entrance fee, ask for the free audio tour to enhance your visit. The on-site bookstore stocks hard-to-find local history tomes.

GREEN CITY MARKET
MARKET

Map p298 (www.greencitymarket.org; 1790 N Clark St; ⊙7am-1pm Wed & Sat May-Oct, ☐22) Stands of purple cabbages, red radishes, green asparagus and other bright-hued produce sprawl through Lincoln Park at Chicago's biggest farmers market. Follow your nose to the demonstration tent, where local cooks such as Top Chef winner Stephanie Izard prepare dishes – say rice crepes with a mushroom gastrique – using market ingredients. In winter the market moves into the Peggy Notebaert Nature Museum (p99) and is held from 8:30am to 1pm on Saturdays only.

✖ EATING

While mega-high-end restaurants such as Alinea are here, Lincoln Park caters to student tastes, too, thanks to the presence of DePaul University. Halsted St, Lincoln Ave and Fullerton Ave are good bets for trendy, flirty eateries. A bit to the south, Old Town is quieter and quainter, run through by Wells St and populated by older diners.

✖ Lincoln Park

ALOHA EATS
HAWAIIAN $

Map p298 (☐773-935-6828; www.alohaeats.com; 2534 N Clark St; mains $7-12; ⊙11am-10pm; MBrown, Purple, Red Line to Fullerton) From *musubis* (rice rolls wrapped in seaweed) to *saimin* (egg noodle soup) to *katsus* (breaded cutlets), it's all about whopping portions of Hawaiian food here. Spam, aka 'the Hawaiian steak,' is the main ingredient in many dishes, including the popular Loco Moco (meat, fried eggs and brown gravy atop rice). Macaroni or fries always arrive on the side. The massive menu includes several tofu and fish options for those watching their girlish figures. The bright-yellow interior and island dishes soothe especially well in winter.

WIENER'S CIRCLE
AMERICAN $

Map p298 (☑773-477-7444; 2622 N Clark St; hot dogs $3-6; ◷10:30am-4am Sun-Thu, to 5am Fri & Sat; ⓂBrown, Purple Line to Diversey) As famous for its unruly, foul-mouthed ambience as its charred hot dogs and cheddar fries, the Wiener Circle is *the* place for late-night munchies. During the day and on weeknights it's a normal hot-dog stand – with damn good food (no less than Rachael Ray and Jerry Springer proclaimed them the best hot dogs in town). The wild show is on weekend eves, around 2am, when the nearby bars close. The f-bombs fly and it can get raucous between staff and customers.

BOURGEOIS PIG
CAFE $

Map p298 (☑773-883-5282; www.thebourgeois pigcafe.com; 738 W Fullerton Ave; mains $7-10; ◷8am-10pm; ⍁; ⓂBrown, Purple, Red Line to Fullerton) An old-style cafe with big, creaking wooden tables and chairs, the Pig serves strong java and whopping sandwiches. It's a convivial place to grab a bite while working through the newspaper or chatting with friends. Tea drinkers and vegetarians will find many options on offer.

FLORIOLE CAFE
BAKERY $

Map p298 (☑773-883-1313; www.floriole.com; 1220 W Webster Ave; items $3-10; ◷7am-5:30pm Tue-Fri, from 8am Sat-Mon; ⓂBrown, Purple, Red Line to Fullerton) The chef got her start selling lemon tarts, twice-baked croissants and rum-tinged *caneles* (pastries with a custard center and caramelized crust) at the Green Market. She now sells her French-influenced baked goods and sandwiches – which use Midwest-sourced meats, cheeses and produce – in an airy, loftlike space punctuated by a big wooden farm table.

PEQUOD'S PIZZA
PIZZERIA $$

Map p298 (☑731-327-1512; www.pequodspizza. com; 2207 N Clybourn Ave; small pizzas from $11; ◷11am-late; ▣9 to Webster) Like the ship in *Moby Dick,* from which this neighborhood restaurant takes its name, Pequod's deep-dish pizza is a thing of legend – head and shoulders above chain competitors because of its caramelized cheese, generous top-

pings and sweetly flavored sauce. The atmosphere is affably rugged, too, with surly waitstaff and graffiti-covered walls.

VIA CARDUCCI
ITALIAN $$

Map p298 (☑773-665-1981; www.viacarducci chicago.com; 1419 W Fullerton Ave; mains $14-20; ◷11am-11pm Mon-Thu, to midnight Fri & Sat, to 10pm Sun; ⓂBrown, Purple, Red Line to Fullerton) The simple southern Italian dishes regularly draw moans of delight from diners at this small trattoria. Red-checkered tablecloths complement the baroque murals and the food leans toward thick tomato-based sauces and amazing sausages. Gluten-free pasta can be substituted in most dishes.

RJ GRUNTS
BURGERS $$

Map p298 (☑773-929-5363; www.rjgruntschi cago.com; 2056 N Lincoln Park West; mains $11-16; ◷11:30am-midnight Mon-Fri, from 10am Sat & Sun; ⍩; ▣22) The very first of the now-ubiquitous Lettuce Entertain You stable of restaurants, RJ Grunts came on to the scene in the 1970s, when Lincoln Park emerged as the young singles' neighborhood of choice. Now, as then, the huge salad bar, burgers and beer are the mainstays.

This is a fun post-zoo lunch spot; even the pickiest kids will find something to love. The awesome milkshakes can be spiked with booze for the adults in the crowd.

CAFE BA-BA-REEBA!
SPANISH $$

Map p298 (☑773-935-5000; www.cafebabareeba. com; 2024 N Halsted St; tapas $5-11; ◷4-10pm Mon-Thu, 11:30am-midnight Fri, 10am-midnight Sat, to 10pm Sun; ⓂBrown, Purple Line to Armitage) At this long-standing, delightfully ersatz tapas joint, the garlic-laced menu changes often but always includes some spicy meats, marinated fish and heaps of hot or cold small plates. For a main event, order one of the paellas ($11 to $13 per person, minimum two people) as soon as you get seated – they take a while to prepare.

PATIO AT CAFE BRAUER
CAFE $$

Map p298 (2021 N Stockton Dr; mains $8-12; ◷11am-9pm Mon-Fri, 8:30am-9pm Sat & Sun; ⍩) Take a break from zoo explorations at pretty Cafe Brauer. It's perfect for an ice-cream cone, flatbread pizza or glass of wine refresher while sitting by the pond.

★ALINEA
MODERN AMERICAN $$$

Map p298 (☑312-867-0110; www.alinearestaurant. com; 1723 N Halsted St; multicourse menu $210-

265; ⊙5:30-9:30pm Wed-Sun; Ⓜ️Red Line to North/Clybourn) Widely regarded as North America's best restaurant, Alinea – helmed by Beard Award–winner Grant Achatz – brings on 20 courses of mind-bending molecular gastronomy. Dishes may emanate from a centrifuge or be pressed into a capsule, à la duck served with a 'pillow of lavender air.' Don't worry: your team of servers will explain it all. The once-in-a-lifetime meal can take upwards of four hours.

There are no reservations. Instead Alinea sells tickets two to three months in advance. Sign up at the website and watch the Facebook page for ticket sales dates. Prices vary by date and time (early weekdays cost less than prime-time weekends). Check the Twitter feed (@Alinea) for possible last-minute seats.

Alinea can modify its menu for vegetarians as long as you provide advance warning. Note: there's no sign on the restaurant's door, so look for the street number.

BALENA
ITALIAN $$$

Map p298 (✆312-867-3888; www.balenachicago.com; 1633 N Halsted St; mains $17-25; Ⓜ️Red Line to North/Clybourn) 'Mamma mia!,' you want to shout after forking into the fat, creamy, roasted mushrooms atop grilled bread. Balena tastes like an Italian grandmother whipped up the wood-fired pizzas, house-cured salumi and saucy pastas. But don't let the rusticness fool you: complex, finessed flavors are at work here. The cavernous, exposed-brick and wood-beam room echoes with chatter and clattering plates.

A huge list of European wines and Prosecco flow by the bottleful. Balena sits across from Steppenwolf Theatre and makes a terrific stop pre- or post-show. Reserve ahead.

BOKA
MODERN AMERICAN $$$

Map p298 (✆312-337-6070; www.bokachicago.com; 1729 N Halsted St; mains $25-35, 7-course menu $85; ⊙from 5pm; Ⓜ️Red Line to North/Clybourn) A Michelin-starred restaurant-lounge hybrid with a seafood-leaning menu, Boka is a pre- and post-theater stomping ground for younger Steppenwolf patrons. Order a cocktail at the bar or slip into one of the booths for small-plate dishes such as mango-laced tabbouleh salad or veal sweetbreads with Moroccan barbecue sauce.

✕ Old Town

LA FOURNETTE
FRENCH $

Map p298 (www.lafournette.com; 1547 N Wells St; items $3-7; ⊙7am-7pm Mon-Sat, to 6pm Sun; Ⓜ️Brown, Purple to Sedgwick) One whiff of the buttery croissants and you're transported across the Atlantic. The chef hails from Alsace in France and he fills his narrow, rustic-wood bakery with bright-hued macarons (purpley passion fruit, green pistachio, red raspberry-chocolate), cheese-infused breads and crust-crackling baguettes. They all beg to be devoured on the spot with a cup of locally roasted Intelligentsia coffee. Staff make delicious soups, crepes, quiches and sandwiches with equal French love.

TWIN ANCHORS
BARBECUE $$

Map p298 (✆312-266-1616; www.twinanchorsribs.com; 1655 N Sedgwick St; mains $16-22; ⊙5-11pm Mon-Thu, to midnight Fri, noon-midnight Sat, noon-10.30pm Sun; Ⓜ️Brown, Purple Line to Sedgwick) Twin Anchors is synonymous with ribs – smoky, tangy-sauced baby backs in this case. The meat drops from the ribs as soon as you lift them. The restaurant doesn't take reservations, so you'll have to wait outside or around the neon-lit 1950s bar, which sets the tone for the place. An almost-all-Sinatra jukebox completes the supper-club ambience.

OLD JERUSALEM
MIDDLE EASTERN $$

Map p298 (✆312-944-0459; www.oldjerusalemchicago.com; 1411 N Wells St; mains $9-15; ⊙11am-10:30pm Sun-Thu, to 11pm Fri & Sat; Ⓜ️Brown, Purple Line to Sedgwick) This friendly Middle Eastern joint has been pumping out falafel and pita sandwiches for more than 30 years. For something leafy try the Greek salad, served with Lebanese flatbread. If the weather's good, get your food to go and feast in nearby Lincoln Park.

BISTROT MARGOT
FRENCH $$$

Map p298 (✆312-587-3660; www.bistrotmargot.com; 1437 N Wells St; mains $19-26; ⊙11:30am-10pm Mon-Fri, 10am-11pm Sat, 10am-9pm Sun; Ⓜ️Brown, Purple Line to Sedgwick) A visit to Bistrot Margot is like a visit to a little Parisian corner bistro in one of the remoter districts. Roast chicken, steak and *frites,* mussels and other coastal shellfish highlight the classic menu. The interior decor mixes dark wood with bright tiles and red booths, and the busy crowd adds to the atmosphere.

There are good daily specials, including half-price wine on Monday and a prix-fixe menu on Wednesday.

SALPICON
MEXICAN $$$

Map p298 (☎312-988-7811; www.salpicon.com; 1252 N Wells St; mains $20-31; ◎from 5pm Mon-Sat, 11am-10pm Sun; Ⓜ Red Line to Clark/Division) Another favorite among Chicago's high-end Mexican restaurants, Priscila Satkoff's place has elevated *ceviche* (seafood marinated in lemon or lime juice, garlic and seasonings) and *chiles rellenos* (stuffed poblano peppers that are batter-fried) to an art. Many other items come slathered in heavenly *mole* (chili and chocolate sauce). The festive interior features high ceilings and bold colors. Create bright colors in your head by trying some of the 60 tequilas, including some rare, oak-barrel-aged numbers.

🍷 DRINKING & NIGHTLIFE

🍸 Lincoln Park

DELILAH'S
BAR

Map p298 (☎773-472-2771; www.delilahschicago.com; 2771 N Lincoln Ave; ◎from 4pm; Ⓜ Brown Line to Diversey) A bartender rightfully referred to this bad-ass black sheep of the neighborhood as the 'pride of Lincoln Ave' – a title earned for the heavy pours and the best whiskey selection in the city. They know their way around a beer list, too, tapping unusual domestic and international suds (though cheap Pabst longnecks are always behind the bar as well).

GOOSE ISLAND BREWERY
BREWERY

Map p298 (☎312-915-0071; www.gooseisland.com; 1800 N Clybourn Ave; ◎from 11am; Ⓜ Red Line to North/Clybourn) Goose Island's popular beers are served in bars and restaurants around Chicago, but it tastes best here at the source. The pub pours the flagship Honker's Ale and 14 or so other potent brews. If you're lucky, the 10% Extra Naughty Goose or Maple Bacon Stout, served with a meaty slice, will be on tap. Four-beer flights are available.

Brewery tours ($10) take place on Saturdays and Sundays and must be reserved in advance. Fine grub complements the brews; special kudos to the Stilton burger and chips.

J PARKER
LOUNGE

Map p298 (www.jparkerchicago.com; 1816 N Clark St; ◎5pm-1am Mon-Thu, from 1pm Fri, from 11:30am Sat & Sun; 🚌22) It's all about the view from the Hotel Lincoln's 13th-floor rooftop bar. And it delivers, sweeping over the park, the lake and downtown skyline. Prepare to jostle with the young and preppy crowd, especially if it's a warm night.

ALIVE ONE
BAR

Map p298 (www.aliveone.com; 2683 N Halsted St; ◎from 5pm; Ⓜ Brown, Purple Line to Diversey) The jukebox is stuffed with hundreds of bootlegged, all-live (get the name?) recordings by The Clash, The Who, Hendrix, Phish and more. The atmosphere converts from jam-absorbing to lounge-like on weekends. A good selection of microbrews flows from the taps.

ROSE'S LOUNGE
BAR

Map p298 (☎773-327-4000; 2656 N Lincoln Ave; ◎from 2pm; Ⓜ Brown, Purple Line to Diversey) Once your eyes adjust to the dark of Rose's, the eclectic bric-a-brac, drop ceiling and dollar brews make it an odd duck among Lincoln Park's yuppie lounges. The ultra-cheap beers are the big draw, bringing in a motley set of spendthrift regulars.

🍸 Old Town

★OLD TOWN ALE HOUSE
BAR

Map p298 (www.theoldtownalehouse.com; 219 W North Ave; ◎3pm-4am Mon-Fri, from noon Sat & Sun; Ⓜ Brown, Purple Line to Sedgwick) Located by the Second City comedy club and the scene of late-night musings since the 1960s, this unpretentious neighborhood favorite lets you mingle with beautiful people and grizzled regulars, seated pint by pint under the nude-politician paintings. Classic jazz on the jukebox provides the soundtrack for the jovial goings-on.

WEEDS
BAR

Map p298 (☎312-943-7815; 1555 N Dayton St; ◎from 4pm, closed Sun; Ⓜ Red Line to North/Clybourn) Weeds has the tenacity of its namesake flora, sticking to its beatnik-meets-bohemia roots for years while the neighborhood gentrified around it. If the walls – or the bras hanging from the ceiling – could talk, you'd hear some strange yarns from the crew who work and drink here.

Weeds hosts open-mic poetry (Monday) and sometimes live music, and you can quaff in the laid-back beer garden.

⭐ ENTERTAINMENT

STEPPENWOLF THEATRE
THEATER

Map p298 (☎312-335-1650; www.steppenwolf. org; 1650 N Halsted St; ⓜRed Line to North/Clybourn) Steppenwolf is Chicago's top stage for quality, provocative theater productions. The Hollywood-heavy ensemble includes Gary Sinise, John Malkovich, Martha Plimpton, Gary Cole, Joan Allen, Tracy Letts and John Mahoney. A money-saving tip: the box office releases 20 tickets for $20 for each day's shows. They go on sale at 11am Monday to Saturday and at 1pm Sunday, and are available by phone.

The legendary troupe was founded by Terry Kinney, Gary Sinise and Jeff Perry in a church basement in 1974. It quickly outgrew one space after another, won a Tony award for regional theater excellence and is now a leading international destination for dramatic arts. The Downstairs Theatre is the main performance space, the Upstairs Theatre is more intimate, and the Garage hosts emerging actors and playwrights.

SECOND CITY
COMEDY

Map p298 (☎312-337-3992; www.secondcity.com; 1616 N Wells St; ⓜBrown, Purple Line to Sedgwick) Second City is where Bill Murray, Tina Fey, Steve Carell, Stephen Colbert and many more honed their wit. Shows take place nightly, filled with hilarious commentaries on life, love, politics and anything else that falls in the crosshairs of the comedians' rapid-fire, hard-hitting humor. Tickets cost $23 to $28 (less on Monday). Turn up after the evening's last show (Friday excluded), and watch the comics improv for free.

SECOND CITY ETC
COMEDY

Map p298 (☎312-337-3992; www.secondcity. com; 1608 N Wells St; ⓜBrown, Purple Line to Sedgwick) Second City's second stage is smaller and often presents more risky work, as actors try to get noticed and make the main stage. Ticket costs are $23 to $28 (same as the main stage).

UP COMEDY CLUB
COMEDY

Map p298 (www.upcomedyclub.com; 230 W North Ave; ⓜBrown, Purple Line to Sedgwick) UP is part of the Second City family and shares the same building (it's on the 3rd floor of Pipers Alley), but it offers a closer, cabaret-style set-up. It also adds stand-up acts by well-known touring comedians to its roster, in addition to sketch revue shows and G-rated matinee improv for kids.

BLUES
BLUES

Map p298 (www.chicagobluesbar.com; 2519 N Halsted St; tickets $7-10; ⓣfrom 8pm; ⓜBrown, Purple, Red Line to Fullerton) Long, narrow and high volume, this veteran blues club draws a slightly older crowd that soaks up every crackling, electrified moment. As one local musician put it, 'The audience here comes out to *understand* the blues.' Big local names like L'il Ed and the Blues Imperials grace the small stage.

KINGSTON MINES
BLUES

Map p298 (www.kingstonmines.com; 2548 N Halsted St; tickets $12-15; ⓣ8pm-4am Mon-Thu, from 7pm Fri & Sat, from 6pm Sun; ⓜBrown, Purple, Red Line to Fullerton) Popular enough to draw big names on the blues circuit, Kingston Mines is so noisy, hot and sweaty that blues neophytes will feel as though they're having a genuine experience – sort of like a gritty Delta theme park. Two stages, seven nights a week, ensure somebody's always on.

The blues jam session from 6pm to 8:30pm on Sundays is free.

LINCOLN HALL
LIVE MUSIC

Map p298 (☎773-525-2501; www.lincolnhallchicago.com; 2424 N Lincoln Ave; ⓣ5pm-2am; ⓣ; ⓜBrown, Purple, Red Line to Fullerton) Owned by the same folks as Schubas (p121), clean-cut

WEEDS POETRY NIGHT

Verse comes in all shapes and sizes at **Weeds Poetry Night** (Map p298; ☎312-943-7815; 1555 N Dayton St; ⓜRed Line to North/Clybourn). Every Monday at 10:30pm a cast of delightfully eccentric poets gets on the tavern's mic to vent about love, sex, war, booze, urban living and pretty much everything in between. Some of it rhymes, some of it rambles, but the proportions make for a pretty cool scene.

Lincoln Hall is larger but with the same acoustically perfect sound. Hyped national indie bands are the main players but, when they're not on, DJs and free movie nights take over. The front room has a kitchen that offers small plates and sandwiches until 10pm.

THEATER ON THE LAKE
THEATER

Map p298 (www.chicagoparkdistrict.com/events /theater-on-the-lake; 2401 N Lake Shore Dr; tickets $18; ⌨151) Set under a canopy of trees in Lincoln Park, with Lake Michigan sparkling in front, the open-air Theater on the Lake brings in edgy, off-Loop companies to put on eight plays in eight weeks (a new show every week of the season). The brilliant performances run from mid-June to mid-August.

VICTORY GARDENS THEATER
THEATER

Map p298 (☑773-871-3000; www.victorygar dens.org; 2433 N Lincoln Ave; MBrown, Purple, Red Line to Fullerton) Long established and playwright-friendly, Victory Gardens specializes in world premieres of plays by Chicago authors. The *Wall St Journal* called it 'one of the most important playwright theaters in the US.' It's located in the historic Biograph Theater, where bank robber John Dillinger – aka Public Enemy Number One – was shot in 1934.

ZANIES
COMEDY

Map p298 (☑312-337-4027; www.chicago.zanies. com; 1548 N Wells St; tickets $10-25; MBrown, Purple Line to Sedgwick) This comedy shack has been booking well-known jokesters for more than three decades. The shows last around two hours and usually include the efforts of a couple of up-and-comers before the main act. The ceiling is low and the seating is cramped, which only adds to the good cheer.

ROYAL GEORGE THEATRE
THEATER

Map p298 (☑312-988-9000; www.theroyalgeor getheatre.com; 1641 N Halsted St; MRed Line to North/Clybourn) The Royal George is actually four theaters in one building. The cabaret venue stages long-running mainstream productions such as *Late Nite Catechism,* a nun-centered comedy. The main stage presents works with big-name stars, and the galleries host various improv and small-troupe works.

FACETS MULTIMEDIA
CINEMA

Map p298 (☑773-281-4114; www.facets.org; 1517 W Fullerton Ave; MBrown, Purple, Red Line to Fuller-

ton) Facets' main business is as the country's largest distributor of foreign and cult films, so it follows that its 'cinematheque' movie house shows interesting, obscure films that would never get booked elsewhere.

APOLLO THEATER
THEATER

Map p298 (☑773-935-6100; www.apollochicago. com; 2540 N Lincoln Ave; MRed, Brown, Purple Line to Fullerton) This midsize theater hosts a variety of productions and improv shows. It's also the home of Emerald City Theatre Company, which stages children's plays.

 SHOPPING

The area around North and Clybourn Aves is thick with urban-living chains such as Pottery Barn and J Crew.

SPICE HOUSE
FOOD & DRINK

Map p298 (☑312-274-0378; www.thespicehouse. com; 1512 N Wells St; ⊙10am-7pm Mon-Sat, to 5pm Sun; MBrown, Purple Line to Sedgwick) A bombardment of peppery fragrance socks you in the nose at this exotic spice house in Old Town, offering delicacies such as black and red volcanic salt from Hawaii and pomegranate molasses among the tidy jars. Best, though, are the house-made herb blends themed after Chicago neighborhoods, including the piquant 'Argyle St Asian Blend,' allowing you to take home a taste of the city.

DAVE'S RECORDS
MUSIC

Map p298 (☑773-929-6325; www.davesrecords chicago.com; 2604 N Clark St; ⊙11am-8pm Mon-Sat, noon-7pm Sun; MBrown, Purple Line to Diversey) With a splatter of colored vinyl decorating the back wall, Dave's feels a little like the setting of Nick Hornby's classic *High Fidelity.* CDs? Forget it. MP3s? Never heard of 'em. Dave's doesn't discriminate with genres, but it's for vinyl purists only.

ROTOFUGI
ARTS & CRAFTS

Map p298 (☑312-491-9501; www.rotofugi.com; 2780 N Lincoln Ave; ⊙11am-7pm; MBrown, Purple Line to Diversey) Rotofugi has an unusual niche: urban designer toys. The spacey, robot-y, odd vinyl and plush items will certainly distinguish you from the other kids on the block. It's also a gallery showcasing artists in the fields of modern pop and illustration art. You can usually find locally designed Shawnimals here.

GREENHEART SHOP ARTS & CRAFTS

Map p298 (☑312-264-1625; www.greenheart shop.org; 1714 N Wells St; ⊙10am-7pm Mon-Fri, to 6pm Sat, to 5pm Sun; Ⓜ Brown, Purple Line to Sedgwick) 🍃 This nonprofit, ecofriendly, fair-trade store stocks chocolate from Ghana, banana-fiber stationery from Uganda, rubber soccer balls from Pakistan and organic cotton baby clothes from, well, Chicago. There's much more, all part of the Center for Cultural Interchange's project that ensures fair wages to artisans.

VOSGES HAUT-CHOCOLAT FOOD & DRINK

Map p298 (☑773 296 9866; www.vosgeschoco late.com; 951 W Armitage Ave; ⊙10am-8pm Mon-Wed, to 9pm Thu-Sat, 11am-6pm Sun; Ⓜ Brown, Purple Line to Armitage) Owner-chocolatier Katrina Markoff has earned a national reputation for her brand by blending exotic ingredients such as curry powder, chilies and wasabi into her truffles, ice cream and candy bars. They sound weird but taste great, as the samples lurking around prove.

The dark-chocolate blends are the sweets to beat, dressed up with sea salt, enchanted mushrooms' and bacon. Wine, beer and coffee are available at the back counter.

CROSSROADS TRADING CO CLOTHING

Map p298 (☑773-296-1000; www.crossroads trading.com; 2711 N Clark St; ⊙11am-8pm Mon-Sat, to 7pm Sun; Ⓜ Brown, Purple Line to Diversey) Crossroads sells funky, name-brand used clothing for men and women that you can count on being in good condition. Lots of jeans usually hang on the racks, including labels such as Seven for all Mankind, Citizens of Humanity and Miss Sixty. Shoes, coats and handbags are also abundant. You can sell or trade items, too.

BARKER & MEOWSKY SPECIALTY

Map p298 (☑773-868-0200; www.barkerandme owsky.com; 1003 W Armitage Ave; ⊙10am-7pm Mon-Fri, to 6pm Sat, noon-5pm Sun; Ⓜ Brown Line to Armitage) Fido and Fluffy get their due here. Sales staff welcome four-legged visitors with a treat from the all-natural pet food stash and then the critters are allowed to commence sniffing up and over the fun apparel, beds and carriers. Top wags go to the Chewy Vuitton purse-shaped squeaky toys and Cubs ball caps, the shop's best sellers.

LORI'S, THE SOLE OF CHICAGO SHOES

Map p298 (☑773-281-5655; www.lorisshoes.com; 824 W Armitage Ave; ⊙11am-7pm Mon-Fri, 10am-6pm Sat, noon-5pm Sun; Ⓜ Brown, Purple Line to Armitage) Lori's caters to shoe junkies, who tear through boxes and tissue paper to get at Franco Sarto, Apepazza and other European brands. The general frenzy morphs into a true gorge-fest during season-ending sales in July/August and January/February; lines can form out the door during these sales.

APPLE STORE ELECTRONICS

Map p298 (www.apple.com; 801 W North Ave; ⊙9am-9pm Mon-Fri, 10am-7pm Sun; 🕿; Ⓜ North/Clybourn) Here's another Apple branch to help with all of your iPhone, iPad and other iNeeds. It's fronted by a plaza with a fountain, tables and chairs where locals hang out and mooch off the free wi-fi.

🏃 SPORTS & ACTIVITIES

NORTH AVE BEACH BEACH

Map p298 (www.cpdbeaches.com; 1600 N Lake Shore Dr; ♿; ☒151) Chicago's most popular strand of sand wafts a southern California vibe. Buff teams spike volleyballs, kids build sandcastles and everyone jumps in for a swim when the sun riots up. Bands rock the steamboat-shaped beach house, which serves ice cream and margaritas in equal measure. A short walk on the curving breakwater yields postcard skyline views.

You can rent kayaks, jet skis, stand-up paddleboards and lounge chairs. Watching dodgeball and roller-hockey leagues collide in the beachside rinks is always entertaining. Lifeguards are on duty throughout summer.

DIVERSEY DRIVING RANGE GOLF

Map p298 (☑312-742-7929; www.cpdgolf.com; 141 W Diversey Pkwy; ⊙7am-11pm; ☒151) If you want to knock a bucket of balls around, this driving range in Lincoln Park will let you whack away to your heart's content. Rental clubs are available and a bucket of balls costs $10 to $15. You can also play an 18-hole round of mini-golf for $9; the scenic course is adjacent to the driving range.

Lake View & Wrigleyville

Neighborhood Top Five

1 Spending an afternoon in the bleachers, hot dog and Old Style beer in hand, hoping for a win at ivy-clad **Wrigley Field** (p112).

2 Making a beer-and-bratwurst detour to the German enclave of **Lincoln Square** (p116).

3 Hearing a soon-to-be-famous band at **Metro** (p121).

4 Joining the thumping nightlife in **Boystown** (p116).

5 Practicing your home-run swing in the batting cages at **Sluggers** (p120).

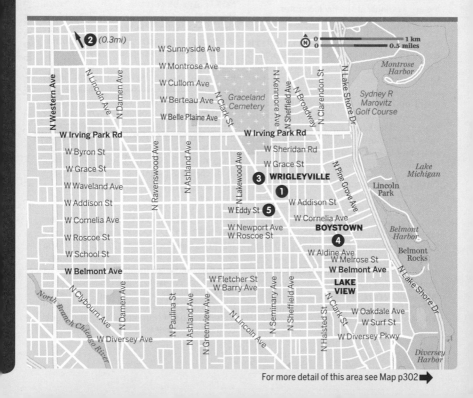

For more detail of this area see Map p302 ➡

Explore Lake View & Wrigleyville

Lake View is the overarching name of this good-time neighborhood, inhabited mostly by 20- and 30-somethings. Wrigleyville is the pocket that surrounds Wrigley Field. It's usually well mannered by day, with an impish dose of carousing in the bars along Clark St by night.

Either the rainbow flags or the abundance of hot, well-dressed men will tip you off when you arrive in Boystown, just east of the ballpark. The well-heeled hub of Chicago's gay community, Boystown bustles on Broadway St during the day and gets hedonistic on Halsted St at night. Head west and you'll run into a wild shopping district centered on Belmont Ave and Clark St. The stores here cater to the lifestyle whims of local goths, punks and kitschy hipsters. Whether you need a nose ring, Fender Telecaster or vintage Morrissey T-shirt, you can count on the endearingly attitude-heavy emporiums to come through for you. The Southport Corridor, along Southport Ave between Belmont Ave and Irving Park Rd, is another rich shopping and entertainment district, but one for those who outgrew their goth lifestyle and now seek designer wares.

For all its copious energy, Lake View has little in the way of historic sights or cultural attractions beyond the ballpark. Just bring your credit cards, your walking shoes and a festive attitude, and you'll be set for an afternoon or evening of fun.

Those wishing to explore further can travel northwest to Lincoln Square, the historic heart of Chicago's German community, rich in cafes and beer gardens.

Local Life

➡ **Hometown Bands** Beat Kitchen (p122) is a popular venue for local bands to play, as is the 'green room' at the Abbey Pub (p122).

➡ **Hangouts** In a tourist heavy neighborhood, the Hungry Brain (p119) and Ten Cat Tavern (p119) stand out as off-the-beaten-path bars where locals go for a relaxing beverage.

➡ **Brunch Time** Even carnivores line up for the French toast and other vegetarian dishes at Victory's Banner (p116), a 'hood hot spot on weekend mornings.

Getting There & Away

➡ **El** Red Line to Addison for Wrigleyville and north Boystown; Red, Brown, Purple Line to Belmont for south Boystown. Brown Line to Western for Lincoln Square.

➡ **Bus** Number 77 plies Belmont Ave.

➡ **Car** Parking is a nightmare. Especially in Wrigleyville, where side streets are resident-only. Take the El!

Lonely Planet's Top Tip

If there's a Cubs game at Wrigley Field, plan on around 30,000 extra people joining you for a visit to the neighborhood. The trains and buses will be stuffed to capacity, traffic will be snarled, and bars and restaurants will be jam-packed. It can be fun... if that's your scene. If not, you might want to visit on a nongame day for a bit more elbow room.

✗ Best Places to Eat

➡ Crisp (p116)
➡ Andy's Thai Kitchen (p118)
➡ HB (p119)
➡ Victory's Banner (p116)
➡ Chilam Balam (p118)

For reviews, see p116 ➡

🍷 Best Places to Drink

➡ Gingerman Tavern (p119)
➡ Hungry Brain (p119)
➡ Ten Cat Tavern (p119)
➡ Globe Pub (p119)
➡ Bar Pastoral (p119)

For reviews, see p119 ➡

☆ Best Places for Live Music

➡ Metro (p121)
➡ Schubas (p121)
➡ Old Town School of Folk Music (p121)
➡ Martyr's (p122)
➡ Constellation (p122)

For reviews, see p121 ➡

LAKE VIEW & WRIGLEYVILLE

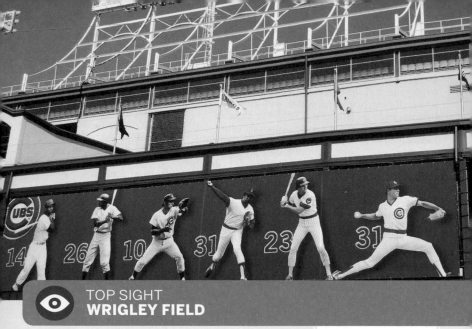

TOP SIGHT
WRIGLEY FIELD

Built in 1914 and named for the chewing-gum guy, Wrigley Field – aka The Friendly Confines – is the second-oldest baseball park in the major leagues. It's filled with legendary traditions and curses, and has a team that suffers from the longest dry spell in US sports history. The hapless Cubbies haven't won a championship since 1908, a sad record unmatched in pro football, hockey or basketball.

The Environs

The ballpark provides an old-school slice of Americana, with a hand-turned scoreboard, ivy-covered outfield walls and an iconic neon sign over the front entrance. The field is uniquely situated smack in the middle of a neighborhood, surrounded on all sides by houses, bars and restaurants. Some lucky building owners can even see into Wrigley from their rooftops.

The stadium's renovation has been the subject of much controversy recently. The owners want to raise big signs and a video scoreboard atop the outfield walls. But neighborhood citizens and businesspeople don't want their view blocked. At press time, it appeared the owners had won the battle, and these (and other) new features will be coming to Wrigley Field.

The Knothole and Tours

If the team is playing a home game you can peep through the 'knothole' – a garage-door-sized opening (with iron bars) on Sheffield Ave. The right-field vantage point is a bit skewed – but it's free.

Fans can also take a 90-minute stadium tour ($25) that goes through the clubhouse, the dugout, the press box and onto the playing field. Tours take place daily during the baseball season, but it's best to go on days when the Cubs are out of town, as you get to

DON'T MISS

- ➡ Photo under neon entrance sign
- ➡ Harry Caray statue
- ➡ Old Style beer and hot dog
- ➡ The Knothole
- ➡ Ballpark tour

PRACTICALITIES

- ➡ Map p302
- ➡ www.cubs.com
- ➡ 1060 W Addison St

see more (many areas are restricted if you tour on a game day). Buy tickets online or at the box office.

The Statues

Statues of Cubs heroes ring the stadium. Ernie Banks, aka 'Mr Cub', stands near the main entrance on Clark St; the shortstop/first baseman was the team's first African American player. Billy 'Sweet-Swinging' Williams wields his mighty bat by the Captain Morgan Club bar on Addison St. Adored third baseman Ron Santo makes a smooth catch beside him. And mythic TV sportscaster Harry Caray dons his barrel-sized eyeglasses in front of the bleacher entrance on Waveland Ave. Caray was known for broadcasting among the raucous bleacher fans while downing a few Budweisers himself. It's said the sculptors mixed a dash of his favorite beer in with the white bronze used for the statue.

The Curse

It started with Billy Sianis, owner of the Billy Goat Tavern. The year was 1945 and the Cubs were in the World Series against the Detroit Tigers. When Sianis tried to enter Wrigley Field with his pet goat to see the game, ballpark staff refused, saying the goat stank. Sianis threw up his arms and called down a mighty hex: 'The Cubs will never win another World Series!' And they haven't.

The Traditions

Old Style beer and a hot dog They're the traditional fare at Wrigley Field.

Home runs hit by the opposing team If you catch a homer slugged by the competition, you're honor-bound to throw it back onto the field.

Seventh inning stretch You gotta stand up in the middle of the seventh inning for the group sing-along of 'Take Me Out to the Ballgame'. Everyone from Mr T to Ozzy Osbourne has led the crooning.

The flag After every game the ballpark hoists a flag atop the scoreboard. A white flag with a blue 'W' indicates a victory; a blue flag with a white 'L' means a loss.

Ball hawks These guys hang out on the corner of Kenmore and Waveland Aves hoping to snag home-run balls that fly out of the stadium. No kids' stuff, this – ball hawks have filed lawsuits when a ball was knocked out of their hands. Depending on who hits the homer, it can be worth a pile of money.

Wait till next year As the typically woeful season wraps up, this is the mantra everyone says. It's Cubbie hope, despite all odds.

BABE'S CALLED SHOT

Babe Ruth's famous 'called shot' happened at Wrigley. During the 1932 World Series, Ruth pointed to center field to show where he was going to homer the next ball. And he did. It's still debated as to whether he called it or was just pointing at the pitcher.

If a ball gets lost in the ivy, it's considered a ground-rule double as long as the outfielder raises his hands to indicate that the ball is lost. If he doesn't, it's considered fair play.

THE WIND

Wrigley Field is known for its havoc wreaking wind patterns caused by nearby Lake Michigan. If the wind is blowing in, it's a pitcher's paradise. If it's blowing out, expect a big day for home runs.

The Bears played at Wrigley from 1921 to 1970. They were called the Staleys for the first season but then renamed themselves to be in sync with the Cubs.

Lake View & Wrigleyville – Wrigley Field

You'll experience more than just a game at Wrigley Field. A tangible sense of history comes alive at the 100-year-old baseball park, thanks to the hand-turned scoreboard, iconic neon entrance sign and time-honored traditions that infuse each inning. Plus the streets around it erupt into one big party during games.

KIM KARPELES / ALAMY ©

CHARLES COOK / GETTY IMAGES ©

1. The park (p112)
Score tickets for a Cubs game at the legendary 'Friendly Confines.'

2. The scoreboard (p112)
The hand-turned scoreboard provides a touch of old-school Americana.

3. Sluggers (p120)
Enjoy a pre-game beer, and even a whack in the batting cages, at this sports bar.

4. Statue of Ron Santo (p113)
Pay tribute to this much loved Cubs third baseman and radio broadcaster.

CHARLES COOK / GETTY IMAGES ©

⊙ SIGHTS

WRIGLEY FIELD STADIUM
See p112.

BOYSTOWN NEIGHBORHOOD
Map p302 (btwn Halsted & Broadway Sts, Belmont Ave & Addison St; MRed Line to Addison) What the Castro is to San Francisco, Boystown is to the Windy City. The mecca of queer Chicago (especially for men), the streets of Boystown are full of rainbow flags and packed with bars, shops and restaurants catering to residents of the gay neighborhood.

ALTA VISTA TERRACE STREET
Map p302 (btwn Byron & Grace Sts; MRed Line to Sheridan) Chicago's first designated historic district is worthy of the honor. Developer Samuel Eberly Gross recreated a block of London row houses on Alta Vista Terrace in 1904. The 20 exquisitely detailed homes on either side of the street mirror each other diagonally and the owners have worked hard at maintaining the spirit of the block.

Individuality isn't dead, however – head to the back of the west row and you'll notice that the back of every house has grown in dramatically different fashions.

✕ EATING

★CRISP ASIAN $
Map p302 (www.crisponline.com; 2940 N Broadway; mains $7-12; ⊙11:30am-9pm; MBrown Line to Wellington) Music blasts from the stereo and cheap, delicious Korean fusions are delivered fresh from the kitchen. The 'Bad Boy Buddha' bowl, a variation on *bibimbap* (mixed vegetables with rice), is one of the best $9 lunches in town. On second thought, maybe that award goes to Crisp's burrito, filled with perfectly fried chicken in a savory soy-ginger sauce.

VICTORY'S BANNER VEGETARIAN $
Map p302 (☑733-665-0227; www.victorysbanner.com; 2100 W Roscoe St; mains $8-11; ⊙8am-3pm, closed Tue; ☑; MBrown Line to Paulina) The tough decision at this revered breakfast house is between the fresh, free-range-egg omelets and the legendary French toast, cooked in rich cream batter and served with peach butter. New Age tunes and muted colors give it a soothing Zen vibe, even when the place is mobbed on weekend mornings.

🏃 Local Life
Lincoln Square Toddle

Lincoln Square is an old German enclave that has blossomed into a Euro-stylish eating, drinking and shopping destination. The action centers on Lincoln Ave northwest of Lake View. Get ready for beer, bratwursts and lots of local color. If you happen by in early September you can sing *Danke Schoen* in the same parade Ferris Bueller did.

❶ Half Acre Tap Room
Half Acre was one of Chicago's craft brewing leaders. The beer earned a cult following and the guys opened the **Half Acre Tap Room** (www.halfacrebeer.com; 4257 N Lincoln Ave; ⊙noon-late Tue-Fri, from 11am Sat & Sun; ☎; MBrown Line to Montrose) at the source. No TVs, no food, no other drinks besides their own megastrong brews. Local hopheads adore it.

❷ Bistro Campagne
Chicago has a lot of French bistros, but not many perfect the balance of fine but unfussy dining the way **Bistro Campagne** (☑773-271-6100; www.bistrocampagne.com; 4518 N Lincoln Ave; mains $18-27; ⊙5:30-9pm Mon-Thu, to 10pm Fri, from 11am Sat & Sun; MBrown Line to Western) does. The neighborhood favorite serves classics such as beef bourguignonne, mussels and chocolate soufflé alongside a robust wine list.

❸ Old Town School
The Old Town School (p121) gets street cred for moving to the neighborhood before it gentrified. Swing into the music shop to blow a harmonica or strum a mandolin. The little cafe whips up healthy, kid-friendly snacks. The first Friday of each month, local musicians and families gather for an open jam session (admission $5), no experience necessary.

❹ Merz Apothecary
Merz Apothecary (☑773-989-0900; www.merzapothecary.com; 4716 N Lincoln Ave; ⊙9am-6pm Mon-Sat; MBrown Line to Western) has been around since 1875. Antique pharmacy jars contain herbs, homeopathic remedies, vitamins and

Entrance to Lincoln Square

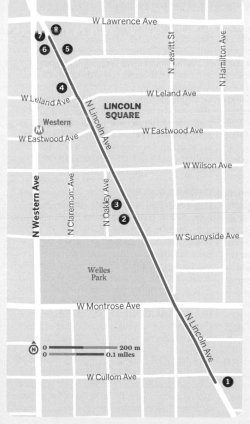

supplements, and the shelves are stacked high with skin care, bath and aromatherapy products from around the world.

5 Huettenbar

Pay homage to the neighborhood's old German roots at the stalwart **Huettenbar** (www.huettenbar.com; 4721 N Lincoln Ave; from 2pm Mon-Fri, from noon Sat & Sun; Brown Line to Western). The kitschy, wood-paneled ambience is straight out of the Black Forest. So are the beers flowing from the taps. A crisp kolsch from Frankfurt and seat by the big open windows, and you're stylin'.

6 Book Cellar

The independent **Book Cellar** (www.bookcellarinc.com; 4736 N Lincoln Ave; 10am-10pm, to 6pm Tue & Sun; Brown Line to Western) is an integral part of the neighborhood. Local book groups hold their meetings here and parents bring in their kids for the weekly story hour (Fridays at 11am). Local authors do readings, while the cafe pours wine and beer.

7 Gene's Sausage Shop

As if the hanging sausages and ripe cheeses lining the shelves at this European market weren't enough, **Gene's** (www.genessausage.com; 4750 N Lincoln Ave; 9am-8pm Mon-Sat, to 4pm Sun; Brown Line to Western) rocks a rooftop beer garden. Sit at communal picnic tables and munch hot-off-the-grill bratwursts while sipping worldly brews. It's sort of a local secret.

8 Timeless Toys

Charming **Timeless Toys** (773-334-4445; www.timelesstoyschicago.com; 4749 N Lincoln Ave; 10am-6pm, to 7pm Thu & Fri, to 6pm Sun; Brown Line to Western) carries high-quality, old-fashioned wares, many made in Germany or other European countries. Have fun playing with the bug magnifiers, microscopes, glitter balls and wooden spinning tops.

LAKE VIEW & WRIGLEYVILLE

PENNY'S NOODLE SHOP
THAI **$**

Map p302 (☑773-281-8222; www.pennysnoodle-shop.com; 3400 N Sheffield Ave; mains $6-9; ⊙11am-10pm Tue-Sun; ⚡; MRed, Brown, Purple Line to Belmont) Despite the presence of several other excellent Asian choices within a few blocks, Penny's attracts crowds most hours of the day and night. People wait outside in all kinds of weather. Maybe these hapless hordes are drawn by the place's minimalist decor, the low prices or – no doubt – the cheap, tasty noodle soups and stir-fries. Penny's is BYOB.

FALAFILL
MIDDLE EASTERN **$**

Map p302 (☑773-525-0052; www.eatfalafill.com; 3202 N Broadway; mains $5-8; ⊙11am-10pm; ⚡; MRed, Brown, Purple Line to Belmont) Buy a falafel sandwich or falafel salad at the counter, then customize it at the topping bar with cilantro chutney, Moroccan olives, *zhug* (hot jalapeno sauce), tabbouleh, pickled ginger and 15 other fresh items. Soup, hummus and sweet-potato fries sum up the side dishes.

CLARK STREET DOG
AMERICAN **$**

Map p302 (☑773-281-6690; www.clarkstdog. com; 3040 N Clark St; mains $3-7; ⊙9am-4am Sun-Thu, to 4am Fri & Sat; MBrown, Purple Line to Wellington) Apart from signature hot dogs, carnivorous delights include the Italian sausage combo – which marries Italian beef *and* Italian sausage on a single soggy bun – and the chili cheese fries. If all the salty meats make you thirsty, head to the adjoining divey Clark Street Bar for some cheap cold ones.

★ANDY'S THAI KITCHEN
THAI **$$**

Map p302 (www.andysthaikitchen.com; 946 W Wellington Ave; mains $8-13; ⊙11am-9:30pm Mon-Fri, noon-9:30pm Sat & Sun; MBrown, Purple Line to Wellington) Little 11-table Andy's earns big praise from foodies who swoon over the authentic Thai menu. Andy is not afraid to use organ parts in his dishes, or to atomically spice them. Standouts among the five pages of menu items include the fish-maw salad, basil preserved egg and boat noodles swimming with beef brisket and pork skin. BYO; cash only.

CHILAM BALAM
MEXICAN **$$**

Map p302 (☑773-296-6901; www.chilambalam-chicago.com; 3023 N Broadway; small plates $9-14; ⊙5-10pm Tue-Thu, to 11pm Fri & Sat; MBrown Line to Wellington) The chef is only in her 20s, but she has already apprenticed under Rick Bayless and brought his 'farm to table' philosophy to this vibrant brick-and-Spanish-tile eatery, which sits below street level. The close-set tables pulse with young foodies ripping into fiery halibut seviche, mushroom empanadas, chocolate-chili mousse and other imaginative fare. It's BYOB. Cash only.

MIA FRANCESCA
ITALIAN **$$**

Map p302 (☑773-281-3310; www.miafrancesca. com; 3311 N Clark St; mains $13-25; ⊙5-10pm Mon-Thu, 5-11pm Fri, 10am-11pm Sat, 10am-10pm Sun; MRed, Brown, Purple Line to Belmont) Diners quickly fill up the room at this family-run Italian bistro (part of a local chain) and energy swirls among the closely spaced tables, topped with white tablecloths and fresh flowers. The handwritten menu features earthy standards – seafood linguine, spinach ravioli, veal medallions – with aggressive seasoning from southern Italy. Other treats include wafer-thin pizzas and flavor-packed polenta.

TANGO SUR
STEAKHOUSE **$$**

Map p302 (☑773-477-5466; www.tangosur. net; 3763 N Southport Ave; mains $15-25; ⊙5-10:30pm Mon-Fri, from 2pm Sat, from noon Sun; MBrown Line to Southport) This candlelit BYO Argentine steakhouse makes an idyllic date location, serving classic skirt steaks and other tender grass-fed options. In addition to the traditional cuts, the chef's special is *bife Vesuvio,* a prime strip stuffed with garlic, spinach and cheese – it's a triumph. In summer, tables outside expand the seating from the small and spare interior.

CHICAGO DINER
VEGETARIAN **$$**

Map p302 (☑773-935-6696; www.veggiediner. com; 3411 N Halsted St; mains $9-14; ⊙11am-10pm Mon-Fri, from 10am Sat & Sun; ⚡; MRed Line to Addison) The gold standard for Chicago vegetarians, this place has been serving barbecue seitan (wheat meat) and tofu stroganoff for decades. The tattooed staff will guide you to the best stuff, including the peanut butter vegan 'supershakes' and the 'Radical Ruben'. Vegans take note: even the pesto for the pasta can be had without a lick of cheese.

VILLAGE TAP
BURGERS **$$**

Map p302 (☑773-883-0817; www.thevillagetap. com; 2055 W Roscoe St; mains $8-11; ⊙5-11pm Mon-Thu, from 3pm Fri, from noon Sat & Sun; MBrown Line to Paulina) Even though it can get overly packed on the weekends, this neighborhood tavern does everything well: food, drink and atmosphere. The friendly bartenders give out free samples of the ever-changing and carefully chosen Midwestern microbrews. The kitchen turns out great burgers, veggie burgers and chicken sandwiches, served with a side of hummus and grilled pita.

Out back the beer garden contains a fountain; inside, the tables enjoy good views of the TVs for ball games.

HB MODERN AMERICAN **$$$**

Map p302 (773-661-0299; www.homebistrochicago.com; 3404 N Halsted St; mains $18-24; 5:30-10pm Tue-Thu, 5-10:30pm Fri & Sat, to 9pm Sun; Red Line to Addison) The monogram stands for 'Home Bistro', where chef-owner Joncarl Lachman serves Dutch-influenced comfort food in a warm wood-and-tile-lined space. Shout-outs go to the exquisite pork chops and the pan-roasted trout. Try to snag a seat by the front window, which entertains with Boystown people-watching. HB is BYOB.

YOSHI'S CAFE JAPANESE **$$$**

Map p302 (773-248-6160; www.yoshiscafe.com; 3257 N Halsted St; mains $18-27; 5-10:30pm Tue-Sat, 11am-9:30pm Sun; Red, Brown, Purple Line to Belmont) Yoshi and Nobuko Katsumura preside over one of the most innovative casual places in town – as they've done for more than two decades – with a changing Japanese- and French-flared menu. They treat all ingredients with the utmost respect, from the salmon to the tofu to the Kobe beef. Service in the low-lit, well-spaced room is every bit as snappy as the food.

🍷⚘ DRINKING & NIGHTLIFE

★**GINGERMAN TAVERN** BAR

Map p302 (3740 N Clark St; from 3pm Mon-Fri, from noon Sat & Sun; Red Line to Addison) A splendid place to pass an evening, this spot features a huge and eclectic beer selection, which is enjoyed by rockers, theater types and other creative folks. It offers respite from the Cubs mania of the rest of the strip. Pool is free on Sunday, Monday and Tuesday (except during Cubs games).

The Metro music club took over ownership recently and technically the name is now 'GMan', though everyone still calls it the Gingerman.

★**HUNGRY BRAIN** BAR

(773-935-2118; 2319 W Belmont Ave; from 8pm Tue-Sun; 77) This off-the-beaten-path little bar charms with its kind bartenders, roving tamale vendors who pop in on occasion and well-worn, thrift-store decor. On Sunday nights it hosts sets of live jazz (cover charge $7) from some of the city's best young players. Cash only.

TEN CAT TAVERN PUB

Map p302 (773-935-5377; 3931 N Ashland Ave; from 3pm; Brown Line to Irving Park) Pool is serious business on the two vintage tables that the pub refelts regularly with material from Belgium. The ever-changing, eye-catching art comes courtesy of neighborhood artists and the furniture is a garage saler's dream. Regulars (most in their 30s) down leisurely drinks at the bar or, in warm weather, head to the beer garden.

GLOBE PUB PUB

Map p302 (773-871-3757; www.theglobepub.net; 1934 W Irving Park Rd; from 11am; Brown Line to Irving Park) This warm, dark-oak pub is ground zero for English soccer and rugby fanatics, since it shows all the international league games on satellite TV. It even opens at 6am for big matches so patrons can watch the action live. The kitchen cooks up a traditional English breakfast daily and the taps flow with ales from the homeland.

BAR PASTORAL WINE BAR

Map p302 (www.pastoralartisan.com/bar-pastoral; 2947 N Broadway; 5-11pm Mon-Thu, 1pm-midnight Fri & Sat, to 9pm Sun; Brown, Purple Line to Wellington) Popular deli minichain Pastoral has added a wine bar to its Lake View shop. Half-glasses are available for $5, which means you can sample widely. The deli's awesome breads and cheeses help soak it up (stick to these rather than the dishes listed on the menu).

DUKE OF PERTH PUB

Map p302 (773-477-1741; www.dukeofperth.com; 2913 N Clark St; from 5pm Mon, from noon Tue-Sun; Brown, Purple Line to Wellington) The UK beers and more than 80 bottles of single-malt scotch are nearly overwhelming at this cozy, laid-back pub. After enough of them, try the fish and chips, which is all-you-can-eat for lunch and dinner for $10.25 on Wednesday and Friday.

GUTHRIE'S   PUB

Map p302 (☎773-477-2900; 1300 W Addison St; ⓧfrom 5pm Mon-Fri, from 2pm Sat & Sun; ⓜRed Line to Addison) A local institution and the perfect neighborhood hangout, Guthrie's remains true to its mellow roots even as the neighborhood goes manic around it. The glassed-in back porch is fittingly furnished with patio chairs and filled with 30- and 40-somethings, and board games abound.

SOUTHPORT LANES   BAR

Map p302 (☎773-472-6600; www.southport-lanes.com; 3325 N Southport Ave; ⓧfrom noon; ⓜBrown Line to Southport) An old-fashioned, four-lane bowling alley with hand-set pins hides inside this busy neighborhood bar and grill. Those who prefer to shoot stick can chalk up at the six regulation pool tables. The main bar features an inspirational mural of cavorting nymphs, and tables sprawl onto the sidewalk in summer.

SMART BAR   CLUB

Map p302 (www.smartbarchicago.com; 3730 N Clark St; ⓧ10pm-4am Wed-Sat; ⓜRed Line to Addison) This downstairs adjunct to Metro (p121) is a dance and music lover's dream, and the DJs are often more renowned than you'd expect the intimate space to accommodate. A who's who of forward-looking break artists, house and trance DJs have held down the turntables.

SLUGGERS   SPORTS BAR

Map p302 (☎773-472-9696; www.sluggersbar.com; 3540 N Clark St; ⓜRed Line to Addison) Practice your home-run swing at Sluggers, a popular bar and grill across from Wrigley Field. Sidestep the shnockered Cubs fans and giant-screen TVs and head to the 2nd floor, where there are four batting cages. Ten pitches cost $1.

MURPHY'S BLEACHERS   SPORTS BAR

Map p302 (☎773-281-5356; www.murphys bleachers.com; 3655 N Sheffield Ave; ⓧfrom 10am Mon-Sat, from 11am Sun; ⓜRed Line to Addison) It's a Cubs game prerequisite to beer up at this well-loved, historic watering hole, only steps away from the entrance to Wrigley Field's bleacher seats. Fans jam into this place like sardines on game day.

CHICAGO BRAUHAUS   BAR

(☎773-784-4444; www.chicagobrauhaus.com; 4732 N Lincoln Ave; ⓧ11am-midnight, closed Tue; ⓜBrown Line to Western) Unlikely as it may seem for a bar, the oompah soundtrack, rosy-cheeked staff and early last call give this spacious Bavarian-themed joint the all-ages appeal of a Disney ride. Dinnertime is best, when the 'world-famous' lederhosen-clad Brauhaus Trio starts bumping and steaming plates of schnitzel seem heaven-sent. Bring your dancing shoes, too – there's polka action nightly. The Brauhaus is located in Lincoln Square.

SIDETRACK   CLUB

Map p302 (www.sidetrackchicago.com; 3349 N Halsted St; ⓧfrom 3pm Mon-Fri, from 1pm Sat & Sun; ⓜRed, Brown, Purple Line to Belmont) Massive Sidetrack thumps dance music for a gay and straight crowd alike. Get ready to belt out your Broadway best at the good-time 'show-tune nights' on Sunday and Monday. The club hosts stand-up comedy on Thursday. If the indoor action gets too much, the huge outdoor courtyard beckons.

SPYNER'S   LESBIAN

(www.spyners.com; 4623 N Western Ave; ⓧfrom 11am; ⓜBrown Line to Western) Lesbian karaoke! Perhaps you didn't know the niche existed. But it does. And it's here, in Lincoln Square. Friday and Saturday nights are the main party. It's a fun scene regardless of your sexual orientation.

BERLIN   CLUB

Map p302 (☎773-348-4975; www.berlinchicago.com; 954 W Belmont Ave; ⓧ10pm-4am Tue, from 5pm Wed-Sun; ⓜRed, Brown, Purple Line to Belmont) Looking for a packed, sweaty dance floor? Berlin caters to a mostly gay crowd midweek, though partiers of all stripes jam the place on weekends. Monitors flicker through the latest video dispatches from cult pop and electronic acts, while DJs take the dance floor on trancey detours.

L&L   BAR

Map p302 (☎773-528-1303; 3207 N Clark St; ⓧfrom 2pm Mon-Fri, from noon Sat & Sun; ⓜRed, Brown, Purple Line to Belmont) The dimly lit L&L is an unapologetic dive bar, complete with curt, seen-it-all staff. It's a great place to duck the Wrigleyville madness. Relax with cheap Pabst beer or a sip from the impressive assortment of Irish whiskey. Cash only.

SPIN
CLUB

Map p302 (☑773-327-7711; www.spin-nightclub.com; 800 W Belmont Ave; ◉from 6pm Mon-Fri, from 4pm Sat, from 2pm Sun; Ⓜ️Red Line to Belmont) Though its clientele consists mostly of gay men in their 20s, Spin also draws hetero men and women on the weekends. Serious dancers hit the floor, while chatty cruisers orbit the large bar by the entrance. Don't miss Spin's shower contest every Friday night, when hopefuls of both genders bare (almost) all. There's also an outdoor beer garden and darts tournaments.

HYDRATE
CLUB

Map p302 (☑773-975-9244; www.hydratechicago.com; 3458 N Halsted St; ◉8pm-4am; Ⓜ️Red Line to Addison) A wild night on the Boystown club circuit requires a visit to this frenzied spot, which boasts an open-air feel (thanks to retractable windows) and a chatty pickup scene (thanks to $1 well drinks). It's not all roses; the service gets rude and the crowds unruly (also thanks to the $1 well drinks).

CLOSET
GAY N LESBIAN

Map p302 (☑773-477-8533; www.thecloset-chicago.com; 3325 N Broadway; ◉4pm-4am Mon-Fri, from noon Sat & Sun; ☎; Ⓜ️Red, Brown, Purple Line to Belmont) One of the few lesbian-centric bars in Chicago, the Closet changes mood and tempo at 2am, when the crowd becomes more mixed, the music gets louder and things get a little rowdier. On Tuesdays there's a ukelele sing-along.

☆ ENTERTAINMENT

★METRO
LIVE MUSIC

Map p302 (www.metrochicago.com; 3730 N Clark St; Ⓜ️Red Line to Addison) For three decades the Metro has been synonymous with loud rock. Sonic Youth and the Ramones in the '80s. Nirvana and Jane's Addiction in the '90s. White Stripes and The Killers in the new millennium. Each night prepare to hear noise by three or four bands who may well be teetering on the verge of superstardom.

SCHUBAS
LIVE MUSIC

Map p302 (☑773-525-2508; www.schubas.com; 3159 N Southport Ave; Ⓜ️Brown Line to Southport) Something of an alternative-country legend, Schubas presents twangy acoustic artists, plus indie rock acts on their way up

JAZZ HOT SPOTS

Sports bars you expect in the neighborhood. Cutting edge jazz music? Not so much. But it's here:

➡ Hungry Brain (p119) – the Sunday Transmission series brings in the young and avant-garde.

➡ Constellation (p122) – improvised music fills the air.

➡ Katerina's (p122) – the jazz is usually a bit more traditional.

(such as My Morning Jacket and the Shins in their early days). Bands play nightly in the cozy back-room club, which is noted for its great sound, thanks to the all-wood construction. A friendly, boisterous bar pours microbrews in the front room.

IO THEATER
COMEDY

Map p302 (☑773-880-0199; www.ioimprov.com; 3541 N Clark St; Ⓜ️Red Line to Addison) iO launched the careers of Tina Fey and Stephen Colbert, along with a host of other well-known comics (many cross over from iO to Second City (p107) before hitting it big). The bawdy shows hinge entirely on audience suggestions and each turn can run 40 minutes or longer. Shows on Wednesday and Sunday are usually just $5.

If you're thoroughly motivated by what you see, iO offers a range of comedy and improv courses to suit every budget. The theater is scheduled to move to new, larger digs at 1501 N Kingsbury St (in Lincoln Park) in late 2014.

COMEDYSPORTZ
COMEDY

Map p302 (☑773-549-8080; www.comedysportzchicago.com; 929 W Belmont Ave; Ⓜ️Red, Brown, Purple Line to Belmont) The gimmick? Two teams compete to make you laugh. It's comedy played like a sport (hence the name). The show is totally improvised, with the audience dictating the action. A referee moderates and the wittiest team 'wins' at the end. You can bring in alcohol from the lobby bar. On Wednesday shows are $2; prime-time weekend shows are $24.

OLD TOWN SCHOOL OF
FOLK MUSIC
LIVE MUSIC

(☑773-728-6000; www.oldtownschool.org; 4544 N Lincoln Ave; ♿; Ⓜ️Brown Line to Western) You can hear the call of the banjos from the street outside this venerable institution, where major national and international acts such as Richard Thompson and Joan Baez play when they come to town. Old Town also hosts superb world music shows, including every Wednesday at 8:30pm when they're free (or a $5 donation if you've got it).

Do-it-yourselfers can take guitar and other musical classes here. Note some concerts (including the Wednesday world music show) take place in Szold Hall, located across the street.

ANNOYANCE THEATRE   COMEDY

Map p302 (www.annoyanceproductions.com; 851 W Belmont Ave; MRed, Brown, Purple Line to Belmont) The Annoyance masterminds naughty and absurd shows, often musicals, such as *Tiny Fascists: A Boy Scout Musical*. Both the shows and the theater itself are of surprisingly high quality. Susan Messing's $5 Thursday night session always provides good yucks.

MARTYRS'   LIVE MUSIC

Map p302 (www.martyrslive.com; 3855 N Lincoln Ave; MBrown Line to Irving Park) Martyrs' is a small, catch-all venue where pretty much anything goes musically: Frank Zappa's former band, a Tom Petty tribute band, a Mexican folk music group. It's also the home of the popular Moth Story Slam: participants get on stage and tell a true story; the best story (and storytelling prowess) wins. The slam is held the last Tuesday of the month. There's mighty fine pub grub to boot.

CONSTELLATION   LIVE MUSIC

(www.constellation-chicago.com; 3111 N Western Ave; ☐77) The producer of Pitchfork Music Festival opened this intimate club, which actually breaks down into two small venues inside. The city's hep-cats come out of the woodwork for the progressive jazz and improvisational music. Many acts are free and none costs more than $15.

LAUGH FACTORY CHICAGO   COMEDY

Map p302 (www.laughfactory.com; 3175 N Broadway; MRed, Brown, Purple Line to Belmont) Newbie comics line up hours in advance for Wednesday's open mic at the Laugh Factory. Such is the cachet of its parent LA club, where everyone from Richard Pryor to Sarah Silverman has tried out jokes. Expect lots of seasoned stand-up acts the rest of the week.

AMERICAN THEATER COMPANY   THEATER

Map p302 (☑773-409-4125; www.atcweb.org; 1909 W Byron St; MBrown Line to Irving Park) ATC has been around for three decades, putting on both new and established works by American playwrights. They usually garner great acclaim and subsequently travel onward to other cities.

ABBEY PUB   LIVE MUSIC

(☑773-478-4408; www.abbeypub.com; 3420 W Grace St; MBlue Line to Addison) The Abbey is two places in one: a club where on-the-verge local and well-known national rock bands play; and a Guinness-pouring Irish pub where guitar and fiddle jam sessions have been known to erupt. The venue is a haul far from the city center, on the northwest side.

KATERINA'S   LIVE MUSIC

Map p302 (☑773-348-7592; www.katerinas.com; 1920 W Irving Park; MBrown Line to Irving Park) Stylish Katerina's hosts soulful jazz, blues and world-music performers nightly. A sophisticated set of 30- and 40-somethings down martinis, fork into food from the Greek-influenced menu and dig the good tunes all night long. Reservations are a good idea.

BEAT KITCHEN   LIVE MUSIC

Map p302 (☑773-281-4444; www.beatkitchen.com; 2100 W Belmont Ave; ☐77) Everything you need to know is in the name – entertaining beats traverse a spectrum of sounds and the kitchen turns out better-than-average dinners. Dine early in the front of the house, since service is unhurried. Music in the homely back room can be funky or jammy, but a crop of Chicago's smart, broadly appealing songwriters dominates the calendar.

MUSIC BOX THEATRE   CINEMA

Map p302 (☑773-871-6604; www.musicboxthea-tre.com; 3733 N Southport Ave; MBrown Line to Southport) It hardly matters what's playing here; the Music Box itself is worth the visit. The perfectly restored theater dates from 1929 and looks like a Moorish palace, with clouds floating across the ceiling under twinkling stars. The art-house films are always first-rate and there's a midnight roster of cult hits such as *The Big Lebowski*. A second, smaller theater shows held-over films.

BREW & VIEW
CINEMA

Map p302 (☎773-929-6713; www.brewview.com; Vic Theater, 3145 N Sheffield Ave; ⓜRed, Brown, Purple Line to Belmont) Even the worst film gets better when you've got a pizza in front of you and a pitcher of beer at your side. As you watch second-run Hollywood releases, you can behave as badly as you would at home – in fact, the cheap midweek drink specials encourage it. You must be 18 or over.

CORN PRODUCTIONS
COMEDY

(☎312-409-6435; www.cornservatory.org; 4210 N Lincoln Ave; ⓜBrown Line to Irving Park) Though Corn occasionally stages something serious, most of its productions are kitschy and inexpensive. One of its recent draws was *Drink!*, lampooning college drinking games. The theater is just west of Lake View in the North Center neighborhood.

 ## SHOPPING

STRANGE CARGO
CLOTHING

Map p302 (www.strangecargo.com; 3448 N Clark St; ⓧ11am-6:45pm Mon-Sat, to 5:30pm Sun; ⓜRed Line to Addison) This retro store stocks hipster wear, platform shoes, wigs and a mind-blowing array of kitschy T-shirts. Staff will iron on decals of Harry Caray, Mike Ditka, the Hancock Center or other local touchstones, as well as Obama, Smurfs and more – all supreme souvenirs.

THREADLESS
CLOTHING

Map p302 (☎773-525-8640; www.threadless.com; 3011 N Broadway; ⓧ11am-8pm Mon-Sat, noon-6pm Sun; ⓜBrown, Purple Line to Wellington) Those seeking the perfect ironic, eccentric, limited-edition T-shirt will find it at Threadless. The company runs an ongoing T-shirt design competition on its website in which designers submit ideas and consumers cast votes (750,000 weekly). The company then releases the winning styles in limited quantities for two weeks. The new designs appear in-store on Friday, before they're posted online on Monday.

Prices range from $15 to $25. Bring back your shopping bag and get $1 off your next purchase. There's a kid-focused outlet at 1905 W Division St in Wicker Park.

ALLEY
CLOTHING & ACCESSORIES

Map p302 (☎773-525-3180; www.thealley.com; 3228 N Clark St; ⓧnoon-10pm Mon-Fri, 11am-

10pm Sat, 11am-8pm Sun; ⓜRed, Brown, Purple Line to Belmont) A skull and crossbones mark the door at this one-stop counterculture shop. The vast emporium offers everything from pot pipes to band posters to human-sized dog collars. Loud, obnoxious punk-rock tees ('I've got the biggest dick in the band' etc), fetish shoes and leatherwear are some of the house specialties.

The scene unfurls through a labyrinth of rooms, including a couple devoted to tattooing and piercing.

CHICAGO COMICS
BOOKS

Map p302 (☎773-528-1983; www.chicagocomics.com; 3244 N Clark St; ⓧnoon-8pm Mon-Fri, from 11am Sat, noon-7pm Sun; ⓜRed, Brown, Purple Line to Belmont) This comic emporium has won the 'best comic-book store in the USA' honor from all sorts of people who should know. Old Marvel *Superman* back issues share shelf space with hand-drawn works by cutting-edge local artists such as Chris Ware, Ivan Brunetti and Dan Clowes (who lived here during his early *Eightball* days). *Simpsons* fanatics will 'd'oh!' with joy at the huge toy selection.

ARCHITECTURAL ARTIFACTS
ANTIQUES

(☎773-348-0622; www.architecturalartifacts.com; 4325 N Ravenswood Ave; ⓧ10am-5pm; ⓜBrown Line to Montrose) This mammoth, 80,000-sq-ft salvage warehouse is a treasure trove that prompts continual mutterings of 'Where on earth did they find *that*?' Italian marionettes, 1920s French mannequins and Argentinean cast-iron mailboxes rest alongside decorative doors, tiles, stained-glass windows, fireplace mantels and garden furnishings. Be sure to step into the free attached Museum of Historic Chicago Architecture (a work in progress).

UNCLE FUN
GIFTS

Map p302 (☎773-477-8223; www.unclefunchicago.com; 1338 W Belmont Ave; ⓧnoon-7pm Mon-Fri, 11am-7pm Sat, 11am-5pm Sun; ⓜBrown Line to Southport) This oddball toy and novelty shop is one of the best spots in Chicago for goofy gifts, kitschy postcards and vintage games. The shelves are overflowing with strange finds such as fake-moustache kits, 3D Jesus postcards and Chinese-made tapestries of the US lunar landing.

UNABRIDGED BOOKSTORE
BOOKS

Map p302 (www.unabridgedbookstore.com; 3251 N Broadway; ⓧ10am-9pm Mon-Fri, to 7pm Sat &

LOCAL KNOWLEDGE

SOUVENIRS

Lake View is a swell neighborhood to pick up unique Chicago souvenirs. Try the following:

➡ Strange Cargo (p123) for a T-shirt with a diagram of what's on a Chicago-style hot dog.

➡ Sports World for a sweatshirt, coffee cup or anything with a Cubs logo.

➡ Chicago Comics (p123) for a hand-drawn magazine made by a local artist.

Sun; MRed, Brown, Purple Line to Belmont) This indie shop is known for its stellar gay and lesbian section (including gay fiction, gay parenting and queer spirituality), as well as travel, sci-fi and children's sections. Staff tape up notes on the shelves next to their recommendations.

BELMONT ARMY

SURPLUS   CLOTHING & ACCESSORIES

Map p302 (773-549-1038; www.belmontarmy. com; 855 W Belmont Ave; ⊙11am-8pm Mon-Sat, noon-6pm Sun; MRed, Brown, Purple Line to Belmont) Don't be fooled by the name – the goods at this sprawling store go well beyond combat gear. Fashion-of-the-moment clothes hang from the 1st floor's racks. A rainbow array of Converse, Vans, Adidas, Dr Martens, Red Wing and sky-high goth shoes fills the 2nd floor's shelves. The 3rd floor is where you finally get to the peacoats and other vintage military wares.

SPORTS WORLD   SOUVENIRS

Map p302 (312-472-7701; www.sportsworldchicago.com; 3555 N Clark St; ⊙9am-6pm; MRed Line to Addison) This store across from Wrigley Field overflows with – that's right, Sherlock – Cubs sportswear. It carries all shapes and sizes of jerseys, T-shirts, sweatshirts and ball caps, plus baby clothes and drink flasks. Surprisingly, the prices aren't bad given the location.

GRAMAPHONE RECORDS   MUSIC

Map p298 (773-472-3683; www.gramaphone records.com; 2843 N Clark St; ⊙noon-9pm Mon-Fri, 11am-8:30pm Sat, noon-6pm Sun; MBrown, Purple Line to Diversey) Gramaphone is one of the hippest record stores in Chicago – you'd have to either be a DJ or be dating a DJ to have heard of most of the hip-hop and electronic music sold here. Along with its collection of trendsetting sounds, Gramaphone offers record needles and DJ supplies, as well as a host of info on upcoming parties.

CHOPPING BLOCK   FOOD & DRINK

(773-472-6700; www.thechoppingblock.net; 4747 N Lincoln Ave; MBrown Line to Western) Let's say your recipe calls for Hungarian cinnamon, gray sea salt and Balinese long pepper. Instead of throwing up your hands in despair after searching the local grocery store and then calling for a pizza delivery, stop in here for specialty foods, high-end cookware and hard-to-find utensils. Chopping Block also offers cooking classes. It's located in Lincoln Square.

MIDWEST STEREO   ELECTRONICS

Map p302 (773-975-4250; 1613 W Belmont Ave; ⊙11am-7pm Mon-Fri, to 6pm Sat; MBrown Line to Paulina) This is a hub for DJ gear, both used and new. If you're looking for a basic mixer or a Technics turntable (or a PA system that will quickly make you the talk of your neighborhood), this is your store.

WINDWARD SPORTS   SPORTS

Map p302 (773-472-6868; www.windward boardshop.com; 3317 N Clark St; ⊙11am-8pm Mon-Sat, noon-6pm Sun; MRed, Brown, Purple Line to Belmont) One-stop shopping for sporty board gear, whether you're into surfing, windsurfing, kiteboarding, snowboarding or skateboarding. Windward carries the requisite apparel labels, too (Quiksilver, Billabong, Split etc). Staff members are clued in to local boarding hot spots. Ask about various beach rentals of windsurfing equipment during the summer.

GAY MART   GIFTS

Map p302 (773-929-4272; www.chicagosgay-mart.com; 3457 N Halsted St; ⊙11am-7:30pm Mon-Sat, noon-6pm Sun; MRed Line to Addison) The Woolworth's of the strip sells toys, novelties, calendars, souvenirs, you name it. One of the top sellers is Billy, the heroically endowed 'world's first out and proud gay doll'. Ken would just wilt in Billy's presence – that is, if Ken had anything to wilt. Lots of Marvel action figures and 'Homo Depot' buttons, too.

EGOIST UNDERWEAR   CLOTHING

Map p302 (www.egoistunderwear.com; 3706 N Halsted St; ⊙11am-8pm Mon-Sat, noon-7pm

Sun; MRed Line to Addison) This boutique in the heart of Boystown specializes in men's designer underwear. Peruse briefs, boxers, G-strings, swimming shorts, V-neck T-shirts and tank tops. Brands include AussieBum and Cocksox.

UNCLE DAN'S   OUTDOOR GEAR
Map p302 (☑773-348-5800; www.udans.com; 3551 N Southport Ave; ⊙10am-7pm Mon-Sat, 11am-6pm Sun; MBrown Line to Southport) This store offers top travel and outdoor gear for those looking to escape the concrete jungle, or at least get some abrasion-reinforced fleece to protect them from the elements. It's a relaxed place to buy hiking boots, camping supplies, backpacks and what-not without the macho posturing that gear stores sometimes give off.

BROWN ELEPHANT
RESALE SHOP   HOMEWARES
Map p302 (☑773-549-5943; 3651 N Halsted St; ⊙11am-6pm; MRed Line to Addison) Proceeds benefit the Howard Brown Health Center, which specializes in health care for the GLBT communities. The shop has a consistently good selection of books, vintage furniture and kitchen items.

YESTERDAY   SPORTS
Map p302 (☑773-248-8087; 1143 W Addison St; ⊙2-6pm Sun-Fri, 1-7pm Sun; MRed Line to Addison) If you've ever actually lived through the classic 'Mom's thrown out all of my baseball cards' tale, you can come here to find out what a fortune you've lost. Old sports memorabilia is the specialty of this shop, which is even older and mustier than some of the goods on sale.

🏃 SPORTS & ACTIVITIES

CHICAGO CUBS   BASEBALL
Map p302 (www.cubs.com; 1060 W Addison St; MRed Line to Addison) The beloved, beleaguered Cubs plays at Wrigley Field. It has been more than a century since the team won the World Series, but that doesn't stop fans and tourists from coming out to see their games. Ticket prices vary, but in general you'll be hard-pressed to get in for under $30. The popular bleacher seats cost around $50. The Upper Deck Reserved (infield) seats, sections 513 to 517, are usually pretty cheap. They're way at the top of the stadium, but have a nice view of the on-field action and Lake Michigan.

Tickets are available at the box office, through the team's website, or by calling ☑800-843-2827 (within Illinois) or ☑866-652-2827 (from out of state).

SYDNEY R MAROVITZ
GOLF COURSE   GOLF
Map p302 (☑312-245-0909; www.cpdgolf.com; 3600 N Recreation Dr (Lake Shore Dr); ☐151) The nine-hole course enjoys sweeping views of the lake and skyline. It is very popular and in order to secure a tee time golfers cheerfully arrive at 5:30am. You can avoid that sort of lunacy by reserving in advance (either online or by phone; no extra fee). Fees are $25 to $28 in summer. You can also rent clubs here.

DIVERSEY-RIVER BOWL   BOWLING
(☑773-227-5800; www.drbowl.com; 2211 W Diversey Ave; lanes per hr $19-33; ☐76) It's nicknamed the 'rock 'n' bowl' for its late-night light show, fog machines and loud music.

WAVELAND BOWL   BOWLING
(☑773-472-5900; www.wavelandbowl.com; 3700 N Western Ave; per person per game $1-5; ⊙9am-1am Sun-Thu, to 3am Fri & Sat; MBrown Line to Addison, then bus 152) Waveland is another alley that fires up fog machine, flashy lights and rock music late at night.

RINK AT WRIGLEY   ICE SKATING
Map p302 (www.rinkatwrigley.com; cnr Clark St & Waveland Ave; ⊙2-8pm Mon-Fri, noon-10pm Sat, 10am-8pm Sun; MRed Line to Addison) The rink takes over the baseball stadium's parking lot in winter. There's an admission fee ($5 to $10) plus skate rental cost (another $5 to $10). Prices vary depending on time and day of the week.

Andersonville & Uptown

Neighborhood Top Five

1 Ambling along **Clark Street**, popping into funky shops by day and drinking and dining in gastronome taverns at night.

2 Listening to jazz and drinking martinis with Al Capone's ghost at the **Green Mill** (p134).

3 Slurping pho and bubble tea on **Argyle Street** (p128).

4 Watching 30 plays in 60 minutes from the offbeat **Neo-Futurists** (p135).

5 Exploring the dunes and magic hedge at **Montrose Beach** (p136).

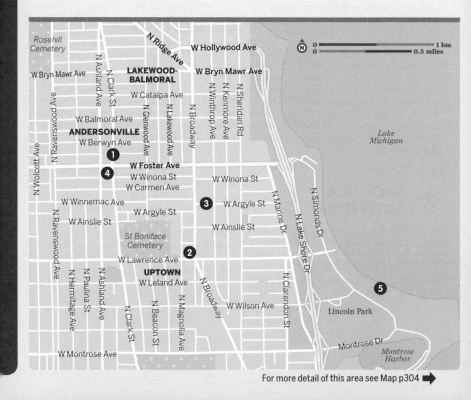

For more detail of this area see Map p304 ➡

Explore Andersonville & Uptown

These northern neighborhoods are good for a delicious browse. Andersonville is an old Swedish enclave centered on Clark St, where timeworn European-tinged business-es and bakeries mix with new foodie restaurants, funky boutiques, vintage shops and gay and lesbian bars. Places like the butter-lovin' Swedish Bakery carry on the legacy of the original inhabitants, but the residential streets are now home mostly to creative types, young professionals and folks who fly the rainbow flag.

Around the corner to the south, Uptown is a whole dif-ferent scene. Argyle St runs through the heart of 'Little Saigon,' filled with pho-serving restaurants and clatter-ing shops selling exotic goods from the homeland. Sever-al historic theaters cluster at N Broadway and Lawrence Ave, including Al Capone's favorite speakeasy, the Green Mill. It's still a timeless venue to hear jazz and to tipple.

Traditional sights are in short supply. You're in the neighborhoods to stroll and window-shop, eat and drink and maybe see a show. Begin in the afternoon and linger on through the night. Or make a full day of it by start-ing at Montrose Beach for surf and sand in the morning. Further north, Devon Ave – a wild mash-up of Indian, Pakistani, Russian and Jewish shops and restaurants – offers a worthy detour for those with more time.

Local Life

➜ **Solstice Party** In mid-June Andersonville harks back to its Swedish roots, and everyone gets together to dance around the maypole and eat lingonberries for Midsommerfest.

➜ **Saturday Salon** Local artists and journalists gather to discuss life on the Green Mill's stage for the Paper Machete (p135) every Saturday.

➜ **Dog Beach** When locals need to let Fido roam and splash, they unleash at Montrose Beach (p136). It is *the* four-legged scene.

Getting There & Away

➜ **El** Red Line to Berwyn (six blocks east of Clark St) for Andersonville. Red Line to Argyle for Argyle St; Red Line to Lawrence for trips to lower Uptown; Red Line to Sheridan for Graceland Cemetery and around.

➜ **Bus** Number 151 runs along Sheridan Rd; bus 22 travels on Clark St.

➜ **Car** Meter and on-street parking are available in Andersonville and Uptown, though it gets congested on weekends.

Lonely Planet's Top Tip

In addition to serving some of the neighborhood's best food, **Hopleaf** (p132) and **Acre** (p132) are fantastic beer bars. Stop in before dinner and enjoy a strong Trappist ale or an unusual microbrew. At Acre you can supplement with $1 oysters from 5pm to 7pm.

Best Places to Eat

➜ Hopleaf (p132)
➜ Big Jones (p133)
➜ Tiztal Cafe (p129)
➜ Tank Noodle (p133)
➜ Swedish Bakery (p129)

For reviews, see p129 ➜

Best Places to Drink

➜ Simon's (p134)
➜ Hamburger Mary's (p134)
➜ Big Chicks (p134)
➜ Crew (p134)
➜ SoFo Tap (p134)

For reviews, see p134 ➜

Best Places for Entertainment

➜ Green Mill (p134)
➜ Neo-Futurists (p135)
➜ Paper Machete (p135)
➜ Carol's Pub (p135)
➜ Black Ensemble Theater (p135)

For reviews, see p134 ➜

◉ SIGHTS

◉ Andersonville

SWEDISH AMERICAN MUSEUM
MUSEUM

Map p304 (☏773-728-8111; www.swedishameri
canmuseum.org; 5211 N Clark St; adult/child
$4/3; ◐10am-4pm Mon-Fri, 11am-4pm Sat & Sun;
Ⓜ Red Line to Berwyn) The permanent collection at this small storefront museum focuses on the lives of the Swedes who originally
settled Chicago. Check out the items people
felt were important to bring with them on
their journey to America; butter churns,
traditional bedroom furniture, religious
relics and more are included. The children's
section lets kids climb around on a steam-
ship and milk fake cows.

ROSEHILL CEMETERY
CEMETERY

(☏773-561-5940; 5800 N Ravenswood Ave;
◐8am-5pm Mon-Sat, 10am-4pm Sun; ☐84)
The entrance gate to Chicago's largest
cemetery is worth the trip alone. Designed
by WW Boyington, the entry looks like a
cross between high Gothic and low Disney. Inside you'll see the graves of plenty
of Chicago bigwigs, from Chicago mayors
and a US vice president to meat man Oscar
Mayer. You'll also find some of the weird-
est grave monuments in the city, including
a postal train and a huge carved boulder
from a Civil War battlefield in Georgia.
More than one ghost story started here;
keep an eye out for vapors as night falls.

LEATHER ARCHIVES & MUSEUM
MUSEUM

(☏773-761-9200; www.leatherarchives.org; 6418
N Greenview Ave; admission $10; ◐11am-7pm Thu
& Fri, to 5pm Sat & Sun; ☐22) Who knew? Ben
Franklin liked to be flogged, and Egypt's
Queen Hatshepsut had a foot fetish. The
museum reveals this and more in its dis-
plays of leather, fetish and S&M subcultures.
The on-site shop sells posters, pins and other
'pervertibles.' It's about 1.5 miles north of
Andersonville, straight up Clark St to Devon
Ave and then a few blocks east.

◉ Uptown

GRACELAND CEMETERY
CEMETERY

Map p304 (☏773-525-1105; www.graceland
cemetery.org; 4001 N Clark St; ◐8am-4:30pm;

Ⓜ Red Line to Sheridan) Graceland Cemetery
is the final resting place for some of the
biggest names in Chicago history, including architects Louis Sullivan and Ludwig
Mies van der Rohe and retail magnate Marshall Field. Most of the notable tombs lie
around the lake, in the northern half of the
121 acres. Pick up a map at the entrance to
navigate the swirl of streets.

Many of the memorials relate to the lives
of the dead in symbolic and touching ways:
National League founder William Hulbert
lies under a baseball; hotelier Dexter Graves
lies under a work titled Eternal Silence; and
George Pullman, the railroad car magnate
who sparked so much labor unrest, lies under a hidden fortress designed to prevent
angry union members from digging him up.

Daniel Burnham, who did so much to
design Chicago, gets his own island. Photographer Richard Nickel, who helped form
Chicago's budding preservation movement
and was killed during the demolition of
his beloved Chicago Stock Exchange Building, has a stone designed by admiring architects. Power couple Potter and Bertha
Palmer also have a doozy memorial.

ARGYLE STREET
STREET

Map p304 (btwn N Broadway & Sheridan Rd;
Ⓜ Red Line to Argyle) It's also known as 'Little Saigon.' Many residents came here as
refugees from the Vietnam War and subsequently filled the storefronts with pho-
serving lunch spots, bubble-tea-pouring
bakeries and shops with exotic goods from
the homeland. The pagoda-shaped Argyle
El station, painted in the auspicious colors
of green and red, puts you in the fishy-
smelling heart of it.

The area is great for a wander (even if it
looks a little scruffy). The businesses spill
out onto N Broadway as well.

ESSANAY STUDIOS
FILM LOCATION

Map p304 (1333-1345 W Argyle St; Ⓜ Red Line to
Argyle) Back before the talkies made silent
film obsolete, Chicago reigned supreme as
the number-one producer of movie magic in
the USA. Essanay churned out silent films
with soon-to-be household names such as
WC Fields and Charlie Chaplin. Filming
took place at the big studio that was here.
Essanay's terra-cotta Indian head logo remains above the door at 1345 Argyle.

These days, the building belongs to a local college. Essanay folded in 1917, about
the time that many of its actors were being

lured to the bright lights of a still-nascent Hollywood. If you see any of the early Essanay films, you'll notice local children performing unintentional cameos, and bits of familiar neighborhoods poking into the edge of 'Caifornia' mesas. It was an era when editing took a back seat to getting the product out the door and into theaters.

HUTCHINSON STREET
DISTRICT
ARCHITECTURE

(MRed Line to Sheridan) Homes here were built in the early 1900s and represent some of the best examples of Prairie School architecture in Chicago. Many residences – including the one at 839 Hutchinson St – are the work of George W Maher, a famous student of Frank Lloyd Wright. Also of note are 817 Hutchinson St and 4243 Hazel St.

In marked contrast to some of Uptown's seedier areas, the district is well-maintained and perfect for a genteel promenade.

EATING

Andersonville

TIZTAL CAFE
BREAKFAST $

Map p304 (4631 N Clark St; mains $7-10; 8am-4pm; 22) Everyone from hipsters nursing hangovers to moms nursing babies pile in to family-run Tiztal for brunch. The chorizo scrambles, gravy-slathered biscuits and country-fried steak are house favorites, along with oatmeal shakes and fresh fruit juices. There are only a dozen tables or so, but they turn over fast.

SWEDISH BAKERY
BAKERY $

Map p304 (773-561-8919; www.swedishbakery. com; 5348 N Clark St; pastries $1.50-4; 6:30am-6:30pm Mon-Fri, to 5pm Sat; ; MRed Line to Berwyn) Locals have been getting in line for custard-plumped eclairs, French silk tortes, chocolate-chip streusels and chocolate-drop butter cookies for more than 75 years. Free samples and coffee help ease the wait. Sometimes it has day-old goodies in stock that sell for half-price. Ask at the counter.

EDGEWATER LOUNGE
PUB $

Map p304 (5600 N Ashland Ave; mains $6-9; noon-2am Sun-Fri, to 3am Sat; 50) The Edgewater is an arty dive bar, rarely crowded, with standout sandwiches such

ARGYLE NIGHT MARKET

The **Argyle Night Market** (Map p304; cnr Broadway & Argyle Sts; 4-8pm Thu late Jun-early Sep; MRed Line to Argyle) offers a spread of street food from local eateries and free entertainment by neighborhood theater troupes and musicians. Oh, and you can buy produce, as well.

as the tangy sloppy joe, lime-marinated cod and grilled pork-loin medallion on rye. Rock-and-roll neighborhood types file in when they need a good, cheap meal with a side of good beer (Belgian, Czech and Midwest craft brews flow from the taps).

FIRST SLICE
CAFE $

Map p304 (www.firstslice.org; 5357 N Ashland Ave; mains $5-10; 10am-9pm Mon-Thu, 10am-10pm Fri, 9am-10pm Sat, 10am-8pm Sun; 50) First Slice not only serves made-from-scratch soups, salads, quiches, sandwiches and eight different flaky-crusted pies daily, but proceeds help supply needy families with fresh, healthy meals. So you're doing good by eating well.

SUNSHINE CAFE
JAPANESE $

Map p304 (773-334-6214; 5449 N Clark St; mains $9-11; 4-9pm Mon-Sat, noon-9pm Sun; MRed Line to Berwyn) Japanese comfort food fries in the pans at this humble storefront. *Gyoza* (dumplings), potato croquettes, *sakiyuki* (a sweet-savory noodle dish with thinly sliced beef and veggies) and *tonkatsu* (breaded pork) are among the most popular dishes. The laid-back staff can help you decide what to order if you're new to the non-sushi scene.

ICOSIUM KAFE
CREPERIE $

Map p304 (5200 N Clark St; crepes $6-10; 10am-9pm Mon-Fri, 8:30am-10pm Sat, 8:30am-9pm Sun; MRed Line to Berwyn) It's crepes galore at this exotic Algerian cafe. The signature dish comes in varieties both sweet (stuffed with figs, Nutella, Belgian chocolate or berries) and savory (stuffed with chicken, smoked salmon or escargot), alongside robust coffee.

KOPI, A TRAVELER'S CAFE
CAFE $

Map p304 (773-989-5674; 5317 N Clark St; mains $7-10; 8am-11pm Mon-Fri, from 9am Sat, from 10am Sun; ; MRed Line to Berwyn) Kopi wafts

LONELY PLANET / GETTY IMAGES ©

1. Swedish pastries (p129)
Enjoy a slice of Scandinavia in Andersonville, a former Swedish enclave.

2. Hindu trinkets, Devon Ave (p132)
Take a wander along this multicultural street, which offers a mash-up of Indian, Pakistani, Russian and Jewish shops and restaurants.

3. Swedish American Museum (p128)
Learn about the Swedes who originally settled Chicago.

4. Hopleaf (p132)
Savor mussels and *frites*, and take your pick from 200 beers.

WORTH A DETOUR

DEVON AVE

Known as Chicago's 'International Marketplace,' Devon Ave is where worlds collide – Indian, Pakistani, Georgian, Russian, Cuban, Hindu, Muslim, Orthodox Jewish – you name the ethnicity and someone from the group has set up a shop or eatery along the street. It's a fun destination for browsing.

Devon at Western Ave is the main intersection. Indian sari and jewelry shops start near 2600 W Devon; to the west they give way to Jewish and Islamic goods stores, while to the east they trickle out into a gaggle of electronics and dollar stores. It's a good place to stock up on low-cost cell phone necessities, luggage and other travel goods. Or just buy an armful of jangly bangles.

While you're here, you've got to stay for a meal. The best curry in the city simmers in Devon's aromatic restaurants. Vegetarians will find scads of options. Local favorites include the following:

Udupi Palace (☏773-338-2152; www.udupipalacechicago.net; 2543 W Devon Ave; mains $9-15; ⊙11:30am-9:30pm; ✐; ▣155) This bustling all-vegetarian South Indian restaurant serves toasty, kite-sized dosas (crepes made with rice and lentil flour) stuffed with all manner of vegetables and spices, along with an array of curries. The room gets loud once it packs with 20-something Anglo hipsters and a young Indian crowd.

Mysore Woodlands (☏773-338-8160; www.mysorewoodlands.com; 2548 W Devon Ave; mains $9-15; ⊙11am-9pm; ✐) It's another South Indian all-veg favorite, where friendly servers deliver well-spiced curries, dosas and iddlies (steamed rice-lentil patties) in the spacious low-lit room.

Sabri Nihari (☏773-465-3272; www.sabrinihari.com; 2502 W Devon Ave; mains $10-15; ⊙noon-midnight; ▣155) Fresh, fresh meat and vegetable dishes, distinctly seasoned, set this Pakistani place apart from its competitors on Devon. Try the 'frontier' chicken, which comes with a plate of freshly cut onions, tomatoes, cucumber and lemon, and enough perfectly cooked chicken for two. For dessert, check out the kheer, a creamy rice pudding.

Devon's epicenter is about 2.5 miles northwest of Andersonville. Take the Red Line to Loyola and transfer to bus 155, or take the Brown Line to Western and then transfer to bus 49B.

---

an Asian trekker-lodge vibe, from the pile of pillows to sit on by the front window to the bean-sprouty sandwiches, lefty clientele and flyer-filled community bulletin board. The little shop in back sells travel books and fair-trade global gifts. Wine goes down the hatch for half-price on Wednesdays.

★**HOPLEAF**   EUROPEAN $$
Map p304 (☏773-334-9851; www.hopleaf.com; 5148 N Clark St; mains $11-26; ⊙noon-11pm Mon-Thu, to midnight Fri & Sat, to 10pm Sun; Ⓜ Red Line to Berwyn) A cozy, European-style tavern, Hopleaf draws crowds for its Montreal-style smoked brisket, cashew-butter-and-fig-jam sandwich, uber-creamy macaroni and Stilton cheese, and the house-specialty *frites* and ale-soaked mussels. It also pours 200 types of brew (30 are on tap), emphasizing craft and Belgian suds.

In winter, a fireplace warms the jam-packed tables full of chattering locals. In summer, everyone heads to the umbrella-shaded patio in the herb garden.

ACRE   MODERN AMERICAN $$
Map p304 (☏773-334-7600; www.acrerestaurant. com; 5308 N Clark St; mains $13-23; ⊙5-10pm Mon-Thu, from 11:30am Fri, from 11am Sat & Sun; Ⓜ Red Line to Berwyn) ✐ Acre isn't doing anything unique with its farm-to-table rainbow trout and sugar snap peas, pork burger with house-cured bacon, and asparagus and mushroom risotto. But it does it well enough to be a neighborhood favorite. A fantastic beer selection flows from 25 taps. And the $1 oysters (from 5pm to 7pm, and after 9pm) may well be the best deal in town.

JIN JU
KOREAN $$

Map p304 (☎773-334-6377; www.jinjurestaurant.com; 5203 N Clark St; mains $12-20; ☺5-9:30pm Tue-Thu, to 11pm Fri & Sat, to 9:30pm Sun; ⓜRed Line to Berwyn) One of only a handful of nouveau Korean restaurants in town, Jin Ju throws a culinary curveball by tempering Korean food to Western tastes. The minimalist candlelit interior of Jin Ju echoes softly with downbeat techno, and the stylish 30-something clientele enjoys mains such as *haemul pajon* (a fried pancake stuffed with seafood) and *kalbi* (beef short ribs).

The drinks menu must is the 'soju tini', a cocktail made with *soju*, a Korean spirit distilled from sweet potatoes.

ANDIE'S
MEDITERRANEAN $$

Map p304 (☎773-784-8616; www.andiesres.com; 5253 N Clark St; mains $12-18; ☺11am-11pm Sun-Thu, to 12:30am Sat & Sun; ☑; ⓜRed Line to Berwyn) Reliable Andie's has anchored Andersonville's restaurant row from the get-go, and it still draws crowds for smooth hummus, dill rice and much more in the cool Mediterranean interior. Gluten-free pita bread arrives in place of regular pita if you ask. There's also a kids menu. Check online for coupons.

LEONARDO'S RESTAURANT
ITALIAN $$

(☎773-561-5028; 5657 N Clark St; mains $14-22; ☺5-10pm Tue-Thu, to 11pm Fri & Sat, to 10pm Sun; ⓜRed Line to Bryn Mawr) A sleek yet quaint atmosphere and delicious traditional Tuscan fare make this a fiercely guarded neighborhood favorite. The champion of the menu is the 18 Hour Ravioli, stuffed with a mouthwatering combination of braised osso bucco and goat cheese, covered in caramelized pearl onions, sage and a succulent demiglace. A whole boneless chicken tops the meat mains.

BIG JONES
AMERICAN $$$

Map p304 (☎773-275-5725; www.bigjoneschicago.com; 5347 N Clark St; mains $17-26; ☺11am-9pm Mon-Thu, to 10pm Fri, from 9am Sat & Sun; ⓜRed Line to Berwyn) Warm, sunny Big Jones puts 'southern heirloom cooking' on the menu, mixing dishes from New Orleans, the Carolina Lowcountry and Appalachia. Choosing among chicken and dumplings, crawfish etouffee and reezy-peezy (vegetables, rice and red pea gravy) is no easy task. The decadent, biscuit-laden brunch draws the biggest crowds. It's best to reserve in advance.

✕ Uptown

BA LE BAKERY
VIETNAMESE $

Map p304 (☎773-561-4424; www.balesandwich.com; 5014 N Broadway; sandwiches $6-9; ☺7:30am-9pm; ⓜRed Line to Argyle) Ba Le serves Saigon-style *banh mi* sandwiches, with steamed pork, shrimp cakes or meatballs on fresh baguettes made right here. The futuristic digs offer several tables to eat at.

TWEET
AMERICAN $$

Map p304 (www.tweet.biz; 5020 N Sheridan Rd; mains $7-12; ☺9am-3pm; ☏; ⓜRed Line to Argyle) ☍ The reimagined breakfast standards are made by former Charlie Trotter's chefs at this cozy morning spot. The Havarti omelet folds in green apple slices and the namesake cheese. The 'Country Benedict' adds two poached eggs and a thick slab of sausage alongside biscuits and gravy for a decadent opening meal. For something lighter, try the organic buckwheat pancakes. Cash only.

TANK NOODLE
VIETNAMESE $$

Map p304 (☎773-878-2253; www.tank-noodle.com; 4953 N Broadway; mains $8-14; ☺8:30am-10pm Mon, Tue & Thu-Sat, to 9pm Sun; ⓜRed Line to Argyle) The official name of this spacious utilitarian eatery is Pho Xe Tang, but everyone just calls it Tank Noodle. The crowds come for *banh mi*, served on crunchy fresh baguette rolls, and the *pho*, which is widely regarded as the city's best. The 200-plus-item menu sprawls on from there and includes *banh xeo* (crispy pancakes), catfish and squid dishes, and a rainbow array of bubble teas.

THAI PASTRY
THAI $$

Map p304 (☎773-784-5399; www.thaipastry.com; 4925 N Broadway; mains $8-14; ☺11am-10pm Sun-Thu, to 11pm Fri & Sat; ⓜRed Line to Argyle) A lunchtime favorite with workers from both Uptown and Andersonville, this Thai restaurant has a window filled with accolades and awards, and the food to back it up. The pad thai is excellent, and the spot-on curries arrive still simmering in a clay pot. For a quick, cheap snack, visit the counter for a baked pastry.

HAI YEN
VIETNAMESE $$

Map p304 (☎773-561-4077; www.haiyenrestaurant.com; 1055 W Argyle St; mains $9-14;

⊙10:30am-10pm Mon, Tue,Thu & Fri, from 9:30am Sat & Sun; Ⓜ️Red Line to Argyle) Many of the dishes at this warm Argyle St eatery require some assembly, pairing shrimp, beef or squid with rice crepes, mint, Thai basil and lettuce. For an appetizer, try the *goi cuon*, fresh rolls of vermicelli rice noodles along with shrimp, pork and carrots. The *bo bay mon* consists of seven (yes, seven) different kinds of beef.

Order sparingly, or ask for some help from your server – like the *bo bay mon*, many of the dishes are large enough to feed an army.

🍷 DRINKING & NIGHTLIFE

SIMON'S BAR
Map p304 (☎773-878-0894; 5210 N Clark St; ⊙from 11am; Ⓜ️Red Line to Berwyn) An Andersonville mainstay that has been around since 1934, Simon's is a dimly lit musicians' watering hole. The jukebox rocks an eclectic menu ranging from Robert Gordon to Elastica to Television to The Clash. In winter, in homage to its Swedish roots, Simon's serves *glogg* (spiced wine punch). A giant neon fish holding a martini glass marks the spot.

HAMBURGER MARY'S BAR
Map p304 (www.hamburgermarys.com/chicago; 5400 N Clark St; ⊙from 11:30am Mon-Fri, from 10:30am Sat & Sun; Ⓜ️Red Line to Berwyn) This is Chicago's outpost of the campy San Francisco–based chain that bills itself as an 'open-air bar and grill for open-minded people.' Yes, it serves well-regarded burgers and weekend brunch in the downstairs restaurant, but the action's on the rowdy, booze-soaked patio. Mary's Rec Room next door brews its own beer and turns on the HDTVs for sports fans. The Attic lounge upstairs hosts cabaret, karaoke and DJs.

BIG CHICKS BAR
Map p304 (www.bigchicks.com; 5024 N Sheridan Rd; ⊙from 4pm Mon-Fri, from 9am Sat, from 10am Sun; 🎱; Ⓜ️Red Line to Argyle) Uptown's Big Chicks has an enjoyable split personality. During the week, the bar is a cozily sedate place for gay and straight to socialize beneath the sizable collection of woman-themed art. On weekends, though, gay men pack the stamp-sized dance floor and boog-

ie until all hours. Every summer Sunday, the bar hosts a free barbecue from 4pm to 6pm.

CREW GAY
Map p304 (www.worldsgreatestbar.com; 4804 N Broadway; ⊙11:30am-late; Ⓜ️Red Line to Lawrence) Sporty Crew offers a change from the usual scene, with good microbrews and 21 hi-def TVs tuned to all the big games. Weekly trivia and karaoke nights slip into the schedule, as does the occasional underwear contest.

ATMOSPHERE GAY
Map p304 (www.atmospherebar.com; 5355 N Clark St; ⊙6pm-late Tue-Fri, from 3pm Sat & Sun; Ⓜ️Red Line to Berwyn) The good-looking boys have a lot of action to choose from at @mosphere: Bored Gaymes on Tuesday (cards, Scrabble) and especially the male go-go dancers Thursday through Sunday. DJs and drag revues also entertain, and there's never a cover charge.

SOFO TAP GAY
Map p304 (www.thesofotap.com; 4923 N Clark St; ⊙5pm-late Mon-Thu, from 3pm Fri, from noon Sat & Sun; Ⓜ️Red Line to Argyle) SoFo is a normal neighborhood bar with a sweet dog-friendly patio. Then again, it also hosts Tuesday night bingo emceed by a drag-queen nun. And if you happen in on Friday night, the vast majority of the male crowd will be shirtless for 'bear' night.

TOUCHE GAY
(www.touchechicago.com; 6412 N Clark St; ⊙5pm-4am Mon-Fri, from 3pm Sat, from noon Sun; 🚌22) Touche caters to the hard-core leather crowd. It's about 1.5 miles north of Andersonville via Clark St, located a few blocks from the Leather Archives & Museum.

☆ ENTERTAINMENT

★GREEN MILL JAZZ
Map p304 (www.greenmilljazz.com; 4802 N Broadway; cover charge $5-15; ⊙noon-4am Mon-Sat, from 11am Sun; Ⓜ️Red Line to Lawrence) The timeless Green Mill earned its notoriety as Al Capone's favorite speakeasy (the tunnels where he hid the booze are still underneath the bar). Sit in one of the curved leather booths and feel his ghost urging you on to another martini. Local and national jazz

artists perform nightly; Sundays also host the nationally acclaimed poetry slam.

NEO-FUTURISTS   THEATER

Map p304 (☑773-275-5255; www.neofuturists.org; 5153 N Ashland Ave; Ⓜ Red Line to Berwyn) The theater is best known for its long-running *Too Much Light Makes the Baby Go Blind*, in which the hyper troupe makes a manic attempt to perform 30 plays in 60 minutes. It runs Friday and Saturday at 11:30pm and Sunday at 7pm. Admission cost is based on a dice throw.

The group puts on plenty of other original works that'll make you ponder and laugh simultaneously. Well worth the northward trek.

PAPER MACHETE   LITERARY

Map p304 (☑773-227-4433; www.thepapermacheteshow.com; 4802 N Broadway; ◎3pm Sat; Ⓜ Brown Line to Western) FREE Poets, musicians, journalists, playwrights, comedians and the occasional trash-talking puppet get together for this weekly 'live magazine' discussing culture, politics and wit. It's held at the Green Mill jazz club at 3pm Saturday.

CAROL'S PUB   LIVE MUSIC

Map p304 (☑773-334-2402; 4659 N Clark St; ▣22) The closest thing Chicago has to a honky-tonk, Carol's Pub offers (at times ironic) boot-stompin', Bud-drinkin' good times to patrons, who come out on weekends to dance like crazy to the house country band.

BLACK ENSEMBLE THEATER   THEATER

Map p304 (☑773-769-4451; www.blackensembletheater.org; 4450 N Clark St; Ⓜ Brown Line to Montrose) This well-established group saw its fledgling production of *The Jackie Wilson Story* attract wide attention and national tours. The focus here has long been on original productions about the African American experience through mostly historical, biographical scripts.

🛍 SHOPPING

WOMEN & CHILDREN FIRST   BOOKS

Map p304 (☑773-769-9299; www.womenandchildrenfirst.com; 5233 N Clark St; ◎11am-7pm Mon & Tue, 11am-9pm Wed-Fri, 10am-7pm Sat, 11am-6pm Sun; 🖶; Ⓜ Red Line to Berwyn) A feminist mainstay, this independent bookstore has been around for over 30 years. Book signings and author events happen most weeks at this welcoming shop, which features fiction and nonfiction by and about women, along with children's books.

ALAMO SHOES   SHOES

Map p304 (☑773-784-8936; www.alamoshoes.com; 5321 N Clark St; ◎9am-8pm Mon-Fri, to 6pm Sat, 10am-6pm Sun; Ⓜ Red Line to Berwyn) This throwback to the 1960s focuses on hip, comfortable shoes for men, women and children. Brands include Dansko, Ecco, Naot, Birkenstock, Keen and Dr Martens, all at good prices. The enthusiastic staffers hop off to the back room and emerge with stacks of boxes until you either find what you want or are entirely walled in by the possibilities.

SCOUT   HOMEWARES

Map p304 (www.scoutchicago.com; 5221 N Clark St; ◎11am-6pm Tue, Wed & Sun, noon-7pm Thu & Fri, noon-5pm Sun; Ⓜ Red Line to Berwyn) With groovy displays of retro tables, chairs, dishware and outdoor gear set up in little scenes throughout the rooms, the owners of this 'urban antique shop' make it difficult to keep your money in your wallet. The classic pieces are all in good repair.

ANDERSONVILLE GALLERIA   ARTS & CRAFTS

Map p304 (☑773-878-8570; www.andersonvillegalleria.com; 5247 N Clark St; ◎11am-7pm Tue-Sat, to 6pm Sun; Ⓜ Red Line to Berwyn) Ninety indie vendors sell their fair-trade and locally made artisan wares in mini-boutiques spread over three floors. Sweets, coffee, clothing, handbags, paintings, photography,

LOCAL KNOWLEDGE

UPTOWN POETRY SLAM

The long-running **Uptown Poetry Slam** (Map p304; www.greenmilljazz.com; 4802 N Broadway; ◎7-11pm Sun; Ⓜ Red Line to Lawrence) birthed the 'performance poetry' genre, and it's still going strong every Sunday night at the Green Mill. Founder Marc Smith continues to host the rollicking event. Watch shaky first-timers take the mic from 7pm to 8pm, then a featured guest raps verse for an hour afterward, and then the slam competition begins in earnest at 9pm. Get your finger snaps ready. There's a $7 cover charge.

ANDERSONVILLE & UPTOWN SHOPPING

jewelry – it's a smorgasbord of cool, crafty goods in a community-oriented marketplace. Support the little guy!

EARLY TO BED EROTICA

Map p304 (📞773-271-1219; www.early2bed.com; 5232 N Sheridan Rd; ⊙noon-7pm Mon & Tue, to 8pm Wed-Sat, to 6pm Sun; Ⓜ Red Line to Berwyn) This low-key, women-owned sex shop is good for novices: it provides explanatory pages and customer reviews throughout the store, so you'll be able to know your anal beads from cock rings from bullet vibes. Also on hand are feather boas, bondage tapes and vegan condoms (made with casein-free latex; casein is a milk-derived product usually used in latex production).

Videos and books round out the offerings – the latter include serious resources such as sex manuals for rape victims.

🏃 SPORTS & ACTIVITIES

MONTROSE BEACH BEACH

(www.cpdbeaches.com; 4400 N Lake Shore Dr; 🚌146) Montrose is one of the city's best beaches. You can rent kayaks, stand-up paddleboards and jet skis. Sometimes you'll see surfers and kitesurfers, and anglers frequently cast here. Sailboats glide in the harbor. The Dock bar and grill provides waterside snacks. A wide, dog-friendly

THE MAGIC HEDGE

The Montrose Point Bird Sanctuary – more commonly known as 'The Magic Hedge' – lies at the southeast edge of Montrose Beach. The bushy area is an important stopover point for migratory birds. More than 300 species have been spotted here, everything from white-crowned sparrows to roosting owls and red-throated loons.

To find the feathery oasis, follow Montrose Ave toward the beach. Take a right at the street by the bait shop, then follow the 'hedge' signs.

beach with a curving breakwater abuts the main beach to the north.

KAYAK CHICAGO KAYAKING

(📞630-336-7245; www.kayakchicago.com; 4400 N Lake Shore Dr; ⊙10am-7pm Wed-Sun; 🚌146) This group rents kayaks and stand-up paddleboards for $20 per hour or $80 per day. Staff also provide lessons. Located in the southeast corner of Montrose Beach.

WILSON SKATE PARK SKATEBOARDING

(cnr W Wilson Ave & N Lake Shore Dr; 🚌146) **FREE** Watch the kids kick-turn and heel-flip at this free facility by Montrose Beach's northern edge.

Wicker Park, Bucktown & Ukrainian Village

Neighborhood Top Five

1 Trawling for treasures – an old Devo record, a vintage pillbox hat, steel-toed boots, a mustache disguise kit – in the shops along **Milwaukee Ave**.

2 Hearing an alt-country band at the **Hideout** (p148).

3 Squeezing into the **Matchbox** (p148) for a gimlet.

4 Digging into a flaky 'flight' at **Hoosier Mama Pie Company** (p145).

5 Perusing the zines at **Quimby's** (p149).

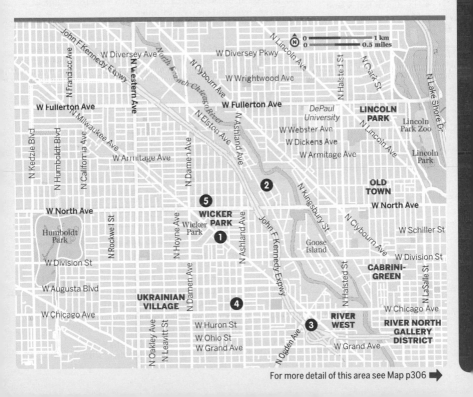

For more detail of this area see Map p306 ➡

Lonely Planet's Top Tip

In summer the neighborhood throws excellent street festivals with big-name bands. Watch for **Do Division** (www.do-division streetfest.com) in early June; **Green Music Fest** (www.greenmusicfest chicago.com) in late June; **West Fest** (www.westfest chicago.com) in mid-July; and the **Hideout Block Party** (www.hideout chicago.com) – the best of the bunch – in early September.

✗ Best Places to Eat

➜ Ruxbin (p146)

➜ Big Star Taqueria (p142)

➜ Irazu (p143)

➜ Handlebar Bar & Grill (p144)

➜ Hoosier Mama Pie Company (p145)

For reviews, see p142 ➜

☐ Best Places to Drink

➜ Matchbox (p148)

➜ Danny's (p146)

➜ Map Room (p146)

➜ Violet Hour (p146)

➜ Bluebird (p147)

For reviews, see p146 ➜

☐ Best Places to Shop

➜ Quimby's (p149)

➜ Dusty Groove (p150)

➜ Una Mae's Freak Boutique (p150)

➜ US #1 (p150)

➜ Reckless Records (p150)

For reviews, see p149 ➜

Explore: Wicker Park, Bucktown & Ukrainian Village

For a taste of artsy young Chicago, wander up Milwaukee Ave near Damen Ave in Wicker Park on a Friday night. You'll pass booming bars, packed restaurants and stages hosting indie rock on one side of the street and shushed underground author readings on the other. By Saturday morning the scene shifts to the dozens of vintage stores, record shops and brunch spots. Buttressed by the slightly fancier Bucktown and slightly scruffier Ukrainian Village, this neighborhood has a lot happening, so strap on some comfortable (hip) sneakers and take it block by block.

Working-class Central and Eastern European immigrants arrived in the late 1800s to work in the factories and breweries that used to be prevalent in the area. Although signs of the community's past are fading fast, there are plenty of traces of the immigrants who founded it, especially in the western reaches of Ukrainian Village. A stroll here will take you past Ukrainian scrawl on shop windows, Orthodox churches and proud, if humble, corner taverns where immigrants have long quenched their thirst.

Milwaukee, North and Damen Aves are the main veins through the neighborhood. Division St is also chockablock. Once a polka-bar-lined thoroughfare known as the 'Polish Broadway,' it's now stuffed with the requisite burger bars and crafty boutiques.

The neighborhood holds very few sights, but you could easily while away the day shopping and the night eating and drinking. And it's definitely Chicago's best 'hood for rock clubs, with the Hideout, Double Door and Empty Bottle leading cool-cat pack.

Local Life

➜ **Weenie Time** At the Vienna Beef Factory Store & Cafe (p143), workers eat franks while discussing last night's baseball game and thumbing through copies of the *Sun-Times* strewn around the room.

➜ **Bar Crafts** The Handmade Market (p152) brings out the crafting community to the Empty Bottle each month.

➜ **Fashion Zone** Several local women's designers have boutiques on Damen Ave as you head north from North Ave.

Getting There & Away

➜ **El** Blue Line to Damen for Bucktown and northern Wicker Park; Blue Line to Division for southern Wicker Park; Blue Line to Chicago for Ukrainian Village.

➜ **Bus** Number 50 runs up Damen Ave; bus 72 runs along North Ave; bus 70 travels along Division St.

➜ **Car** Meter and free on-street parking are at a premium in Wicker Park and Bucktown; they're more available in Ukrainian Village.

👁 SIGHTS

👁 Wicker Park & Bucktown

WICKER PARK   PARK
Map p306 (btwn N Damen Ave, W Schiller St & N Wicker Park Ave; MBlue Line to Damen) Sure, Chicago invented the zipper and Twinkie, but the city's true legacy is a strange softball game invented here almost a century ago. Aptly named, 16-Inch Softball uses the same rules as normal softball, but with shorter games, a bigger, squishier ball and no gloves or mitts on the fielders. Wicker Park is a prime place to see this unique sport in action. And for travelers suffering withdrawal from the pooch left at home, Wicker Park's dog park is a great way to get in some quality canine time.

NELSON ALGREN'S HOUSE   HISTORIC SITE
Map p306 (1958 W Evergreen Ave; MBlue Line to Damen) You can't go inside, but on the 3rd floor of this apartment building, writer Nelson Algren created some of his greatest works about life in the once down-and-out neighborhood. He won the 1950 National Book Award for his novel *The Man with the Golden Arm,* about a drug addict hustling on Division St near Milwaukee Ave (a half-mile southeast).

Other insights Algren picked up in the 'hood: 'Never play cards with a man called Doc. Never eat at a place called Mom's. Never sleep with a woman whose troubles are worse than your own' – classic advice he relayed in *A Walk on the Wild Side.* His short *Chicago: City on the Make* summarizes 120 years of thorny local history and is the definitive read on the city's character.

POLISH MUSEUM OF AMERICA   MUSEUM
Map p306 (✆773-384-3352; www.polishmuseumofamerica.org; 984 N Milwaukee Ave; admission $7; ⊙11am-4pm, closed Thu; MBlue Line to Division) If you don't know Pulaski from a pierogi, this is the place to get the scoop on Polish culture. It's one of the oldest ethnic museums in the country, crammed with traditional Polish costumes, WWII artifacts, ship models and folk art pieces. Head up to the 2nd floor and ring the doorbell to get buzzed in.

The curator can give you a personalized tour, since you'll likely be the only one here. It's a fine opportunity to learn about the Poles who helped shape Chicago, which has one of the world's largest Polish communities. (Casimir Pulaski, by the way, was a Polish hero in the American Revolution who was known as the 'father of the American cavalry' and the guy who saved George Washington's life at the Battle of Brandywine; a pierogi, meanwhile, is a Polish dumpling.)

👁 Ukrainian Village

UKRAINIAN INSTITUTE OF MODERN ART   MUSEUM
Map p306 (✆773-227-5522; www.uima-chicago.org; 2320 W Chicago Ave; ⊙noon-4pm Wed-Sun;

LOCAL KNOWLEDGE

WICKER PARK & UKIE VILLAGE GALLERIES

These neighborhoods are great places to seek out emerging talent. Several artists live and work in the landmark **Flat Iron Building** (Map p306; www.flatironartsgroup.com; 1579 N Milwaukee Ave; MBlue Line to Damen) and host a monthly First Friday open house, which also offers reasonably priced art for purchase. Keep an eye on telephone poles around the area for flyers detailing the latest shows and open-houses in the 'hood. Other good art museums:

Intuit: the Center for Intuitive and Outsider Art (Map p306; www.art.org; 756 N Milwaukee Ave; admission $5; ⊙11am-6pm Tue-Sat, to 7:30pm Thu; MBlue Line to Chicago) Behold the museum-like collection of folk art, including watercolors by famed local Henry Darger. In fact, Intuit has recreated his studio, complete with comic books and welded-can sculptures.

Monique Meloche Gallery (Map p306; www.moniquemeloche.com; 2154 W Division St; ⊙11am-6pm Tue-Sat; MBlue Line to Division) One of Chicago's tastemakers, it features provocative paintings, neon and mixed media. If nothing else, have a look at the 'wall' that shows works through huge windows to engage passersby on Division St.

CHARLES COOK / GETTY IMAGES ©

1. Danny's (p146)
Pop in for a relaxed early evening drink, or boogie at an impromptu dance party on the weekend.

2. North Ave, Wicker Park (p142)
Enjoy the food and nightlife scenes on this bustling commercial street.

3. Flat Iron Building (p139)
Sniff out the talent at the monthly First Friday open houses, where resident artists' works are for sale.

4. Myopic Books (p150)
Trawl three floors of used books, with a coffee hit in between.

CHARLES COOK / GETTY IMAGES ©

CHURCHES OF UKRAINIAN VILLAGE

Take a minute to wander by these beauties, whose majestic domes pop out over the neighborhood's treetops:

St Nicholas Ukrainian Catholic Cathedral (Map p306; 773-276-4537; www.st-nicholaschicago.org; 2238 W Rice St; 66) The less traditional of the main churches. Its 13 domes represent Christ and the Apostles. The intricate mosaics – added to the 1915 building in 1988 – owe their inspiration to the Cathedral of St Sophia in Kiev.

Saints Volodymyr & Olha Church (Map p306; 312-829-5209; www.stsvo.org; 739 N Oakley Blvd; 66) Was founded by traditionalists from St Nicholas, who broke away over liturgical differences and built this showy church in 1975. It makes up for its paucity of domes (only five) with a massive mosaic of the conversion of Grand Duke Vladimir of Kiev to Christianity in AD 988.

Holy Trinity Russian Orthodox Cathedral (Map p306; 773-486-6064; www.holytrinitycathedral.net; 1121 N Leavitt St; 70) Looks like it was scooped straight out of the Russian countryside and deposited here. But famed Chicago architect Louis Sullivan actually designed the 1903 stunner and its octagonal dome, front bell tower, and stucco and wood-framed exterior. Czar Nicholas II helped fund the structure, which is now a city landmark. Cathedral staff give tours of the gilded interior by appointment on weekdays.

66) **FREE** Step into the bright white storefront and make a choice. To the right is the permanent collection of mod, colorful paintings and sculpture (which rotates a few times per year). To the left are the playful and provocative temporary exhibits, done in various media. While most artists are Ukrainian, plenty of other locals get shelf space, too.

The small galleries make for a quick and easy browse. Afterward, keep the Ukrainian theme going by checking out the resplendent churches nearby.

Wicker Park & Bucktown

BIG STAR TAQUERIA MEXICAN $
Map p306 (www.bigstarchicago.com; 1531 N Damen Ave; tacos $3-4; 11:30am-2am; Blue Line to Damen) Once a filling station, now a taco-serving honky-tonk bar helmed by a big-name Chicago chef (Paul Kahan). So goes gentrification in Wicker Park. The place gets packed, but damn, those tacos are worth the wait – pork belly in tomato-guajillo chili sauce and lamb shoulder with *queso fresco* (creamy white cheese) accompany the specialty whiskey list.

If the table-studded patio is too crowded, order from the walk-up window. Cash only.

SULTAN'S MARKET MIDDLE EASTERN $
Map p306 (773-235-3072; www.chicagofalafel.com; 2057 W North Ave; mains $4-9; 10am-10pm Mon-Sat, to 9pm Sun; ; Blue Line to Damen) Steps from the Blue Line, this Middle Eastern spot is a neighborhood favorite with meat-free delights such as falafel sandwiches, spinach pies and a sizable salad bar. Carnivores can come in, too; many swear by the chicken shawarma.

PODHALANKA POLISH $
Map p306 (773-486-6655; 1549 W Division St; mains $5-10; 9am-8pm Mon-Sat, 10am-7pm Sun; Blue Line to Division) Since you're in the middle of the old 'Polish Broadway' area, why not eat like they did in the old days? This hole-in-the-wall holdover from the era serves up massive portions of potato pancakes, pierogi, dill-flecked borscht and other Polish fare on red vinyl seats as Pope JP2 stares from the wall.

BELLY SHACK FUSION $
Map p306 (www.bellyshack.com; 1912 N Western Ave; mains $9; 11:30am-9pm Tue-Thu & Sun, to 10pm Fri & Sat; Blue Line to Western) It may have a wee menu and an impersonal, industrial-metallic ambience. But that hasn't stopped Belly Shack from receiving a Michelin Bib Gourmand award (bestowed upon great food for great value). The chefs

meld their Korean and Puerto Rican heritages in fat-flavored sandwiches such as the Boricua, a take on the jibarito, with tofu, chicken or beef kissed by hoisin sauce in plantain 'bread.'

LETIZIA'S NATURAL BAKERY   BAKERY $

Map p306 (☑773-342-1011; www.superyummy.com; 2144 W Division St; sandwiches $6-8, pizzas from $20; ⊗6am-7pm Mon-Sat, from 7am Sun; ☎; Ⓜ Blue Line to Division) Early risers can get their fix of fantastic baked goods here starting at 6am, and everyone else can swing by at a more reasonable hour for Letizia's crunchy, toasty panini, slices of gourmet pizza and cups of mind-expanding coffee. The patio with plush seats wins kudos in summer.

VIENNA BEEF FACTORY
STORE & CAFE   AMERICAN $

(☑773-435-2277; www.viennabeef.com; 2501 N Damen Ave; mains $3-6; ⊗6am-4pm Mon-Fri, 10am-3pm Sat; ☐50) A true Chicago hot dog uses a Vienna Beef weenie, and this factory is where they're made. There's no better place to indulge than right at the source, in the employee cafeteria. Grab a tray, go through the line, then join hair-netted workers at the tables. The shop in front sells well-priced cases of franks, as well as superb meaty T-shirts, posters and condiments.

MARGIE'S   DESSERT $

Map p306 (☑773-384-1035; www.margiesfinecandies.com; 1960 N Western Ave; mains $4-8; ⊗9am-midnight; ☀; Ⓜ Blue Line to Western) Margie's has held court at Bucktown's edge for over 90 years, dipping ice-cream sundaes for everyone from Al Capone to the Beatles (check the wall photos). Sure, you can admire the marble soda fountain and the booths with mini-jukeboxes. But the star is the hot fudge, unbelievably thick, rich and bountiful, served in its own silver pot. Burgers and sandwiches are just clumsy foreplay to the 50 massive sundaes on offer.

MILK & HONEY   CAFE $

Map p306 (☑773-395-9434; www.milkandhoneycafe.com; 1920 W Division St; mains $7-9; ⊗7am-4pm Mon-Fri, 8am-5pm Sat, to 4pm Sun; Ⓜ Blue Line to Division) A bright, stylish cafe, Milk & Honey has become the hangout du jour for discerning neighborhood socialites. The orange brioche French toast rocks the breakfast menu, while the

thick-cut bacon, lettuce and tomato sandwich and crab-cake baguette please the lunch crowd. The fireplace and small list of beer and wine soothe when the weather blows.

ALLIANCE BAKERY   BAKERY $

Map p306 (☑773-278-0366; www.alliance-bakery.com; 1736 W Division St; items $2-5; ⊗6am-9pm Mon-Sat, from 7am Sun; ☎; Ⓜ Blue Line to Division) Order your macaroons, red-velvet cupcakes and other creamy-frosted goodies in the bakery, then take them to the 'lounge' next door (or out to the sidewalk tables) and make like a local by hanging out, reading or tap-tap-tapping on your laptop using the free wi-fi.

LAZO'S TACOS   MEXICAN $

Map p306 (☑773-486-3303; www.lazostacos.com; 2009 N Western Ave; mains $4-11; ⊗24hr; Ⓜ Blue Line to Western) The quintessential taco stop after a long night of drinking.

★ IRAZU   LATIN AMERICAN $$

Map p306 (☑773-252-5687; www.irazuchicago.com; 1865 N Milwaukee Ave; mains $9-14; ⊗11:30am-9:30pm Mon-Sat; Ⓜ Blue Line to Western) Chicago's unassuming lone Costa Rican eatery turns out burritos bursting with chicken, black beans and fresh avocado, and sandwiches dressed in a heavenly, spicy-sweet vegetable sauce. Wash them down with an *avena* (a slurpable oatmeal milkshake). For breakfast, the *arroz con huevos* (peppery eggs scrambled into rice)

LOCAL KNOWLEDGE

SOUP AND BREAD DINNERS

The Hideout hosts a groovy dinner series at 5:30pm Wednesdays. From January to mid-April, **Soup and Bread** (www.soupandbread.net) offers a free meal of – yes – homemade soup and bread. Local foodies, musicians and artists take turns making the wares. Donations are collected and go to local food banks.

From late June until early September, the action morphs into a cookout and Veggie Bingo. You pay a few bucks to play, and winners receive organic produce as prizes. Proceeds support community gardens.

The jolly shindigs attract a big crowd, so don't be late.

WICKER PARK, BUCKTOWN & UKRAINIAN VILLAGE EATING

relieves hangovers. Irazu is BYO with no corkage fee. Cash only.

HANDLEBAR BAR & GRILL   INTERNATIONAL $$

Map p306 (☎773-384-9546; www.handlebar-chicago.com; 2311 W North Ave; mains $9-14; ◷10am-midnight Mon-Thu, to 2am Fri & Sat, to 11pm Sun; ☍; Ⓜ︎Blue Line to Damen) The cult of the bike messenger runs strong in Chicago, and this restaurant-bar is a way station for tattooed couriers and locals who come for the strong, microbrew-centric beer list, vegetarian-friendly food (including West African groundnut stew and tofu fajitas) and festive back beer garden.

PIECE   PIZZERIA $$

Map p306 (☎773-772-4422; www.piecechicago.com; 1927 W North Ave; small pizzas from $12; ◷11am-10:30pm Mon-Thu, to 12:30am Fri & Sat, to 10pm Sun; Ⓜ︎Blue Line to Damen) The thin flour-dusted crust of 'New Haven–style' pizza at this spacious Wicker Park microbrewery offers a welcome reprieve from the city's omnipresent deep-dish version. The best is the white variety – a sauceless pie dressed simply in olive oil, garlic and mozzarella – which makes a clean pairing with brewer Jon Cutler's award-winning beer.

The easygoing, sky-lit ambience changes after dark, when ball games beam down from ubiquitous flat screens, an occasional band plugs in, and the 30-something patrons get a bit more boisterous.

SCHWA   MODERN AMERICAN $$$

Map p306 (☎773-252-1466; www.schwarestaurant.com; 1466 N Ashland Ave; 9-course menu $110; ◷5:30-9:30pm Tue-Sat; Ⓜ︎Blue Line to Division) The fact that chef Michael Carlson worked at Alinea is apparent in his avant-garde, nine-course menu that redefines American comfort food via such dishes as apple-pie soup. The setup is progressive, too, with chefs also acting as servers. The intimate room is bookended by black wood floors and has a mirrored ceiling. Make reservations well in advance.

TRENCHERMAN   MODERN AMERICAN $$$

Map p306 (☎773-661-1540; www.trenchermen.com; 2039 W North Ave; mains $21-28; ◷5:30-10pm Mon-Thu, to 11pm Fri & Sat, 6-9pm Sun, 10am-2pm Sat & Sun; Ⓜ︎Blue Line to Damen) Trencherman defies easy description. Imagine steam-punk decor set in an old Turkish bathhouse. Imagine unconventional flavor mash-ups such as chocolate-cured ham, chai tofu ice cream and pickle tots (the tangy love child of fried pickles and tater tots). It's bizarre, playful, exotic, inspired – you'll think of more adjectives after tipping back one of the divine cocktails (or two).

HOT CHOCOLATE   AMERICAN $$$

Map p306 (☎773-489-1747; www.hotchocolate-chicago.com; 1747 N Damen Ave; mains $15-26; ◷11:30am-2pm Wed-Fri, from 10am Sat & Sun, 5:30-late Tue-Sun; Ⓜ︎Blue Line to Damen) ☍ 'Come for dessert, stay for dinner' might be the motto at this mod Bucktown restaurant helmed by renowned pastry chef Mindy Segal. With six rich kinds of hot chocolate available (they're like dipping your mug into Willy Wonka's chocolate river), along with mini brioche doughnuts, you may forget to order the other food on offer.

The sustainably sourced entrées – say, buffalo milk ricotta crepes or a lamb sausage sandwich – change often.

KENDALL COLLEGE DINING ROOM   MODERN AMERICAN $$$

Map p306 (☎312-752-2328; www.kendall.edu; 900 N North Branch St; 3-course menu lunch/dinner $18/29; ◷hours vary; ☐8, Ⓜ︎Blue Line to Grand) The School of Culinary Arts at Kendall College has turned out a host of local cooking luminaries and this classy space with river and skyline views is where they honed their skills. Students prepare and serve inventive contemporary American dishes, with forays into French and international fusion styles, all of which come with white-glove service at fantastic value.

Call ahead for reservations (and note the hours vary depending on the school term schedule). It's located on Goose Island, west of the Gold Coast, near where Chicago Ave meets Halsted St.

MIRAI SUSHI   JAPANESE $$$

Map p306 (☎773-862-8500; www.miraisushi.com; 2020 W Division St; rolls $5-9, dishes $8-15; ◷5-10pm Sun-Thu, to 11pm Fri & Sat; Ⓜ︎Blue Line to Division) This high-energy restaurant has a higher-energy lounge upstairs; both are packed with happy, shiny Wicker Park residents enjoying some of the freshest sushi in the area. From the trance-hop electronic music to the young, black-clad staff, Mirai is where connoisseurs of sashimi and *maki* (rolled sushi) gather to throw back cocktails between savory morsels of yellowtail and shiitake tempura lightly fried to perfection.

✖ Ukrainian Village

★**HOOSIER MAMA
PIE COMPANY** DESSERTS $

Map p306 (☎312-243-4846; www.hoosier-mamapie.com; 1618 ½ Chicago Ave; slices $4; ◷8am-7pm Tue-Fri, 9am-5pm Sat, 10am-4pm Sun; ⊠Blue Line to Chicago) There's a statistic saying one out of five people has eaten an entire pie solo. Hoosier Mama is your place to do it. Pastry chef Paula Haney hand rolls and crimps her dough, then plumps it with fruit or creamy fillings. Favorites include the banana cream, chocolate chess (nicknamed the 'brownie pie') and classic apple (flavored with Chinese five-spice powder).

Fridays she offers a pie 'flight' (three small slices for $7) for eat-in diners. Seating is limited in the itty-bitty storefront.

BLACK DOG GELATO DESSERTS $

Map p306 (www.blackdogchicago.com; 859 N Damen Ave; gelato from $3.50; ◷2-10pm Fri-Sun, mid-May–Oct; ⊠50) All hail the oddball masterpieces that come forth from this little shop. Will it be the goat-cheese cashew caramel flavor or the sesame fig chocolate chip? What about the bacon-studded, booze-tinged, chocolate Whiskey Gelato Bar? You can also find the gelato at big-name restaurants around town.

LA PASADITA MEXICAN $

Map p306 (www.pasadita.com; 1132 N Ashland Ave; mains $3-9; ◷9am-3am; ⊠Blue Line to Division) The national press crowned La Pasadita's burrito as one of America's 10 best. They are absolutely behemoth and delicious. But cheapos prefer the tacos. You can make a meal on two fat ones, plus get a drink and basket of nacho chips, for under $6. It explains why 20-something hipsters, TV repair guys, and Latino families with kids all pile in here. Just to confuse you, La Pasadita has another branch a few steps away at 1140 N Ashland. Same menu. Same prices. And both places get busy late at night.

BARI FOODS DELI $

Map p306 (☎312-666-0730; www.bariitaliansubs.com; 1120 W Grand Ave; sandwiches $5-8; ◷8am-6:30pm Mon-Sat, to 2pm Sun; ⊠Blue Line to Grand) This Italian grocery store and butcher cuts a mean salami. If you're planning a picnic, drop by and pick up a 9in sub sandwich or two (the Italian meatball is particularly scrumptious) and a nice bottle of earthy red.

THE SWEETEST TREATS

The neighborhood is rich in sugar. The best places to spike your insulin:

➡ Hoosier Mama Pie Company – sniff out what's cooling on the racks.

➡ Hot Chocolate – sip the ridiculously rich namesake beverage.

➡ Margie's (p143) – ladle on the thick hot fudge.

➡ Alliance Bakery (p143) – pray it has the donuts made of croissant dough (aka cronuts).

➡ Black Dog Gelato – lick a Whiskey Gelato Bar.

FLO MEXICAN $$

Map p306 (☎312-243-0477; www.flochicago.com; 1434 W Chicago Ave; mains $9-14; ◷8:30am-10pm Tue-Thu, 8:30am-11pm Fri, 9am-11pm Sat, to 9am-3pm Sun; ⊠Blue Line to Chicago) Think you've had a good breakfast burrito before? Not until you've eaten here. The Southwestern-bent dishes and jovial staff at this brunch hot spot draw hordes of late-rising neighborhood hipsters on the weekend. Tart, potent margaritas and fish tacos take over after dark, but the breakfast foods are the main draw.

TWISTED SPOKE AMERICAN $$

Map p306 (☎312-666-1500; www.twistedspoke.com; 501 N Ogden Ave; mains $9-14; ◷11am-late Mon-Fri, from 9am Sat & Sun; ⊠Blue Line to Grand) Don't let the motorcycle theme, burly burgers and steel finishing intimidate you: behind the macho facade at this popular brunch spot are artful dishes better calibrated for nesting yuppies than hardscrabble Hell's Angels. If the smoky-sweet BBQ Kobe Brisket isn't tough enough for you, order the unfortunately named 'Road Rash' Bloody Mary extra spicy, and chomp your way through its array of harpooned veggies.

BITE CAFE INTERNATIONAL $$

Map p306 (☎773-395-2483; www.bitecafe-chicago.com; 1039 N Western Ave; mains $10-15; ◷9am-2am; ✐; ⊠49) Join the shaggy rockers reading graphic novels and eating lemon ricotta French toast for breakfast, falafel sandwiches for lunch or coq au vin for dinner. The small room is industrial-chic, with sky-blue chairs around plain wood tables, and funky artwork peppering exposed brick walls.

Up until 8:30pm, you can bring booze over from the Empty Bottle (p149) bar/music venue next door to accompany meals (or BYO with no corkage fee).

HONEY 1 BBQ BARBECUE $$
Map p306 (www.honey1bbq.com; 2241 N Western Ave; half-slab ribs $11.50; ☺11am-9:30pm Tue-Thu, to 11pm Fri & Sat, noon-8pm Sun; ⓂBlue Line to Western) Pork is king at Honey 1, where the meat is slow-cooked over a hickory-wood fire. The namesake honey figures prominently in the sassy sauce. The rib tips rock, and the lunch specials are a steal. The no-frills joint even lets you bring in your own brewskis.

MR BROWN'S LOUNGE JAMAICAN $$
Map p306 (☑773-278-4445; www.mrbrowns-lounge.com; 2301 W Chicago Ave; mains $11-18; ☺4pm-2am Tue-Fri, from noon Sat & Sun; ☐66) Named after a Jamaican folklore tale that Bob Marley adapted into a song, this bar-restaurant cooks up such Jamaican staples as jerk chicken and stewed oxtail along with American riffs such as 'island-style' macaroni and cheese. Wash it down with a spicy rum punch. DJs spin reggae and dance-hall tunes on weekends. Ya, mon.

TECALITLAN MEXICAN $$
Map p306 (☑312-384-4285; 1814 W Chicago Ave; mains $6-13; ☺10am-midnight Sun-Thu, to 3am Fri & Sat; ☐66, ⓂBlue Line to Chicago) Weighing in at more than a pound, the *carne asada* (roast meat) burrito with cheese is not just one of the city's best food values, it's one of the city's best foods. Add the optional avocado and you'll have a full day's worth of food groups wrapped in a huge flour tortilla. The *horchata* (a rice-based beverage made with water, sugar, cinnamon, vanilla and lime) is creamy and refreshing.

★RUXBIN MODERN AMERICAN $$$
Map p306 (☑312-624-8509; www.ruxbinchicago.com; 851 N Ashland Ave; mains $25-30; ☺5:30-10pm Tue-Sat, to 9pm Sun; ⓂBlue Line to Division) ✐ The passion of the brother-sister team who run Ruxbin is evident in everything from the warm decor made of found items, such as antique theater seats and church pews, to the artfully prepared flavors in dishes such as the pork-belly salad with grapefruit, cornbread and blue cheese. It's

a wee place of just 32 seats, and BYO. Reservations accepted for Sunday only.

GREEN ZEBRA VEGETARIAN $$$
Map p306 (☑312-243-7100; www.greenzebra-chicago.com; 1460 W Chicago Ave; small plates $7-13; ☺5:30-9:30pm Mon-Thu, 5-10pm Fri & Sat, to 9pm Sun; ✐; ⓂBlue Line to Chicago) ✐ Chicago doesn't offer many opportunities for chic vegetarian fare, which may explain why Beard-award-winning chef Shawn McClain's slick restaurant has been so successful for the past decade. The menu focuses on creative seasonal odes to meatless fare. Rich broths, unconventional curries and dumplings all make appearances. It's a small-plate setup, so you'll have to order three or four to make a meal.

🍷 DRINKING & NIGHTLIFE

🍷 Wicker Park & Bucktown

DANNY'S BAR
Map p306 (1951 W Dickens Ave; ☺from 7pm; ⓂBlue Line to Damen) Little Danny's is a hipster magnet, featuring a comfortably dim and dog-eared atmosphere and occasional DJ sets of Stax 45s. Blessedly TV-free, Danny's is a great place to come for conversation early in the evening, or to shake a tail feather at an impromptu dance party on the weekend.

MAP ROOM BAR
Map p306 (www.maproom.com; 1949 N Hoyne Ave; ☺from 6:30am Mon-Fri, from 7:30am Sat, from 11am Sun; 🕏) At this map- and globe-filled 'travelers' tavern,' artsy types sip coffee by day and suds from the 200-strong beer list by night. Board games and *National Geographics* are within reach.

VIOLET HOUR COCKTAIL BAR
Map p306 (☑773-252-1500; www.theviolethour.com; 1520 N Damen Ave; ☺from 6pm; ⓂBlue Line to Damen) This nouveau speakeasy isn't marked, so look for the poster-covered, wood-panel building and the door topped by a yellow lightbulb. Inside, high-backed booths, chandeliers and long velvet drapes provide the backdrop to elaborately engi-

neered cocktails in which homemade bitters are applied with an eyedropper over six varieties of ice. As highbrow as it sounds, it's quite welcoming and accessible.

BLUEBIRD BAR

Map p306 (☑773 486 2473; www.bluebird chicago.com; 1749 N Damen Ave; ⊘from 5pm; ⓜBlue Line to Damen) Rustic Bluebird's candlelit bar, oak tables and exposed brick walls give it a casually romantic, good-for-a-first-date ambience. The lengthy, well-curated beer list focuses on small-batch and global pours, and there are several wines available by the glass. To quell the stomach, order a cheese or charcuterie plate or perhaps a Belgian chocolate waffle.

GOLD STAR BAR BAR

Map p306 (☑773-227-8700; 1755 W Division St; ⊘from 4pm; ⓜBlue Line to Division) A vestige from the days when Division St was 'Polish Broadway,' the Gold Star remains a divey winner, drawing a posse of bike messengers – and people who dress like them – for cheapie libations and a great metal-and-punk jukebox.

WORMHOLE COFFEE CAFE

Map p306 (www.thewormholecoffee.com; 1462 N Milwaukee Ave; ⊘7am-11pm; 🛜; ⓜBlue Line to Damen) The Wormhole is pretentious in an endearing way. Take the seasonal drinks such as autumn's Harrison Gourd (espresso and sweet-potato whipped cream) and winter's Mayan Melk (white hot chocolate, lavender syrup and cracked-pepper marshmallow): pompous, but also cutely delicious. Students and hipsters caffeinate while staring at their laptops amid movie kitsch (yes, that is a Delorean car in front).

LUSH WINE AND SPIRITS WINE BAR

Map p306 (www.lushwineandspirits.com; 1412 W Chicago Ave; ⊘noon-10pm Sun-Thu, to 11pm Fri & Sat; ⓜBlue Line to Chicago) Lush is a local mini-chain that is part wine shop and part wine bar. Buy a bottle on the one side, then take it over to the other and sit at the butcher-block tables in a decibel-friendly, Euro-style ambience. It's all very economical, especially during the free tastings on Sundays from 2pm to 5pm.

DEBONAIR SOCIAL CLUB CLUB

Map p306 (☑773-227-7990; 1575 N Milwaukee Ave; ⊘from 10pm Mon-Thu, from 9pm Fri-Sun;

ⓜBlue Line to Damen) It's mostly a younger, hipster crowd dancing their asses off at Debonair. The main action takes place on the upstairs floor. That's where Monday's youth-friendly Rehab party draws big crowds for the can't-sit-still oldies mash-ups, hard rock and new electro. The down-stairs floor is less hot and packed, though still grooving with rock or whatnot. Reggae and burlesque shows entertain on other nights.

ED & JEAN'S BAR

Map p306 (2032 W Armitage Ave; ⊘hours vary; ⓜBlue Line to Damen) It's one of the city's classic dive bars, where the wood paneling, kitschy knickknacks and 'shot-ana-beer' orders impart authentic Chicago character. There's no phone number, and the hours are at Ed and Jean's whim, so it's good to have a backup plan such as nearby Danny's or the Map Room.

RAINBO CLUB BAR

Map p306 (☑773-489-5999; 1150 N Damen Ave; ⊘from 4pm; ⓜBlue Line to Damen) The center for Chicago's indie elite during the week, the boxy, dark-wood Rainbo Club has an impressive semicircular bar and one of the city's best photo booths. The service is slow and the place goes a little suburban on weekends, but otherwise it's an excellent place to hang out with artsy locals.

FILTER CAFE

Map p306 (☑773-904-7819; 1373 N Milwaukee Ave; ⊘7am-9pm Mon-Thu, to 7am-8pm Fri & Sat, 8am-9pm Sun; 🛜; ⓜBlue Line to Division or Damen) Linger over good coffee at thrift-store tables and couches along with all the laptop-toting writers tapping out their screenplays. The in-house roasting system uses oil from the coffee beans to run the machine. Cash only.

RODAN LOUNGE

Map p306 (☑773-276-7036; www.rodanchicago.com; 1530 N Milwaukee Ave; ⊘from 6pm Mon-Thu, from 2pm Fri, from 11am Sat & Sun; ⓜBlue Line to Damen) This sleek, cinematic spot for 30-somethings slides from restaurant mode to bar mode around 10pm. Arty videos courtesy of Chicago artists are projected on the back wall, and the space often hosts interesting live collaborations between electronic composers and video artists.

♀ Ukrainian Village

MATCHBOX   COCKTAIL BAR
Map p306 (770 N Milwaukee Ave; ⊘from 4pm; ⓂBlue Line to Chicago) Lawyers, artists and bums all squeeze in for retro cocktails. It's as small as – you got it – a matchbox, with about 10 barstools; everyone else stands against the back wall. Barkeeps make the drinks from scratch. Favorites include the pisco sour and the ginger gimlet, ladled from an amber vat of homemade ginger-infused vodka.

HAPPY VILLAGE   BAR
Map p306 (☑773-486-1512; www.happyvillagebar.com; 1059 N Wolcott Ave; ⊘from 4pm Mon-Fri, from noon Sat & Sun; ⓂBlue Line to Division) The sign boasting the 'happiest place in the east village' seems like an understatement on a summer evening when a strolling tamale vendor appears on the vine-covered patio here – then it's the happiest place on Earth. Don't get too sauced before entering the table-tennis room adjoining the bar; the competition is fierce.

RICHARD'S BAR   BAR
Map p306 (☑312-421-4597; 725 W Grand Ave; ⊘from 8am Mon-Fri, from 9am Sat, from noon Sun; ⓂBlue Line to Grand) The younger of the two main bartenders in this timeless dive is in his 70s. The bar – with its tall, humming refrigerated coolers for to-go orders and a strange mix of Rat Pack and *Saturday Night Fever* on the jukebox – feels like something out of a Jim Jarmusch movie.

Hang around long enough and the owner may bring out a huge platter of food for everyone. Otherwise Richard's fare consists of hard-boiled eggs served in a shot glass.

INNERTOWN PUB   BAR
Map p306 (☑773-235-9795; 1935 W Thomas St; ⊘from 3pm; ⓂBlue Line to Division) A cigar-smoking moose and a bronze bust of Elvis overlook the crowd of artsy regulars playing pool and drinking cheap at this lovably divey watering hole. Order a Christmas Morning, a delightful shot of hot espresso and chilled Rumplemintz.

OLA'S LIQUOR   BAR
Map p306 (☑773-384-7259; 947 N Damen Ave; ⊘from 7am Mon-Sat, from 11am Sun; ☐50) This classic 'slashie' – the term for a bar/liquor

store combo, where the bar is stashed in the back room – has hours catering to third-shift locals and the most indomitable night owls. Order the advertised *zimne piwo* (Polish for 'cold beer') and blast some tunes on the juke in the same language.

BEAUTY BAR   CLUB
Map p306 (☑312-226-8828; www.thebeautybar.com/chicago; 1444 W Chicago Ave; ⊘from 5pm; ⓂBlue Line to Chicago) The owners of the Empty Bottle had a hand in this venue. The interior is an imported and restored late-1960s beauty salon from New Jersey. 'Martinis and manicures' are the shtick, and you can get the latter anytime for $10. Genre-spanning DJs spin nightly. If the Beauty Bar sounds familiar, it's because it's part of a chain with outposts in several US cities.

FUNKY BUDDHA LOUNGE   CLUB
Map p306 (☑312-666-1695; www.funkybuddha.com; 738 W Grand Ave; ⊘closed Mon-Wed; ⓂBlue Line to Grand) The Buddha shakes with hip-hop and house music (plus chunks of funk, neosoul and old-school rap). It's usually a mixed crowd dancing in the room, which is unobnoxiously decorated with antique lighting, mural-covered walls and big ol' Buddhas.

☆ ENTERTAINMENT

☆ Wicker Park & Bucktown

★HIDEOUT   LIVE MUSIC
Map p306 (www.hideoutchicago.com; 1354 W Wabansia Ave; ⊘7pm-late Tue & Sat, from 4pm Wed-Fri, varies Sun & Mon; ☐72) Hidden behind a factory at the edge of Bucktown, this two-room lodge of indie rock and alt-country is well worth seeking out. The owners have nursed an outsider, underground vibe, and the place feels like the downstairs of your grandma's rumpus room. Music and other events (bingo, literary readings etc) take place nightly. Tickets cost between $5 and $15.

DOUBLE DOOR   LIVE MUSIC
Map p306 (www.doubledoor.com; 1572 N Milwaukee Ave; ⓂBlue Line to Damen) Alternative rock that's *just* under the radar finds a home at

this former liquor store, which still has the original sign out front and remains a landmark around the Wicker Park bustle. The cachet is such that groups such as the Rolling Stones have plugged in too.

CHOPIN THEATRE
THEATER
Map p306 (☑773-278-1500; www.chopintheatre.com; 1543 W Division St; Ⓜ Blue Line to Division) Looking for a tasty slice of Chicago fringe theater? Maybe something oddball, thought provoking or just plain silly? Chopin is the place. The city's best itinerant companies, such as House Theatre and Theater Oobleck, often turn up here.

HOUSE THEATRE
THEATER
Map p306 (www.thehousetheatre.com; 1543 W Division St; Ⓜ Blue Line to Damen) By throwing out the rule book, 'Chicago's most exciting young theater company' *(Tribune)* presents a mix of quirky, funny, touching shows written by untrained playwrights. Magic, music and good old-fashioned storytelling usually tie in somehow. House typically performs at the Chopin Theatre, but sometimes it turns up in offbeat locations (such as a hotel room) as well.

SUBTERRANEAN
LIVE MUSIC, CLUB
Map p306 (☑773-278-6600; www.subt.net; 2011 W North Ave; Ⓜ Blue Line to Damen) DJs spin hip-hop and other styles to a trendy crowd at this place, which looks slick inside and out. The cabaret room upstairs draws good indie rock bands and hosts popular open-mic events.

PHYLLIS' MUSICAL INN
LIVE MUSIC
Map p306 (☑773-486-9862; 1800 W Division St; ☺from 4pm; Ⓜ Blue Line to Division) One of the all-time great dives, this former Polish polka bar features scrappy up-and-coming bands nightly. It's hit or miss for quality, but you've got to applaud them for taking a chance. If you don't like the sound you can always slip outside to the bar's basketball court for relief. Cheap brewskis, to boot.

TRAP DOOR THEATRE
THEATER
Map p306 (☑773-384-0494; www.trapdoortheatre.com; 1655 W Cortland St; ☑9) This ragtag operation once had to hold a fundraiser to purchase a bathroom for its tiny theater, but it is now drawing bigger audiences for its consistently great productions of European avant-garde plays and originals.

DAVENPORT'S PIANO BAR & CABARET
LIVE MUSIC
Map p306 (☑773-278-1830; www.davenportspianobar.com; 1383 N Milwaukee Ave; ☺from 7pm, closed Tue; Ⓜ Blue Line to Damen) Old standards get new interpretations and new songs are heard for the first time at this swanky place on a rather lonely stretch of Milwaukee Ave. The front room is a fun, inclusive (read: sing-along) place, with the back reserved for more fancy pants cabaret events (where singing along will get you thrown out). There's a two-drink minimum.

☆ Ukrainian Village

EMPTY BOTTLE
LIVE MUSIC
Map p306 (www.emptybottle.com; 1035 N Western Ave; ☺5pm-late Mon-Wed, from 3pm Thu & Fri, from 11am Sat & Sun; ☑49) Chicago's music insiders fawn over the Empty Bottle, the city's scruffy, go-to club for edgy indie rock, jazz and other beats. Monday's show is usually a freebie by a couple of up-and-coming bands. You won't even have to spend much on booze – cans of Pabst are $1.50. Plus there's a cool photo booth in back.

CHICAGO DRAMATISTS THEATRE
THEATER
Map p306 (☑312-633-0630; www.chicagodramatists.org; 1105 W Chicago Ave; Ⓜ Blue Line to Chicago) For a visit to the heart of Chicago's dramatic scene, step into this small, functional theater space, a testing ground for Chicago's new playwrights and plays. It's no surprise that this embracing environment has earned stunning results; current resident playwrights are Emmy nominee Susan Lieberman and Nambi E Kelly.

SHOPPING

⬛ Wicker Park & Bucktown

QUIMBY'S
BOOKS
Map p306 (www.quimbys.com; 1854 W North Ave; ☺noon-9pm Mon-Thu, to 10pm Fri & Sat, to 7pm Sun; Ⓜ Blue Line to Damen) The epicenter of Chicago's comic and zine worlds, Quimby's is one of the linchpins of underground culture in the city. Here you can find everything from crayon-powered punk-rock manifestos to slickly produced graphic

ⓘ NEIGHBORHOOD RESOURCE

Check the website of the **Wicker Park & Bucktown Chamber of Commerce** (www.wickerparkbucktown.com) for neighborhood events and deals at local restaurants, bars and shops.

novels. It's a groovy place for cheeky literary souvenirs and bizarro readings.

DUSTY GROOVE   MUSIC

Map p306 (☎773-342-5800; www.dustygroove.com; 1120 N Ashland Ave; ☺10am-8pm; ⓜBlue Line to Division) Old-school soul, Brazilian beats, Hungarian disco, bass-stabbing hip-hop – if it's funky, Dusty Groove (which also has its own record label) stocks it. Flip through stacks of vinyl, or get lost amid the tidy shop's CDs. Be sure to check out the dollar bin.

UNA MAE'S FREAK BOUTIQUE   CLOTHING

Map p306 (☎773-276-7002; www.unamaeschicago.com; 1528 N Milwaukee Ave; ☺noon-8pm Mon-Fri, 11am-8pm Sat, noon-7pm Sun; ⓜBlue Line to Damen) It's unlikely that the solid suburban women who once wore the pillbox hats and fine Republican cloth coats on sale here would have ever thought of themselves as freaks. Along with the vintage wear, Una Mae's has a collection of new, cool-cat designer duds and accessories for both men and women.

MYOPIC BOOKS   BOOKS

Map p306 (☎773-862-4882; www.myopicbookstore.com; 1564 N Milwaukee Ave; ☺9am-11pm; ⓜBlue Line to Damen) Sunlight pours through the windows at Myopic, one of the city's oldest and largest used bookstores. It rambles through three floors, serves coffee, and hosts poetry readings (usually on Saturday evenings) and experimental music (on Monday evenings). In other words, it's perfect.

US #1   CLOTHING

Map p306 (☎773-489-9428; 1460 N Milwaukee Ave; ☺noon-7pm; ⓜBlue Line to Damen) Rack after rack of '70s bowling, Hawaiian and western-wear shirts, as well as towers of secondhand jeans, including big-name brands, cram this vintage shop.

RECKLESS RECORDS   MUSIC

Map p306 (☎773-235-3727; www.reckless.com; 1532 N Milwaukee Ave; ☺10am-10pm Mon-Sat, to 8pm Sun; ⓜBlue Line to Damen) Chicago's best indie-rock record and CD emporium allows you to listen to everything before you buy. It's certainly the place to get your finger on the pulse of the local, *au courant* underground scene. There's another outlet in the Loop at 26 E Madison St.

BORING STORE   SPECIALTY

Map p306 (☎773-772-8108; www.notasecretagentstore.com; 1331 N Milwaukee Ave; ☺11am-6pm; ♿; ⓜBlue Line to Division) The big orange sign out front will have you scratching your head, but do yourself a favor and step inside (don't worry, those 25 surveillance cameras pointed at you are harmless). The place sells crazy spy gear! Mustache disguise kits, underwater voice amplifiers, banana-shaped cases to hide your cell phone in – it's genius.

Better yet: profits from sales go toward supporting the after-school writing and tutoring programs that take place on-site at nonprofit group 826CHI.

LOMOGRAPHY   ELECTRONICS

Map p306 (www.lomography.com; 1422 N Milwaukee Ave; ☺11am-7pm Sun-Fri, to 9pm Sat; ⓜBlue Line to Damen) A camera shop where all the cameras use film? How retro! Lomography offers terrifically cool analog photo devices, plus the store develops film and holds photography workshops.

CITY SOLES   SHOES

Map p306 (☎773-489-2001; www.citysoles.com; 2001 W North Ave; ☺10am-7pm Mon-Sat, 11am-6pm Sun; ⓜBlue Line to Damen) It's one of the hippest men's and women's shoe stores in Chicago. The vast range of kicks services pretty much the entire neighborhood: punks, young housewives and old Polish women alike. There are blowout sales a couple of times per year.

PENELOPE'S   CLOTHING & ACCESSORIES

Map p306 (☎773-395-2351; www.shoppenelopes.com; 1913 W Division St; ☺11am-7pm Mon-Sat, noon-6pm Sun; ⓜBlue Line to Division) Named after the owners' ridiculously cute pug, Penelope's is a warm boutique for 20- and 30-somethings. It offers both men's and women's fashions (they're new but look thrift-store bought) along with housewares, jewelry and nifty gifty things.

T-SHIRT DELI   CLOTHING

Map p306 (☎773-276-6266; www.tshirtdeli.com; 1739 N Damen Ave; ☺11am-7pm Mon-Fri, to 6pm

Sat. to 5pm Sun; Ⓜ️Blue Line to Damen) They take the 'deli' part seriously: after they cook (ie iron a retro design on) your T-shirt, they wrap it in butcher paper and serve it to you with potato chips. Choose from heaps of shirt styles and decals, of which Mao, Sean Connery, Patty Hearst and a red-white-and-blue bong are but the beginning.

BEADNIKS
ARTS & CRAFTS

Map p306 (☎773-276-2323; www.beadniks.com/chicago; 1937 W Division St; ⊙11am-9pm Mon-Sat, to 7pm Sun; Ⓜ️Blue Line to Division) Incense envelops you at the door, and you know right away you're in for a hippie treat. Mounds of worldly baubles rise up from the tables. African trade beads and Thai silver-dipped beads? Got 'em. Bright-hued stone beads, ceramic beads, glass beads? All present. For $3 the kindly staff will help you string your choices into a necklace. Or take a workshop (two to three hours, $10 to $60) and learn to wield the pliers yourself; they take place several evenings throughout the week. The website has the schedule.

4 MILES 2 MEMPHIS
CLOTHING & ACCESSORIES

Map p306 (www.4miles2memphis.com; 1734 W North Ave; ⊙11am-7pm Tue-Sat, to 5pm Sun; Ⓜ️Blue Line to Damen) If you've seen the TV reality show *American Pickers*, you'll recognize the shop's owner. She takes old silk, lace and other vintage materials and upcycles them into rock-and-roll jackets, shirts, T-shirts and jewelry.

MS CATWALK
CLOTHING & ACCESSORIES

Map p306 (☎773-235-2750; www.mscatwalk.com; 2042 N Damen Ave; ⊙2-7:30pm Wed-Fri, 10am-6pm Sat, 11am-4pm Sun; Ⓜ️Blue Line to Damen) Ms Catwalk stocks fun, flirty clothing and garnishes for women. T-shirts feature images from Buddha to Supergirl to Junior Mints candies; hoodies, low-rise corduroy pants and big silvery bags accessorize your selection.

UPRISE SKATEBOARDS
SPORTS

Map p306 (☎773-342-7763; www.upriseskateboards.com; 1820 N Milwaukee Ave; ⊙noon-7pm Mon-Sat, to 5pm Sun; Ⓜ️Blue Line to Western) Looking for a Street Sweeper or a pair of Lakais? Uprise is the city's top spot for skateboarders to pick up gear, boards and tips on the local scene. Drop in for a rad T-shirt and to find out where the action is. No attitude here: they're friendly and patient with newbies.

RED BALLOON CO
CHILDREN

Map p306 (☎773-489-9800; www.theredballoon.com; 1940 N Damen Ave; ⊙10am-6pm Mon-Sat, 11am-5pm Sun; Ⓜ️Blue Line to Damen) When hipsters get good jobs and start having kids, this is where they outfit the li'l pups. Adorable clothes, classic children's books and '50s-style wooden block toys prevail in the cozy space.

AKIRA
CLOTHING & ACCESSORIES

Map p306 (☎773-489-0818; www.shopakira.com; 1814 W North Ave; ⊙11am-9pm Mon-Sat, to 7pm Sun; Ⓜ️Blue Line to Damen) Several fashion design students work here, staffing the denim bar, which is stocked with more than 20 different brands of jeans. There's a focus on up-and-coming and newly popular lines. This particular location is women-oriented, but two other Akira shops – one for men's clothing and one for shoes – hover on the same block.

MILDBLEND SUPPLY CO
CLOTHING

Map p306 (www.mildblend.com; 1342 N Milwaukee Ave; ⊙11am-8pm Mon-Sat, noon-6pm Sun; Ⓜ️Blue Line to Division) Stacks and racks of premium denim fill this shop, which feels a bit like a country store. Staff will hem any jeans you buy at the sewing machines on-site.

JOHN FLUEVOG SHOES
SHOES

Map p306 (☎773-772-1983; www.fluevog.com; 1539-1541 N Milwaukee Ave; ⊙11am-7pm Mon-Fri, 11am-8pm Sat, noon-6pm Sun; Ⓜ️Blue Line to Damen) Bold and colorful shoes by the eccentric designer are the order of the day at this close-out haven. They come as

LOCAL KNOWLEDGE

VINTAGE & THRIFT SHOPS

The stretch of Milwaukee Ave heading southeast from North Ave holds the mother lode of vintage and thrift shops, with lots of funky shoe stores thrown in for good measure. Within a quarter-mile you'll pass more than 10 hot spots, including US #1, Una Mae's and **Buffalo Exchange** (Map p306; ☎773-227-9558; www.buffaloexchange.com; 1478 N Milwaukee Ave; ⊙11am-8pm Sun-Thu, to 9pm Fri & Sat; Ⓜ️Blue Line to Damen), where, as long as you have some suitably fashionable threads of your own to trade, you don't even need cash.

tough-girl chunky or sex-kitten pointy as you like, and there are equally hip selections for men.

VIVE LA FEMME
CLOTHING & ACCESSORIES

Map p306 (☑773-772-7429; www.vivelafemme.com; 2048 N Damen Ave; ⊙11am-7pm Mon-Fri, to 5pm Sat & Sun; MBlue Line to Damen) Plus-size shops for women are often woefully lacking in style. Not so at Vive La Femme, where larger women can find sassy and classy designs in sizes 12 to 24.

PAPER DOLL
GIFTS

Map p306 (☑773-227-6950; www.paperdollchicago.com; 2027 W Division St; ⊙11am-7pm Tue-Fri, to 6pm Sat, to 5pm Sun; MBlue Line to Damen) Stationery rules the house at Paper Doll, and many a Wicker Park thriftster has ordered her wedding cards or baby annoucements from the mod assortment on hand. Kitschy gifts round out the inventory.

FREE PEOPLE
CLOTHING & ACCESSORIES

Map p306 (☑773-227-4871; www.freepeople.com; 1464 N Milwaukee Ave; ⊙11am-7pm Mon-Sat, to 6pm Sun; MBlue Line to Damen) Owned by the same parent company as Urban Outfitters (young hipster styles) and Anthropologie (older feminine styles), Free People lands in the middle with boho-chic tank tops, cardigan sweaters, herringbone jackets and patterned dresses.

🏠 Ukrainian Village

HANDMADE MARKET
ARTS & CRAFTS

Map p306 (☑773-276-3600; www.handmadechicago.com; 1035 N Western Ave; ⊙noon-4pm Oct-Apr; ☐49) Held the second Saturday of the month at the Empty Bottle (p149), this event showcases Chicago crafters who make funky glass pendants, knitted items, handbags, scarves, journals and greeting cards. The bar serves drinks throughout the event, for those who enjoy sipping while shopping.

WICKER PARK, BUCKTOWN & UKRAINIAN VILLAGE SHOPPING

Logan Square & Humboldt Park

Neighborhood Top Five

1 Biting into a fig-and-goat-cheese-slathered elk sausage while admiring weenie-themed art after meeting the pope of encased meats at **Hot Doug's** (p155).

2 Flicking through sweet vinyl and playing vintage Donkey Kong at **Logan Hardware** (p163).

3 Strolling around the lagoon and munching Puerto Rican snacks in **Humboldt Park** (p155).

4 Hearing a fret-bending set by local bluesmen at **Rosa's Lounge** (p162).

5 Perusing thousands of oddball badges at the **Busy Beaver Button Museum** (p155).

For more detail of this area see Map p310 ➡

Lonely Planet's Top Tip

Pack your patience for Logan Square's rich restaurant scene. Most places do not take reservations, so you'll have to wait an hour or more to fork into that goji berry pheasant sausage. Try to arrive right at opening time. Otherwise, hit the bar. At **Kuma's Corner** (p156) and **Longman & Eagle** (p160), you can order meals at the bar if you snag a seat.

✕ Best Places to Eat

→ Hot Doug's (p155)

→ Longman & Eagle (p160)

→ Reno (p156)

→ Kuma's Corner (p156)

→ Lula Cafe (p160)

For reviews, see p155 ➡

⬤ Best Places to Drink

→ Revolution Brewing (p161)

→ Billy Sunday (p161)

→ Small Bar (p162)

→ Quenchers Saloon (p162)

→ Scofflaw (p162)

For reviews, see p161 ➡

☆ Best Places for Entertainment

→ Whistler (p162)

→ Rosa's Lounge (p162)

→ Logan Theatre (p163)

→ Prop Thtr (p163)

→ Elastic Arts Foundation (p163)

For reviews, see p162 ➡

Explore: Logan Square & Humboldt Park

Sights are few and far between in Logan Square and Humboldt Park. No matter. You're here to eat, drink and see a show. Many of Chicago's best restaurants are tucked in along the neighborhood's tree-shaded boulevards. These aren't high-falutin' places, but rather boisterous taverns and small storefronts dishing out inventive fare (Michelin-starred, in some cases) at reasonable prices. Add in retro dive bars, sudsy brewpubs and thrifty gin lounges for sipping, plus artsy music clubs for entertainment, and you've got a stellar Chicago night out.

Logan Square is the hipster haven, home to artists and stylish types who've moved in among the Latino families. Gentrification continues its relentless push here, but thanks to Logan's community gardens, neighborhood-run farmers market and preservation efforts, the area has more or less held on to its dignity. Longman & Eagle, Hot Doug's, Lula Cafe and several other must-eats serve during the day, but nighttime is when the action peaks.

Humboldt Park, to the south, is rougher around the edges. It's still heavily Puerto Rican, as the giant flag sculptures and island-food cafes along Division St attest. The eponymous park is the area's focal point. Morning or afternoon is the best time to visit.

Local Life

→ **Free Stuff** Just north of Lula Cafe (p160), there are a couple of newspaper boxes that front W Logan Blvd. Inside are free books and DVDs. Go ahead: take one or leave one. Residents swap 'em all the time.

→ **Heavy Drinking** To slake thirst, the neighborhood hot spot is the 2300 block of N Milwaukee Ave. At press time, three new bars and a craft distillery were slated to open, joining Revolution Brewing (p161), Cole's (p162) and a couple of awesome coffee shops.

→ **Sausages** Longman & Eagle (p160) hosts a pop-up sausage restaurant at its Offsite Bar (across the patio from the main venue) every Saturday starting at 11am.

Getting There & Away

→ **El** Most Logan Square destinations can be reached via the Blue Line stations at Logan Square and California.

→ **Bus** For Humboldt Park destinations, you'll need a bus. Number 70 travels along Division St to the heart of the park. Bus 72 along North Ave, bus 73 along Armitage Ave and bus 74 along Fullerton Ave are also useful.

→ **Car** Street parking isn't bad, although it can get tight around Logan Square near Lula Cafe.

⊙ SIGHTS

HUMBOLDT PARK
PARK

Map p310 (www.chicagoparkdistrict.com; 1440 N Humboldt Dr; ⊡70 or 72) This 207-acre park, which lends its name to the surrounding neighborhood, comes out of nowhere and gobsmacks you with Mother Nature. A lagoon brushed by native plants takes up much of the green space, and birdsong flickers in the air. The 1907 Prairie School **boathouse** rises up from the lagoon's edge and serves as the park's showpiece.

A gravel path takes off from the boathouse and circles the water, where you'll sometimes see people fishing. Across the street, on the northwest corner of Humboldt Dr and Division St, lies the **Formal Garden**, rich with jelly-bean-colored flower beds and bison sculptures (by Edward Kemeys, the gent who hewed the Art Institute lions). It's a fine place to sit and smell the roses. Just south, the Institute of Puerto Rican Arts and Culture has cool free exhibits ongoing.

The park was built in 1869 and named for German naturalist Alexander von Humboldt. Landscape architect Jens Jensen gave it its 'prairie style' design, using native plants and stone, in the early 1900s. The park has gone through some rough times since then. It has only come into its own again in the past decade. While it's family filled by day, it's still pretty rough and best avoided at night (unless there's a free outdoor movie or music event happening).

Street vendors and food trucks sell fried plantains, meat dumplings and other Puerto Rican specialties around the park's edges. Many congregate on Kedzie Ave at North Ave and at Hirsch St – sniff them out for a picnic. The annual Riot Fest punk music bash takes over the park in mid-September.

For more in-depth explorations, including the park's wee waterfall, wind turbine and picnic island, download the free audio tour at www.chicagoparkdistrict.com/audio-tours/humboldt-park.

INSTITUTE OF PUERTO RICAN ARTS AND CULTURE
MUSEUM

Map p310 (☏773-486-8345; www.iprac.org; 3015 W Division St; ◷10am-5pm Tue-Fri, to 3pm Sat; ⊡70) **FREE** The Institute fills the old horse stables in Humboldt Park. It's worth a stroll inside to see what free art and cultural exhibits are showing.

PASEO BORICUA
STREET

Map p306 (Division St, btwn Western Ave & Mozart St; ⊡70) Paseo Boricua, aka the Puerto Rican Passage, is a mile-long stretch of Division St stuffed with Puerto Rican shops and restaurants. It's marked at either end by a 45-ton, steel **Puerto Rican flag sculpture** that arches over the road; the eastern flag stands near Western Ave, while the western one is at Mozart Ave.

This area has long been the epicenter of Chicago's 113,000-strong Puerto Rican community.

ILLINOIS CENTENNIAL MEMORIAL COLUMN
MONUMENT

Map p310 (Logan Blvd & Milwaukee Ave, intersection of Kedzie Blvd; ⓂBlue Line to Logan Square) What's that giant phallic thing in the middle of the road, causing traffic to swerve every which way? Excellent question. Most locals have no idea. Turns out it's a monument commemorating the 100th anniversary of Illinois' statehood, built in 1918 by a gent named Henry Bacon – the same architect who created the Lincoln Memorial in Washington DC.

The eagle atop the Doric column echoes that on the Illinois state flag. The reliefs of Native Americans, explorers, farmers and laborers represent the great changes the state experienced during its first century.

BUSY BEAVER BUTTON MUSEUM
MUSEUM

Map p310 (www.buttonmuseum.org; 3279 W Armitage Ave; ◷10am-4pm Mon-Fri; ⊡73) Even George Washington gave out campaign buttons, though in his era they were the sew-on kind. Pin-back buttons came along in 1896. Badge-making company Busy Beaver chronicles its history in displays holding thousands of the little round mementos. They tout everything from Dale Bozzio to Bozo the clown, Cabbage Patch Kids to Big Rock Point Nuclear Plant.

They're fascinating to browse (especially Washington's button), and the hipster office staff is totally gracious about letting you gawk over their desks where the framed cases hang. Ring the doorbell to enter.

EATING

★HOT DOUG'S
AMERICAN $

(☏773-279-9550; www.hotdougs.com; 3324 N California Ave; mains $3-9; ◷10:30am-4pm

LOGAN SQUARE & HUMBOLDT PARK SIGHTS

Mon-Sat; Ⓜ️Blue Line to California to bus 52) Doug is the most famous weenie maker in town, and deservedly so. He serves multiple hot-dog styles (Polish, bratwursts, Chicago) cooked multiple hot-dog ways (char grilled, deep fried, steamed). Confused? He'll explain it all. While the chatty Cubs lover is renowned for his gourmet 'haute dogs' – say blue-cheese pork with cherry cream sauce or sesame-ginger duck – his old-school, Chicago-style frankfurter remains the top seller.

On Friday and Saturday, Doug offers his popular fries cooked in duck fat. Unless you arrive before 10:45am, the line will be snaking out the door no matter what day it is. Don't worry: it's a good-natured gathering, with folks even known to burst into a group sing-along. Cash only.

BANG BANG PIE SHOP DESSERTS $

Map p310 (www.bangbangpie.com; 2051 N California Ave; slices $5; ⊘7am-7pm Tue-Fri, 9am-5pm Sat, 9am-4pm Sun; Ⓜ️Blue Line to California) Count on fruit, cream and chocolate pie variations daily. Will it be chocolate peanut butter or Kentucky bourbon fudge you take to the sunlit, butcher-board tables? Will it be blood orange or key lime you fork into while sitting in the garden's Adirondack chairs? Almost better than pie are Bang Bang's hulking biscuits, especially after a slathering with the condiment bar's jams and herbed butter.

RENO AMERICAN $$

Map p310 (www.renochicago.com; 2607 N Milwaukee Ave; mains $8-14; ⊘7am-11pm Mon-Thu, to 1am Fri, 9am-1am Sat, 9am-11pm Sun; 🛜; Ⓜ️Blue Line to Logan Square) 🍴 Reno is Logan Square's de facto community center, thanks to its reasonable prices and wood-fired bagels and pizzas. Stylishly scruffy residents pull up a chair at the reclaimed wood tables and peck away at their laptops while munching egg-and-maple-fennel-sausage sandwiches by day, and Gruyere-and-butternut-squash-topped pizzas and pastas by night. Cash only.

Reno also has a full bar and pours particularly lovely reds and whites – a perk of owning Telegraph Wine Bar next door.

KUMA'S CORNER BURGERS $$

(📞773-604-8769; www.kumascorner.com; 2900 W Belmont Ave; mains $12-13; ⊘11:15am-11:45pm Mon-Wed, to 12:45am Thu-Sat, 11:45am-11:45pm Sun; 🚍77) This place is ridiculously busy and

🏃 Local Life
Logan & Humboldt Boulevard Stroll

The four broad green boulevards – Logan, Kedzie, Palmer and Humboldt – that stripe the neighborhood are so impressive they're an official city landmark. Built in 1869, they roll through the heart of the community, past whimsically styled, century-old manors; modern cool-cat shops; and the lagoon-dotted park where locals go out to play.

❶ Fuel Up at Reno
Breakfast, lunch or dinner – Reno (p156) does it right. Staff make just about everything in-house with organic ingredients. Linger along with everyone else over the bottomless cups of coffee and free wi-fi (the java morphs to beer and wine as the day progresses).

❷ Rally at the Monument
Logan Square's centerpiece is the 68ft Illinois Centennial Memorial Column (p155) erected (OK, bad pun) in 1918 to mark 100 years of statehood. On sunny days folks scramble through the take-your-life-in-your-hands traffic circle to loll on the surrounding grass, people-watch and nibble goodies from the Sunday farmers market.

❸ Get Fashionable
Wolfbait & B-girls (p163) sells funky women's wear and accessories by 170 local designers. Weren't you looking for a hand-dyed repurposed minidress made from men's boxer shorts? The name, incidentally, comes from the 1950s guidebook *Chicago Confidential* that defines 'wolfbait' as girls who moved to the city looking for success, and 'B-girls' as what they sometimes turn into.

❹ City Lit Pit Stop
City Lit (Map p310; www.citylitbooks.com; 2523 N Kedzie Blvd; ⊘11am-8pm Tue-Fri, 10am-7pm Sat, 10am-5pm Sun; Ⓜ️Blue Line to Logan Square) is a modern, generalist bookstore that often hosts readings by local authors. A Logan resident opened the shop in 2012. Grab a novel and cozy up by the fireplace. The children's section is particularly rich.

Humboldt Park (p155)

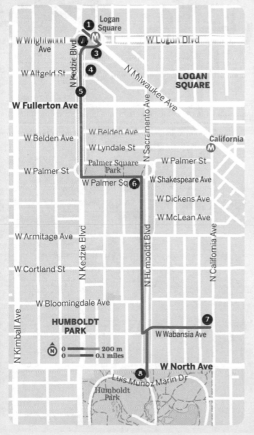

⑤ Kedzie's Mansions

Meander on **Kedzie Boulevard**, a prime example of the area's wide, leafy thoroughfares. Several mansions stand sentry; the best ones are on the street's west side. European immigrants who made their fortunes in Chicago built the manors at the turn of the century. Unwelcome by the Gold Coast's old-money millionaires, the nouveau riche had to move out here.

⑥ Schwinn's House

At 2128 N Humboldt Blvd (aka the southwest corner of Palmer and Humboldt) a gent named Ignaz Schwinn used to roll his two-wheeler out of the driveway. Alas, the original Schwinn mansion is gone now, but the neighborhood's many cyclists tip their cap when passing by, as Ignaz pretty much invented the modern bike (with 40 patents to prove it).

⑦ Plantain Pileup

Follow your nose to Borinquen Restaurant (p160), wellspring of the *jibarito* sandwich. It'll probably be crowded with Puerto Rican families, elderly couples and neighborhood tough guys chomping down in unison on the mealy, garlicky signature item dribbling out of two fried plantain slices of 'bread.' Pack breath mints for the aftermath.

⑧ Go Fish

Humboldt Blvd runs smack into Humboldt Park (p155). Stroll around the lagoon, fish and munch Puerto Rican snacks from the food carts. To really go native, bring a folding chair or blanket, plop it under a shade tree and lick your fresh-bought coconut popsicle.

Logan Square & Humboldt Park – Hipster Haven

Whenever something new and cool opens – be it a craft whiskey maker, a pop-up sausage restaurant, a thrifty gin lounge, a record shop with an attached video-game museum – it opens here. And even though it's the hottest 'hood in town, it remains refreshingly low-key.

1. Longman & Eagle (p160)

Belly up at the bar while contemplating the menu at this Michelin-starred tavern.

2. Wolfbait & B-girls (p163)

Check out local designers in action, then take your pick of their unique wares.

3. Kuma's Corner (p156)

Heavy-metal music meets burgers at this loud and proud joint.

4. Hot Doug's (p155)

From gourmet 'haute dogs' to classic Chicago-style frankfurters, Doug is the king of weenies.

FARMERS MARKET & NIGHT MARKET

The **Logan Square Farmers Market** (Map p310; www.logansquarefarmers-market.org; 3107 W Logan Blvd; ☉10am-3pm Sun mid-May–Oct; MBlue Line to Logan Square) is one of Chicago's best. The neighborhood operates it (versus the city), so it marches to its own progressive beat. Live music, free yoga classes and prepared foods from surrounding restaurants join the usual vendor line-up of fruits, veggies, eggs and flowers. In winter the market moves to the lobby of the Congress Theater (2135 N Milwaukee Ave).

The city-run **Logan Square Night Market** (Map p310; 3100 W Palmer Square; ☉5-9pm Wed late Jun-early Sep; MBlue Line to California) also offers produce and snacks from local eateries, but it ratchets up the entertainment with free performances by neighborhood theater troupes and musicians. It's held in Palmer Square Park.

head-bangingly loud, and it attracts the tattooed set for its monster 10oz burgers, each named for a heavy-metal band and hefted onto a pretzel-roll bun. The results can be straightforward (Black Sabbath comes blackened with chili and pepper jack), esoteric (Led Zeppelin is piled with pulled pork, bacon, cheddar and pickles) or whimsical (Judas Priest has bacon, blue cheese, fruit and nuts).

There's a mac 'n' cheese menu for vegetarians, and beer and bourbon for all. Be warned: on winter days there's no outside seating, so the prime-time wait can be two hours. There is another Kuma's outpost in Lincoln Park (at 666 W Diversey Ave), but the original is best.

BORINQUEN RESTAURANT   PUERTO RICAN **$$**

Map p310 (☎773-227-6038; www.borinquenon-california.net; 1720 N California Ave; mains $6-13; ☉11am-10pm Sun-Thu, to midnight Fri & Sat; MBlue Line to California) The story goes that Borinquen owner Juan 'Peter' Figueroa created his signature dish after reading an article in a Puerto Rican newspaper about a sandwich that subbed plantains for bread – a flash of inspiration that birthed the *jibarito*, a popular dish that piles steak, let-

tuce, tomato and garlic mayo between two thick, crisply fried plantain slices. The idea caught on, and the *jibarito* is all the rage at local Puerto Rican eateries. It's the marquee item at Borinquen, though more traditional Puerto Rican fare is also available at the homey family spot.

FEED   SOUTHERN **$$**

Map p310 (☎773-489-4600; www.feedrestaurantchicago.com; 2803 W Chicago Ave; mains $7-13; ☉8am-10pm Mon-Fri, 9am-10pm Sat, 9am-9pm Sun; ☐66) With red-checked tablecloths, a free-play jukebox piled with classic rock and country, and a menu of southern home cookin', Feed has the chipper feel of a lost *Hee Haw* set. All the framed portraits of poultry allude to the house specialty – juicy, tender rotisserie chicken – but the sides, including hand-cut fries, corn pudding and mac 'n' cheese, are equally stellar. Bulging fruit pie and vanilla-wafer banana pudding follow for dessert. Cash only; BYOB.

CHICAGO DINER   VEGETARIAN **$$**

Map p310 (www.veggiediner.com; 2333 N Milwaukee Ave; mains $9-14; ☉11am-10pm Mon-Fri, from 10am Sat & Sun; ☑; MBlue Line to California) Chicago's favorite, long-standing vegetarian restaurant expanded from Lake View and opened a fancier branch in Logan Square.

★**LONGMAN & EAGLE**   AMERICAN **$$$**

Map p310 (☎773-276-7110; www.longmanandeagle.com; 2657 N Kedzie Ave; mains $17-29; ☉9am-2am; MBlue Line to Logan Sq) Hard to say whether this shabby-chic tavern is best for eating or drinking. Let's say eating, since it earned a Michelin star for its beautifully cooked comfort foods such as vanilla brioche French toast for breakfast, wild-boar sloppy joes for lunch and maple-braised pork shank for dinner. There's a whole menu of juicy small plates, too. Reservations not accepted.

Luckily, you can drink well while waiting. Belly up at the bar for hard-to-find bourbons and whiskeys, and suck 'em down via a house-curated flight or a flight of your own making. A six-room inn fills the tavern's 2nd floor.

LULA CAFE   AMERICAN **$$$**

Map p310 (☎773-489-9554; www.lulacafe.com; 2537 N Kedzie Ave; mains $19-28; ☉9am-10pm Sun-Mon & Wed-Thu, to 11pm Fri & Sat; ☑; MBlue Line to Logan Square) 🍴 Funky, arty Lula led the way for Logan Square's dining scene, and appreciative neighborhoodies still crowd in for the seasonal, locally sourced menu. Even the muffins here are something to drool over, and that goes double for lunch items such as pasta *yiayia* (bucatini pasta with Moroccan cinnamon, feta and garlic) and dinners such as striped bass with pine-nut-peppered orzo. Mondays offer a prix-fixe three-course Farm Dinner ($38). There's also a six-course vegetarian tasting menu ($45).

YUSHO
JAPANESE $$$

Map p310 (☑773-904-8558; www.yusho-chicago.com; 2853 N Kedzie Ave; small plates $9-14; ⊙5-10pm Mon-Thu, to midnight Fri & Sat, noon-8pm Sun; ⓂBlue Line to Logan Square) The cook at Yusho was Charlie Trotter's executive chef for 14 years, so he knows his way around a kitchen. The focus here is *yakitori*, or grilled Japanese street food. Small plates of tofu and chrysanthemum, tuna and taro root, and duck breast and mushrooms hit the unadorned wood tables and booths. You'll need a few dishes to make a meal. The daily draught cocktail and wildly flavored soft-serve ice cream round out the flavorgasm. Yusho is a great date place (and yes, it does take reservations). There's a prix-fixe special on Sundays: a noodle dish, drink and dessert for $20.

FAT RICE
INTERNATIONAL $$$

Map p310 (☑773-661-9170; www.eatfatrice.com; 2957 W Diversey Ave; mains $18-28; ⊙6-10pm Tue-Sat, ⓂBlue Line to Logan Square) Fat Rice ladles out the unusual flavors of Portugal and its former colonies. The signature dish, from which the restaurant takes its name, is a rich paella-esque casserole of roast pork, chicken thighs, thick sausage slices, huge prawns, clams, hard-boiled eggs, olives, chilies and pickled peppers. It's meant to be shared (and is served as part of a four-course prix-fixe menu for $35 per person).

Single-serving casseroles and stir fries, as well as spicy, coconutty small plates and white wintermelon soup, also hit the tables. Fat Rice doesn't take reservations, so expect to wait.

🍷⚓ DRINKING & NIGHTLIFE

REVOLUTION BREWING
BREWERY

Map p310 (☑773-227-2739; www.revbrew.com; 2323 N Milwaukee Ave; ⊙from 11am Mon-Fri, from 10am Sat & Sun; ⓂBlue Line to California) Raise

SMOQUE BBQ

Squeaky-clean, family-friendly **Smoque** (☑773-545-7427; www.smoquebbq.com; 3800 N Pulaski Rd; mains $9-20; ⊙11am-9pm, to 10pm Fri & Sat, closed Mon; ⓂBlue Line to Irving Park) is all about slow-cooked meats. The baby-back and St Louis–style ribs are what line 'em up: they're smoked over oak and applewood and soaked in a tangy, slightly sweet sauce. The brisket and pulled pork aren't far behind in making carnivores swoon. Drisket-flecked baked beans, cornmeal-crusted mac 'n' cheese, freshly cut fries and citrusy coleslaw round out the menu. It's BYO so bring a few brewskis to complement the meaty goodness. Smoque is a couple of miles northwest of Logan Square, easily reached three Blue Line stations onward at Irving Park.

your fist to Revolution, a massive, industrial-chic brewpub that fills glasses with heady beers such as the 7% Eugene porter (named for Eugene Debs, the leader of Chicago's Pullman strike in 1894). The suds are high quality – the brewmaster led the way for Chicago's exploding craft-beer scene. The *haute* pub grub includes fig-and-pancetta pizza and bacon-fat popcorn with fried sage.

Revolution also has a **tap room** (⊙2-10pm Wed-Sat) nearby at 3340 N Kedzie Ave. It's not usually as crowded as the brewpub, and offers a relaxed atmosphere for hop-heads to knock back pints. Free brewery tours at 6pm are an added bonus.

BILLY SUNDAY
COCKTAIL BAR

Map p310 (www.billy-sunday.com; 3143 W Logan Blvd; ⊙from 5pm; ⓂBlue Line to Logan Square) Tastemakers at *Details* magazine named this cocktail haven one of the best new bars in the country. Spiced kola nut, rhubarb sherbet and pineapple bitters are among the ingredients shaken and stirred into Billy's high-end gins, bourbons and other booze. Old-timey portraits hang on the walls; sconces give the small room a warm glow. Most drinks cost around $10.

A small menu of gastronome snacks – such as crispy, malt-vinegar-doused pig ears, and Things in Jars, such as whipped garbanzo beans with pickled pistachio –

helps soak up the libations. Note it's easy to miss the bar's entrance, as the sign isn't very prominent.

SMALL BAR
BAR

Map p310 (☑773-509-9888; www.thesmallbar. com; 2956 N Albany Ave; ☺from 4pm Mon-Fri, from noon Sat & Sun; MBlue Line to Logan Square) Its ace jukebox, affordable food menu and kindly staff make this unpretentious gem an easygoing place to spend an evening in the neighborhood. The mirror behind the bar dates back to 1907. Alas, there's no easy public transport to get here, so you'll have to walk a half-mile or so from the El. There's a sister Small Bar in Wicker Park.

SCOFFLAW
COCKTAIL BAR

Map p310 (www.scofflawchicago.com; 3201 W Armitage Ave; ☺from 5pm; ☐73) Scofflaw is a gin joint – literally. The bar specializes in boutique, small-batch gins mixed into gimlets, martinis and other cocktails that get creative with juniper. It's mostly a 30-something crowd sipping from mismatched glassware and kicking back in vintage French armchairs by the fireplace. That may sound preciously hipster, but the cozy bar's vibe is more rebellious thrift store.

QUENCHERS SALOON
BAR

Map p310 (☑773-276-9730; www.quenchers. com; 2401 N Western Ave; ☺from noon Sun-Fri, from 11am Sat; ☎; ☐74) At the Logan Square/ Bucktown border, Quenchers peddles a global selection of nearly 300 beers from more than 40 nations. Locals, artisans, laborers and visiting brew masters enjoy Earle Miller's hospitality (and his tater-tot pizza and chili). There's entertainment nightly, with rock bands, literary readings and improv comedy all on the agenda.

COLE'S
BAR

Map p310 (www.coleschicago.com; 2338 N Milwaukee Ave; ☺from 5:30pm Mon-Fri, from 4pm Sat & Sun; MBlue LIne to California) Cole's is a dive bar with nifty free entertainment. Young scenesters flock in to shoot pool and swill Midwest microbrews (Bell's, Two Brothers) in the front room. Then they head to the back-room stage where bands and DJs do their thing. On Wednesdays the popular comedy open mic (9:30pm) takes over. Hopefully, the 90-year-old comic will be telling dirty jokes...

LATE BAR
CLUB

(www.latebarchicago.com; 3534 W Belmont Ave; ☺from 10pm Tue-Sat; MBlue Line to Belmont) Late Bar is off the beaten path on a forlorn stretch of Belmont Ave surrounded by auto repair shops and Polish bars, though it's easy to get to via the El. Two DJs opened the club, and its weird, new-wave vibe draws fans of all stripes: mods, hooligans, rockers, punks, goths, scooterists and more. Saturday's Planet Earth alt/postpunk dance nights are popular.

CALIFORNIA CLIPPER
BAR

Map p310 (☑773-384-2547; www.californiaclipper.com; 1002 N California Ave; ☺from 8pm; ☐52) The Clipper's retro linoleum and Naugahyde decor hasn't changed much since it opened in 1937. Guys in bowling shirts and ladies in thrift-store dresses dig the cheap cocktails and weekend bands (often alt-country tinged). Eventually curiosity will lead you to try the house drink: the purple martin, a fizzy mix of grape soda and coconut rum.

WHIRLAWAY LOUNGE
BAR

Map p310 (☑773-276-6809; www.whirlaway.net; 3224 W Fullerton Ave; ☺from 4pm; MBlue Line to Logan Square) With threadbare couches and broken-in board games, this neighborhood fave has the homey charm of your uncle's '70s rumpus room – if your uncle had loads of young hip pals with an insatiable thirst for Pabst.

☆ ENTERTAINMENT

WHISTLER
LIVE MUSIC

Map p310 (☑773-227-3530; www.whistlerchicago.com; 2421 N Milwaukee Ave; ☺from 6pm Mon-Thu, from 5pm Fri-Sun; MBlue Line to California) FREE Hometown indie bands, jazz combos and DJs rock this wee, arty bar most nights. There's never a cover charge, but you'd be a shmuck if you didn't order at least one of the swanky cocktails or craft beers to keep the scene going. Whistler is also a gallery: the front window showcases local artists' work. The first Monday of each month is the very fun 'movieoke' event (like karaoke, only you act along with the movie scenes playing on the screen behind you).

ROSA'S LOUNGE
BLUES

Map p310 (☑773-342-0452; www.rosaslounge. com; 3420 W Armitage Ave; ☺from 8pm Tue-

Sat; 🚌73) Rosa's is an unadorned, real-deal blues club that brings in top local talent and dedicated fans to a somewhat derelict Logan Square block. The location is isolated from easy public transportation; a taxi is probably the best way to get here. Tickets range from $7 to $15.

LOGAN THEATRE — CINEMA
Map p310 (www.thelogantheatre.com; 2646 N Milwaukee Ave; Ⓜ Blue Line to Logan Square) The 1915 movie palace has been recently renovated and now shows both mainstream and art-house flicks a few weeks after their initial run (so tickets are cheap). Cult classics screen late-night on weekends. Bonus: local craft beers flow from the theater's bar so you can sip well while viewing.

PROP THTR — THEATER
(📞773-539-7838; www.propthtr.org; 3502 N Elston Ave; 🚌152) This long-running storefront venue presents fresh stage adaptations of literary works by serious writers, from Nabokov to William Burroughs. The well-executed productions are typically dark in theme. Prop also hosts the annual fringe Rhinoceros Theater Festival.

ELASTIC ARTS FOUNDATION — PERFORMING ARTS
Map p310 (📞773-772-3616; www.elasticrevolution.com; 2nd fl, 2830 N Milwaukee Ave; Ⓜ Blue Line to Logan Square) The calendar at Elastic Arts is far-reaching and impossible to pin down – one day will see a funk band, the next an experimental video screening, and the next will see an improvised jazz performance by a cutting-edge international ensemble. Tickets rarely cost more than $8.

FACTORY THEATER — THEATER
(📞312-409-3247; www.thefactorytheater.com; 3504 N Elston Ave; 🚌152) Factory has been staging ridiculous and marginally serious plays for more than two decades. It still maintains a nervy, irreverent edge that makes its schedule a must for Chicago theater and comedy fans.

🛍 SHOPPING

★LOGAN HARDWARE — MUSIC
Map p310 (www.logan-hardware.com; 2532 W Fullerton Ave; ⏱noon-9pm Mon-Sat, to 7pm Sun; 🚌74) Logan Hardware is a used record store with a little something extra in its back room: the **Vintage Arcade Museum**. So after flicking through bins of rock, funk and Chicago-band LPs – and scoring, say, a bluesy Chess Records 45 – you celebrate with a knockdown game of Donkey Kong, Ms Pac-Man, Dolly Parton pinball or 30 other whirring, beeping '80s games.

They're all free to play, though remember: music purchases are what keep the place in business.

WOLFBAIT & B-GIRLS — CLOTHING, ACCESSORIES
Map p310 (📞312-698-8685; www.wolfbaitchicago.com; 3131 W Logan Blvd; ⏱10am-7pm Mon-Sat, to 4pm Sun; Ⓜ Blue Line to Logan Square) Old ironing boards serve as display tables; tape measures, scissors and other designers' tools hang from vintage hooks. You get that crafting feeling as soon as you walk in, and indeed, Wolfbait & B-girls both sells the wares (tops, dresses, handbags and jewelry) of local indie designers and serves as a working/sewing studio for them.

Near West Side & Pilsen

NEAR WEST SIDE | PILSEN | WEST LOOP | GREEKTOWN | LITTLE ITALY

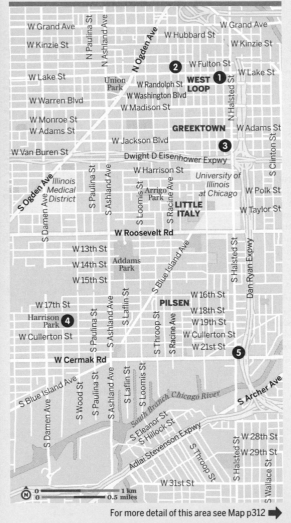

Neighborhood Top Five

❶ Forking into a decadent meal by a celebrity chef at one of the mega-hot restaurants in the **West Loop** (p171).

❷ Wanding around forklifts and warehouses to find art hubs such as **Mars Gallery** (p170).

❸ Yelling *'opa'* as the waiter sets your cheese aflame at a taverna in **Greektown** (p172).

❹ Admiring psychedelic paintings and colorful folk art at the **National Museum of Mexican Art** (p167).

❺ Slouching into a booth alongside Pilsen's bohemian crowd at **Skylark** (p175).

For more detail of this area see Map p312 ➡

Explore: Near West Side & Pilsen

Just west of the Loop is, well, the West Loop. It's akin to New York City's Meatpacking District, with chic restaurants, clubs and galleries poking out between meat-processing plants. The area is booming, and it seems like a new hot chef opens a restaurant (or two) here weekly. By day it's still a serious food-supply zone filled with forklifts and delivery trucks. At night it turns up the glamor. Stroll along the main veins of W Randolph St and W Fulton Market and you'll get the drift.

The Near West Side also includes the ethnic neighborhoods of Greektown (along Halsted St) and Little Italy (along Taylor St). Neither has much in the way of sights, but gustatory tourists will revel in the delicious offerings.

To the southwest lies Pilsen, the center of Chicago's Mexican community. A trip to this colorful, mural-splashed neighborhood is like stepping into a foreign country. Spend an afternoon poking around the bakeries, taquerias and impressive art museum. Chicago's hipster underground also has been moving in, so you'll find some great bohemian bars and restaurants if you linger into the evening.

Local Life

→ **Vintage Jackpot** Local fashionistas scour the shops along 18th St between Halsted St and Ashland Ave. See www.facebook.com/vintageon18th for locations.

→ **Rowdy Skaters** The Windy City Rollers (p177) attract a raucous home crowd to their games at UIC Pavilion.

→ **Tube Socks & Tacos** Maxwell Street Market (p176) draws a local crowd of junk hounds and Mexican street-food fans.

Getting There & Away

→ **El** Pink Line to 18th St for Pilsen; Green, Pink Lines to Morgan or Clinton for the West Loop; Blue Line to UIC-Halsted for Greektown; Pink Line to Polk or Blue Line to Racine for Little Italy.

→ **Bus** For United Center, buses 19 (game-day express) and 20 run along Madison St; they return to the Loop via Washington St. Number 8 travels along Halsted St through Greektown and Pilsen.

→ **Taxi** If you don't want to bother with public transport, the West Loop and Greektown are only 1.25 miles west of the Loop, making them a fairly cheap ride. And cabs are easy to hail in the neighborhoods.

→ **Car** It can be tough to find parking in the West Loop and Greektown, but valets abound. Street parking is pretty easy in Little Italy and Pilsen.

Lonely Planet's Top Tip

You'll need to make reservations months in advance (at least) for hot restaurants such as **Next** (p172) and **Girl and the Goat** (p172). But if you can't get in, you can still sample the wares of chefs Grant Achatz and Stephanie Izard. Try **Aviary** (p175), Achatz's cocktail bar, and **Little Goat** (p171), Izard's diner.

 **Best Places to Eat**

→ Little Goat (p171)
→ Publican Quality Meats (p171)
→ Sweet Maple Cafe (p173)
→ Meli Cafe (p173)
→ Don Pedro Carnitas (p174)

For reviews, see p171 →

Best Places to Drink

→ Aviary (p175)
→ Haymarket Pub & Brewery (p175)
→ Skylark (p175)
→ Simone's (p175)
→ Beer Bistro (p175)

For reviews, see p175 →

Best Places to Shop

→ Randolph Street Market (p176)
→ Blommer Chocolate Store (p176)
→ Groove Distribution (p176)
→ Athenian Candle Co (p176)
→ Working Bikes Cooperative (p177)

For reviews, see p176 →

NEAR WEST SIDE & PILSEN

◉ SIGHTS

◉ Near West Side

HAYMARKET SQUARE   HISTORIC SITE
Map p312 (Desplaines St, btwn Lake & Randolph Sts; MGreen, Pink Line to Clinton) The odd bronze statue of guys on a wagon marks the spot where the world's labor movement began. So the next time you take a lunch break or go home after your eight-hour workday, thank Haymarket Sq, which you're now standing upon. Striking factory workers held a meeting here on May 4, 1886. Bombs, deaths, anarchists and hangings ensued. The statue is meant to depict the speaker's platform at the rally.

HARPO STUDIOS   TV LOCATION
Map p312 (www.oprah.com; 1058 W Washington Blvd; MGreen, Pink Line to Morgan) For 25 years *The Oprah Winfrey Show* taped at this studio, which the media queen owns. But in 2011 she packed up and left town for LA. The studio technically is still in business, though not much goes on. Fans occasionally drop by to snap a picture with the 'Harpo Studios' sign at the corner of W Randolph and N Carpenter Sts.

THREEWALLS   GALLERY
Map p312 (www.three-walls.org; 119 N Peoria St; ☺11am-5pm Tue-Sat; MGreen Line to Morgan) This West Loop gallery is so groovy it has CSA (community-supported art), where you buy a 'share' and receive an allotment of art (maybe a handwoven placement and ceramic dish). It sponsors lectures and performances, too.

BATCOLUMN   MONUMENT
Map p312 (600 W Madison St; MGreen Line to Clinton) Artist Claes Oldenburg – known for his gigantic shuttlecocks in Kansas City and oversized cherry spoon in Minneapolis – delivered this simple, controversial sculpture to Chicago in 1977. The artist mused that the 96ft bat 'seemed to connect earth and sky the way a tornado does.' Hmm... See it for yourself in front of the Harold Washington Social Security Center.

CHICAGO FIRE
DEPARTMENT ACADEMY   HISTORIC SITE
Map p312 (☎312-747-7239; 558 W DeKoven St; MBlue Line to Clinton) Rarely has a building been placed in a more appropriate place: the fire department's school stands on the very spot where the 1871 fire began – between Clinton and Jefferson Sts. Although there's no word on whether junk mail still shows up for Mrs O'Leary, the academy trains firefighters so they'll be ready the next time somebody, or some critter, kicks over a lantern.

OLD ST PATRICK'S CHURCH   CHURCH
Map p312 (☎312-648-1021; www.oldstpats. org; 700 W Adams St; MBlue Line to Clinton) A Chicago fire survivor, this 1852 church is not only the city's oldest but also one of its fastest-growing. Old St Pat's is best known for its World's Largest Block Party, a weekend-long bash in early July with big-name rock bands where Catholic singles can flirt. It's famed for matchmaking: more than 100 couples have met in the crowd and eventually married. Such social programs have certainly boosted Old St Pat's membership, which has gone from four (yes, four) in 1983 to thousands three decades later. The domed steeple signifies the Eastern Church; the spire signifies the Western Church. There's a beautifully restored Celtic-patterned interior.

UNITED CENTER STADIUM

Map p312 (☎312-455-4650; www.unitedcenter.
com; 1901 W Madison St; ☑19 or 20) The United
Center arena is home to the Bulls and the
Blackhawks, and is the venue for special
events such as the circus. The statue of an
airborne Michael Jordan in front of the
east entrance pays a lively tribute to the
man whose talents financed the edifice.
The area is OK by day but gets a bit edgy at
night – unless there's a game, in which case
cops are everywhere to ensure public safety.

GARFIELD PARK CONSERVATORY GARDENS

(☎312-746-5100; www.garfieldconservatory.org;
300 N Central Park Ave; ⊙9am-5pm, to 8pm
Wed; Ⓜ Green Line to Conservatory) FREE Built
in 1907, these 4.5 acres under glass are
the Park District's pride and joy. Designer
Jens Jensen intended for the palms, ferns
and other plants to recreate Chicago's prehistoric landscape. Today the effect continues – all that's missing is a rampaging
stegosaurus. Newer halls contain displays
of seasonal plants that are especially spectacular in the weeks before Easter.

Kids can get dirty with roots and seeds
in the Children's Garden. Between May and
October the outdoor grounds are open, including the Demonstration Garden, which
shows urbanites how to grow veggies, keep
bees and compost in city plots; and the
Monet Garden, which adapts the impressionist painter's colorful garden at Giverny,
France. If you drive, lock up: the neighborhood isn't the safest.

◉ Pilsen

NATIONAL MUSEUM OF MEXICAN ART MUSEUM

Map p312 (☎312-738-1503; www.nationalmus-
eumofmexicanart.org; 1852 W 19th St; ⊙10am-
5pm Tue-Sun; Ⓜ Pink Line to 18th St) FREE
Founded in 1982, this vibrant museum – the
largest Latino arts institution in the USA –
has become one of the city's best. The vivid
permanent collection sums up 1000 years of
Mexican art and culture through classical
paintings, shining gold altars, skeleton-rich
folk art, beadwork and much more. Don't
miss the psychedelic 'semen-acrylic' painting (that's, um, bodily fluids mixed with
pigments).

The turbulent politics and revolutionary leaders of Mexican history are well
represented, including works about Cesar

ⓘ PILSEN RESOURCE

Check the calendar of **Pilsen Portal**
(www.pilsenportal.org) for the lowdown
on street fairs, gallery exhibitions and
free art and dance workshops in the
neighborhood.

Chavez and Emiliano Zapata. The museum
also sponsors readings by top authors and
performances by musicians and artists. If
you are in town during the fall, be sure to
check out the exhibits and celebrations re-
lating to November 1, the Day of the Dead, a
traditional Mexican holiday that combines
the festive with the religious. The events
take place for a month on either side of
the day. The on-site store is a winner, with
brightly painted Mexican crafts filling the
shelves.

CHICAGO ARTS DISTRICT GALLERY

Map p312 (www.chicagoartsdistrict.org; 1821
S Halsted St; ☑8) Pilsen's art galleries are
known collectively as the Chicago Arts District. There are 20 or so galleries, and they
tend to be small, artist-run spaces with erratic hours. Many cluster around 18th and
Halsted Sts.

The best time to visit is on Second Fridays, when the galleries stay open late on the
second Friday of each month. Galleries welcome patrons with wine, snacks, and freshly
hung paintings and photos. It's free, and
takes place between 6pm and 10pm. Pick up
a map at the office at 1821 S Halsted St.

COOPER DUAL LANGUAGE ACADEMY MURAL

Map p312 (1645 W 18th Pl; Ⓜ Pink Line to 18th)
Check out the exterior wall of this school,
the canvas for a 1990s tile mosaic that
shows a diverse range of Mexican images,
from a portrait of farmworker advocate
Dolores Huerta to the Virgin of Guadalupe.
Each summer, art students add more panels to the mural.

ST ADALBERT CHURCH CHURCH

Map p312 (www.stadalbertchicago.com; 1650 W
17th St; Ⓜ Pink Line to 18th) The 1914 St Adalbert Church features 185ft steeples and is
a good example of the soaring religious
structures built by Chicago's ethnic populations through thousands of small donations from parishioners, who would cut
family budgets to the bone to make their

Near West Side & Pilsen – Pilsen Murals

Murals are a traditional Mexican art form, and they're splashed all over Pilsen's buildings. They're on schools, on churches, on storefronts, on the El stations. Whatever the image – a sun, the Virgin of Guadalupe, Che Guevara, abstract gauchos or beady-eyed skeletons – count on it being wildly colorful.

BRUCE LEIGHTY / GETTY IMAGES ©

KIM KARPELES / ALAMY ©

1. *Increibles las Cosas que Se Ven* mural
Jeff Zimmermann's vivid 1999 mural is located at W 19th St and S Ashland Ave.

2. Pilsen neighborhood
Colour-popping murals dot this neighborhood, the center of Chicago's Mexican community.

3. Cooper Dual Language Academy (p167)
The exterior wall is the canvas for a tile mosaic that is added to each summer by art students.

4. Casa Aztlan
Historical figures frame the entrance mural to this community center (1831 S Racine Ave).

KIM KARPELES / ALAMY ©

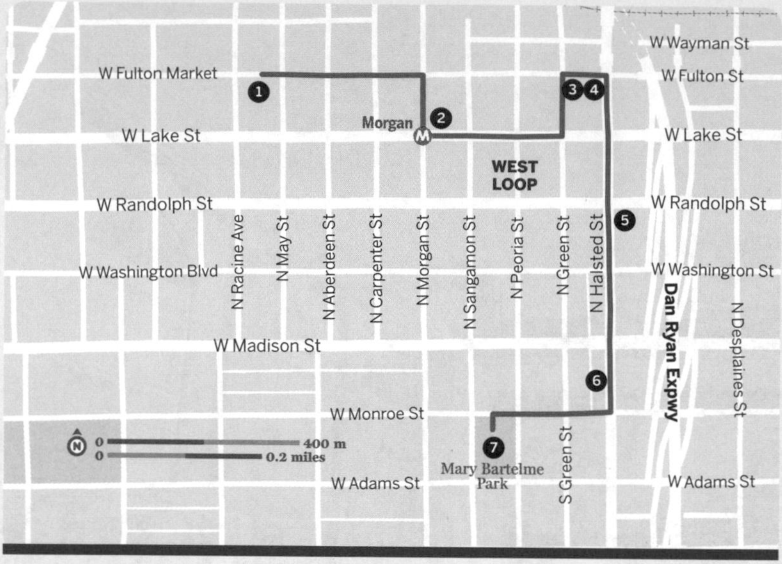

Local Life
West Loop Wander

The West Loop has exploded in the last few years with hot-chef restaurants and condos carved from old meatpacking warehouses. Meat is still the main biz around here, and you're guaranteed to see at least one bloody-apron-clad worker or forklift driver as you traverse the galleries, shops and mega-stylish eateries.

1 Cool-Cat Gallery
Pop-art-filled **Mars Gallery** (Map p312; www.marsgallery.com; 1139 W Fulton Market; ⏲noon-6pm Wed, Fri & Sat, to 7pm Thu; Ⓜ Green Line to Morgan) is pure fun, from the plaid-tie-wearing cat who roams the premises (he's the assistant manager, according to the sign) to the building's offbeat history (it was an egg factory, then a club where the Ramones played). Weird bonus: it sits atop an energy vortex.

2 Spooky Gallery
Packer Schopf Gallery (Map p312; ☎312-226-8984; www.packergallery.com; 942 W Lake St; ⏲11am-5:30pm Tue-Sat; Ⓜ Green Line to Morgan) carves out its niche in 'pop surrealism,' with spooky, offbeat artists including horror filmmaker (and painter) Clive Barker on the roster.

3 Meat Treat
Neighborhood dwellers come to Publican Quality Meats (p171) for its supply of smoked chorizo and maple breakfast sausage. Then they pull up a chair in the small restaurant in the back and linger over beer and artisanal sandwiches. In summer, the crowd spills out to streetside tables.

4 Glazed and Infused
It is perhaps the greatest name ever for a doughnut shop. **Glazed and Infused** (Map p312; www.goglazed.com; 813 W Fulton Market; doughnuts $2-3; ⏲7am-2pm Mon-Thu, to 5pm Fri, to 3pm Sat & Sun; Ⓜ Green, Pink Line to Morgan) has popped up in three other neighborhoods besides the West Loop, and no wonder. That first bite of the vanilla crème brûlée doughnut, when you crunch into the delicate sugar crust, hooks you for life. The next one down the hatch is the toffee-glazed yeast ring, then the banana cream cheese…

5 Historic Suds
Haymarket Pub & Brewery (p175) provides a nice dose of local history. It's located near where the 1886 Haymarket labor riot

Haymarket Memorial sculpture by Mary Brogger, in Haymarket Square (p166)

took place, and the brewery's suds have affiliated names, such as the Mathias Imperial IPA (named after the first police officer to die in the melee) and the Speakerswagon Pilsner.

❻ Grocery Grazing

West Loopers shop for their groceries at multi-level **Mariano's** (Map p312; www.marianos.com; 40 S Halsted St; ☺6am-10pm; ⓂBlue Line to UIC-Halsted). You can almost make a meal from all the free samples: a handful of pita chips here, a little slice of pizza in the next aisle. Pick up something cool to drink or a gelato at the cafe to take for a picnic in the park.

❼ Park Stroll

The neighborhood's stroller-pushing families and dog-walking hipsters get their exercise in **Mary Bartelme Park** (Map p312; 115 S Sangamon St; ⓂBlue Line to UIC-Halsted). Five off-kilter stainless-steel arches form the gateway in; kids play in the mist that the sculptures release in summer. Grassy mounds dot the park and provide good lookout points to view the Willis Tower rising in the distance.

weekly contribution. The rich ornamentation in the interior glorifies Catholic Polish saints and religious figures.

ST PIUS CHURCH   CHURCH

Map p312 (www.stpiusvparish.org; 1919 S Ashland Ave; ⓂPink Line to 18th) The Poles had St Adalbert's; the Irish had St Pius, a Romanesque revival edifice built between 1885 and 1892. Its smooth masonry contrasts with the rough stones of its contemporaries. A mural of parishioners eating corn while Jesus looks on graces the exterior.

✖ EATING

✖ West Loop

★LITTLE GOAT   DINER $$

Map p312 (www.littlegoatchicago.com; 820 W Randolph St; mains $8-12; ☺7am-2am; 🐶✍; ⓂGreen, Pink Line to Morgan) Stephanie Izard opened a diner for the foodie masses across the street from her ever-booked main restaurant, Girl and the Goat (p172). Sit on a vintage twirly stool and order off the all-day breakfast menu. Better yet, try lunchtime favorites such as the goat sloppy joe with mashed potato tempura or the pork belly on scallion pancakes. Heavenly smelling bread baked on-site and bottomless cups of strong coffee add to the awesomeness. Plus it serves late at night. The diner offers a great way to sample Izard's much-ballyhooed fare, since it's hard to get into her signature eatery. The menu is massive. No reservations; expect a wait during peak brunch and lunch times.

PUBLICAN QUALITY MEATS   DELI $$

Map p312 (www.publicanqualitymeats.com; 825 W Fulton Market; mains $8-12; ☺11am-5:30pm Mon-Sat, to 5pm Sun; ⓂGreen, Pink Line to Morgan) 🍃 This butcher shop/32-seat eatery is the casual, cheaper sibling to the nearby Publican (p172). Grab a seat at the blocky tables in back and bite into an artisanal sandwich of delicately cured meat on just-baked bread. The line-up changes weekly, but might include the beefy meatball sandwich or thick-cut bacon, lettuce and tomato on sourdough. A tidy beer and wine list accompanies the fare. Before leaving, browse the shelves of locally made condiments and spice mixes; they make great gifts for foodies.

AVEC
MEDITERRANEAN $$

Map p312 (📞312-377-2002; www.avecrestaurant.com; 615 W Randolph St; mains $15-21; ⊘3:30pm-midnight Mon-Thu, to 1am Fri & Sat, from 11am Sun; MGreen, Pink Line to Clinton) Feeling social? This casual cousin to neighboring Publican (p172) gives diners a chance to rub elbows at eight-person communal tables. The mini-room looks a heck of a lot like a Finnish sauna and fills with noisy chatter as stylish urbanites pile in. The bacon-wrapped dates are the menu's must. The squid-ink pasta and salumi plates beg for your fork, as well. No reservations.

WISHBONE
AMERICAN $$

Map p312 (📞312-850-2663; www.wishbone-chicago.com; 1001 W Washington Blvd; mains $8-17; ⊘7am-3pm Mon, 7am-9pm Tue-Fri, 8am-10pm Sat, 8am-3pm Sun; MGreen, Pink Line to Morgan) They call it 'Southern reconstruction cooking,' which means such items as corn muffins, cheese grits, fried chicken, buttermilk rolls and crawfish patties top the tables. Wishbone sits a block from Oprah's studio, and indeed it's her kind of folksy, down-home, gravy-laden place. Wacky chicken and egg artwork splashes across the wall in the cavernous room, which was once a Goodyear Tire garage.

GIRL AND THE GOAT
MODERN AMERICAN $$$

Map p312 (📞312-492-6262; www.girlandthegoat.com; 809 W Randolph St; small plates $9-13; ⊘4:30-11pm Mon-Fri, to midnight Sat & Sun; 📞; MGreen, Pink Line to Morgan) 🍴 Top Chef winner Stephanie Izard's restaurant rocks. The soaring ceilings, polished wood tables and cartoony art on the walls offer a convivial atmosphere where local beer and house-made wine hit the tables along with unique small plates such as scallops with brown butter kimchi. Goat dishes figure prominently, of course; Izard buys her signature meat from a local farm. Reservations are almost impossible unless you book months in advance. Try for walk-in seats before 5pm or see if anything opens up at the bar.

NEXT
INTERNATIONAL $$$

Map p312 (📞312-226-0858; www.nextrestaurant.com; 953 W Fulton Market; multicourse menu from $125; ⊘5:30-9:30pm Wed-Sun; MGreen, Pink Line to Morgan) Grant Achatz's West Loop restaurant, which opened in 2011, remains one of the hottest tickets in town. And we mean it literally – you need a ticket to dine at Next, which operates like a time machine. It started by serving an eight-course French meal from 1906 Paris, but every three months the whole thing changes: new era, new menu, new decor. Sign up for tickets at the website as early as possible. Prices vary by date, time and menu (early weekdays cost less than prime-time weekends), and you pay when you book. Check the Facebook feed for possible last-minute seats.

PUBLICAN
AMERICAN $$$

Map p312 (📞312-733-9555; www.thepublicanrestaurant.com; 837 W Fulton Market; mains $19-25; ⊘3:30-10:30pm Mon-Thu, 3:30-11:30pm Fri, 10am-11:30pm Sat & Sun; MGreen, Pink Line to Morgan) 🍴 Set up like a swanky beer hall with urbanites young and old sitting across from each other at long communal tables, Publican specializes in oysters, hams and fine suds – all from small family farms and microbrewers. So you'll know your pork shoulder is from Dyersville, Iowa; your orange-honey turnips from Congerville, Illinois; and your oysters from Bagaduce River, Maine. Many locals think the weekend brunch is the best around – Publican does indeed know its bacon.

BLACKBIRD
MODERN AMERICAN $$$

Map p312 (📞312-715-0708; www.blackbirdrestaurant.com; 619 W Randolph St; mains $30-42; ⊘11:30am-2pm & 5:30-10pm Mon-Thu, 11:30am-2pm & 5:30-11pm Fri, 5:30-11pm Sat, 5:30-10pm Sun; MGreen, Pink Line to Clinton) 🍴 This buzzy, chic dining destination for Chicago's young and wealthy perches atop best-of lists for its exciting, notably seasonal menu. The warm-ups – like the chilled spring pea and tofu soup, roasted soft-shell crab with rye berries, and house-made prosciutto – are a perfect introduction to the visionary mains, which pair well with the short, careful wine list. The chef offers an eight-course tasting menu for $120, and there's a prix-fixe lunch for $22.

🍴 Greektown

MR GREEK GYROS
GREEK $

Map p312 (📞312-906-8731; 234 S Halsted St; mains $6-9; ⊘24hr; MBlue Line to UIC-Halsted) 'The Mr' is a classic gyros joint. While the fluorescent lighting and plastic decor may lack charm, the gyros have a beauty of their own. Carnivores: this is definitely your place in the 'hood for late-night eats, as the

UIC students, club goers and occasional bum will attest.

MELI CAFE BREAKFAST **$$**

Map p312 (312-454-0748; www.melicafe.com; 301 S Halsted St; mains $10-15; 6am-3pm; Blue Line to UIC-Halsted) Meli is the Greek word for 'honey,' and it's apt for this sweet breakfast spot. Skillet dishes made from cage-free eggs (served over a bed of potatoes), goat-cheese and fig omelets, and the decadent French toast (made from challah bread dipped in vanilla-bean custard) start the day off right. Meli is also a juice bar, so you can gulp beverages from wheat-grass shots to banana-maple smoothies.

KARYN'S ON GREEN VEGETARIAN **$$**

Map p312 (312-226-6155; www.karynsongreen. com; 130 S Green St; mains $15-17; 11:30am-10pm Tue-Thu, to 3pm Sun; ; Blue Line to UIC-Halsted) Karyn Calabrese, who owns two other local restaurants, is Chicago's queen of raw foods, but this stylish place is her first foray into cooked fare. Her mission: to make vegan dining sexy. And she does a heckuva job in the loungey, low-lit room. Menu items include chicken legs, meatloaf, crab and salmon – but of course, they're vegan re-interpretations of the classics. The full bar pours more than 30 organic and sustainable wines and cocktails.

PARTHENON GREEK **$$**

Map p312 (312-726-2407; www.theparthenon. com; 314 S Halsted St; mains $13-25; 11am-11pm; ; Blue Line to UIC-Halsted) The Parthenon has anchored Greektown since 1968, hearing countless yells of 'opa' to accompany the flaming saganaki (sharp, hard cheese cut into wedges or squares and fried). Greeks returning to the city from their suburban retreats have made the Parthenon a favorite. Vegetarians and gluten-free eaters will find lots of options. A plus for drivers: there's free valet service.

ARTOPOLIS BAKERY & CAFE GREEK **$$**

Map p312 (312-559-9000; www.artopolis-chicago.com; 306 S Halsted St; mains $9-15; 9am-midnight Mon-Thu, to 1am Fri & Sat, 10am-midnight Sun; Blue Line to UIC-Halsted) Like a good Greek salad, this place has many ingredients. It's one of the city's top bakeries – many of the nearby Randolph St joints get their bread here. It's a cafe-bar that opens onto the street, with wine-laden tables along the front. And it's a food bar with classics like spinach pie that you can eat in or get to go.

✕ Little Italy

AL'S #1 ITALIAN BEEF ITALIAN **$**

Map p312 (312-226-4017; www.alsbeef.com; 1079 W Taylor St; mains $4-8; 9am-11pm Mon-Thu, 9am-midnight Fri, 10am-midnight Sat; Blue Line to Racine) Piled high with savory beef that soaks through the thick bun, Al's inexpensive sandwich is one of Chicago's culinary hallmarks. This is the original location of the local chain, which has now spread beyond the city. It might not be the place to grab lunch if you want to get off your feet – there are no tables, only a stand-up counter.

MARIO'S ITALIAN **$**

Map p (1068 W Taylor St; drinks $1-4; 10am-midnight, closed Oct-Apr; ; Blue Line to Racine) At this cheerful box of a shop, super Italian ice comes loaded with big chunks of fresh fruit, which keeps crowds coming in the summer. The owners have been serving the slushy goodness for a half century. Lemon tops the list.

★ SWEET MAPLE CAFE AMERICAN **$$**

Map p312 (312-243-8908; www.sweetmaplecafe.com; 1339 W Taylor St; mains $9-12; 7am-2pm; Blue Line to Racine) The creaking floorboards, matronly staff and soulful home cookin' lend the Sweet Maple Cafe the bucolic appeal of a Southern roadside diner. The signature dishes – inch-thick banana (or, seasonally, peaches and cream) pancakes, cheddar grits and fluffy, freshly baked biscuits that come smothered in spicy sausage gravy – earn the superlatives of locals. The egg dishes, sturdy muffins and lunch sandwiches are done with equal aplomb. If you only have time for one breakfast in the city, this is the place.

TUFANO'S VERNON PARK TAP ITALIAN **$$**

Map p312 (312-733-3393; www.tufanosrestaurant.com; 1073 W Vernon Park Pl; mains $11-19; 11am-10pm Tue-Thu, 11am-11pm Fri, 4-11pm Sat, 3-9pm Sun; Blue Line to UIC-Halsted) Still family run after three generations, Tufano's serves old-fashioned, hearty Italian fare for modest prices. The blackboards carry a long list of daily specials, which can include such wonderful items as pasta with garlic-crusted broccoli. Amid the usual celebrity photos on the wall you'll see some really nice shots of Joey DiBuono, his family and their patrons through the decades. Cash only.

MANNY'S DELI
DELI $$

Map p312 (☑312-939-2855; www.mannysdeli. com; 1141 S Jefferson St; mains $9-15; ⊙6am-8pm Mon-Sat; Ⓜ Blue Line to Clinton) Chicago's politicos and seen-it-all senior citizens get in the cafeteria-style line at Manny's for the towering pastrami and corned-beef sandwiches, matzo-ball soup, potato pancakes and other deli staples. Know what you want before you join the fast-moving queue. The newspaper clippings on the wall provide a dose of city history – or you could just eavesdrop on the table next to you to hear deals being brokered that'll be tomorrow's front-page stories.

CHEZ JOEL
FRENCH $$$

Map p312 (☑312-226-6479; www.chezjoelbistro. com; 1119 W Taylor St; mains $17-27; ⊙4-10pm Tue-Thu, 11am-11pm Fri & Sat, 11am-10pm Sun; Ⓜ Blue Line to Racine) Whether you're dining outside under the big oak tree or tucked in a cozy corner, the atmosphere and exceptional French fare make Chez Joel a romantic favorite, though an odd duck among the predominantly Italian stretch of Taylor St. The menu is anchored by bistro favorites such as duck-leg *confit* and *coq au vin*, complemented by an extensive wine list.

ROSEBUD
ITALIAN $$$

Map p312 (☑312-942-1117; www.rosebud-restaurants.com; 1500 W Taylor St; mains $16-26; ⊙11am-10:30pm Mon-Thu, to 11:30pm Sat, from noon Sat & Sun; Ⓜ Pink Line to Polk) This location in Little Italy is the first branch of an empire of quality Italian restaurants that has spread throughout the city. It is popular with politicos and old-school Taylor St Italians, who slurp down colossal piles of pasta and spinach gnocchi soaked in red sauces. Bring a big appetite.

✕ Pilsen

DON PEDRO CARNITAS
MEXICAN $

Map p312 (1113 W 18th St; tacos $1.50-2; ⊙6am-6pm Mon-Fri, 5am-5pm Sat, 5am-3pm Sun; Ⓜ Pink Line to 18th) At this no-frills meat den, a man with a machete salutes you at the front counter. He awaits your command to hack off pork pieces, then wraps the thick chunks with onion and cilantro in a fresh tortilla. You then devour the taco at the tables in back. Goat stew and tripe add to the meaty menu. Cash only. Lines twist out the door on weekends.

CAFE JUMPING BEAN
CAFE $

Map p312 (☑312-455-0019; 1439 W 18th St; mains $5-9; ⊙6am-10pm Mon-Fri, 7am-7pm Sat & Sun; ☎; Ⓜ Pink Line to 18th St) The ramshackle cafe will make you feel like a regular as soon as you step through the door. It serves excellent hot focaccia sandwiches, baked goods and strong coffee to the 20- and 30-something crowd of local bohemians. Chess and domino games are always breaking out. The comfy confines make it an excellent spot for whiling away a couple of hours with a mocha, soaking up Pilsen's colorful surroundings.

HONKY TONK BBQ
BARBECUE $$

Map p312 (☑312-226-7427; www.honkytonk-bbqchicago.com; 1800 S Racine Ave; mains $8-18; ⊙4pm-late Tue-Sun; Ⓜ Pink Line to 18th St) Art-colored walls and a swell beer and wine list separate Honky Tonk from its Chicago barbecue brethren. It's a fun atmosphere, with live country music some nights and imaginative, changing side dishes such as candied bacon and empanadas with shiitake mushrooms. That's all gravy, though, for the signature wood-roasted pork, beef and chicken.

NUEVO LEON
MEXICAN $$

Map p312 (☑312-421-1517; 1515 W 18th St; mains $10-15; ⊙7am-midnight; Ⓜ Pink Line to 18th St) There may be a lot of gringos here, but there's even more Latino families. Festive Nuevo Leon is Pilsen's best-known restaurant. Outstanding tacos, tamales and enchiladas hit the tables, though the dish most likely to blow any meat eater's taste buds is the *assado de puerco* – tender roast pork served with homemade flour tortillas. The breakfast is also excellent. Cash only.

NIGHTWOOD
MODERN AMERICAN $$$

Map p312 (☑312-526-3385; www.nightwood-restaurant.com; 2119 S Halsted St; mains $19-32; ⊙5:30-10pm Mon-Thu, 5:30-11pm Fri & Sat, 9am-2:30pm Sun; ☷8) ✒ Staff members handwrite the menu each day based on what local farmers have provided to the chefs: maybe chicken with grits and red kale, or thick-cut hand-made pasta with Hungarian wax peppers. It has the same owners as oh-so-hip Lula Cafe (p160) in Logan Square, but they've intensified their commitment to sustainably produced foods here at Nightwood. The warm, wood-toned room sports an open kitchen, and there's a big patio for alfresco dining.

DRINKING & NIGHTLIFE

West Loop

AVIARY
COCKTAIL BAR

Map p312 (www.theaviary.com; 955 W Fulton Market; ⊘from 6pm Tue-Sat; MGreen, Pink Line to Morgan) The Aviary won the James Beard Award for best cocktails in the nation. The ethereal drinks are like nothing you've laid lips on before. Some arrive with Bunsen burners, others with a slingshot you use to break the ice. They taste terrific, whatever the science involved. It's wise to make reservations online. The man behind the booze is Grant Achatz. Aviary sits beside his hot restaurant Next (p172), though the bar is more in spirit (pun!) with his Lincoln Park restaurant, Alinea (p104). Drinks cost around $20 each.

HAYMARKET PUB & BREWERY
BREWERY

Map p312 (www.haymarketbrewing.com; 737 W Randolph St; ⊘11am-2am; MGreen, Pink Line to Clinton) Fresh-from-the-tank beers and a good craft selection flow from the 24 taps at cavernous, barrel-strewn Haymarket. That's all fine and delicious, but the brewery then goes a step beyond to please hopheads by hosting the Drinking and Writing Theater on-site. That's right: a troupe devoted entirely to exploring 'the connection between creativity and alcohol.' Check the website for the schedule. Bands play on the weekends, and there's a monthly story slam. The brewery sits near Haymarket Sq, the historic labor riot site, hence the name.

BEER BISTRO
BAR

Map p312 (☏312-433-0013; www.thebeerbistro. com; 1061 W Madison St; ⊘from 11am; ☐19 or 20) This bar near United Center fills with Bulls and Blackhawks fans, and it even runs a shuttle to the arena on game days. Ninety global beers (most in bottles) comprise the

swill, and TVs flashing the requisite games circle the big room.

JOHNNY'S ICE HOUSE EAST
SPORTS BAR

Map p312 (www.johnnysicehouse.com; 1350 W Madison St; ⊘from noon; MGreen, Pink Line to Ashland) Johnny's is an ice rink, which explains why you can practically see your breath in the attached bar. The wood-paneled, neon-lit room is prime for watching Blackhawks games and knocking back Labatt's (Johnny's is supposedly the state's biggest seller of the beer).

At Johnny's other ice house, further west at 2550 W Madison St, you can see the Blackhawks in person: they practice at the facility and it's open for free public viewing. Check the Hawks' website for the schedule.

CITY WINERY
WINE BAR

Map p312 (www.citywinery.com; 1200 W Randolph St; ⊘from 4pm Mon-Fri, from 2pm Fri, from noon Sat & Sun; MGreen, Pink Line to Morgan) City Winery pours on the grape theme, with casks and tanks of wine everywhere you look. It's very Sonoma decor-wise, with a vine-strewn, open-air patio and exposed blond brick in the airy interior rooms. The menu sprawls through 400 reds and whites, including several housemade vintages that are on tap. Can't decide? Try a flight.

The winery also has a small theater that books well-known singer-songwriter types.

Pilsen

SKYLARK
BAR

Map p312 (☏312-948-5275; www.skylarkchicago. com; 2149 S Halsted St; ⊘from 4pm; ☐8) The Skylark is a bastion for artsy drunkards, who slouch into big booths sipping on strong drinks and eyeing the long room. They play pinball, snap pics in the photo booth and scarf down the kitchen's awesome tater tots. It's a good stop after the Pilsen gallery hop. Cash only.

SIMONE'S
BAR

Map p312 (www.simonesbar.com; 960 W 18th St; ⊘from 11:30am; ☏; MPink Line to 18th) A distinct neighborhood hot spot, Simone's packs in the young and beautiful from around Pilsen. Recycled and found materials comprise the cool decor inside; a large patio beckons outside. Bartenders shake up delicious cocktails, and the kitchen cooks well-priced worldly comfort foods.

NEAR WEST SIDE & PILSEN DRINKING & NIGHTLIFE

⭐ ENTERTAINMENT

REDMOON THEATER
THEATER

Map p312 (📞312-850-8440; www.redmoon.org; 2120 S Jefferson St; 🚌8) The interaction of humans and puppets is key to the magical, haunting adaptations of classic works such as *Moby Dick* and new commissions like *The Princess Club,* a fairly twisted look at children's fairy tales. The innovative non-profit troupe, headed up by performance artists Blair Thomas and Jim Lasko, never fails to mesmerize. Redmoon is the creative force behind the new Great Chicago Fire Festival in October.

UIC PAVILION
CONCERT VENUE

(525 S Racine Ave; Ⓜ Blue Line to Racine) This venue at the University of Illinois at Chicago (UIC) is used mostly for concerts, though women's roller-derby teams also do battle inside.

🛍 SHOPPING

BLOMMER CHOCOLATE STORE
FOOD & DRINK

(📞312-492-1336; 600 W Kinzie St; ☺9am-5pm Mon-Fri, to 1pm Sat; Ⓜ Blue Line to Grand) Often in the Loop, a smell wafts through that's so enticing you'd shoot your own mother in the kneecaps to get to it. It comes from Blommer Chocolate Factory, which provides the sweet stuff to big-time manufacturers such as Fannie May and Nabisco. Luckily, the wee attached store sells a line of Blommer's own goodies straight to consumers. The dark-chocolate-covered almonds reign supreme, and there's a sweet selection of retro candies including Zots, Pop Rocks and Zagnut bars.

GROOVE DISTRIBUTION
MUSIC

Map p312 (📞312-997-2375; www.groovedis.com; 346 N Justine St; ☺noon-7pm Tue-Fri; Ⓜ Green, Pink Line to Ashland) Whenever you're at a club, dancing to the beat, Groove is likely the source of the music. The company provides record stores around the world with downtempo, mashups, dubstep, nu jazz, cosmic disco and lotsa that Chicago specialty – house – both on vinyl and CD. You can shop right in the warehouse, which is exactly what discerning DJs do.

ATHENIAN CANDLE CO
CRAFT

Map p312 (📞312-332-6988; www.atheniancandle. com; 300 S Halsted St; ☺9:30am-6pm, closed Wed & Sun; Ⓜ Blue Line to UIC/Halsted) Whether

---

LOCAL KNOWLEDGE

NEAR WEST SIDE MARKETS

The neighborhood hosts a couple of stellar bazaars. They're a study in contrasts.

Maxwell Street Market (Map p312; 800 S Desplaines St; ☺7am-3pm Sun; Ⓜ Blue Line to Clinton) FREE is the working man's place. Starting early in the morning, hundreds of vendors set up outdoor stalls that sell everything from Jesus statues to 10 packs of tube socks to power tools. The market draws thrifty foodies who come for the homemade churros, tamales and other Mexican noshes, but mostly it draws folks seeking cheap clothing, electronics and junk galore.

Don't be fooled by the name: the market is not on Maxwell St, though it was for decades until gentrification forced it onward. It now stretches along Desplaines St between Harrison and Roosevelt Rds. The city runs the market and adds to the festivities with free fitness classes and the occasional band or dance group.

Randolph Street Market (Map p312; www.randolphstreetmarket.com; 1350 W Randolph St; admission $10; ☺10am-5pm Sat, to 4pm Sun, last weekend of the month; Ⓜ Green, Pink Line to Ashland) is styled on London's Portobello Market and is nicknamed 'the Barneys of Vintage.' The monthly market sprawls indoors and out and has an entrance fee. Hip shoppers make a day of it, trawling the antiques and vinyl swap. Then they settle in with a snack and glass of vino to hear the live bands.

Much of the action takes place inside the beaux-arts Plumbers Hall, where more than 200 sellers hock collectibles, costume jewelry, furniture, books, Turkish rugs and pinball machines. One of the coolest facets is the Indie Designer Market, where fledgling designers sell their one-of-a-kind skirts, shawls, handbags and other pieces. A free trolley picks up patrons downtown by the Water Works Visitor Center hourly. You can save a few bucks if you buy your admission ticket online.

you're hoping to get lucky at bingo, remove a jinx or fall in love, this Greektown store promises to help with its array of candles, incense, love potions and miracle oils. Though it has been making candles for Orthodox churches on-site since 1919, the owners aren't devoted to one religion: you'll find Buddha statues, Pope holograms, Turkish evil-eye stones and tarot cards.

WORKING BIKES
COOPERATIVE   OUTDOOR GEAR
(☎773-847-5440; www.workingbikes.org; 2434 S Western Ave; ⊗noon-7pm Wed & Thu, to 5pm Fri & Sat; ⓜPink Line to Western) This nonprofit group trawls local landfills and scrap yards for junked bikes, then brings them back to its warehouse and refurbishes them. Half get sold in the storefront shop; proceeds enable the group to ship the rest to developing countries. It's a great deal – you'll get a sturdy, well-oiled machine for the bargain price of about $100. If you're planning on renting a bike for more than a few days, consider buying one of the co-op's two-wheelers instead. When you're finished, you can donate it back.

🏃 SPORTS & ACTIVITIES

CHICAGO BULLS   BASKETBALL
Map p312 (www.nba.com/bulls; 1901 W Madison St; 🚌19, 20) They may not be the mythical champions of yore, but the Bulls are still well loved and draw good crowds. Tickets are available through the United Center box office – located at Gate 4 on the building's east side – and at Ticketmaster outlets. On game days, there's a special express bus (number 19) on Madison St that heads west to the stadium.

CHICAGO BLACKHAWKS   HOCKEY
Map p312 (www.chicagoblackhawks.com; 1901 W Madison St; 🚌19, 20) Tickets have become difficult to get, with lots of sellouts since the team's recent Stanley Cup wins (in 2010 and 2013). The box office and Ticketmaster do the honors. Be sure to arrive in time for the national anthem at the game's start. The raucous, ear-splitting rendition is a tradition. Express bus number 19 plies Madison St on game days.

WINDY CITY ROLLERS   SPECTATOR SPORT
Map p312 (www.windycityrollers.com; 525 S Racine Ave; tickets $20; ⓜBlue Line to Racine) The bang-'em-up sport of roller derby was born in Chicago in 1935, and it has made a comeback in recent years thanks to the battlin' beauties of the Windy City Rollers. Players boast names such as Sassy Squatch and Juanna Rumbel, and there is a fair amount of campy theater surrounding the bouts. But the action and the hits are real. Matches take place once a month at the UIC Pavilion from late January to mid-June.

PILSEN MURAL TOURS   WALKING TOUR
(☎773-342-4191; per group 1½hr tour $125) Pilsen is full of traditional Mexican murals. Local artist Jose Guerrero leads a highly recommended tour that takes in the most impressive works. Call to arrange an excursion.

South Loop & Near South Side

Neighborhood Top Five

1 Sizing up Sue the T-rex, the towering totem poles and magnificent mummies at the **Field Museum** (p180).

2 Seeing beluga whales and reef sharks swim by the glass windows at **Shedd Aquarium** (p181).

3 Viewing the stars and Chicago skyline from **Adler Planetarium** (p182).

4 Nibbling chestnut cakes and almond cookies at bakeries in **Chinatown**.

5 Hearing the best bluesmen in the biz bend frets at **Buddy Guy's Legends** (p189).

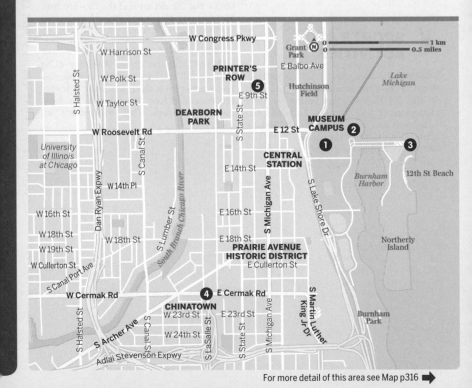

For more detail of this area see Map p316 →

Explore: South Loop & Near South Side

What you'll see when you come to the South Loop – and come you will, since this is where the Field Museum, the Shedd Aquarium and Adler Planetarium sit on the lakeshore – is a whole lot of shiny newness. The neighborhood went development crazy in recent years with high-rise condos and Columbia College's expansion, so it's also home to loads of young urbanites. The Museum Campus itself is lovely, jutting out into the blue-green lake and providing skyline views. Tranquil 12th St Beach and Northerly Island offer escapes if the crowds get to be too much.

Blues fans will want to make the pilgrimage further south to the old Chess Records site, a humble building where Muddy Waters and Howlin' Wolf plugged in their amps. History buffs will appreciate mansion-filled Prairie Ave between 16th and 20th Sts. The area around Chess, which abuts the massive McCormick Place convention center, is slated to be developed into an entertainment district with restaurants and music venues. Keep an eye on this space.

To top off the wealth of offerings, the neighborhood is also home to Chicago's small but busy Chinatown, where pork buns, steaming bowls of noodles and imported wares reward an afternoon of exploring.

Local Life

➡ **Global Dance Party** Learn to salsa, rumba or tango with Chicagoans at SummerDance (p190).

➡ **Chinatown Square** The plaza and mall are at their wonderful noisiest on weekends, when neighborhood families swarm in to eat and shop.

➡ **Blues Heaven** Locals stop by Willie Dixon's Blues Heaven (p186) to see who's plugging in for the free Thursday night concerts.

Getting There & Away

➡ **Bus** Number 146 goes to the Museum Campus/Soldier Field; bus 1 goes to Prairie Ave and sights on S Michigan Ave. In summer, bus 130 joins the action, running between State St in the Loop and the Museum Campus.

➡ **El** Red Line to Harrison for Printer's Row and the photography museum; Red Line to Cermak-Chinatown for Chinatown.

➡ **Metra** Roosevelt Rd stop for Museum Campus/Soldier Field; 18th St for Prairie Ave Historic District; 23rd St for McCormick Place.

➡ **Car** The Museum Campus boasts plenty of lot parking (from $15 per car on nonevent days); meter parking is available but scarce in the South Loop, and readily available in Near South Side.

Lonely Planet's Top Tip

In summer it's a good idea to buy advance tickets for the Shedd Aquarium, the most popular of the Museum Campus attractions. It's less necessary for the Field Museum unless there's an all-the-rage exhibit going on. For the Adler Planetarium and for the Shedd and Field in winter, there's no need for e-tickets. Save yourself the service charges.

Best Places to Eat

➡ Sweet Station (p188)
➡ Yolk (p188)
➡ Lao Sze Chuan (p189)
➡ Panozzo's (p188)
➡ Lawrence's Fisheries (p189)

For reviews, see p188 ➡

Best Places to Drink

➡ Little Branch Cafe (p189)
➡ Weathermark Tavern (p189)

For reviews, see p189 ➡

Best Places to Shop

➡ ShopColumbia (p190)
➡ Giftland (p191)
➡ Woks N Things (p191)
➡ Loopy Yarns (p190)
➡ Aji Ichiban (p191)

For reviews, see p190 ➡

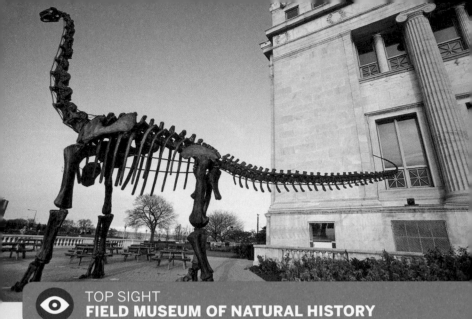

TOP SIGHT
FIELD MUSEUM OF NATURAL HISTORY

The mammoth Field Museum houses everything but the kitchen sink – beetles, mummies, gemstones, Bushman the stuffed ape. The collection's rock star is Sue, the largest Tyrannosaurus rex yet discovered. She's 13ft tall, 41ft long, and she menaces the main floor with ferocious aplomb. The galleries beyond hold 20 million other artifacts, tended by a slew of PhD-wielding scientists, as the Field remains an active research institution.

After communing with Sue, dino lovers should head up to the Evolving Planet exhibit on the 2nd floor, which has more of the big guys and gals. You can learn about the evolution of the species and watch staff paleontologists clean up fossils in the lab. There's even a mask that lets you see the world through a trilobite's eyes.

'Inside Ancient Egypt' is another good exhibit that recreates an Egyptian burial chamber on three levels. The mastaba (tomb) contains 23 actual mummies and is a reconstruction of the one built for Unis-ankh, the son of the last pharaoh of the Fifth dynasty, who died at age 21 in 2407 BC. The bottom level, with its twisting caverns, is especially worthwhile. Those reeds growing in the stream are real.

Other displays that merit your time include the polished Hall of Gems, the Northwest Coast and Arctic Peoples totem pole collection (many of which were shipped to Chicago for the 1893 World's Expo), and the largest man-eating lion ever caught (he's stuffed and standing sentry on the basement floor).

The basic admission fee covers all of the above. To see bells and whistles such as the 3-D movie or any of the special exhibits, it'll cost $8 more ($6 for kids). The various shops inside the museum are chock-full of dino gear.

DON'T MISS

→ Sue the T-rex
→ Hall of Gems
→ Totem poles
→ Mummies
→ Lions of Tsavo

PRACTICALITIES

→ Map p316
→ ☎312-922-9410
→ www.fieldmuseum.org
→ 1400 S Lake Shore Dr
→ adult/child $15/10
→ ⊙9am-5pm
→ ♿
→ ▣146, 130

TOP SIGHT
SHEDD AQUARIUM

A huge assortment of finned, gilled, amphibious and other aquatic creatures swims within the kiddie-mobbed, marble-clad confines of the John G Shedd Aquarium. Though it could simply rest on its superlative exhibits – say, beluga whales in a 4-million-gallon tank – the Shedd makes a point of trying to tie concepts of ecosystems, food webs and marine biology into its presentation of super-cool animals.

Permanent exhibits include the Oceanarium, which mimics ocean conditions off the northwest coast of North America. The beluga whales – cute creatures from the pint-sized end of the whale scale – are the star attraction. Pacific white-sided dolphins, sea lions and sea otters also frolic inside. Don't linger only on the main floor – you can go underneath and watch the mammals from below through viewing windows.

The Wild Reef exhibit will have sharkophiles and sharko-phobes equally entranced: over two dozen sharks cut through the waters in a simulation of a Philippines reef ecosystem. Penguins toddle around the Polar Play Zone in all their adorableness. And you've got to stop by the Caribbean Reef to look for Nickel, the sea turtle with the buoyant butt (the effect of a boating accident).

The 4-D theater costs $4 extra. The stingray touch tank, jellyfish exhibit and odd aquatic show each cost $5 extra.

You might want to pony up for advance-purchase tickets in summer. The regular admission line can be long (30 to 60 minutes). That sucks with little ones, especially if the weather is steamy. Buying online beforehand lets you avoid the outdoor queue, but there is a $5 surcharge (via Ticketmaster) per ticket.

While not widely promoted, there's also a 'general admission' ticket (fish and turtle tanks only; no sharks, whales or dolphins) for adult/child $8/6.

DON'T MISS
→ Beluga whales
→ Sharks
→ Penguins
→ Nickel the sea turtle

PRACTICALITIES
→ Map p316
→ ☎312-939-2438
→ www.sheddaquarium.org
→ 1200 S Lake Shore Dr
→ adult/child $29/20
→ ⊙9am-6pm Jun-Aug, to 5pm Sep-May
→ 🚼
→ 🚌146, 130

TOP SIGHT

ADLER PLANETARIUM & ASTRONOMY MUSEUM

Space enthusiasts will get a big bang out of the Adler, the first planetarium built in the western hemisphere. Cosmic films are shown in the digital theaters and use gaming-like technology (and real satellite data) to propel you around Earth and into star clusters. Cool interactive exhibits allow you to simulate events such as a meteor hitting the globe. Kids gravitate to the Planet Explorers gallery, where they can climb over a spacey landscape and 'launch' a rocket.

Adler's astronomers bring out their big honkin' telescopes to let you view the sun on Mondays and Thursdays at 10:30am. They also give occasional 3-D lectures, for which you receive special eyeglasses to watch presentations, such as 'Where supernovas come from.'

Basic admission includes the exhibits, telescope viewings and lectures; you can cover the place in less than two hours. The groovy films cost extra ($10 for one show, $16 for two). If you're only going to see one, make it 'Welcome to the Universe' for an astronaut's-eye view of the cosmos.

There's also much to see outside the Adler, and for free. Check out how the 1930s building has 12 sides, one for each sign of the zodiac. A 12ft **sundial** (Map p316) by sculptor Henry Moore marks the time near the main entrance. In the front median, the bronze **Copernicus statue** (Map p316) shows 16th-century Polish astronomer Nicolaus Copernicus holding a compass and a model of the solar system. But the best thing about the Adler's entrance? The front steps. Get your camera ready, because this is Chicago's primo skyline view. The steps are also a renowned spot for lovers to smooch.

The Adler is a good option if the next-door Shedd Aquarium is overrun, as the scene here is usually much quieter.

DON'T MISS

➡ Telescope viewings
➡ Sundial by Henry Moore
➡ Awesome city view from front steps
➡ Immersive sky show

PRACTICALITIES

➡ Map p316
➡ ☎312-922-7827
➡ www.adlerplanetarium.org
➡ 1300 S Lake Shore Dr
➡ adult/child $12/8
➡ ⊙9:30am-6pm Jun-Aug, 10am-4pm Sep-May
➡ 👪
➡ ◻146, 130

 **SIGHTS**

South Loop

SHEDD AQUARIUM   AQUARIUM
See p181.

**FIELD MUSEUM OF
NATURAL HISTORY**   MUSEUM
See p180.

**ADLER PLANETARIUM
& ASTRONOMY MUSEUM**   MUSEUM
See p182.

NORTHERLY ISLAND   PARK
Map p316 (1400 S Lynn White Dr; ☐146 or 130)
Northerly Island was once the busy commuter airport known as Meigs Field. Now
it's a prairie-grassed park with walking
trails, fishing, birdwatching and an outdoor concert venue.

The shift from runway to willowy grasses
has its root in a controversial incident that
reads a little like a municipal spy thriller,
complete with midnight operatives and surprise bulldozings. To sum it up: Mayor Richard M Daley wanted the land for a park;
businesses wanted to keep it for their private
planes. A standoff ensued. Then, one dark
night in March 2003, Daley fired up the
heavy machinery and razed the airfield while
the city slept. His reasoning? Terrorists could
attack Chicago with tiny planes launched
from Meigs; the airfield was a security liabil-
ity. Why it couldn't be jackhammered during
daylight hours was never answered. But by
2005 the controversy had died down, and
Chicagoans were out in force, happily exploring this beautiful piece of lakefront that had
been off-limits for a half-century.

SOLDIER FIELD   STADIUM
Map p316 (☐312-235-7152; www.soldierfield.
net; 1410 S Museum Campus Dr, tours adult/
child $15/4; ☐146 or 130) Built between 1922
and 1926 to pay homage to WWI soldiers,
this oft-renovated edifice has been home
to everything from civil-rights speeches by
Martin Luther King Jr to Brazilian soccer
games. It got its latest UFO-landing-upon-
a-Greek-ruin look in a controversial 2003
makeover. The Bears now play football
here. Stadium tours are available; advance
booking is required by phone or online.

Before the 2003 renovation, Soldier
Field's architecture was so noteworthy
it was named a National Historic Landmark. Unfortunately, the landmark lacked

LOCAL KNOWLEDGE

PRINTER'S ROW ARCHITECTURE

Chicago was a center for printing at the turn of the 20th century, and the rows of
buildings on S Dearborn St from W Congress Pkwy south to W Polk St housed the
heart of the city's publishing industry. By the 1970s the printers had left for more
economical quarters elsewhere, and the buildings had been largely emptied out.

In the late 1970s savvy developers saw the potential in these derelicts, and one
of the most successful gentrification projects in Chicago began. The following de-
scribes some of the notable buildings in the area as you travel from north to south.

Mergenthaler Lofts (Map p316; 531 S Plymouth Ct) A snazzy renovation of this building, the 1886 headquarters for the legendary linotype company, included the artful
preservation of a diner storefront.

Pontiac Building (Map p316; 542 S Dearborn St) A classic 1891 design by Holabird &
Roche, the Pontiac features the same flowing masonry surfaces as the firm's famed
Monadnock Building in the Loop.

Second Franklin Building (Map p316; 720 S Dearborn St) A 1912 factory, it shows the
history of printing on its tiled facade. The roof slopes to allow for a huge skylight over
the top floor where books were hand bound (the building existed long before fluores-
cent lights or high-intensity lamps). The large windows on many of the other buildings
in the area served the same purpose.

Dearborn St Station (Map p316; 47 W Polk St) Once the Chicago terminal of the Santa
Fe Railroad, the 1885 building used to be the premier station for trains to and from
California. Today it merely sees the trains of parent-propelled strollers from the Dear-
born Park neighborhood, built on the site of the tracks to the south.

South Loop & Near South Side – Family-Friendly South Loop

Where to begin for family fun? The Shedd Aquarium's beluga whales? The Field Museum's hulking dinosaurs? The Adler Planetarium's lunar landscape to climb over? If the indoors gets to be too much, parkland and a beach surround the museums, so kids have space to romp and burn off steam.

2

CHARLES COOK / GETTY IMAGES ©

4

RICHARD NOWITZ / NATIONAL GEOGRAPHIC SOCIETY / CORBIS ©

1. Shedd Aquarium (p181)
Commune with dolphins, whales, sharks and other creatures from the deep.

2. Caribbean Reef Exhibit (p181)
Stop by this exhibit at Shedd Aquarium and look for Nickel, the sea turtle with the buoyant butt.

3. 12th St Beach (p191)
Take time out from sightseeing with a swim at this secluded beach.

4. Field Museum (p180)
Among 20 million artifacts, the museum boasts Sue, the largest Tyrannosaurus rex yet discovered.

3

PETER TITMUSS / ALAMY ©

corporate skyboxes and giant bathrooms, so the city (the venue is owned by the park district) decided it was time for a change. The new look met almost unanimous derision when it was unveiled; critics quickly dubbed it 'the Mistake on the Lake.' The landmark folks agreed and whacked it from their list, saying it jeopardized the national landmark integrity. And that was that.

OLMEC HEAD NO 8   MONUMENT

Map p316 (🖥146 or 130) Staring out from the Field Museum's lawn, Olmec Head No 8 is a replica of one of many sculptures the Olmec people carved in Veracruz, Mexico, c 1300 BC. Scholars believe the colossal heads are likenesses of revered Olmec leaders. This guy's noggin weighs in at 1700lb.

MUSEUM OF CONTEMPORARY PHOTOGRAPHY   MUSEUM

Map p316 (📞312-663-5554; www.mocp.org; Columbia College, 600 S Michigan Ave; ⊙10am-5pm Mon-Wed, Fri & Sat, 10am-8pm Thu, noon-5pm Sun; Ⓜ Red Line to Harrison) FREE This museum focuses on American photography since 1937, and is the only institution of its kind between the coasts. The permanent collection includes the works of Debbie Fleming Caffery, Mark Klett, Catherine Wagner, Patrick Nagatani and 500 more of the best photographers working today. Special exhibitions (also free) augment the rotating permanent collection.

SPERTUS INSTITUTE   CULTURAL CENTER

Map p316 (📞312-322-1700; www.spertus.edu; 610 S Michigan Ave; ⊙10am-5pm Sun-Wed, to 6pm Thu, to 3pm Fri; Ⓜ Red Line to Harrison) FREE Located in a glassy mod facility, Spertus is a center for Jewish learning and culture. The institute often has special exhibits with an art or cultural focus on display in its 1st floor vestibule gallery.

CHINATOWN TOUR

The **Chicago Chinese Cultural Institute** (www.chinatowntourchicago.com; 1hr tour $10) offers a guided walking tour covering the neighborhood's history, architecture and cultural highlights. Departure is at 10am Friday through Sunday in summer from Three Happiness Restaurant at 2130 S Wentworth Ave. You must reserve in advance.

⊙ Chinatown

Chicago's small but busy Chinatown is an easy 10-minute train ride from the Loop. Take the Red Line to the Cermak-Chinatown stop, which puts you between the neighborhood's two distinct parts: Chinatown Square (an enormous bilevel strip mall) unfurls to the north along Archer Ave, while Old Chinatown (the traditional retail area) stretches along Wentworth Ave to the south. Either zone allows you to graze through bakeries and shop for the requisite Hello Kitty trinkets.

PING TOM MEMORIAL PARK   PARK

Map p316 (300 W 19th St) Ping Tom Memorial Park offers dramatic city-railroad-bridge views. In summer, Chicago Water Taxi runs a groovy boat down the Chicago River from Michigan Ave (the dock is on the bridge's northwest side, by the Wrigley Building) to the park. It costs $4 one way ($5 on weekends), and takes 25 minutes.

ON LEONG BUILDING   BUILDING

Map p316 (2216 S Wentworth Ave) Built in 1928, the grand structure is a fantasy of Chinese architecture that makes good use of glazed terra-cotta details. Note how the lions guarding the door have twisted their heads so they don't have to risk bad luck by turning their backs to each other. The building is now called the Pui Tak Center and provides ESL classes and other community programs.

⊙ Near South Side

WILLIE DIXON'S BLUES HEAVEN   HISTORIC BUILDING

Map p316 (📞312-808-1286; www.bluesheaven.com; 2120 S Michigan Ave; tours $5-10; ⊙11am-4pm Mon-Fri, noon-2pm Sat; 🚌1) From 1957 to 1967, the humble building at 2120 S Michigan Ave was Chess Records, the seminal electric blues label. It's now called Willie Dixon's Blues Heaven Foundation, named for the bassist who wrote most of Chess's hits, and it's open for tours. Free blues concerts rock the side garden on summer Thursdays at 6pm.

The Chess brothers, two Polish Jews, ran the recording studio that saw – and heard – the likes of Muddy Waters, Bo Diddley, Koko Taylor and others. Chuck Berry recorded four top-10 singles here, and the Rolling Stones named a song '2120 S Michigan Ave' after a recording session at this spot in 1964. (Rock trivia buffs will know that the Stones named themselves after the Muddy Waters song 'Rolling Stone.')

But within a few decades, the building had fallen by the wayside and was on the chopping block until Dixon's family bought it. It opens for tours most days, and small groups of hard-core blues fans trickle in for the pilgrimage through the old offices and studios. It's pretty ramshackle, with few original artifacts on display. Still, when Willie's grandson hauls out the bluesman's well-worn standup bass and lets you take a pluck, it's pretty cool...

The hours can be erratic, so it's wise to call first to make sure someone is on site. There are two types of tour: the short one ($5, which is 25 minutes and our recommendation), and the long one ($10, which adds a 45-minute video to the mix).

PRAIRIE AVENUE
HISTORIC DISTRICT   ARCHITECTURE

Map p316 (🚌1) In the late 1800s, Prairie Ave between 16th and 20th Sts is where Chicago's millionaires lived in their mansions. Today the district is good for a stroll. Some of the homes have been preserved as museums; others are intriguing to admire from the outside. A footbridge over the train tracks links the area to Burnham Park and the Museum Campus.

Prairie Ave was millionaire's row until the vice and industry of the nearby Levee District (four blocks west) got too close for comfort. By 1900 the crème de la crème had packed up and moved north to the Gold Coast. The neighborhood endured years of decline until the Chicago Architecture Foundation stepped in to help restore various buildings.

Nifty ones to check out from the street (they're privately owned, so you can't go in) include the **William K Kimball House** (Map p316; 1801 S Prairie Ave), which dates from 1892 and is modeled after a 15th-century French château. Both it and the Romanesque **Joseph G Coleman House** (Map p316; 1811 S Prairie Ave) now serve as the incongruous headquarters for the US Soccer Federation. Limestone puts a glitzy facade on the brick **Elbridge G Keith House** (Map p316; 1900 S Prairie Ave), an 1870 home.

CLARKE HOUSE MUSEUM   MUSEUM

Map p316 (📞312-326-1480; www.clarkehousemuseum.org; 1827 S Indiana Ave; tours adult/child $10/6, Wed free; ⏰tours noon & 2pm Wed-Sun;

🚌1) The Henry B Clarke House is the oldest structure in the city. When Caroline and Henry Clarke built the imposing Greek revival home in 1836, log cabins were still the rage in Chicago residential architecture. The interior has been restored to the period of the Clarkes' occupation, which ended in 1872. One-hour tours delve into the family's life and times.

During the past 170-plus years the house has been moved twice to escape demolition. The present address is about as close as researchers can get to its somewhat undefined original location.

GLESSNER HOUSE MUSEUM   MUSEUM

Map p316 (📞312-326-1480; www.glessnerhouse.org; 1800 S Prairie Ave; tours adult/child $10/6, Wed free; ⏰tours 1pm & 3pm Wed-Sun; 🚌1) The 1887 John J Glessner House is the premier survivor of the Prairie Avenue Historic District. Much of the interior is reminiscent of an English manor house, with heavy wooden beams and other English-style details. Additionally, more than 80% of the current furnishings are authentic, thanks to the Glessner family's penchant for family photos. One-hour tours take it all in.

Famed American architect Henry Hobson Richardson designed the beautiful composition of rusticated granite. The L-shaped house surrounds a sunny southern courtyard.

CHICAGO WOMEN'S PARK   PARK

Map p316 (1827 S Indiana Ave; 🚌1) Fronting on Prairie Ave, with the Glessner House to the north and the Clarke House to the west, this 4-acre park has a French garden, a fountain and winding paths. It also has a notorious past. The Fort Dearborn battle, in which a group of local Native Americans rebelled against the incursion of white settlers, is thought to have occurred on this very spot on August 15, 1812.

MCCORMICK PLACE
BUILDING

Map p316 (📞312-791-7000; www.mccormick-place.com; 2301 S Lake Shore Dr, main entrance on S Martin Luther King Jr Dr; Ⓜ Metra to 23rd St) Called 'the Mistake on the Lake' before Soldier Field (p183) stole the title, the McCormick Place convention center is an economic engine that drives up profits for the city's hotels, restaurants, shops and airlines. 'Vast' isn't big enough to describe it. The 2.7 million sq ft of meeting space spreads out over four halls, making this the largest convention center in the country. As usual, it's undergoing an expansion to increase restaurant and hotel capacity.

✖ EATING

✖ South Loop

YOLK
BREAKFAST $

Map p316 (📞312-789-9655; www.eatyolk.com; 1120 S Michigan Ave; mains $8-12; ☺6am-3pm Mon-Fri, from 7am Sat & Sun; ♿; Ⓜ Red, Orange, Green Line to Roosevelt) This diner is worth the long wait – you'll dig into the best traditional breakfast in the South Loop. The omelets include lots of healthy options (the Iron Man is made from egg whites and comes loaded with veggies and avocado), and sweets lovers have stacks of cinnamon-roll French toast and peach-cobbler crepes to drench in syrup. Scores of big salads and burgers are on hand for those inclined to order lunch.

PANOZZO'S
ITALIAN $

Map p316 (📞312-356-9966; www.panozzos.com; 1303 S Michigan Ave; mains $8-10; ☺10am-8pm Tue-Fri, 10am-5pm Sat & Sun; Ⓜ Red, Orange, Green Line to Roosevelt) Stock your picnic basket for the Museum Campus at Panozzo's. Head to the deli counter in the back where staff prepare hulking hot (house-made meatball) and cold (prosciutto and mozzarella) sandwiches, plus lasagna, rice balls and roasted chicken. Grab a bottle of wine, Italian cookies or cheeses to accompany your selection.

EPIC BURGER
BURGERS $

Map p316 (📞312-913-1373; www.epicburger.com; 517 S State St; mains $6-9; ☺11am-10pm Mon-Thu, to 11pm Fri & Sat, 10am-9pm Sun; Ⓜ Brown, Orange, Purple, Pink Line to Library) 🥐 This sprawling, sunny-orange restaurant brings ecoconscious fast-food eaters the goods they crave: burgers made with all-natural beef, no hormones or antibiotics, topped with cage-free organic eggs and nitrate-free bacon; preservative-free buns; vanilla-bean-speckled milkshakes; and no petroleum-based packaging. The loud music and flat-screen TVs draw a student crowd from the surrounding college campuses in the South Loop.

CHICAGO CURRY HOUSE
INDIAN $$

Map p316 (📞312-362-9999; www.curryhouse-online.com; 899 S Plymouth Ct; mains $10-19; ☺11am-10pm; ♿; Ⓜ Red Line to Harrison) Even if it's just standard Indian food in a standard Indian restaurant ambience, the Curry House provides a nice option for the South Loop and offers a rare bonus: Nepalese dishes. Standouts include *aloo tama bodi* (potatoes and black-eyed peas) and *khasi ko maasu* (goat meat on the bone). Sample them at the lunch buffet. A full bar helps wash it all down.

CHICAGO FIREHOUSE
AMERICAN $$$

Map p316 (📞312-786-1401; www.chicagofire-house.com; 1401 S Michigan Ave; mains $20-35; ☺11:30am-10pm Mon-Fri, from 9:30am Sat & Sun; Ⓜ Red, Orange, Green Line to Roosevelt) Situated in a carefully restored turn-of-the-century firehouse, this place offers traditional American cuisine. Ribs and steaks headline the show. Head to the leafy patio when the weather permits.

✖ Chinatown

SWEET STATION
CHINESE $

Map p316 (www.mysweetstation.com; 2101 S China Pl; mains $5-10; ☺8am-4am Mon-Thu, 24hr Fri & Sat, to 2am Sun; Ⓜ Red Line to Cermak-Chinatown) Join the young, hip Asian crowd chowing down at Sweet Station in Chinatown Sq. Slide into a booth, flip on the table's flat-screen TV, then settle in to examine the massive menu. It sprawls through a global medley including Portuguese pork-chop sandwiches, Hong Kong–style baked spaghetti, Szechuan hot pots, curried tofu and good ol' French toast.

When the weather blows, it's hard to beat a warm egg-custard tart and glass of almond milk for breakfast. Bonus for late-night types: Sweet Station serves into the wee hours (and all night long on Friday and Saturday).

LAWRENCE'S FISHERIES SEAFOOD $

Map p316 (☏312-225-2113; www.lawrences-fisheries.com; 2120 S Canal St; mains $6-12; ⊗24hr; ⓜRed Line to Cermak-Chinatown) There's not much to look at inside this 24-hour joint, but the window at the end of the long dining room frames a stunning scene of the Willis Tower over the Chicago River. Not that you have much option but to stand agape once your order arrives – delicious treats such as popcorn shrimp, oysters and fish and chips are stalwarts.

Frog legs and scallops round out the menu of batter-crusted goodies from the sea. At night the parking lot outside of this typically family-oriented joint is a prime location for locals to sit on car hoods and shop for suspiciously current DVDs.

WAN SHI DA BAKERY CHINESE $

Map p316 (☏312-225-1133; 2229 S Wentworth Ave; items $1-3; ⊗7am-8pm; ⓜRed Line to Cermak-Chinatown) Offering the best, and cheapest à la carte lunch in Chinatown, this bright little bakery has fluffy barbecue-pork buns, hot-dog buns (a Chinese variation on the pig in a blanket), bite-sized egg-custard tarts, coconut and winter-melon pastries and some dim-sum fare. It's available to go, or to scarf down by the handful at the no-frills tables in the back.

The more weather-beaten sister bakery across the street, Chiu Quon Bakery, has a nearly identical menu and more tourist foot traffic. Cash only.

LAO SZE CHUAN CHINESE $$

Map p316 (☏312-326-5040; www.tonygourmetgroup.com; 2172 S Archer Ave; mains $12-20; ⊗10:30am-midnight; ⓜRed Line to Cermak-Chinatown) Lao Sze Chuan is the most authentic option in heavily touristy Chinatown Sq. The house special is the three-chili chicken, which is tender and very spicy, though the extensive menu has excellent hot pots alongside dishes from the far reaches of the Szechuan province. If the choices are overwhelming, look for advice from watchful chef and owner 'Tony' Xiao Jun Hu.

JOY YEE'S NOODLE SHOP ASIAN $$

Map p316 (☏312-328-0001; www.joyyee.com; 2139 S China Pl; mains $8-15; ⊗11:30am-10:30pm; ♿; ⓜRed Line to Cermak-Chinatown) Folks line up for bubble teas packed with fresh fruit at this brightly colored, hip cafe in Chinatown Sq. Do yourself a favor, though, and save one of the deliciously sweet drinks for dessert after a bowl of udon, *chow fun* (rice noodles) or chow mein.

PHOENIX CHINESE $$

Map p316 (☏312-328-0848; www.chinatown-phoenix.com; 2131 S Archer Ave; mains $14-21; ⊗9am-10pm Mon-Fri, from 8am Sat & Sun; ⓜRed Line to Cermak-Chinatown) Though better sit-down dinner experiences in Chinatown are abundant, the draw here is the excellent dim sum. Small plates of *char siu bao* (barbecued pork buns), shrimp-filled rice noodles, egg custards and other popular vitals roll around the dining room in a seemingly endless parade of carts.

The language barrier can be an issue, so keep in mind that if it looks like chicken feet, it probably is.

🍺 DRINKING & NIGHTLIFE

LITTLE BRANCH CAFE CAFE

Map p316 (☏312-360-0101; www.littlebranchcafe.com; 1251 S Prairie Ave; ⊗7am-7pm Mon & Tue, 7am-10pm Wed-Fri, 8am-7pm Sat & Sun; 🍴; ⓜRed, Orange, Green Line to Roosevelt) A good fortifier after the Museum Campus, Little Branch is probably better known for its food than its drinks, but it does indeed have a bar. And that bar stirs hot toddies, Irish coffees and gin-filled Corpse Revivers, and serves a small roster of wines and beers. The cafe hides in a residential complex.

WEATHERMARK TAVERN PUB

Map p316 (www.weathermarktavern.com; 1503 S Michigan Ave; ⊗11:30am-late Mon-Fri, from 10:30am Sat & Sun; ⓜRed, Orange, Green Line to Roosevelt) While Weathermark is one of the least obnoxious of the South Loop's upscale pubs, it does get in your face with its nautical theme and rum-based 'sailor's rations.' Still, we forgive it because the bar also pours hard-to-find local microbrews such as Three Floyd's Zombie Dust. The place packs 'em in for Bears games and Thursday trivia night.

☆ ENTERTAINMENT

★ BUDDY GUY'S LEGENDS BLUES

Map p316 (www.buddyguys.com; 700 S Wabash Ave; tickets Sun-Thu $10, Fri & Sat $20; ⊗from 5pm Mon & Tue, from 11am Wed-Fri, from noon Sat & Sun; ⓜRed Line to Harrison) Top local and

FREE BLUES AT BUDDY'S

Buddy Guy's Legends (p189) hosts free, all-ages acoustic performances from noon to 2pm Wednesday through Sunday. Listen in while having lunch (the club doubles as a Cajun restaurant) or a drink at the bar.

national blues acts wail on the stage of local icon Buddy Guy. The man himself plugs in his ax during a multishow residency in January; keep an eye on the website for details (tickets usually go on sale in November). The location is a bit rough around the edges, but the acts are consistently excellent.

SUMMERDANCE MUSIC

Map p316 (☑312-742-4007; www.chicagosummerdance.org; 601 S Michigan Ave; ☺6pm Thu-Sat, 4pm Sun late Jun–mid-Sep; ⓂRed Line to Harrison) FREE Boogie at the Spirit of Music Garden in Grant Park with a multiethnic mash-up of locals. Bands play rumba, samba and other world beats preceded by fun dance lessons – all free.

JAZZ SHOWCASE JAZZ

Map p316 (www.jazzshowcase.com; 806 S Plymouth Ct; ☺from 8pm Mon-Sat, from 4pm Sun; ⓂRed Line to Harrison) The Jazz Showcase, set in a gorgeous room in historic Dearborn Station, is Chicago's top club for national names. In general, local musicians take the stage Monday through Wednesday, with visiting jazz cats blowing their horns Thursday through Sunday. Tickets cost $20 to $35.

REGGIES ROCK CLUB LIVE MUSIC

Map p316 (☑312-949-0121; www.reggieslive.com; 2109 S State St; ☺from 11am; ⓂRed Line to Cermak-Chinatown) Bring on the punk and the all-ages shows. Graffitied Reggies books mostly touring hard-core bands at the Rock Club. Next door, Reggies Music Joint is for folks 21 and older, and hosts more mainstream (we use that term loosely) live music nightly, as well as trips to see the White Sox, the Bears and other sports teams.

DANCE CENTER AT COLUMBIA COLLEGE DANCE

Map p316 (☑312-344-8300; www.colum.edu/dancecenter; 1306 S Michigan Ave; ⓂGreen, Or-

ange Line to Roosevelt) More than an academic institution, the Dance Center is one of the most focused collegiate modern dance programs in the country and has carved out a fine reputation. The on-site theater attracts quality performers from beyond Chicago and hosts everything from tap jams to classical Indian dance.

PAVILION AT NORTHERLY ISLAND CONCERT VENUE

Map p316 (☑312-540-2668; ☐146 or 130) Northerly Island's grassy environs and skyline backdrop make a splendid place to see a touring band such as Jimmy Buffet or Phish. The outdoor concert venue was supposed to be temporary when it opened a decade ago, but as the years roll by and the bands keep plugging in, it appears the pavilion is here to stay.

🛍 SHOPPING

🛍 South Loop

SHOPCOLUMBIA ARTS & CRAFTS

Map p316 (☑312-369-8616; www.colum.edu/shopcolumbia; 1st fl, 623 S Wabash Ave; ☺11am-5pm Mon-Fri; ⓂRed Line to Harrison) This is Columbia College's student store, where artists and designers in training learn how to market their wares. The shop carries original pieces spanning all media and disciplines: clothes, jewelry, prints, mugs, stationery and more. Proceeds help individual students earn income, and part goes toward student scholarships. It's attached to the college's student center and coffee-slinging cafe.

LOOPY YARNS ARTS & CRAFTS

Map p316 (☑312-583-9276; www.loopyyarns.com; 47 W Polk St; ☺11am-7pm Mon-Fri, 10am-6pm Sat, noon-5pm Sun; ⓂRed Line to Harrison) This isn't your grandma's knitting shop. Loopy Yarns caters mostly to students from the nearby Art Institute, so the books, patterns, needles, hooks and designer yarns are about as hip as they come. Beginners can learn to knit or crochet in a workshop (two hours $90, materials included).

Advanced practitioners can learn more complex techniques while making a fair-isle hat or flip-top mittens (two hours $20 to $60, materials not included). Check the website for the schedule.

SANDMEYER'S BOOKSTORE BOOKS
Map p316 (www.sandmeyersbookstore.com; 714 S Dearborn St; ⊙11am-6:30pm Mon-Fri, to 5pm Sat, to 4pm Sun; MRed Line to Harrison) It's not big, it's not flashy and it doesn't host many author events. Instead this small Printer's Row spot offers an old-school bookstore experience of creaking wood floors and jazz piping softly through the speakers while you browse tomes of all types.

⛩ Chinatown

GIFTLAND GIFTS
Map p316 (☎312-225-0088; 2212 S Wentworth Ave; ⊙10am-7pm; MRed Line to Cermak-Chinatown) After you see it, you'll wonder how you've lived without it: a toast-scented Hello Kitty eraser. Giftland stocks a swell supply of pens, stationery, coin purses and backpacks donning the images of Kitty as well as Mashimaro, Pucca, Doraemon and other Asian cartoon characters.

WOKS N THINGS HOMEWARES
Map p316 (☎312-842-0701; 2234 S Wentworth Ave; ⊙10am-7pm; MRed Line to Cermak-Chinatown) This busy store carries every kind of utensil and cookware you could want – pots, pans, wok brushes, knives. Don't miss the baseball-bat-shaped chopstick holders.

AJI ICHIBAN FOOD & DRINK
Map p316 (☎312-328-9998; www.ajiichiban-usa.com; 2117-A S China Pl; ⊙11am-8pm Mon-Fri, 10am-9pm Sat & Sun; MRed Line to Cermak-Chinatown) The front sign at this Asian snack and candy store says 'Munchies Paradise,' and so it is. Sweet and salty treats fill the bulk bins, from dried salted plums to chocolate wafer cookies, roasted fish crisps to fruity hard candies. It's all packaged in cool, cartoony wrappers, with plenty of samples out for grabs. Located in Chinatown Sq.

TEN REN TEA & GINSENG CO FOOD & DRINK
Map p316 (☎312-842-1171; www.tenren.com; 2247 S Wentworth Ave; ⊙9:30am-7pm; MRed Line to Cermak-Chinatown) Ten Ren is *the* place to buy green, red, white and black teas, plus the teacups and teapots to serve them in. It also sells thirst-quenching bubble teas at the counter.

HOYPOLOI HOMEWARES
Map p316 (☎312-225-6477; www.hoypoloigallery.com; 2235 S Wentworth Ave; ⊙noon-8pm Wed-Sun; MRed Line to Cermak-Chinatown) Hoypoloi is more upscale than most Chinatown stores – it's actually a gallery filled with Asian artwork, glassware, funky lamps and other interior items. The wind-chime selection wins kudos.

BUDDHIST TEMPLE GIFT SHOP GIFTS
Map p316 (☎312-881-0177, www.ibfachicago.org; 2249 S Wentworth Ave; ⊙9am-6pm; MRed Line to Cermak-Chinatown) Follow your nose into this quiet, incense-wafting storefront to contemplate charms and necklaces (for good luck and happiness), books on how to meditate, Buddha statues and other spiritual items.

🏃 SPORTS & ACTIVITIES

CHICAGO BEARS FOOTBALL
Map p316 (www.chicagobears.com; 1410 S Museum Campus Dr; ☐146, 130) Da Bears, Chicago's NFL team, tackle at Soldier Field from September through January. Tickets are hard to come by, and are available only through Ticketmaster. Arrive early on game days and wander through the parking lots – you won't believe the elaborate tailgate feasts people cook up from the back of their cars. And for crissake, dress warmly.

12TH STREET BEACH BEACH
Map p316 (www.cpdbeaches.com; 1200 S Linn White Dr; ☐146, 130) A path runs south from the Adler Planetarium to 12th St Beach, where there are good views of the lake and the fishermen who are likely to be casting there. Despite the beach's proximity to the Museum Campus and its zillions of visitors, the crescent-shaped sand sliver remains bizarrely (but happily) secluded.

There aren't many amenities besides a bathhouse and a taco stand. Beach bonus: if you can't get tickets to see your favorite band at the Pavilion at Northerly Island, you can sit here and still hear the tunes.

SLEDDING HILL SNOW SPORTS
Map p316 (☎235 7000; 1410 S Museum Campus Dr; ☐146 or 130) The Park District operates a free, 33ft sledding hill on the southeast side of Soldier Field in winter; bring your own gear. A snow-making machine is fired up when the weather doesn't cooperate.

Hyde Park & South Side

HYDE PARK | BRIDGEPORT | BRONZEVILLE

Neighborhood Top Five

1 Gawking at the eye-popping stained glass and horizontal design of **Robie House** (p194), Frank Lloyd Wright's Prairie-style masterpiece.

2 Exploring the U-boat, doll house and mock tornado at the **Museum of Science & Industry** (p195).

3 Strolling by **Obama's house** (p197) and the other distinctive architecture in Kenwood.

4 Seeking out the stage where Louis Armstrong played at **Meyers Ace Hardware Store** (p200).

5 Losing yourself in the labyrinth at **57th Street Books** (p204).

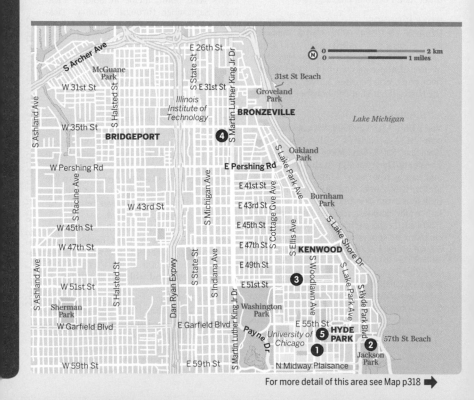

For more detail of this area see Map p318 ➡

Explore: Hyde Park & South Side

The South Side is huge, but most of the sights are concentrated in three areas: Hyde Park, home to the gargoyle-cluttered University of Chicago; Bridgeport, a traditional Irish neighborhood that has become a pocket of cool, sprinkled with artists studios and hip restaurants; and Bronzeville, the historic heart of Chicago's black arts and cultural scene.

In Hyde Park, the intersection of 57th St and S University Ave is a great place to start exploring the neighborhood. That'll put you close to the brainy bookstores, Frank Lloyd Wright's Robie House and the site where the atomic age began. You could spend a day here easily. Architecture buffs and black-history enthusiasts should block out an afternoon for Bronzeville. Bridgeport's bars and White Sox baseball games make it ideal for an evening visit.

Beyond these areas, explorers will find neighborhoods that are slowly piecing things together in the shadow of some of the country's bleakest housing projects, the neglected flip side of the immaculately groomed Chicago pictured in tourist brochures. Around 74th and 75th Sts you'll find a stretch of soul food, blues and jazz, but you'll need a car to get there.

Local Life

→ **Third Fridays** The monthly open studios night that Bridgeport Art Center (p200) and Zhou B Art Center (p200) sponsor has become one of the city's coolest soirees.

→ **Community Bar** The name doesn't lie at Maria's Packaged Goods and Community Bar (p203): it really is a communal watering hole. Schaller's Pump (p204) is the old-school version down the road.

→ **Neighborhood News** For years neighborhood folks – including a gent named Barack Obama – have gathered to gossip while forking into Southern-style biscuits, bacon and pot pies at Valois Cafeteria (p201).

Getting There & Away

→ **Bus** Number 6 runs from State St in the Loop to Hyde Park (it's relatively quick since it goes express between 11th and 47th Sts). Bus 8 motors along Hasted St for Bridgeport.

→ **El** Green Line to 35th-Bronzeville-IIT for Bronzeville and the Illinois Institute of Technology sights. Red Line to Sox-35th for the ballpark.

→ **Metra** 55th-56th-57th St station for Hyde Park, 51st-53rd St station for Kenwood.

→ **Car** Hyde Park can be tight. Free parking is available on the street and in university parking lots after 4pm weekdays and all day on weekends. Bridgeport and Bronzeville shouldn't be a problem.

Lonely Planet's Top Tip

Don't be put off by the distance of these southern neighborhoods from downtown. They're all easy to reach by public transportation, especially Hyde Park, and the sights, bookshops, bars and restaurants offer a true, exceptional slice of Chicago. Really, where else are you going to see President Obama's bulletproof-glass-encased barber chair?

✖ Best Places to Eat

→ Pleasant House Bakery (p203)

→ Nana (p203)

→ Valois Cafeteria (p201)

→ Soul Vegetarian East (p203)

→ Medici (p203)

For reviews, see p201

🍷 Best Places to Drink

→ Maria's Packaged Goods and Community Bar (p203)

→ Jimmy's Woodlawn Tap (p203)

→ Bernice's Tavern (p203)

→ Schaller's Pump (p204)

For reviews, see p203

⊙ Best Museums

→ Robie House (p194)

→ Museum of Science & Industry (p195)

→ Smart Museum of Art (p196)

→ Oriental Institute (p196)

→ DuSable Museum of African American History (p196)

For reviews, see p196

TOP SIGHT
ROBIE HOUSE

Robie House is one of the most famous dwellings in the world. Designed by Frank Lloyd Wright, it's the masterpiece of his Prairie School style, and it's often listed among the most important structures in American architecture. The low horizontal planes and dramatic cantilevers were meant to mirror the Midwestern landscape, and they're ornamented by 174 exquisite stained- and leaded-glass doors and windows.

Frederick C Robie, a forward-thinking businessman who dealt in bicycle parts and early auto machinery, was only 28 years old when he commissioned Wright to build a mod house for his family. Wright designed it in his Oak Park studio between 1908 and 1909, but he wasn't around for the majority of the construction, as he had packed up and moved to Europe with his mistress by then. His associates finished the building, and the Robies moved into the home in 1910. Their residency was short-lived, however. After 14 months, financial and marital problems forced them to sell the house. It was threatened with demolition several times, until it became a landmark under Mayor Richard J Daley in the 1950s.

Docents provide one-hour tours, roughly every half-hour from June through October, and hourly otherwise. They go room to room explaining Wright's design concept in each space and how he achieved it. Note how the furniture repeats the building's forms, and how the colors link to the autumnal prairie palette.

Robie House has been undergoing renovation for several years, but the tours work around it. Advance tickets are highly recommended; call or go online.

Robie House also does lots of children's programming. The 'Wright 3' tours on Saturday at 1:30pm are based on the same-named children's novel and use junior guides to take families through the mysterious spaces.

DON'T MISS

➜ Exterior view against the horizon
➜ Stained glass everywhere
➜ Cantilevered roofs
➜ Fireplace
➜ Children's tours

PRACTICALITIES

➜ Map p318
➜ ☏312-994-4000
➜ www.gowright.org
➜ 5757 S Woodlawn Ave
➜ adult/child $15/12
➜ ⊙11am-3pm Thu-Mon
➜ 🚌6, Ⓜ Metra to 55th-56th-57th

 TOP SIGHT
MUSEUM OF SCIENCE & INDUSTRY

Sure, the permanent exhibits of this enormous museum examine just about every aspect of life on Earth, but its pleasures are in the details: chicks struggling to peck their way out of shells in the baby-chick hatchery, the whimsical little high jinks of wooden puppets in the Cabaret Mechanical Theatre and the minuscule furnishings in Colleen Moore's fairy castle. If you want to go big, explore the German U-boat captured during WWII.

Level 1 holds the U-boat, which is pretty freaking impressive. It's given the Hollywood treatment with blue spotlights moving over it and dramatic music swelling in the background. An interactive kiosk lets you try to break codes. There's plenty more to see around the sub, but the highlight is going on board and touring the cramped quarters. Tours cost $8 extra; tickets are available at the exhibit-side kiosk. The Space Center (with rockets and the Apollo 11 lunar module), the fairy castle and Farm Tech (with huge tractors to climb and fake cows to milk) are other Level 1 highlights.

Level 2 rolls out lots of trains. 'Science Storms' lets you conjure a mock tornado and simulate a tsunami rolling toward you. Or submerge into the life-sized shaft of a coal mine ($8 extra). The baby chicks also peck on this floor.

Level 3 hangs cool old German dive bombers and English Spitfires from the ceiling. 'You! The Experience' has a giant 3D heart to walk through and the infamous body slices (cadavers displayed in half-inch-thick pieces).

The museum's main building served as the Palace of Fine Arts at the landmark 1893 World's Expo, which was set in surrounding Jackson Park. When you've had your fill at the museum, the park makes an excellent setting to recuperate.

DON'T MISS

→ U-505 submarine
→ Fairy castle
→ Science Storms' tornadoes and tsunamis
→ Body slices

PRACTICALITIES

→ ☎773-684-1414
→ www.msichicago.org
→ 5700 S Lake Shore Dr
→ adult/child $18/11
→ ⏱9:30am-5:30pm Jun-Aug, reduced Sep-May
→ ♿
→ 🚌6, Ⓜ Metra to 55th-56th-57th

⊙ SIGHTS

⊙ Hyde Park

ROBIE HOUSE   ARCHITECTURE
See p194.

**MUSEUM OF SCIENCE
& INDUSTRY**   MUSEUM
See p195.

UNIVERSITY OF CHICAGO   UNIVERSITY
Map p318 (www.uchicago.edu; 5801 S Ellis Ave; ⊟6, MMetra to 55th-56th-57th) Faculty and students have racked up more than 80 Nobel prizes within U of C's hallowed halls. The campus is well worth a stroll, offering grand Gothic architecture and good free museums.

The economics and physics departments lay claim to most of the awards. Merton Miller, a U of C economics faculty member and a Nobel winner himself, explained the string of wins to the *Sun-Times*: 'It must be the water; it certainly can't be the coffee.'

The university's classes first met on October 1, 1892. John D Rockefeller was a major contributor to the institution, donating more than $35 million, calling it 'the best investment I ever made in my life.' The original campus was constructed in an English Gothic style.

Highlights of a walkabout include the **Rockefeller Memorial Chapel** (Map p318; rockefeller.uchicago.edu; 5850 S Woodlawn), the exterior of which will send sculpture lovers into paroxysms of joy – the facade bears 24 life-sized religious figures and 53 smaller ones, with even more inside. Check the website for carillon and tower tours, and yoga and meditation classes. The **William Rainey Harper Memorial Library** (Map p318; 1116 E 59th St) is another must-see. The long row of arched, two-story windows bathes the 3rd-floor reading room with light and an almost medieval sense of calm. The **Bond Chapel** (Map p318; 1050 E 59th St) is equally serene. Built in 1926, the exquisite 300-seat chapel is the harmonious creation of the architects, sculptors, woodcarvers and glassmakers who worked together on the project.

The university is also where the nuclear age began: Enrico Fermi and his Manhattan Project cronies built a reactor and carried out the world's first controlled atomic reaction on December 2, 1942. The **Nuclear Energy sculpture** (Map p318; S Ellis Ave btwn E

56th & E 57th Sts), by Henry Moore, marks the spot where it blew its stack.

SMART MUSEUM OF ART   MUSEUM
Map p318 (☎773-702-0200; http://smart-museum.uchicago.edu; 5550 S Greenwood Ave; ☉10am-5pm Tue-Sun; ⊟6, MMetra to 55th-56th-57th) FREE Named after the founders of *Esquire* magazine, who contributed the start-up money, this is the official fine arts museum of the university. The collection holds 5000 years' worth of fine arts. Twentieth-century paintings and sculptures, central European expressionism and East Asian art are the strong suits. De Goya, Warhol and Kandinsky are just a few of the big-name artists hanging around. Frank Lloyd Wright's table and chairs mix in for good measure. It only takes a half-hour or so to see the galleries. After that, grab a drink or bite at the front cafe. From September through mid-June, the museum stays open until 8pm on Thursdays.

ORIENTAL INSTITUTE   MUSEUM
Map p318 (www.oi.uchicago.edu; 1155 E 58th St; suggested donation $10; ☉10am-6pm Tue & Thu-Sat, to 10am-8:30pm Wed, noon-6pm Sun; ⊟6, MMetra to 55th-56th-57th) The University of Chicago's famed archaeologists – Indiana Jones supposedly was based on one – cram their headquarters with antiquities they've unearthed from Egypt, Nubia, Persia and Mesopotamia. King Tut is the star, standing 17ft tall, weighing 6 tons and lording over more mummies, clay tablets and canopic jars than you can shake a papyrus scroll at. There's no pressure at all for the suggested donation, so if you don't have it, don't fret.

**DUSABLE MUSEUM OF AFRICAN
AMERICAN HISTORY**   MUSEUM
Map p318 (☎773-947-0600; www.dusable-museum.org; 740 E 56th Pl; adult/child $10/3, Sun free; ☉10am-5pm Tue-Sat, noon-5pm Sun; ⊟4) This was the first independent museum in the country dedicated to African American art, history and culture. The collection features African American artworks and photography, permanent exhibits that illustrate African Americans' experiences from slavery through the Civil Rights movement, and rotating exhibits that cover topics such as Chicago blues music or the Black Panther movement.

Housed in a 1910 building, the museum takes its name from Chicago's first perma-

LOCAL KNOWLEDGE

OBAMA'S HOUSE & KENWOOD HISTORIC ARCHITECTURE

Kenwood, which abuts Hyde Park to the north, has become a tour-bus favorite since a certain resident got elected president. Hefty security means you can't get close to **Obama's house** (Map p318; 5046 S Greenwood Ave), but you can stand across the street on Hyde Park Blvd and try to glimpse over the barricades at the redbrick Georgian-style manor. Many historic buildings are nearby. Across the street, the **KAM Synagogue** (Map p318; 1100 E Hyde Park Blvd) is a domed masterpiece in the Byzantine style with acoustics that are said to be perfect. The house at **4944 S Woodlawn Ave** (Map p318) was once home to Muhammad Ali, and Nation of Islam leader Louis Farrakhan currently lives in the 1971 **Elijah Muhammad House** (Map p318; 4855 S Woodlawn Ave). The sites are about three quarters of a mile north of the university.

nent settler, Jean Baptiste Pointe du Sable, a French Canadian of Haitian descent.

JACKSON PARK PARK
(6401 S Stony Island Ave; ☒6) This 543-acre, lagoon-filled green space fringes Hyde Park to the east. Historically, it's where the city held the 1893 World's Expo, when Chicago introduced the world to wonders such as the Ferris wheel, moving pictures and the zipper. Boat harbors, beaches, the Osaka Garden and a golf course are all part of the mix today. A long strip of land called the Midway Plaisance connects Jackson Park to Washington Park to the west; the Plaisance is home to an ice rink and college students kicking around soccer balls.

OSAKA GARDEN GARDENS
Map p318 (Jackson Park; ☒6) **FREE** Enchanted Osaka Garden floats in Jackson Park. Birds flit through the sunlight, turtles swim in the lagoons, and stone-cut lanterns dot the exotic landscape, which you'll likely have to yourself. It's located on the north end of the Wooded Island and accessed by the bridge there. From the Museum of Science & Industry, walk south toward 59th St and you'll see it.

HYDE PARK ART CENTER GALLERY
Map p318 (www.hydeparkart.org; 5020 S Cornell Ave; ☺10am-8pm Mon-Thu, 10am-5pm Fri & Sat, noon-5pm Sun; ☒6, ⓂMetra to 51st-53rd) Hyde Park Art Center shows contemporary works by Chicagoans – many of them students (current or graduated) of the center's classes. Check the schedule, as sometimes various groups offer walking or cycling tours that depart from here.

HYDE PARK HAIR SALON BUILDING
Map p318 (5234 S Blackstone Ave; ☒6, ⓂMetro to 51st-53rd) You can visit Obama's barber

Zariff and the bulletproof-glass-encased presidential barber chair at the Hyde Park Hair Salon. Staff don't mind if you come in and take a look.

⊙ Bridgeport

A traditionally Irish, working-class neighborhood, Bridgeport has emerged as a hot spot for art centers and nifty bars and restaurants. Halsted St, from 31st St south to 43rd St, is Bridgeport's main drag. Most of the neighborhood lies west of the huge train embankment that itself is west of US Cellular Field. However, Bridgeport extends north of the park all the way to Chinatown.

PALMISANO PARK PARK
(2700 S Halsted St; ☒8) Opened on the site of an old limestone quarry, Palmisano Park unfurls an urban prairie landscape with great views of the Chicago skyline. Locals come here to fish for bluegill in the lagoon in summer and sled the hills in winter. The winding walkways, made of recycled construction debris, are great for a stroll anytime.

UNION STOCKYARDS GATE HISTORIC SITE
(850 W Exchange Ave; ☒8) The gate was once the main entrance to the vast stockyards where millions of cows and hogs met their ends each year. During the 1893 World's Expo the stockyards were a popular tourist draw, with nearly 10,000 people a day making the trek here to stare, awestruck, as the butchering machine took in animals and spat out blood and meat.

The value of those slaughtered in 1910 was an enormous $225 million. While sanitary conditions eventually improved from the hideous levels documented by Upton Sinclair; during the Spanish-American war

Hyde Park & South Side – Lofty Heights

Maybe it's the architecture that has inspired colleagues at the University of Chicago to win more than 80 Nobel prizes. It's certainly grandiose, with Gothic spires soaring into the sky and thick, turreted buildings fronting leafy quadrangles. Even Frank Lloyd Wright felt the vibe; he launched the Prairie style here.

1. University of Chicago (p196)
Stroll among the grand, ivy-clad buildings of this prestigious center of learning.

2. College life
Grab a book and a strong coffee and play student in one of the campus cafes.

3. Robie House (p194)
Don't miss Frank Lloyd Wright's Prairie School masterpiece, one of the most famous dwellings in the world.

4. Rockefeller Memorial Chapel (p196)
This university chapel will delight architecture buffs with its facade bearing 77 religious figures.

American soldiers suffered more casualties because of bad cans of meat from the Chicago packing houses than because of enemy fire. The gate lies a block west of the 4100 block of S Halsted St.

BRIDGEPORT ART CENTER   ARTS CENTER
(www.bridgeportart.com; 1200 W 35th St; 🚌8) The old Spiegel Catalog Warehouse holds more than 50 artists' studios. The best time to come is on the third Friday of the month when the studios open to the public for a big ta-do between 6pm and 10pm. Otherwise you'll need to make an appointment to visit. The exception is **Coyle & Herr** (☉10am-5pm Tue-Sat, 11am-4pm Sun), a 1st-floor shop that sells nifty recycled furniture. Enter on the north side off Racine Avenue.

ZHOU B ART CENTER   ARTS CENTER
(www.zhoubartcenter.com; 1029 W 35th St; 🚌8) Like Bridgeport Art Center, which sits one block west, Zhou B fills a massive old warehouse with galleries and studios. It also participates in the popular Third Friday Open Studios event starting at 7pm.

A trendy, Asian-style lounge with drinks and occasional live music operates on the

1st floor. A great gallery to check out is **4Art** (☉10am-6pm Tue-Sat) on the 4th floor, which exhibits mod works in a variety of media.

◉ Bronzeville

Once home to Louis Armstrong and other notables, Bronzeville thrived as the vibrant center of black life in the city from 1920 to 1950, boasting an economic and cultural strength akin to New York's Harlem. Shifting populations, urban decay and the construction of a wall of public housing along State St led to Bronzeville's decline. In the last decade many young urban professionals have moved back to the neighborhood, and South Loop development stretches almost all the way here. Still, be careful at night; it's not a good place to be walking around after dark.

**ILLINOIS INSTITUTE
OF TECHNOLOGY**   UNIVERSITY
(📞312-567-5014; www.miessociety.org; 3201 S State St; tours $10; Ⓜ Green Line to 35th-Bronzeville-IIT) Famed architect Ludwig Mies

LOCAL KNOWLEDGE

BLUES & JAZZ SHRINES

You won't find the two spots listed below on the usual tourist itinerary, but hard-core music fans will want to make the effort.

Jazz aficionados often seek out the unassuming **Meyers Ace Hardware Store** (315 E 35th St). Why? Because in the 1920s and '30s the building was the Sunset Cafe, where all the greats gigged. Imagine Louis Armstrong blowing his trumpet over by the socket wrenches. Or Earl Hines hammering the piano, down in the plunger aisle. And that was just the house band. Benny Goodman, Jimmy Dorsey and Bix Beiderbecke all launched their careers at the Sunset.

While Chicago landmarked the building, there's no hint of its past life – no plaque marking the spot or jazz tchotchkes for sale. But if David Meyers, the store's owner, is around and not too busy, he'll take you into the back office, which was once the stage. The original red-tinged mural of jazz players splashes across the wall. He'll bring out a box of yellowing news articles about the club and Armstrong's sheet music. He'll even autograph a plunger for you.

A few decades later and a few miles south, a different sound played in the night air – literally different. Guitars screamed and bass lines rolled at new decibel levels, because Muddy Waters and friends had plugged in their amps. So began the electric blues.

At **Muddy Waters' house** (4339 S Lake Park Ave), impromptu jam sessions with pals such as Howlin' Wolf and Chuck Berry erupted in the front yard. Waters, of course, was Chicago's main bluesman, so everyone who was anyone came to pay homage. Waters lived here for 20 years, until 1974, but today the building stands vacant in a lonely, tumbledown lot. Preservationists have been working hard to to ensure it's spared from the wrecking ball. A sign commemorates the spot.

You'll need wheels to reach Waters' home, and it's easiest if you have them for Meyers' store (which is about a block from the Supreme Life Building). Daytime is best for visits, as the 'hoods can be edgy at night.

van der Rohe designed many of the campus' modern buildings. Download a free map for DIY wanderings. Better yet, docents lead 90-minute tours (10am Monday to Friday, 10:30am Saturday and Sunday); departure is from the welcome center in the McCormick Tribune Campus Center. The center also rents audio tours (same price) from 10am to 3pm.

A world-class leader in technology, industrial design and architecture, the Illinois Institute of Technology (IIT) owes much of its look to Mies van der Rohe, who fled the Nazis in Germany for Chicago in 1938. From 1940 until his retirement in 1958, Mies designed 22 IIT buildings that reflected his tenets of architecture, combining simple, black-metal frames with glass and brick infills. The look became known as the International Style. The star of the campus and Mies' undisputed masterpiece is **SR Crown Hall** (3360 S State St), appropriately home to the College of Architecture. The building, close to the center of campus, appears to be a transparent glass box floating between its translucent base and suspended roof. At night it glows from within like an illuminated jewel.

Mies isn't the only architectural hero whose works are on display at IIT. In 2003 the campus opened two other buzz-worthy buildings. Dutch architect Rem Koolhaas designed the McCormick Tribune Campus Center with its simple lines and striking en-tubing of the El tracks that run overhead. This is Koolhaas' only building in the USA. Just south of the Campus Center is the Helmut Jahn-designed **State Street Village** (cnr 33rd & State Sts). Jahn studied at IIT in his younger days, and his strip of rounded glass-and-steel residence halls is a natural progression from the works of the modernist bigwigs he learned from while here.

SUPREME LIFE BUILDING HISTORIC BUILDING

(3501 S Martin Luther King Jr Dr; ⓂGreen Line to 35th-Bronzeville-ITT) The 1930s Supreme Life Building was the spot where John H Johnson Jr, the publishing mogul who founded *Ebony* magazine, got the idea for his empire, which includes *Jet* and other important titles serving African Americans. There's a little **neighborhood visitors center** that sells old albums and trinkets behind the bank here; enter from 35th St.

VICTORY MONUMENT MONUMENT

(3500 S Martin Luther King Dr; ⓂGreen Line to 35th-Bronzeville-ITT) In the median at 35th St and Martin Luther King Jr Dr, the Victory Monument was erected in 1928 in honor of the African American soldiers who fought in WWI. The figures include a soldier, a mother and Columbia, the mythical figure meant to symbolize the New World.

ROBERT W ROLOSON HOUSES ARCHITECTURE

(3213-3219 S Calumet Ave; ⓂGreen Line to 35th-Bronzeville-ITT) Examples of stylish architecture from the past can be found throughout Bronzeville, and you can see some fine homes along two blocks of Calumet Ave between 31st and 33rd Sts, an area known as 'the Gap.' The buildings here include Frank Lloyd Wright's only row houses, the Robert W Roloson Houses.

IDA B WELLS HOUSE HISTORIC BUILDING

(3624 S Martin Luther King Jr Dr; ⓂGreen Line to 35th-Bronzeville-ITT) One of scores of Romanesque houses that date from the 1880s, the Ida B Wells House is named for its 1920s resident. Wells was a crusading journalist who investigated lynchings and other racially motivated crimes. She coined the line: 'Eternal vigilance is the price of liberty.'

PILGRIM BAPTIST CHURCH CHURCH

(☎312-842-5830; 3301 S Indiana Ave; ⓂGreen Line to 35th-Bronzeville-ITT) Gospel music got its start at Pilgrim Baptist Church, originally built as a synagogue from 1890 to 1891. Unfortunately, the opulent structure burned to the ground (barring these few exterior walls) in 2006 when a roof repairman lost control of his blowtorch.

GREATER SALEM BAPTIST CHURCH CHURCH

(☎773-874-2325; 215 W 71st St; 🚌29) Gospel fans can make the pilgrimage to the Greater Salem Baptist Church where gospel great Mahalia Jackson was a lifelong member.

EATING

Hyde Park

VALOIS CAFETERIA SOUTHERN $

Map p318 (☎773-667-0647; 1518 E 53rd St; mains $5-11; ⊗5:30am-10pm; ⓂMetra to 51st-53rd) It's a

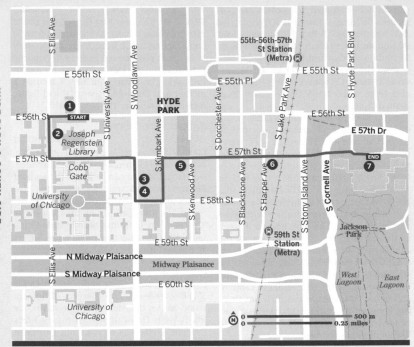

Neighborhood Walk
Higher Learning

START SMART MUSEUM OF ART
FINISH MUSEUM OF SCIENCE & INDUSTRY
LENGTH 0.25 MILES, FIVE HOURS INCLUD-
ING BROWSING TIME

You can learn a lot walking around the University of Chicago's Hyde Park campus and beyond.

Start by brushing up on your art acumen at the ❶ **Smart Museum of Art** (p196). Exhibits here explore the tension between realism and abstraction. Learn about artists from Europe and the Americas, especially during the 20th century, including Mexican painter Diego Riviera.

Around the corner you'll come to a real hot spot. Under the Stagg Field Stadium on the university campus, in secret, scientists initiated the first self-sustaining controlled nuclear reaction on December 2, 1942 – the precursor to the atomic bomb. Today, the spot is marked by the bronze, skull-like ❷ **Nuclear Energy Sculpture** (p196) flanking a tennis court.

Onward to the ❸ **Seminary Cooperative Bookstore** (p204), an awesomely academic institution where you'll find no less than eight different versions of War and Peace on the shelves. Next door, Frank Lloyd Wright's ❹ **Robie House** (p194) rises up and provides an excellent opportunity to educate yourself on Prairie School architecture.

All this thinking has probably made you hungry. Replenish at student-favorite ❺ **Medici** (p203) with an apple and blue cheese baguette. Continuing east on 57th St you'll pass more bookstores. No matter what subject you want to study – astronomy, architecture, rocket science – you're likely to find a secondhand book about it at ❻ **Powell's** (p204).

Finally you'll come to the ❼ **Museum of Science & Industry** (p195). The only German U-505 on US soil is part of a multimedia, multimillion-dollar exhibit – a fine way to improve your WWII sea-warfare knowledge. You can also explore a full-scale coal mine or manipulate the direction and speed of a tornado.

mixed crowd at Valois. In fact, the clientele is so socioeconomically diverse that a U of C sociology professor wrote a well-known book about it, titled *Slim's Table*. It seems hot, fast, Southern-style dishes including French toast, bacon, biscuits, pot pies and patty melts attract all kinds – even Barack Obama, who used to chow down here regularly. It's a real-deal cafeteria, so know what you want before reaching the front of the fast-moving line. Cash only.

SOUL VEGETARIAN EAST VEGETARIAN **$$**
(☑773-224-0104; www.originalsoulvegetarian.com; 205 E 75th St; mains $8-13; ☺11am-9pm Mon-Thu, 11am-10pm Fri, from 8:30am Sat & Sun; ☑) Finding soul food that meets the tenets of the vegan diet is such a rarity that the creative barbecue sandwiches and dinner plates at this comfy South Side place have earned a national reputation. It is attached to a juice bar so you can get your wheatgrass fix, too. You'll need wheels to get here.

MEDICI CAFE **$$**
Map p010 (☑773-667-7394; www.medici57.com; 1327 E 57th St; mains $8-14; ☺7am-10pm Mon-Fri, from 8am Sat & Sun; ☂☑♨; ☑6, Ⓜ Metra to 55th 56th 57th) The menu of thin-crust pizzas, sandwiches and salads draws U of C students to this colorful cafe and bakery. For breakfast, try the 'eggs espresso,' made by steaming eggs in an espresso machine. Heaps of gluten-free and vegetarian options are available. After your meal, check the vast bulletin board out front. It's the perfect place to size up the character of the community and possibly find the complete works of John Maynard Keynes for sale, cheap.

LEM'S BAR-B-Q HOUSE BARBECUE **$$**
(☑773-994-2428; www.lemsque.com; 311 E 75th St; mains $9-14; ☺1pm-1am Mon, Wed, Thu & Sun, to 3am Fri & Sat) Lem's is revered for its smoky-sauced rib tips, which come cushioned between a bed of fries and topping of white bread slices. You'll need a car to get here. Cash only.

✗ Bridgeport

PLEASANT HOUSE BAKERY BAKERY **$**
(www.pleasanthousebakery.com; 964 W 31st St; mains $8-10; ☺11am-9pm Tue-Thu, to 10pm Fri & Sat, 10am-8pm Sun; ☑8) Follow your nose to Pleasant House, which bakes tall, fluffy, savory pies. The blackboard lists the daily flavors, say chicken and chutney, steak and ale, or kale and mushroom. You can eat in at the handful of tables, but many folks take their pies to go and indulge over a beer at Maria's Packaged Goods and Community Bar next door.

NANA MODERN AMERICAN **$$**
(☑312-929-2486; www.nanaorganic.com; 3267 S Halsted St; mains $15-20; ☺9am-2:30pm daily, 5-9:30pm Wed-Sun; ☑; ☑8) 🍴 This convivial little gem received a Michelin Bib Gourmand award for great food offered at great value. It whips up yummy organic breakfasts (try the poached egg and chorizo 'nanadict') by day, and sandwiches and no-fuss dinners by candlelit night. Many dishes have a Latin twist, such as the pork chop with yucca and rum-pickled pineapple.

🍸 DRINKING & NIGHTLIFE

MARIA'S PACKAGED GOODS AND COMMUNITY BAR BAR
(http://communitybar.wordpress.com; 960 W 31st St; ☺from 4pm; ☂; ☑8) Owner Ed works the cozy back room bar furnished with vintage reclaimed decor, while mom Maria works the front liquor store. Both offer a fantastic craft beer selection that Bridgeport's nouveau hipsters greedily suck down. DJs spin most nights, or there's other arty entertainment (Ed also owns a nearby gallery and 'experimental cultural center'). The bar even has a discount card: drink 10 beers, and your 11th one is free. Maria's is Bridgeport's finest, a great stop after the neighborhood gallery hop or a White Sox game.

JIMMY'S WOODLAWN TAP BAR
Map p318 (☑773-643-5516; 1172 E 55th St; ☺from 10:30am Mon-Fri, from 11am Sat & Sun; Ⓜ Metra to 55th-56th-57th) Some of the geniuses of our age have killed plenty of brain cells right here in one of Hyde Park's few worthwhile bars. The place is dark and beery, and a little seedy. But for thousands of University of Chicago students deprived of a thriving bar scene, it's home. Hungry? The Swissburgers are legendary. Cash only.

BERNICE'S TAVERN BAR
(☑312-326-9460; 3238 S Halsted St; ☺from 3pm Mon & Wed-Fri, from 11am Sat & Sun; ☑8, Ⓜ Red

Line to Sox-35th) A motley assemblage of local artists and neighborhood regulars haunts this workaday Bridgeport tavern, where the eclectic calendar includes wild, wacky bingo sessions on Wednesdays. Order a *Starka*, a honey-flavored liqueur every bit as Lithuanian as the owners.

SCHALLER'S PUMP BAR
(773-376-6332; 3714 S Halsted St; ⏱from 11am Mon-Fri, from 4pm Sat, from 3pm Sun; 8, MRed Line to Sox-35th) Schaller's is Chicago's oldest continually operating tavern and is conveniently located across the street from the 11th Ward Democratic offices in Bridgeport. Old neighborhood men sip Dewars and soda at the bar, families order burgers and butt steak at the white-clothed tables, and there's nary a microbrew in sight. Cash only.

It's a fine place to toast the city's infamous politicos (both Mayor Daleys have imbibed here) or the White Sox, whose ballpark is a short toss away.

⭐ ENTERTAINMENT

COURT THEATRE THEATER
Map p318 (773-753-4472; www.courttheatre. org; 5535 S Ellis Ave; 6, MMetra to 55th-56th-57th) A classical company hosted by the University of Chicago, the Court focuses on great works from the Greeks to Shakespeare, and various international plays not often performed in the USA. The 2013 season saw August Wilson's *Jitney* and Molière's *The Misanthrope* among the lineup.

LEE'S UNLEADED BLUES BLUES
(www.leesunleadedblues.com; 7401 S South Chicago Ave; ⏱from 8pm Thu-Sun) Far off the tourist path and buried deep on the South Side, Lee's is a genuine juke joint with sweet blues. The local crowd dresses in their finest threads, and everyone jams until dawn. The cover is $5. You'll need wheels to get here.

MUNTU DANCE THEATER OF CHICAGO DANCE
(773-602-1135; www.muntu.com) The word *muntu* means 'the essence of humanity' in Bantu. This company was founded in 1972 to perform African and American dances that draw on ancient and contemporary movement. The fiery performances of traditional dances from West Africa are an essential part of Muntu's signature. It performs at venues around town, including many in Hyde Park.

SHOPPING

There's a great selection of bookstores around the University of Chicago campus.

57TH STREET BOOKS BOOKS
Map p318 (773-684-1300; www.semcoop. com; 1301 E 57th St; ⏱10am-8pm; 6, MMetra to 55th-56th-57th) A serious university demands a serious bookstore, and as you descend the stairs to this basement-level shop you'll know you're in the right place. Its labyrinth of low-slung rooms makes up the kind of old-fashioned bookstore that goes way deeper than the popular titles. It has excellent staff picks. Seminary Cooperative is its sister shop selling academic tomes.

SEMINARY COOPERATIVE BOOKSTORE BOOKS
Map p318 (773-752-4381; www.semcoop.com; 5751 S Woodlawn Ave; ⏱8:30am-8pm Mon-Fri, 10am-6pm Sat, noon-6pm Sun; 6, MMetra to 55th-56th-57th) This is the bookstore of choice for several University of Chicago Nobel Prize winners, including Robert Fogel, who says, 'For a scholar, it's one of the great bookstores of the world.' The shop recently moved from its subterranean warren of 50-plus years to this sprawling sunny spot next to Robie House. It's owned by the same folks as 57th Street Books.

POWELL'S BOOKS
Map p318 (773-955-7780; www.powellschicago. com; 1501 E 57th St; ⏱9am-11pm; 6, MMetra to 55th-56th-57th) This leading store for used books can get you just about any title ever published. Shelf after heaving shelf prop up the well-arranged stock. Staff often put a box of free books outside by the entrance. They may be semi-tattered or in a foreign language, but then again, you may find a treasure to take away.

🏃 SPORTS & ACTIVITIES

CHICAGO WHITE SOX BASEBALL
(www.whitesox.com; 333 W 35th St; tickets $20-70; MRed Line to Sox-35th) The White Sox play

> **WORTH A DETOUR**
>
> ## CHICAGO FIRE
> ....
>
> The city's pro soccer team, the **Chicago Fire** (☑888-657-3473; www.chicago-fire.com; Toyota Park, 71st St & Harlem Ave, Bridgeview; tickets $20-50), plays March through October at Toyota Park in southwest suburban Bridgeview. Tickets are available through Ticketmaster, and are fairly easy to come by. It's a pretty good haul to reach the stadium. If you get to Midway Airport via the Orange Line, you can catch the suburban Pace Bus number 386 Toyota Park Express, which runs on game days only. The full trip from the Loop will likely take an hour or so.

at US Cellular Field (aka the Cell, though often referred to by its pre-corporate-sponsorship name, Comiskey Park). Less loved than the Cubs despite their 2005 World Series win, the Sox resort to more promotions (free hot dogs, fireworks etc) and cheaper tickets to lure fans to their southerly location. Tickets are half-price most Mondays.

Tickets are available through the team's website, at the ballpark box office or at any Ticketmaster outlet. Sellouts aren't usually an issue. The Cell sports a couple of cool features, such as the Bullpen Bar, where you sip your beer practically right on the field; and the pet check, which allows dog owners to bring Fido to the game and drop him off with a babysitter for a fee.

63RD ST BEACH　　　　　　BEACH
(www.cpdbeaches.com; 6300 S Lake Shore Dr; ☐6) This expanse of sand abutting Jackson Park contains a stately restored beach house with dramatic breezeways. It's next to a yacht harbor, and exudes a charm lacking at beaches with more modern – and mundane – facilities. Kids love the splashy, interactive water fountains. There are a couple of bars and grills for refreshments. Lifeguards patrol in summer.

57TH ST BEACH　　　　　　BEACH
Map p318 (www.cpdbeaches.com; 5700 S Lake Shore Dr; ☐Metra to 55th-56th-57th) Just across Lake Shore Dr from the Museum of Science & Industry, 57th St Beach features an expanse of clean, golden sand. Surfers say it's the best beach to hang-ten.

JACKSON PARK GOLF COURSE　　GOLF
(☑773-667-0524; www.cpdgolf.com; 6401 S Richards Dr; ☐6, Ⓜ Metra to 63rd) The district's only 18-hole course is moderately challenging. Public fees range from $27 to $30. Reservations are recommended. There's also a driving range.

Day Trips from Chicago

Oak Park p207
Tour Frank Lloyd Wright's studio and see a slew of homes he designed for his neighbors. Ernest Hemingway's birthplace is here, too.

Indiana Dunes p209
Sunny beaches, woodsy trails, ranger-guided walks and towering sand dunes feature at this national and state park combination.

Milwaukee p210
Wisconsin's biggest city has a stellar lineup of beer, motorcycles, world-class art and a ballpark of racing sausages.

Saugatuck & Douglas p212
These artsy towns boom in summer thanks to their golden beaches, piney breezes, fruit pies and their welcome one, welcome all mindset.

Galena p213
Quaint it is, with perfectly preserved, Civil War–era streets set amid rolling, cow-dotted hills by the Mississippi River.

Oak Park

Explore

This suburb spawned two famous sons: novelist Ernest Hemingway was born here, and architect Frank Lloyd Wright lived and worked here from 1889 to 1909. The town's main sights revolve around the men. For Hemingway, a low-key museum and his birthplace provide an intriguing peek at his formative years. For Wright, the studio where he developed the Prairie style is the big draw, as is a slew of surrounding houses he designed for his neighbors. Ten of them cluster within a mile along Forest and Chicago Aves (gawking must occur from the sidewalk since they're privately owned). You could easily spend an afternoon here.

The Best...

➡ **Sight** Frank Lloyd Wright Home & Studio (p208)

➡ **Place to Eat** Hemmingway's Bistro (p208)

Top Tip

Stop by the Oak Park Visitors Center and buy an architectural site map ($4.25), which gives the locations of all the Wright-designed houses in the area.

Getting There & Away

➡ **Car** Take I-290 west, exiting north on Harlem Ave; take Harlem Ave north to Lake St and turn right. There's a parking garage a few blocks down the road.

➡ **El** From downtown Chicago, take the CTA Green Line to its terminus at the Harlem stop, which lands you about a quarter-mile from the visitors center. The trip (one way $3) takes 20 minutes; be aware that the train traverses some bleak neighborhoods before emerging into Oak Park's wide-lawn splendor.

Need to Know

➡ **Area Code** ☑708

➡ **Location** 10 miles west of the Loop

➡ **Oak Park Visitors Center** (☑000-625-7275; www.visitoakpark.com; 1010 W Lake St; ☺10am-5pm)

WORTH A DETOUR

ROUTE 66

America's 'Mother Road' kicks off in downtown Chicago on Adams St, just west of Michigan Ave. Within a three hour drive you can see some vintage bits. Sadly, most of the original Route 66 has been superseded by I-55 in Illinois, though the old road still exists in scattered sections often paralleling the interstate. Keep an eye out for brown 'Historic Route 66' signs, which pop up at crucial junctions to mark the way.

The first primo stop rises from the cornfields 60 miles south in Wilmington. Here the Gemini Giant – a 28ft fiberglass spaceman – stands guard outside the **Launching Pad Drive In** (810 E Baltimore St). The restaurant is now shuttered, but the statue remains a quintessential photo op. To reach it, exit I-55 at Joliet Rd, and follow it south as it becomes Hwy 53 into town.

Motor 45 miles onward to Pontiac and the trinket-and-photo-filled **Route 66 Hall of Fame** (☑815-844-4566; 110 W Howard St; admission free; ☺9am-5pm Mon-Fri, 10am-4pm Sat & Sun). Cruise another 50 miles to Shirley and **Funk's Grove** (☑309-874-3360; www.funksmaplesirup.com; ☺9am-5pm Mon-Fri, from 10am Sat, from noon Sun), a pretty 19th-century maple syrup farm and nature preserve (exit 154 off I-55).

Ten miles later you'll reach the throwback hamlet of Atlanta. Pull up a chair at the **Palms Grill Cafe** (☑217-648-2233; www.thepalmsgrillcafe.com; 110 SW Arch St; pie slices $3; ☺5am-8pm), where thick slabs of gooseberry, sour cream raisin and other retro pies tempt from the glass case. Then walk across the street to snap a photo with **Tall Paul**, a sky high statue of Paul Bunyan clutching a hot dog.

The state capital of Springfield, 50 miles farther on, has several more sights including the **Cozy Dog Drive In** (www.cozydogdrivein.com; 2935 S 6th St; mains $2-4.50; ☺8am-8pm Mon-Sat), reputed birthplace of the corn dog.

For more information, see **Illinois Route 66 Scenic Byway** (www.illinoisroute66.org). And should you decide to keep on truckin', it's a lazy 2200 miles onward to the route's end in Los Angeles.

⊙ SIGHTS

FRANK LLOYD WRIGHT
HOME & STUDIO
ARCHITECTURE

(☎312-994-4000; www.gowright.org; 951 Chicago Ave; adult/child/camera $15/12/5; ☺11am-4pm) This is where Wright lived and worked from 1889 to 1909. Tour frequency varies, from every 20 minutes on summer weekends to every hour or so in winter. The hour-long walk-through reveals a fascinating place, filled with the details that made Wright's style distinctive. The Studio also offers guided neighborhood walking tours, as well as a self-guided audio version.

ERNEST HEMINGWAY MUSEUM
MUSEUM

(☎708-848-2222; www.ehfop.org; 200 N Oak Park Ave; adult/child $10/8; ☺1-5pm Sun-Fri, from 10am Sat) Despite Hemingway calling Oak Park a 'village of wide lawns and narrow minds,' the town still pays homage to him at this museum. Exhibits begin with his middle-class Oak Park background and the innocent years before he went off to find adventure. The ensuing displays focus on his writings in Spain and during WWII.

Admission tickets also provide entry to his **birthplace** (339 N Oak Park Ave; ☺1-5pm Sun-Fri, from 10am Sat) across the street.

MOORE HOUSE
ARCHITECTURE

(333 N Forest Ave) Of the many homes Wright designed in the 'hood, Moore House is particularly noteworthy. First built in 1895, it's Wright's bizarre interpretation of an English manor house. In his later years, Wright called the house 'repugnant' and said he had only taken the commission because he needed the money. He claimed he walked out of his way to avoid passing it.

UNITY TEMPLE
ARCHITECTURE

(☎708-383-8873; www.utrf.org; 875 Lake St; adult/child $10/8; ☺10:30am-4:30pm Mon-Fri, 10am-2pm Sat, 1-4pm Sun) It's another one of Frank Lloyd Wright's architectural wonders, built in 1909. Explore at your leisure on a self-guided look-around, or check the schedule for occasional guided tours.

✗ EATING

HEMMINGWAY'S BISTRO
FRENCH $$$

(www.hemmingwaysbistro.com; 211 N Oak Park Ave; mains $20-30; ☺7am-10pm) Fork in to all the French classics – coq au vin, caussoulet, bouillabaisse – at this cozy little bistro across from the Hemingway Museum. If nothing else, drop in and sit at the bar for a glass of wine.

Indiana Dunes

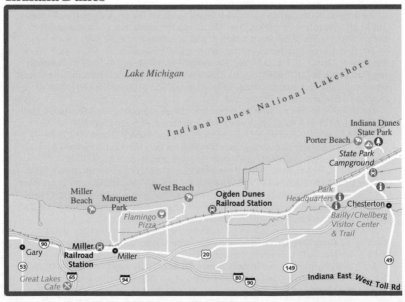

Indiana Dunes

It can provide beach details; a schedule of ranger-guided walks and activities; and hiking, biking and birding maps.

Explore

Sunny beaches, rustling grasses and woodsy campgrounds are Indiana Dunes' claim to fame. Unfurling 21 miles of Lake Michigan shoreline, the area is popular on summer days with sunbathers from Chicago and towns throughout northern Indiana. The area is also noted for its plant variety: everything from cacti to pine trees sprouts here. Hiking trails meander up the dunes and through the woodlands. Oddly, all this natural bounty lies smack-dab next to smoke-belching factories, which you'll also see at various vantage points. Visit in the morning and linger on into the afternoon.

The Best...

➡**Sight** Indiana Dunes National Lakeshore

➡**Place to Eat** Great Lakes Cafe (p210)

➡**Place to Drink** Flamingo Pizza (p210)

Top Tip

The best place to start is the **Dorothy Buell Visitor Center** (☑219-926-7561; Hwy 49; ⏰8:30am-6:30pm Jun-Aug, to 4:30pm Sep-May).

Getting There & Away

➡**Car** Take I-90 east out of Chicago to Indiana (be prepared to pay about $7 worth of tolls). After Gary take exit 21 to merge onto I-94 east (toward Detroit). Soon after, take exit 22B to merge onto US 20 toward Porter. Parking is difficult on weekends; try West Beach (per car $6). Driving takes one hour from Chicago.

➡**Metra South Shore Line trains** (www.nictd.com) make the journey from Millennium Station in the Loop. It's about 75 minutes to the Dune Park or Beverly Shores stops (one way $7.25 to $8.25). Note that both stations are about a 1.5 mile walk from the beach.

Need to Know

➡**Area Code** ☑219

➡**Location** 45 miles southeast of the Loop

➡**Porter County Convention & Visitors Bureau** (www.indianadunes.com)

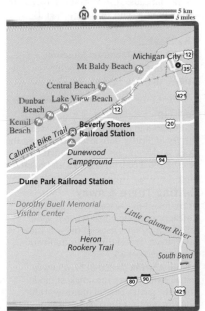

⊙ SIGHTS

INDIANA DUNES NATIONAL LAKESHORE   PARK

(☑800-959-9174, 219-926-7561; www.nps.gov/indu) Swimming is allowed anywhere along the shore. A short walk away from the beaches, several hiking paths crisscross the dunes and woodlands. The best are the **Bailly–Chellberg Trail** (2.5 miles) that winds by a still-operating 1870s farm, and the **Heron Rookery Trail** (2 miles), where blue herons flock. **Mt Baldy** is the top dune to climb, though it was closed at press time due to unstable sand.

INDIANA DUNES STATE PARK   PARK

(☑219-926-1952; www.dnr.in.gov/parklake; per car $10) The state park is a 2100-acre, shoreside pocket within the national lakeshore; it's located at the end of Hwy 49, near Chesterton. It has more amenities, but also more regulation and more crowds (plus the vehicle entry fee). Wintertime brings out the cross-country skiers; summertime brings out the hikers. Seven trails zigzag over the landscape; No 4, up Mt Tom, rewards with Chicago skyline views.

SLEEPING IN INDIANA DUNES

Dunewood Campground (☑219-395-8914; www.nps.gov/indu; campsites $18; ⊘Apr-Oct) The national lakeshore's seasonal campsites are rustic (no electricity) and first come, first served (no reservations).

Indiana Dunes State Park Campground (☑866-622-6746; www.camp.in.gov; campsites $19-36; ⊘year-round) These campsites are modern and fairly close to the beach. Reserve in advance in summertime.

Tryon Farm Guesthouse (☑219-879-3618; www.tryonfarmguesthouse.com; r incl breakfast $135-170; ✳@🐾) This four-room B&B nestles in a turn-of-the-20th-century farmhouse near Michigan City.

✖ EATING & DRINKING

GREAT LAKES CAFE   CAFE $
(201 Mississippi St; mains $6-9; ⊘5am-3pm Mon-Fri, 6am-1pm Sat; ⏲) This colorful Greek family diner sits right in front a steel mill, whose workers pile in for the cheap, hearty pancakes, meatloaf, butterfly shrimp, bacon-pecan brownies and whatever else features on the dry-erase board of daily specials.

LUCREZIA   ITALIAN $$$
(☑219-926-5829; www.lucreziacafe.com; 428 S Calumet Rd; mains $18-28; ⊘11am-10pm Sun-Thu, to 11pm Fri & Sat) It's a homey favorite for Italian staples, in Chesterton.

FLAMINGO PIZZA   BAR
(8341 Locust Ave; ⊘from 11am) Yes, you can get pizza and lake perch (mains $9 to $15) but it's the bar that beckons at Flamingo: a cozy watering hole where you sit elbow-to-elbow with older locals. The good beers are a bonus to the ambience. Located near West Beach.

⚐ SPORTS & ACTIVITIES

WEST BEACH   BEACH
(per car $6) West Beach, nearest to Gary, draws fewer crowds than the other beaches and features a number of nature hikes and trails. It's also the only beach with life-guards. There's a snack bar and cool Chicago vistas.

**CAMP STOP
GENERAL STORE**   BICYCLE RENTAL
(www.campstopgeneralstore.com; 2 W Dunes Hwy; per hr/day $5/30; ⊘9am-9pm Mon-Sat, to 6pm Sun) The store serving Dunewood Campground (p210) also rents bikes. It's located across the tracks from the Beverly Shores train stop. From here, it's a short ride to the nearest beach. Be sure to turn left onto Lake Front Dr for a quick detour past the 'Century of Progress homes,' five offbeat remnants from the 1933 Chicago World's Fair.

Milwaukee

Explore
Beer, brats and bowling? Of course Milwaukee has them. But attractions like the Calatrava-designed art museum, bad-to-the-bone Harley-Davidson Museum, and stylish eating and shopping 'hoods have added a groovy layer to Wisconsin's largest city. In summertime, festivals let loose revelry by the lake. And where else will you see racing sausages? Milwaukee rocks any time, but especially during weekends.

The Best...
➡ **Sight** Harley-Davidson Museum
➡ **Place to Eat** Comet Cafe (p212)
➡ **Place to Drink** Best Place (p212)

Top Tip
Many bars and restaurants host a traditional fish fry on Friday. Join locals celebrating the work week's end over a communal meal of beer-battered cod, French fries and coleslaw.

Getting There & Away
➡ **Car** Take I-90/94 west from downtown Chicago, and follow I-94 when it splits off. The interstate goes all the way into Milwaukee. Travel time is around two hours; tolls cost $5.

➡ **Train** Amtrak (☑800-872-7245; www.amtrak.com) is often the quickest mode given the snail's pace of highway traffic. The *Hiawatha* train runs seven times daily to/from Chicago ($24, 1½ hours). The main **station** (433 W St Paul Ave) is downtown.

Getting Around

The **Milwaukee County Transit System** (www.ridemcts.com; fare $2.25) provides efficient local bus service. Bus 31 goes to Miller Brewery; bus 90 goes to Miller Park. Catch them along Wisconsin Ave.

Need to Know

➡**Area Code** ☏414

➡**Location** 92 miles north of Chicago

➡**Milwaukee Convention & Visitors Bureau** (☏800-554-1448; www.visitmilwaukee.org)

◉ SIGHTS

HARLEY-DAVIDSON MUSEUM   MUSEUM
(☏877-436-8738; www.h-dmuseum.com; 400 W Canal St; adult/child $18/10; ⊙9am-6pm Fri-Wed, to 8pm Thu May-Oct, reduced hours Nov-Apr) Hundreds of motorcycles show the styles through the decades, including the flashy rides of Elvis and Evel Knievel. You can sit in the saddles of various bikes (on the bottom floor, behind the Design Lab), as well as get a minilesson on how to ride (by the front entrance). Even nonbikers will enjoy the place.

MILWAUKEE ART MUSEUM   MUSEUM
(☏414-224-3200; www.mam.org; 700 N Art Museum Dr; adult/child $15/12; ⊙10am-5pm Tue, Wed & Fri-Sun, to 8pm Thu Sep-May) Even those who aren't usually museum-goers will be struck by this lakeside museum, which features a stunning winglike addition by Santiago Calatrava. It soars open and closed every day

at 10am, noon and at closing time, which is wild to see. There are fabulous folk and outsider art galleries, and a sizable collection of Georgia O'Keeffe paintings.

MILLER BREWING COMPANY   BREWERY
(☏414-931-2337; www.millercoors.com; 4251 W State St; ⊙10:30am-3:30pm Mon-Sat, to 4:30pm summer) **FREE** Though the mass-produced beer may not be your favorite, the factory impresses with its sheer scale: you'll visit the packaging plant where 2000 cans are filled each minute, and the warehouse where a half-million cases await shipment. And then there's the generous tasting session at the tour's end, where you can down three full-size samples. Don't forget your ID.

LAKEFRONT BREWERY   BREWERY
(☏414-372-8800; www.lakefrontbrewery.com; 1872 N Commerce St; 1hr tours $7; ⊙9am-4:30pm Mon-Thu, to 9pm Fri, 11am-4:30pm Sat, noon-4:30pm Sun) This well-loved brewery, across the river from bar-laden Brady St, has afternoon tours, but the best time to visit is on Friday nights when there's a fish fry, 16 beers to try and a polka band letting loose. Tour times vary throughout the week, but there's usually at least a 2pm and 3pm walk-through.

✖ EATING & DRINKING

MILWAUKEE PUBLIC MARKET   MARKET $
(www.milwaukeepublicmarket.org; 400 N Water St; ⊙10am-8pm Mon-Fri, 8am-7pm Sat, 10am-6pm Sun; ☎) Located in the Third Ward, it stocks mostly prepared foods – cheese, chocolate, beer, tacos and frozen custard. Take them

---

SLEEPING IN MILWAUKEE

County Clare Irish Inn (☏414-272-5273; www.countyclare-inn.com; 1234 N Astor St; r incl breakfast $129-179; ℗ ❋ ☎) Rooms have a snug Irish-cottage feel, with four-poster beds, white wainscot walls and whirlpool baths. There's free parking and an on-site Guinness-pouring pub, of course.

Brewhouse Inn & Suites (☏414-810-3350; www.brewhousesuites.com; 1215 N 10th St; r incl breakfast $189-229; ❋ @ ☎) It's a new hotel in the renovated Pabst Brewery. Each of the large chambers has steampunk decor, a kitchenette and free wi-fi. It's at downtown's far west edge. Parking costs $26 a day.

Iron Horse Hotel (☏888-543-4766; www.theironhorsehotel.com; 500 W Florida St; r from $189-259; ℗ ❋ ☎) Classy, loft-style rooms fill this old factory building. Motorcycle riders get special perks. Car parking costs $25 a day.

upstairs where there are tables, free wi-fi and $1 used books.

★COMET CAFE   AMERICAN $$

(www.thecometcafe.com; 1947 N Farwell Ave; mains $8-12; ⊙10am-10pm Mon-Fri, from 9am Sat & Sun; ☑) Students, young families, older couples and bearded, tattooed types pile in to the rock and roll Comet for gravy-smothered meatloaf, mac 'n' cheese, vegan gyros and hangover brunch dishes. It's a craft-beer-pouring bar on one side, and retro-boothed diner on the other.

BEST PLACE   BAR

(www.bestplacemilwaukee.com; 901 W Juneau Ave; ⊙noon-midnight Thu-Sat, to 6pm Sun) Join the locals knocking back beers and massive whiskey pours at this small tavern in the former Pabst Brewery headquarters. A fireplace warms the cozy, dark-wood room; original murals depicting Pabst's history adorn the walls.

UBER TAP ROOM   BAR

(www.ubertaproom.com; 1048 N Old 3rd St; ⊙11am-8pm Sun-Wed, to 10pm Thu, to 11pm Fri & Sat) It's touristy, in the thick of Old World 3rd St and attached to the Wisconsin Cheese Mart, but it's a great place to sample local fare. Thirty Wisconsin beers flow from the taps, and cheese from the state's dairy bounty accompanies. Themed plates (ie spicy cheeses, stinky cheeses etc) cost $8 to $12.

☆ ENTERTAINMENT

MILLER PARK   BASEBALL

(www.brewers.com; 1 Brewers Way) The Brewers play baseball at fab Miller Park, which has a retractable roof and real grass. The 'Racing Sausages' star in the middle of the 6th inning. To the uninitiated, that's five people in foam-rubber meat costumes – including Hot Dog, Bratwurst and Chorizo – who sprint around the ballpark's perimeter, vying for sausage supremacy. It's located near S 46th St.

Saugatuck & Douglas

Explore

Saugatuck is one of Michigan's most popular resort areas, known for its strong arts community, numerous B&Bs and gay-friendly vibe. Douglas is its twin city a mile or so south, and they've pretty much sprawled into one. It's a touristy but funky place, with ice-cream-licking families, yuppie boaters and martini-drinking gay couples sharing the waterfront. Galleries and shops fill the compact downtown core. Weekends bring out the masses.

The Best...

➡**Activity** Saugatuck Chain Ferry

➡**Place to Eat** Crane's Pie Pantry

➡**Place to Drink** Saugatuck Brewing Company

Top Tip

Don't forget that Michigan is on Eastern Standard Time, one hour ahead of Chicago.

Getting There & Away

➡**Car** Take I-90 east toward Indiana for about 30 miles. After Gary, merge onto I-94 east, and stay on it for 65 miles. After Benton Harbor, merge onto I-196/US 31 north, and take it for about 40 miles, until

WORTH A DETOUR

WINERIES & ANTIQUES AROUND SAUGATUCK

The roads around Saugatuck are ripe for exploration. **Antiquing** prevails on the Blue Star Hwy running south for 20 miles. The odd shops often look like just a bunch of junk in someone's front yard, but pull up at the right time and that old traffic light or Victorian sled can be yours for a song. **Blueberry U-pick farms** share this stretch of road and make a juicy stop, too. And several wineries cluster in the area. The **Lake Michigan Shore Wine Trail** (www.lakemichiganshorewinetrail.com) provides a downloadable map of vineyards and tasting rooms. Most are signposted off the highway.

the Saugatuck/Douglas exit. Travel time is around 2½ hours; tolls cost $7.

Need to Know

➡**Area Code** ☎269

➡**Location** 140 miles northeast of Chicago

➡**Saugatuck/Douglas CVB** (www.saugatuck.com)

 EATING & DRINKING

CRANE'S PIE PANTRY   BAKERY $

(☎269-561-2297; www.cranespiepantry.com; 6054 124th Ave; pie slices $4; ☺9am-8pm Mon-Sat, from 11am Sun May-Oct, reduced hours Nov-Apr) For dessert buy a bulging slice at Crane's, or pick apples and peaches in the surrounding orchards. It's in Fennville, 3 miles south on the Blue Star Hwy, then 4 miles inland on Hwy 89.

WICKS PARK BAR & GRILL   AMERICAN $$

(☎269-857-2000; www.wickspark.com; 449 Water St; mains $11-25; ☺11:30am-9pm) Located by the chain ferry, Wicks gets props for its lake perch and live music.

SAUGATUCK BREWING COMPANY   BREWERY

(www.saugatuckbrewing.com; 2948 Blue Star Hwy; ☺11am-10pm Sun-Thu, to 11pm Fri & Sat) Locals like to hang at this Douglas pub and sip the house made suds. There's live music various nights and occasional beer-brewing classes.

 **SPORTS & ACTIVITIES**

SAUGATUCK CHAIN FERRY   BOAT RIDE

(end of Mary St; one way $1; ☺9am-9pm late May-early Sep) The best thing to do in Saugatuck is also the most affordable. Jump aboard the clackety Saugatuck Chain Ferry, and the operator will pull you across the Kalamazoo River.

OVAL BEACH   BEACH

(Oval Beach Rd; ☺9am-10pm) Life guards patrol the long expanse of fine sand. There are bathrooms and concession stands, though not enough to spoil the peaceful, dune-laden scene. It costs $6 to park. Or you

can walk from the chain ferry: head right from the dock to Mt Baldhead (a 200ft-high sand dune), huff up the stairs and then race down the other side to the beach.

SAUGATUCK DUNE RIDES   ADVENTURE TOUR

(☎269-857-2253; www.saugatuckduneride.com; 6495 Blue Star Hwy; adult/child $18/10; ☺10am-7:30pm Mon-Sat, from 11:30am Sun, closed late Oct-late Apr) Can't get enough sand? The Saugatuck Dune Rides provide a half-hour of good, cheesy fun zipping over nearby mounds.

Galena

Explore

Wee Galena spreads across wooded hillsides near the Mississippi River, amid rolling, barn-dotted farmland. Red-brick mansions line the streets, left over from the town's heyday in the mid-1800s, when local lead mines made it rich. Even with all the touristy B&Bs, fudge and antique shops, there's no denying the Galena's beauty. Throw in cool kayak trips and backroad drives, and you've got a lovely, slow-paced getaway. Summer and fall weekends see the most action.

The Best...

➡**Sight** Ulysses S Grant Home (p214)

➡**Place to Eat** 111 Main (p214)

➡**Place to Drink** VFW Hall (p214)

SLEEPING IN GALENA

Grant Hills Motel (☑877-421-0924; www.granthills.com; 9372 US 20; r $70-100; ❇❋❄) It's a no-frills option 1.5 miles east of town, with countryside views, an outdoor pool and a horseshoe pitch.

Ryan Mansion B&B (☑815-776-0608; www.ryanmansiongalena.net; 11373 US 20; r incl breakfast $90-160; ❇❄) Parlors, marble fireplaces and a library of historic tomes stuff this Victorian country estate 2 miles northwest of town.

DeSoto House Hotel (☑815-777-0090; www.desotohouse.com; 230 S Main St; r $128-200; ❇❄) ❀ Grant and Lincoln stayed in the well-furnished rooms here, and you can too. The hotel dates from 1855.

Top Tip
Most of the historic sites, restaurants and shops are walkable from the visitor center, so ditch your car in the public parking lot there (per day $5).

Getting There & Away
➜**Car** Take I-90 west out of Chicago (tolls apply). Just before Rockford, follow US 51 and I-39 heading south for 3 miles, and then merge onto US 20 west, which runs all the way into hilly Galena. The drive takes about three hours.

Need to Know
➜**Area Code** ☑815
➜**Location** 165 miles northwest of Chicago
➜**Visitor Center** (☑877-464-2536; www.galena.org; 101 Bouthillier St; ◷9am-5pm)

◉ SIGHTS

ULYSSES S GRANT HOME
MUSEUM

(☑815-777-3310; www.granthome.com; 500 Bouthillier St; adult/child $5/3; ◷9am-4:45pm Wed-Sun Apr-Oct, reduced hours Nov-Mar) The Ulysses S Grant Home was a gift from local Republicans to the victorious general at the Civil War's end. Grant lived here until he became the country's 18th president.

✖ EATING & DRINKING

111 MAIN
AMERICAN $$

(☑815-777-8030; www.oneelevenmain.com; 111 N Main St; mains $17-25; ◷4-9pm Mon-Thu, 11am-10pm Fri & Sat, 11am-9pm Sun) Meatloaf, pork and beans and other Midwestern favorites arrive at the table, using ingredients sourced from local farms.

FRITZ AND FRITES
FRENCH, GERMAN $$

(☑815-777-2004; www.fritzandfrites.com; 317 N Main St; mains $17-22; ◷4-9pm Tue & Wed, from 11:30am Thu-Sun) This romantic little bistro offers a compact menu of both German and French classics. Dig in to mussels with champagne sauce or maybe a tender schnitzel.

VFW HALL
BAR

(100 S Main St; ◷from 4pm) The VFW Hall provides a sublime opportunity to sip cheap beer and watch TV alongside veterans of long-ago wars. Don't be shy: as the sign out front says, the public is welcome.

✦ SPORTS & ACTIVITIES

FEVER RIVER OUTFITTERS
OUTDOORS

(☑815-776-9425; www.feverriveroutfitters.com; 525 S Main St; ◷10am-5pm, closed Tue-Thu early Sep-late May) Outdoors enthusiasts should head to this shop, which rents canoes, kayaks, bicycles and snowshoes. It also offers guided tours, such as two-hour kayak trips ($45 per person, equipment included) on the Mississippi River.

SHENANDOAH RIDING CENTER
HORSEBACK RIDING

(☑815-777-2373; www.shenandoahridingcenter.com; 200 N Brodrecht Rd; 1hr ride $45) Saddle up at Shenandoah. It offers trail rides through the valley for all levels of riders. The stables are 8 miles east of Galena.

STAGECOACH TRAIL
DRIVING TOUR

The Stagecoach Trail is a 26-mile ride on a narrow, twisty road en route to Warren. Pick it up by taking Main St northeast through downtown; at the second stop sign go right (you'll see a trail marker). And yes, it really was part of the old stagecoach route between Galena and Chicago.

Sleeping

Chicago's lodgings rise high in the sky, many in architectural landmarks. Snooze in the building that gave birth to the skyscraper, or in one of Mies van der Rohe's boxy structures, or in a century-old art deco masterpiece. Huge business hotels, B&Bs and hostels blanket the cityscape too. But nothing comes cheap...

Seasons & Prices

The high-season apex is June to August, when festivals and tourism peak. But Chicago hosts loads of business conventions, so demand – and prices – can skyrocket during odd times the rest of the year too. Book well in advance to avoid unpleasant surprises. Prices are lowest December to February.

Hotels

There are roughly 100,000 hotel rooms in Chicago, seemingly on every corner in the Loop, Near North and the Gold Coast in particular. All big-box chains have outposts (usually several) here. Most are geared to conventioneers. Groovy boutique hotels abound, as do uber-luxury hotels catering to rock stars and business tycoons.

B&Bs

Chicago has several B&Bs and they're typically cheaper than big hotels. Set in elegant old row houses and graystones, they cluster in the Gold Coast, Wicker Park and Lake View. They're generally casual, with self-serve breakfast. Many have two- to three-night minimum stays.

Hostels

Chicago has one **Hostelling International** (www.hiusa.org) property and several independent hostels that do not require membership. Since 2012, there has been a boom of the latter in fun, outlying neighborhoods such as Wicker Park and Wrigleyville. Browse listings at **Hostels.com** and **Hostelworld.com**.

Apartments

Vacation rentals in apartments are a good deal in Chicago, especially if your stay coincides with a big convention that ratchets up hotel prices. Try **Vacation Rental By Owner** (www.vrbo.com) and **www.airbnb.com**.

Amenities

In-room wi-fi, air-conditioning and a private bathroom are standard, unless noted otherwise. Here are some other general guidelines:

TOP END

On-site concierge services, fitness and business centers, restaurants, bars and room service are all par for the course. There's often a fee for in-room wi-fi ($10 to $15), while it's free in the lobby. Breakfast is rarely included.

MIDRANGE

Rooms have a phone, cable TV and free wi-fi; many also have a mini-refrigerator, microwave and hairdryer. Often a small fitness center is on-site. Rates often include a continental breakfast.

BUDGET

Hostels comprise this category. Expect dorms, shared bathrooms, free wi-fi and continental breakfast. Staff often organize outings to local sights and entertainment venues.

Pets

A fair number of Chicago hotels allow pets, but they charge a $50 to $100 nonrefundable cleaning fee. In this book, we have used the 🐾 icon to denote places that not only permit pets, but waive fees and/or provide special programs for our four-legged friends.

NEED TO KNOW

Price Ranges

$$$ more than $200 a night

$$ $100–200 a night

$ less than $100 a night

Tax

Chicago's room tax is 16.4%.

Parking Costs

Figure on $45 to $55 per day downtown for in-and-out privileges.

Tipping

➜ **Hotel bellhops** $2 per bag

➜ **Housekeeping staff** $2 to $5 daily

➜ **Parking valets** At least $2

➜ **Room service** 15% to 20%

➜ **Concierges** Up to $20 (for securing last-minute restaurant reservations, sold-out show tickets etc)

Check-In/Check-Out

Normally 3pm/11am. Many places will allow early check-in if the room is available (or will store your luggage if not).

Websites

➜ **Lonely Planet** (hotels. lonelyplanet.com) Find reviews and make bookings.

➜ **Chicago Bed & Breakfast Association** (www.chicago-bed-breakfast.com) Represents 18 properties.

➜ **Hotel Tonight** (www. hoteltonight.com) National discounter with last-minute deals.

Lonely Planet's Top Choices

Acme Hotel (p221) Downtown's grooviest boutique, complete with lava lights.

Hotel Burnham (p218) History, architecture and yoga gear mash up in slick rooms.

Urban Holiday Lofts (p229) It's more apartment than hostel, wafting the buzzy Bucktown vibe.

Gold Coast Guest House (p225) A wonderfully laid-back B&B in the city's priciest 'hood.

Willows Hotel (p228) Peachy rooms fill this dapper little spot.

Best by Budget

$

Urban Holiday Lofts (p229) Live like a local in Bucktown, surrounded by cool cafes.

HI-Chicago (p218) You can't beat the Loop location and free city tours.

Wrigley Hostel (p227) Brand new guesthouse right by the famed baseball park.

Chicago Parthenon Hostel (p230) Well-run, brightly painted spot in Greektown.

$$

Gold Coast Guest House (p225) Three-story townhome with a secret garden.

Willows Hotel (p228) Stylish boutique evoking the French countryside.

Buckingham Athletic Club Hotel (p218) Expansive rooms and a gym with lap pool, hiding downtown.

Wicker Park Inn (p229) Sunny pastel-colored B&B with a sweet tooth.

House of Two Urns (p229) Quirky, artist-run B&B in Wicker Park.

$$$

Hotel Burnham (p218) Free wine and chaise lounges where Al Capone's dentist once worked.

Acme Hotel (p221) Indie-cool urbanites dig the funky art and industrial decor.

Radisson Blu Aqua Hotel (p219) Mod, blond-wood rooms with balconies and views.

Hotel Lincoln (p227) Fun, from 'wall of bad art' kitsch to pedicab service.

Best for Architecture Buffs

Hotel Burnham (p218) In the landmark Reliance Building, which laid the groundwork for modern skyscraper design.

Radisson Blu Aqua Hotel (p219) In the undulating Aqua Tower, the world's tallest structure designed by a woman.

Renaissance Blackstone (p231) In a neoclassical, beaux-arts beauty known as the 'hotel of presidents.'

Hard Rock Hotel (p220) In the art deco, champagne-bottle-esque Carbide & Carbon building.

Best for Families

Embassy Suites Chicago – Lakefront (p223) Large rooms a few blocks from Navy Pier.

Days Inn Lincoln Park North (p227) Good-value digs near the park, zoo and beaches.

Essex Inn (p230) Close to the Museum Campus, plus a massive pool for post-sightseeing splashes.

Residence Inn by Marriott (p227) Laundry, kitchen and location near American Girl and Lego shops.

Where to Stay

Neighborhood	For	Against
Loop	Cool boutique and architectural hotels. Convenient to the parks, festival grounds, museums and theater district. Easy transport access to anywhere in the city.	Limited eating and drinking options after dark.
Near North & Navy Pier	The most lodging-packed 'hood. Bars, restaurants and big-box stores are everywhere.	Lots of chain hotels. Can be crowded, noisy and pricey.
Gold Coast	Chichi environs. Close to both downtown and the lakefront. Shopping bonanza at your doorstep.	Expensive.
Lincoln Park & Old Town	Characterful lodgings. A short walk to the park, zoo and beaches. Fun nightlife.	A bit removed from downtown's sights.
Lake View & Wrigleyville	Good-value boutique hotels and B&Bs surrounded by rollicking bars, restaurants and music clubs.	Main areas can be congested and rowdy at night.
Andersonville & Uptown	Tranquillity in a residential, gay-friendly neighborhood.	Far from the top-draw sights.
Wicker Park & Bucktown	Hostels and B&Bs away from the tourist masses. Area has a real neighborhood feel. Near buzzy nightlife and trendy shops.	About a 15-minute El ride to get downtown and some properties are a 15-minute walk from the El station.
Logan Square & Humboldt Park	Authentic neighborhood vibe. Indie-cool cafes, bars and shops nearby.	Isolated from downtown and the lakefront.
Near West Side & Pilsen	Near restaurant-laden Greektown and the West Loop's hot eateries.	Lonely area at night, cut off from the Loop by the highway.
South Loop & Near South Side	Well positioned near the Museum Campus, Grant Park, lakefront and Loop attractions. Prices can be cheaper.	Not lively at night; bars and restaurants are in short supply.
Hyde Park & South Side	Low prices.	Far flung from downtown and just about everything else.

SLEEPING

SAVING STRATEGIES

In peak season it's hard to find a room for less than $200 per night. Here are a few ways to cut costs:

➡ **Free parking** Look for properties with free parking and you'll save a good $50 per day downtown. Lodgings in outlying neighborhoods, such as Lake View and Wicker Park, often have free or lower cost parking lots (closer to $20 per day). We've noted the handful of downtown properties with free parking in our reviews.

➡ **Biddings sites** Try Priceline or Hotwire. 'River North' and 'Mag Mile' yield the most listings. Certain properties turn up often; we've mentioned which in our reviews.

➡ **Free wi-fi** While free wi-fi is common, many business-oriented hotels still charge for it. We tell you in the reviews which places add the fee.

➡ **Leave downtown** Prices decrease as you move out to Lincoln Park, Lake View, Wicker Park and the South Loop.

⌨ The Loop

HI-CHICAGO
HOSTEL $

Map p290 (☑312-360-0300; www.hichicago.org; 24 E Congress Pkwy; dm incl breakfast $30-36; P ✳ @ 🛜; MBrown, Orange, Purple, Pink Line to Library) Chicago's best hostel is immaculate, conveniently placed in the Loop, and offers bonuses like a staffed information desk, free volunteer-led tours and discount passes to museums and shows. The simple dorm rooms have six to 12 beds and most have attached baths. The smattering of private rooms cost about $100 per night.

In the morning, toast, cereal and pastries await in the enormous dining room; make meals whenever you want using the fully equipped kitchen. The giant common area buzzes with guests using the free wi-fi (available throughout the building), playing Ping-Pong, and chatting up the concierge to plan their day. Linens provided, but bring your own lock.

BUCKINGHAM ATHLETIC CLUB HOTEL
BOUTIQUE HOTEL $$

Map p290 (☑312-663-8910; www.bac-chicago. com; 440 S LaSalle St; r incl breakfast $169-209; P ✳ 🛜 ✹; MBrown, Orange, Purple, Pink Line to LaSalle) Tucked onto the 40th floor of the Chicago Stock Exchange building, this 21-room hotel is not easy to find. The benefit if you do? It's quiet (on weekends and evenings especially) and has expansive views south of town. Elegant rooms here are so spacious they'd be considered suites elsewhere. Lots of freebies add to the Buckingham's beauty, including free access to the namesake gym with lap pool. There's free continental breakfast and free wi-fi, to boot.

CENTRAL LOOP HOTEL
HOTEL $$

Map p290 (☑312-601-3525; www.centralloop-hotel.com; 111 W Adams St; r $149-249; P ✳ @ 🛜; MBrown, Orange, Purple, Pink Line to Quincy) The Central Loop is in a good location (the name doesn't lie) and has good prices if you're stuck paying rack rates. It's accessorized for business-oriented guests, though not so useful for families given the rooms' smallish size. A fine pub pours drinks downstairs. The owners have a similar property called **Club Quarters** (75 E Wacker Dr) at the northern fringe of the Loop.

★HOTEL BURNHAM
BOUTIQUE HOTEL $$$

Map p290 (☑312-782-1111; www.burnhamhotel. com; 1 W Washington St; r $269-399; P ✳ @ 🛜✹; MBlue Line to Washington) The proprietors brag that the Burnham has the highest guest return rates in Chicago; it's easy to see why. Housed in the landmark 1890s Reliance Building (precedent for the modern skyscraper), the superslick Burnham woos architecture buffs. Mahogany writing desks and chaise lounges furnish the bright, butter-colored rooms. Blue velvet headboards make you feel like you're sleeping in a tufted jewel box.

Like other Kimpton-brand hotels, this one has complimentary wi-fi, wine happy hours and yoga gear to borrow. For an only-in-Chicago experience, try to nab room 809, where Al Capone's dentist and partner in crime drilled teeth.

RADISSON BLU AQUA HOTEL   HOTEL $$$

Map p290 (☑312-565-5258; ww.radissonblu.com/aquahotel-chicago; 221 N Columbus Dr; r $269-349; P❄@☎☒; MBrown, Orange, Green, Purple, Pink Line to State/Lake) Radisson Blu's clean-lined rooms occupy floors 1 to 18 of the rippling, 82-story Aqua Tower. Chambers come in two styles: the Scandinavian-like 'naturally cool' (our preference), with light wood floors, blond built-in cabinets and big white bathrooms; and 'mansion house' rooms with darker colors and aqua carpet. Request your choice when booking. Upgrading to a room with a balcony (around $25) is well worth it.

There's free wi-fi throughout. Service is top-notch, as is the fitness center with indoor and outdoor pools, a running track and half-basketball court. Renowned local architect Jeanne Gang designed Aqua, which was completed in 2010 to much acclaim. It's the world's tallest building designed by a woman.

HOTEL MONACO   BOUTIQUE HOTEL $$$

Map p290 (☑866-610-0081, 312-960-8500; www.monaco-chicago.com; 225 N Wabash Ave; r $269-399; P❄@☎☒; MBrown, Orange, Green, Purple, Pink Line to State/Lake) Free goldfish on request and a geometric, deco-inspired interior help polish the Monaco's cool-daddy-o vibe. Rooms are big and boldly colored, with at least one window providing a nook to sit and watch the street action below. Amenities such as pet sitters and dog beds for pooches, cribs and child-safety kits for families, and a good fitness facility and free wi-fi for businessfolk, ensure the Monaco draws a mixed crowd. There's a free-wine happy hour each evening (as per all Kimpton-brand properties).

WIT   BOUTIQUE HOTEL $$$

Map p290 (☑312-467-0200; www.thewithotel.com; 201 N State St; r $255-385; P❄@☎; MBrown, Orange, Green, Purple, Pink Line to State/Lake) One of the Loop's hottest properties, the design-savvy Wit draws holidaying hipsters and business travelers with its viewtastic rooms, swanky rooftop bar and private movie theater. The green-glass tower glints in a sweet spot between the Theater District and the river. Each chamber features vast windows and eco-amenities like dual-flush toilets and energy-efficient heating and lighting.

Wi-fi is free in the lobby, though there's a fee for in-room service. The hotel is part of the Doubletree chain.

HAMPTON MAJESTIC
CHICAGO THEATER DISTRICT   HOTEL $$$

Map p290 (☑312-332-5052; www.hampton-majestic.com; 22 W Monroe St; r incl breakfast $169-279; P❄@☎; MRed, Blue Line to Monroe) You know what you're getting at a Hampton, and it's a solid deal at this property, which sits atop the landmark Bank of America Theatre. The 135 rooms are painted a dramatic deep red and punctuated with downy-white beds. Freebies include a simple hot breakfast buffet each morning, cookies in the evening, a small fitness center and free wi-fi. It's surprisingly quiet and intimate for being above a Broadway venue.

PALMER HOUSE HILTON   HISTORIC HOTEL $$$

Map p290 (☑800-445-8667, 312-726-7500; www.palmerhousehiltonhotel.com; 17 E Monroe St; r $179-369; P❄@☎☒; MBrown, Orange, Green, Purple, Pink Line to Adams, Red Line to Monroe) The Palmer House has been around since 1875 and the lobby still has an 'Oh my God' opulence – Tiffany chandeliers, ceiling frescoes – that makes a look-see imperative. The 1600-plus guest rooms give off a more updated vibe: most are spacious, done up in funky chartreuse and red decor, with geometric-print drapes and carpet. The Art Institute and Millennium Park are within spitting distance.

Chicago millionaire Potter Palmer set many worldwide records when he opened the property (first to use electric lighting, first to have in-room telephones, invention of the brownie...). Today it remains the nation's oldest hotel in continual operation. Its huge size makes it a convention favorite, which is why prices fluctuate wildly. Wi-fi costs $13 per day.

HOTEL ALLEGRO   HOTEL $$$

Map p290 (☑800-643-1500, 312-236-0123; www.allegrochicago.com; 171 W Randolph St; r $269-349; P❄@☎☒; MBrown, Orange, Purple, Pink Line to Washington) Hotel Allegro is part of the fun and flirty Kimpton chain. The 483 rooms sport a retro luxury cruise ship look, with funky patterned wallpaper and carpet in royal blue and snowy white tones. It's dramatic – which makes sense for a hotel right next to the Cadillac Palace Theater and its Broadway crowd.

Flat-screen TVs, free wi-fi, free evening wine receptions and free yoga gear round out the stylish package.

HYATT REGENCY CHICAGO   HOTEL $$$

Map p290 (📞800-233-1234, 312-565-1234; www.chicagoregency.hyatt.com; 151 E Wacker Dr; r $179-299; P ✳ @ 🛜; MBrown, Orange, Green, Purple, Pink Line to State/Lake) With 2019 rooms and five restaurants and bars, the riverside Hyatt Regency is Chicago's biggest hotel and typically filled with conventioneers. They should be thrilled with the $168 million revamp, completed in 2013, that modernized the joint. Rooms are still vanilla, but they're now vanilla with brand spankin' new beds, chairs, bathroom fixtures and tech-savvy work spaces.

Drinkers rejoice that the hotel has the longest freestanding bar in North America (so it claims). Lots of specials keep all those rooms filled during nonconvention times. Wi-fi costs $13 per day.

SWISSÔTEL CHICAGO   HOTEL $$$

Map p290 (📞888-737-9477, 312-565-0565; www. swissotelchicago.com; 323 E Wacker Dr; r $239-319; P ✳ @ 🛜; MBrown, Orange, Green, Purple, Pink Line to Randolph) Water vistas are just part of the attraction at this triangular-shaped, mirrored-glass high-rise at the confluence of river and lake. Businessfolk like the rooms' ample, well-appointed workstations. Families love the oversized layouts, separate shower and tub, and special kids' suites with colorful furnishings and toys. The hotel shows up a lot on discount booking sites. Summer weekends sell out fast.

Note that the fitness center with indoor pool costs $10 per day, while wi-fi costs $5 per day.

SILVERSMITH   HISTORIC HOTEL $$$

Map p290 (📞312-372-7696; www.silversmith-chicagohotel.com; 10 S Wabash Ave; r $179-279; P ✳ @ 🛜; MBrown, Orange, Green, Purple, Pink Line to Madison) Another Loop architectural gem, this one was built in 1894. Although the exterior was designed by Daniel Burnham's architects firm, the hotel's interior recalls Frank Lloyd Wright: the chunky wood furniture has a distinct Prairie School charm. Too bad that windows overlook the El tracks, or face right onto another building. Ah well – it's a small price to pay for the core Loop location. The Art Institute and Millennium Park are steps away. Wi-fi is free.

HARD ROCK HOTEL CHICAGO   HOTEL $$$

Map p290 (📞866-966-5166, 312-345-1000; www. hardrockhotelchicago.com; 230 N Michigan Ave; r $259-399; P ✳ @ 🛜; MBrown, Orange, Green, Purple, Pink Line to State/Lake) The Hard Rock tries hard to prove it rocks – DJs work the lobby lounge, staff will loan you an electric guitar to wail in your room, rock star photos pop up everywhere (including the bathroom where you might find, say, David Bowie staring out over your toilet). Considering that, the standard-sized, steel-gray rooms are relatively staid. The young and stylish clientele doesn't seem to mind, though. And the architecture is stunning: the hotel sits inside the landmark art-deco Carbide & Carbon Building, supposedly modeled after a gold-foiled champagne bottle. Wi-fi costs $13.50 per day.

FAIRMONT   LUXURY HOTEL $$$

Map p290 (📞866-540-4408, 312-565-8000; www.themillenniumparkhotel.com; 200 N Columbus Dr; r $279-499; P ✳ @ 🛜; MBrown, Orange, Green, Purple, Pink Line to State/Lake) Millennium Park here you come. All 687 luxury rooms and suites here are as close to the statues and fountains as you can stay. Upgrade to a deluxe room to get a park or lake view. Those near the top of the hotel's 45 stories are the best. Accents such as Asian ceramics combine with French empire chairs to create soft – if a bit stodgy – surrounds. Allergy sufferers can book one of the 22 hypoallergenic rooms. Wi-fi costs $14; premium (faster) wi-fi takes it up to $24.

RENAISSANCE CHICAGO DOWNTOWN HOTEL   HOTEL $$$

Map p290 (📞800-468-3571, 312-372-7200; www. renaissancehotels.com; 1 W Wacker Dr; r $289-489; P ✳ @ 🛜🏊; MBrown, Orange, Green, Purple, Pink Line to State/Lake) Don't be fooled by the bland exterior. Step into the lobby, where modern art, sink-right-in couches and lively earth tones exude warmth and style. Rooms are pretty typical contemporary stuff, but those with a water view (about $50 extra) have bay windows overlooking the skyline and the adjacent river. Conventioneers populate most of the 513 rooms. Wi-fi costs $15 per day.

W CHICAGO CITY CENTER   HOTEL $$$

Map p290 (📞877-946-8357, 312-332-1200; www. wchicagocitycenter.com; 172 W Adams St; r $269-379; P ✳ @ 🛜; MBrown, Orange, Purple, Pink

Line to Quincy) You expect urban-hip from the W brand and that's what you get here. The small, sleek black-and-white rooms can seem stark, but the bedding is uber-comfy. The soaring 'living room' (lobby/bar) feels a little like a dance club, especially when the neon-lit desks flash and the bass-heavy music gets pumping. Service is top-notch, with excellent concierges who can work miracles for reservations. Wi-fi costs $15 per day.

WYNDHAM BLAKE CHICAGO
BOUTIQUE HOTEL $$$

Map p290 (☎312-986-1234; www.hotelblake.com; 500 S Dearborn St; r $169-279; P ✳ @ 🛜; MBlue Line to LaSalle) The old customs house building has found new life as a boutique hotel at the Loop's southern edge. It's a unique location midway between downtown's core and the Museum Campus, though not much goes on in the evenings. The modern black-and-red furnishings are spread out in the well-sized rooms; the bathrooms are flat-out huge. Wi-fi is free.

If rates swing up to the high end of the spectrum you'll probably get better bang for your buck elsewhere.

🛏 Near North & Navy Pier

BEST WESTERN RIVER NORTH
HOTEL $$

Map p292 (☎800-780-7234, 312-467-0800; www.rivernorthhotel.com; 125 W Ohio St; r $169-249; P ✳ @ 🛜🏊; MRed Line to Grand) Well-maintained rooms with maple veneer beds and desks, coupled with free parking (!), free wi-fi, an indoor pool and sundeck overlooking the city, make this great value for downtown. Families in particular dig the straightforward, seven-story hotel, given its proximity to several kid-friendly restaurants.

OHIO HOUSE MOTEL
MOTEL $$

Map p292 (☎866-601-6446, 312-943-6000; www.ohiohousemotel.com; 600 N LaSalle St; r $129-159; P ✳ @ 🛜; MRed Line to Grand) First the good news about this retro 1960s motel: free parking! And a biscuit-serving, nouveau diner on site. And a great location in River North close to transport and loads of restaurants to the east (though it's still ragged to the west). Free wi-fi, too. Now the less-good news: the rooms are basic, kind of dingy and thin-walled. Still, it's a killer deal for the area.

INN OF CHICAGO
HOTEL $$

Map p292 (☎800-557-2378, 312-787-3100; www.innofchicago.com; 162 E Ohio St; r $165-229; P ✳ @ 🛜; MRed Line to Grand) It tries hard to be trendy with a clubby lobby and cocktail lounge. Rooms come in 'contemporary' style (lime-green accents, mod Jetsonslike chair) or 'traditional' style (beige striped wallpaper, officelike furniture). They're all pretty darn small. Wi-fi costs $5 to $15 per day, depending on speed.

All in all, the Inn is not particularly good value, but it often has rooms when other places are sold out. It's an OK option in that case (or if you find a low price on a booking site).

RED ROOF INN
HOTEL $$

Map p292 (☎800-733-7633, 312-787-3580; www.redroof-chicago-downtown.com; 162 E Ontario St; r $159-219; P ✳ @ 🛜; MRed Line to Grand) If you snag one of the lower rates it might be worth your while to stay at this hotel, which is steps from the Michigan Ave shopping bonanza. But just how much money are you willing to pay for faded, stuffy rooms with barely enough space to walk around two beds? Wi-fi is free.

HOWARD JOHNSON INN
MOTEL $$

Map p292 (☎800-446-4656, 312-664-8100; www.hojo.com; 720 N LaSalle St; r $169-229; P ✳ @ 🛜🏊; MBrown, Purple Line to Chicago) Ah, the outdated charm of a cheap motel. At least this one's in the city and on the edge of respectable. Sure, the rooms could use a serious re-do. If you care about decor more than free parking (yes, *free*), look elsewhere. You'll have to walk 10 minutes or so to hit the Near North's mother lode of bars and restaurants.

★ACME HOTEL
BOUTIQUE HOTEL $$$

Map p292 (☎312-894-0800; www.acmehotelcompany.com; 15 E Ohio St; r $179-309; P ✳ @ 🛜; MRed Line to Grand) Urban bohemians are loving the Acme for its indie-cool style at (usually) affordable rates. The 130 rooms mix industrial fixtures with retro lamps, mid-century furniture and funky modern art. They're wired up with free wi-fi, good speakers, smart TVs and easy connections to stream your own music and movies. Graffiti and neon and lava lights decorate the common areas.

The excellent location puts you between the Magnificent Mile (the N Michigan Ave shopping haven, a few blocks east) and the Theater District (about a half-mile south).

HOTEL PALOMAR
HOTEL $$$

Map p292 (℡877-731-0505, 312-755-9703; www. hotelpalomar-chicago.com; 505 N State St; r $199-309; P✳@⊕⊛⊛; MRed Line to Grand) Here we go again: an excellent property in the Kimpton chain (like the Burnham, the Monaco and the Allegro, all in the Loop). Note of distinction: the 17-story, 261-room Palomar has a green roof, Chicago's first for a hotel. Arty decor – little sculptures, original paintings on the wall – add to the fashionable but businesslike scheme. There's an indoor rooftop pool and a free wine hour each evening.

IVY HOTEL
BOUTIQUE HOTEL $$$

Map p292 (℡312-335-5444; www.exploreivy.com; 233 E Ontario St; r $179-279; P✳@⊕; MRed Line to Grand) The 63-room Ivy parcels out its chambers so there are just five per floor, making it feel exceptionally intimate. The sleek and chic rooms offer platform beds, bathrooms with big soaking tubs and eco-friendly bamboo flooring. It's a newer hotel and as it tries to gain traction it shows up often on booking sites with good deals. Take advantage. Wi-fi is free.

JAMES
HOTEL $$$

Map p292 (℡312-337-1000; www.jameshotels.com; 55 E Ontario St; r $209-319; P✳@⊕⊛; MRed Line to Grand) Low and loungey chairs sidle up to oversized tripod lamps. Porthole windows allow you to peep through sliding bathroom doors. Hep cats and fans of Mid-Century Modern design love it here. But everyone can appreciate the little luxuries: organic bath products, Turkish cotton towels, a bar that has half bottles instead of minis, a real-deal gym, free wi-fi…

An overwhelmingly gracious staff helps work out any service kinks, like rooms not being ready on time.

HOTEL FELIX
HOTEL $$$

Map p292 (℡312-447-3440; www.hotelfelixchicago.com; 111 W Huron St; r $169-279; P✳@⊕; MRed Line to Chicago) 🏊 Opened in 2009, the 225-room, 12-story Felix is downtown's first hotel to earn eco-friendly LEED certification (Leadership in Energy and Environmental Design; silver status, to be exact). The earth-toned, mod-furnished rooms are small but efficiently and comfortably designed. It's more of a place for urban hipsters than families, but who doesn't enjoy a rainfall showerhead, soft Egyptian cotton sheets and free wi-fi?

ALOFT CHICAGO CITY CENTER
HOTEL $$$

Map p292 (℡312-661-1000; www.aloftchicagocitycenter.com; 515 N Clark St; r $199-279; P✳@⊕; MRed Line to Grand) A new option that opened in summer 2013, this hotel offers the chain's typical compact, efficiently designed minimalist rooms. They sport a bookish, library look here, with big windows and all the electronics you need. The clubby, game-filled lobby (another Aloft staple) is prime for mingling. Wi-fi is free.

If the hotel is full, well, it happens to be attached to two other new properties that might be options: family-oriented Fairfield Inn & Suites and business-focused Hyatt Place.

AMALFI HOTEL CHICAGO
BOUTIQUE HOTEL $$$

Map p292 (℡877-262-5341, 312-395-9000; www.amalfihotelchicago.com; 20 W Kinzie St; r incl breakfast $249-359; P✳@⊕; MRed Line to Grand) There's lots to love at the Amalfi beyond the modern-design-driven, warm-toned rooms. Each floor lays out its own sumptuous spread of pastries, fruit and yoghurt every morning. In the evening you can munch free hors d'oeuvres and sip two free cocktails in the lounge. CDs and DVDs are available to borrow at any time to play in your in-room entertainment center. Wi-fi is free.

VIRGIN HOTEL

The most buzzed about new place to get into bed is **Virgin Hotel** (Map p290; www.virginhotels.com; 203 N Wabash Ave; P✳@⊕; MBrown, Orange, Green, Purple, Pink Line to State/Lake). Billionaire Richard Branson chose Chicago to open his first guesthouse. He's transforming the 27-story, art deco landmark Dearborn Bank Building into a decadent, trendy, 250-room property with free wi-fi throughout. The four-star hotel is slated to open in the first half of 2014. More Virgin hotels will follow around the globe.

HOTEL CASS
BOUTIQUE HOTEL $$$

Map p292 (☏800-799-4030, 312-787-4030; www.
casshotel.com; 640 N Wabash Ave; r incl breakfast
$209-369; P✳@☎; MRed Line to Grand) Expensive hardwoods, Kohler fixtures and
other upscale treatments transformed what
was an aging 1920s hotel into a Holiday Inn
Express–affiliated boutique. Small room
spaces are maximized with modern flair:
hanging flat-screen TVs, mod C-shaped
tables and armless couches. The breakfast
bar includes bacon, eggs and a few other
hot items. Wi-fi is free.

HAMPTON INN & SUITES
CHICAGO DOWNTOWN
HOTEL $$$

Map p292 (☏800-426-7866, 312-832-0330,
www.hamptonsuiteschicago.com; 33 W Illinois St;
r incl breakfast $179-289; P✳@☎☒; MRed
Line to Grand) Thick oak desks and angular
leaded-glass lamps give the lobby a Prairie
School feel. But the Frank Lloyd Wright influence is less apparent once you get to the
contemporary rooms dominated by fluffy
white duvet-covered beds. Several are studio and one-bedroom suites with kitchens.
The 12-story property offers Hampton's
requisite free wi-fi, a small indoor pool and
hot (if spare) breakfast buffet.

HILTON GARDEN INN
HOTEL $$$

Map p292 (☏800-774-1500, 312-595-0000; www.
hiltongardeninn.com; 10 E Grand Ave; r $189-269;
P✳@☎☒, MRed Line to Grand) Part of the
stalwart chain, this outpost near the Magnificent Mile caters to business travelers,
families and holidaying couples in equal
measure. Rooms are decent-sized and good
quality, with free wi-fi. Meaty smells waft
up from the Weber Grill restaurant downstairs. Rates vary wildly, so you may get a
steal.

DOUBLETREE
MAGNIFICENT MILE
HOTEL $$$

Map p292 (☏312-787-6100; www.doubletreemag
mile.com; 300 E Ohio St; r $179-269; P✳@☎☒;
MRed Line to Grand) Relax on your window
seat and look out at the sliver of a lake view
many rooms have here in Streeterville, near
Navy Pier. If you're not looking for anything
fancy (ie average space, generic faux-wood
decor), you've found it. But there is a 50,000
sq ft athletic club, an outdoor pool and free
wi-fi in the lobby (in-room connectivity will
cost you). The three-star property pops up
at lower rates on discount booking websites
quite often.

ALLERTON HOTEL
HISTORIC HOTEL $$$

Map p292 (☏312 440 1500; www.theallertonhotel.
com; 701 N Michigan Ave; r $189-279; P✳@☎;
MRed Line to Chicago) High atop the Italianate
red-brick facade shines the red neon Allerton
Tip Top sign, a reminder of the hotel's past.
From the 1920s to the '50s, the penthouse
Tip Top Club was a happening place. All the
big bands and early radio stars played here.
Thankfully, the Allerton's rooms have leaped
into modern times with marble bathrooms,
flat-screen TVs and comfy bedding.

Standard rooms are by no means large
(and the 'classic' rooms are downright tiny),
but they can be a bargain off-peak. It's a
prime location right on the Mag Mile. Wi-fi
costs $10 per day.

EMBASSY SUITES CHICAGO –
LAKEFRONT
HOTEL $$$

Map p292 (☏866-866-8095, 312-836-5900;
www.chicagoembassysuiteslakefront.com; 511
N Columbus Dr; ste incl breakfast $209-289;
P✳@☎☒; MRed Line to Grand) This Embassy displays the chain's typical hallmarks: all
the units are two-room suites (living room
with sofa bed in front, bedroom in back);
there's always a cooked-to-order bacon,
egg and pancake breakfast each morning;
there's free wine each evening; and there's
an indoor, kiddie-mobbed pool. Families
dig the location between Michigan Ave and
Navy Pier. It may leave little to the imagination, but this outpost of the chain does a
fine job with all the basics. Wi-fi costs $15
per day.

EMBASSY SUITES CHICAGO –
DOWNTOWN
HOTEL $$$

Map p292 (☏800 362 2779, 312 943 3800; www.
embassysuiteschicago.com; 600 N State St; ste
incl breakfast $199-279; P✳@☎☒; MRed
Line to Grand) This hotel rises a mere half-mile west of the Embassy Suites Lakefront
(yes, the latter is closer to the water). It's
the same deal – large rooms, free cooked-to-order breakfast, indoor pool etc – particularly beloved by families. This property
sometimes has slightly cheaper prices than
its sibling.

AVENUE CROWNE PLAZA HOTEL
HOTEL $$$

Map p292 (☏877-227-6963, 312-787-2900; www.
avenuehotelchicago.com; 160 E Huron St; r $199-
309; P✳@☎☒; MRed Line to Chicago) Guests
cite the Avenue's classy yet unfussed vibe,
its large rooms and the try-hard staff as the
reasons to book in here. The small heated

rooftop pool and sundeck offer cool views. The hotel's rainbow-hued 'KidSuites' rooms are impressive, with beanbag chairs, drawing easels and other toys for children. Wi-fi costs $10 per day.

INTERCONTINENTAL CHICAGO   HOTEL $$$

Map p292 (☎800-327-0200, 312-944-4100; www.icchicagohotel.com; 505 N Michigan Ave; r $235-399; P❀@☎☒; MRed Line to Grand) The InterContinental's two towers have a split personality. The Historic Tower's 315 rooms waft an elegant, heavily draped look, with thick brocades and sumptuous silks. The Grand Tower's 477 rooms are newer and fresh off a 2013 rehab that brightened the spaces with spiffy fabrics and added more outlets and USB ports for the many business travelers who stay here.

The ornate, original tower was built in 1929 as the Medinah Athletic Club. Period architecture and decor grace the premises, best known for the mosaic-tiled indoor pool where Hollywood goddess Esther Williams swam. Ask the concierge for the iPod audio tour that lets you explore the building.

LANGHAM HOTEL   LUXURY HOTEL $$$

Map p292 (☎312-923 9988; chicago.langham-hotels.com; 330 N Wabash Ave; r from $450; P❀@☎☒; MRed Line to Grand) Early starchitect Ludwig Mies van der Rohe designed the 52-story, black-box building originally. His grandson remade the lower floors into the Langham in 2013. The mega-swank, 316-room property features some of the biggest chambers in the city; they start at 516 sq ft and go up from there. Groovy sculptures and modern art dot the common areas. The building's upper floors house the American Medical Association. There's free wi-fi throughout.

PENINSULA   LUXURY HOTEL $$$

Map p292 (☎866-288-8889, 312-337-2888; www.peninsula.com; 108 E Superior St; r from $450; P❀@☎☒; MRed Line to Chicago) The over-the-top Peninsula is among Chicago's top addresses. Equestrian statues and marquetry furnishings decorate the neoclassical rooms. Two-story walls of glass enclose the pool, where you can swim after your essence-of-rubies spa facial. How's the service? Buttoned down. This is where Hollywood stars check in when they come to town.

PARK HYATT   LUXURY HOTEL $$$

Map p292 (☎800-633-7313, 312-335-1234; www.parkchicago.hyatt.com; 800 N Michigan Ave; r from $400; P❀@☎☒; MRed Line to Chicago) Want every inch of your suite covered in rose petals, with candles lit and your bath water run? They've done it before at this ask-and-it-shall-be-granted luxury flagship of the locally based Hyatt chain. From the miniature TVs in the bathroom to the butler and the courtesy car service, no expense has been spared.

Bow-shaped tubs hide behind rolling window shades in some rooms so you can soak and still admire the view. Terrace kings have small balconies looking out across the street to the Water Tower and the lake beyond. C'mon – if it's good enough for U2 when they rock through town, you know it's got street cred.

TRUMP HOTEL & TOWER   LUXURY HOTEL $$$

Map p292 (☎877-458-7867, 312-588-8000; www.trumpchicagohotel.com; 401 N Wabash Ave; r from $450; P❀@☎☒; MBrown, Orange, Green, Purple, Pink to State) Donald opened his glassy Chicago handiwork, which rose to be the city's second-tallest building, in 2008. The manly, earth-toned rooms are high in the sky with floor-to-ceiling windows, and most have kitchens full of stainless-steel appliances. The views are sweet and service is as polished as you'd expect.

W CHICAGO LAKESHORE   HOTEL $$$

Map p292 (☎312-943-9200; www.wchicago-lakeshore.com; 644 N Lake Shore Dr; r $239-379; P❀@☎☒; ☒66) The W has an earthy aesthetic that feels entirely appropriate here on the lakefront. You can see the water from telescopes by the windows in the elevator bays, from 'spectacular' rooms and 'fantastic' suites. Navy Pier and oceanlike expanses stretch before you while you run on the treadmill or lie on the pool deck. The small Whisky Sky bar glows from the 33rd floor. Wi-fi costs $15 per day.

FOUR POINTS CHICAGO DOWNTOWN   HOTEL $$$

Map p292 (☎800-368-7764, 312-981-6600; www.fourpointschicago.com; 630 N Rush St; ste $189-289; P❀@☎☒; MRed Line to Grand) Constructed in 2005, this Sheraton-affiliated hotel has more soundproofing and less wear than many of the other big name chains in town. Every room has microwaves, minifridges, coffee makers and free wi-fi that come standard. (Balconies and whirlpool tubs cost extra.) It's within easy walking distance to loads of food and drink options.

CHICAGO MARRIOTT HOTEL HOTEL $$$
Map p292 (☏800-228-9290, 312-836-0100; www.marriott.com; 540 N Michigan Ave; r $179-309; P❋@🛜🌊; MRed Line to Grand) A Magnificent Mile address is the primary draw card of this 46-story behemoth. The standard rooms are smaller than what you expect at these rates. The downy duvets and flatscreen TVs will do, though.

🛏 Gold Coast

OAK 112 HOSTEL $
Map p296 (☏312-804-3677; www.oak112.com; 112 W Oak St; incl breakfast dm $30-45, r from $120; P❋🛜; MRed Line to Clark/Division) Tucked in an old row house on a leafy residential street, Oak 112 is operated by the same folks as Bucktown's Urban Holiday Lofts (p229) and features similar freebies, including continental breakfast, wi-fi and El fare from the airport. With just eight rooms, it's a smaller, quieter hostel than the others in town. You certainly won't find anything cheaper in the Gold Coast.

There's no sign, just a strip of tape over the door buzzer with the property's name. Bike rentals are available for $20 per day.

★GOLD COAST GUEST HOUSE B&B $$
Map p296 (☏312-337-0361; www.bbchicago.com; 113 W Elm St; r incl breakfast $129-229; ❋@🛜; MRed Line to Clark/Division) Innkeeper Sally Baker has been making stays memorable for more than 20 years. She'll lead you to a happy-hour bargain on lobster, make a discounted tour reservation or guide you to the local grocery store. Her 1873 classic threestory townhouse has a delightful secret garden, and four rooms made light and airy by muted taupes, blues and creams.

Self-serve coffee, juices, breads and cheeses are among the breakfast choices. Help yourself to sodas and snacks around the clock. Wi-fi and computer use are free, parking (on street with permit) is $25 per day. She also rents apartments nearby. No children under 10.

TREMONT HOTEL HOTEL $$
Map p296 (☏866-716-8139, 312-751-1900; www.tremontchicago.com; 100 E Chestnut St; r $139-

229; P❋🛜; MRed Line to Chicago) Here are the Tremont's pros: you're steps from the Magnificent Mile in a ritzy neighborhood and the property often turns up dirt cheap on Hotwire. Do the rooms tend toward faded upholstery and peeling wallpaper? Yes, but you can help the situation by asking for a room with good natural light at check-in.

Old-school touches, like the parlor that's studded with leather chairs and has a fireplace, evoke nostalgia, as does the on-site meaty restaurant of former Bears coach Mike Ditka. Look elsewhere if room prices slide toward the high end of the range. Starwood Hotels–affiliated.

PUBLIC BOUTIQUE HOTEL $$$
Map p296 (☏312-787-3700; www.publichotels.com; 1301 N State Pkwy; r $189-315; P❋🛜; MRed Line to Clark/Division) Pop-hotelier Ian Schrager took over the old Ambassador East Hotel and gave it a minimalist chic touch. Rooms are done up in a 'no-color palette' (aka light beige). Walls are bare except for a giant flat-screen TV, an oversize clock and cow photos (a nod to Chicago's historic stockyards). Stylish urbanites are digging it in droves. Wi-fi is free.

You'll get the vibe as soon as you enter the swanky white lobby, which leads to the 'library' with its limestone fireplace and beautiful people sipping coffee by day and vino by night. Or make like Frank Sinatra and Mick Jagger by hitting the glamorous Pump Room bar/restaurant.

RAFFAELLO CHICAGO BOUTIQUE HOTEL $$$
Map p296 (☏800-898-7198, 312-943-5000; www.chicagoraffaello.com; 201 E Delaware Pl; r $189-279; P❋@🛜; MRed Line to Chicago) If only you could live in the creamy, silkdraped modernity of these rooms. Oh, wait, you can – they're condominiums, too. Suites have microwaves and minifridges in marble cooking centers, plus roomy seating areas or separate living rooms. King and double rooms are smaller, but they have similar upscale amenities, such as rainforest shower heads and high-thread-count linens.

A smart rooftop lounge and Italian seafood restaurant tempt on-site. Wi-fi is free in the lobby, but $10 per day in-room.

SOFITEL CHICAGO WATER TOWER HOTEL $$$
Map p296 (☏800-763-4835, 312-324-4000; www.sofitel-chicago.com; 20 E Chestnut St; r $199-350; P❋@🛜; MRed Line to Chicago) The Sofitel looks a little like some state-of-the-art Mac

CONVENTION CRAZINESS

When huge conventions trample through town, beware. You'll be competing with an extra 25,000 people or so for hotel rooms, which will skyrocket in price. In general, spring and fall are the busiest convention times. Check Choose Chicago's convention calendar (www.choosechicago.com/meeting-professionals/convention-calendar) to see what's on when. The following are some of the largest events when room prices will make you weep:

➡ International Home and Housewares Show – three nights in mid-March

➡ National Restaurant Association – three nights in mid-May

➡ American Society of Clinical Oncologists (ASCO) – five nights in late May/early June

➡ Radiological Society of North America – five nights in late November/early December

computing device from the outside, its triangular glass tower leaning gracefully forward into space. Inside, stylish staff members tend to stylish 30- and 40-something guests, who come here for the minimalist vibe (think blond wood and rectangular lines). A lot of Europeans check in. Wi-fi costs $15 per day.

Sometimes the hotel also shows up on discount booking sites where you can score a great deal.

FLEMISH HOUSE   B&B $$$

Map p296 (☎312-664-9981; www.innchicago.com; 68 E Cedar St; r incl breakfast $200-250; ✴🛜; MRed Line to Clark/Division) A wall full of framed line drawings, coffered panels and rosette woodwork, an exquisite porcelain collection atop the armoire – you can tell that one of the co-owners of this 1892 row house is an architect. Travelers check into these self-service apartments (with full kitchens) for the quiet. Don't expect the typical B&B socializing; breakfast supplies are stocked in the fridge before you arrive.

The closest parking is in a lot a couple of blocks away. No children under six.

WALDORF ASTORIA
CHICAGO   LUXURY HOTEL $$$

Map p296 (☎312-646-1300; www.waldorfastoria-chicagohotel.com; 11 E Walton St; r from $400; P✴@🛜✴✴; MRed Line to Chicago) The Waldorf routinely tops the list for Chicago's best uber-luxury hotel. It models itself on 1920s Parisian glamor and we gotta say: it delivers. Rooms are large – they have to be, to hold the fireplaces, the bars, the marble soaking tubs, the beds with 460-thread-

count sheets and the fully wired work spaces and other techno gadgets.

There's a fancy gym with a lap pool, a high-rolling bar and a couple of spiffy restaurants. Wi-fi is free.

HOTEL INDIGO   BOUTIQUE HOTEL $$$

Map p296 (☎800-972-2494, 312-787-4980; www.goldcoastchicagohotel.com; 1244 N Dearborn St; r $179-259; P✴@🛜; MRed Line to Clark/Division) The Indigo feels more like your perky friend's apartment than a hotel. Rooms feature hardwood floors, white furniture and neon green, orange and yellow accent fabrics, while a macro photo wall mural of something, er, indigo (like blueberries) watches over it all. The location is quieter than most other Gold Coast places, yet it's still within easy walking distance of shopping, nightlife and the lakefront.

DRAKE HOTEL   HISTORIC HOTEL $$$

Map p296 (☎800-553-7253, 312-787-2200; www.thedrakehotel.com; 140 E Walton St; r $209-329; P✴@🛜; MRed Line to Chicago) Queen Elizabeth, Winston Churchill, Charles Lindbergh, Dean Martin, Princess Di... the Reagans, the Bushes, the Clintons... Who hasn't stayed at the elegant Drake Hotel since it opened in 1920? The grande dame commands a striking location at the north end of Michigan Ave, near Oak St Beach. Embroidered gold silk coverlets and Grecian urn lamps are almost as impressive as the water views from the junior suites.

Whether enjoying lobster in the Cape Cod Room (as Marilyn Monroe did) or swirling a Manhattan in the Coq d'Or bar, you'll feel like somebody special too. Guests tend to be older or members of the many weddings the Drake hosts. Wi-fi costs $13 per day.

WESTIN MICHIGAN AVENUE   HOTEL $$$

Map p296 (📞888-625-5144, 312-943-7200; www. westin.com/michiganave; 909 N Michigan Ave, entrance on E Delaware Pl; r $199-319; P ❄ @ 🛜; MRed Line to Chicago) The Magnificent Mile location – we're talking smack on the Mag Mile, by all the high-end shops – is the main selling point. While the Westin's rooms are decent sized and offer comfy beds, they feel like being in an office cubicle with their beige, corporate vibe. Indeed, the 752 rooms often fill with convention-goers.

The good news is that rates drop in off-peak times to keep the many rooms filled. Wi-fi costs $13 per day. Lake views are available for a premium.

RESIDENCE INN BY MARRIOTT   HOTEL $$$

Map p296 (📞866-596-7890, 312-943-9800; www.marriott.com; 201 E Walton St; r incl breakfast $179-279; P ❄ @ 🛜; MRed Line to Chicago) What to say about a generic extended-stay hotel... Well, it's got all the extras families crave: DIY kitchens, laundry facilities, free wi-fi and hot breakfast buffet. They'll even run out and buy groceries for you. Studios, one and two bedrooms available. No pool, though – sorry, kids (though Oak St Beach is nearby) – but it does have weekday happy hours.

WHITEHALL HOTEL   HISTORIC HOTEL $$$

Map p296 (📞866-753-4081, 312-944-6300; www.thewhitehallhotel.com; 105 E Delaware Pl; r $179-289; P ❄ @ 🛜; MRed Line to Chicago) Tallyho, my good chap, we're off on the fox hunt. This old-world hotel speaks with a decidedly British accent thanks to cozy rooms, hunting-dog paintings and vintage mahogany furniture. It's popular with wedding parties; you'll often see gown-clad beauties flowing by. The property was looking pretty run-down, but at press time was being refurbished with new paint, carpeting and flat-screen TVs. Michigan Ave is superbly close.

🛏 Lincoln Park & Old Town

CHICAGO GETAWAY HOSTEL   HOSTEL $

Map p298 (📞773-929-5380; www.getawayhostel.com; 616 W Arlington Pl; incl breakfast dm

$32-36, r from $90; P ❄ @ 🛜; 🚌22, MBrown, Purple, Red Line to Fullerton) The fun, social Getaway Hostel continues to spruce up. It attracts mostly a college-aged crowd who strum the house guitars, lounge on leather couches, sip beer on the patio and head out to nightlife-rich Clark and Halsted Sts (the hostel is equidistant between the two). Staff organize outings (like pub crawls) throughout the week. Continental breakfast and wi-fi are free.

Rooms have a fresh, bright-hued coat of paint. Dorms are single sex, sleeping six to 12 people. The private rooms are small and either have a full bathroom, a half bathroom or share one down the hall.

DAYS INN LINCOLN PARK NORTH   HOTEL $$

Map p302 (📞773-525-7010; www.daysinnchicago.net; 644 W Diversey Pkwy; r incl breakfast $125-185; P ❄ @ 🛜; 🚌22) This well-maintained chain hotel is a favorite of both families and touring indie bands, providing good service and value-added perks such as free health club access, wi-fi and hot waffle breakfasts. It's an easy amble to the lakefront's parks and beaches, and a 15-minute bus ride to downtown. It's right at the hustle-bustle intersection of Broadway, Clark St and Diversey Pkwy.

HOTEL LINCOLN   BOUTIQUE HOTEL $$$

Map p298 (📞312-254-4700; www.hotellincolnchicago.com; 1816 N Clark St; r $179-319; P ❄ @ 🛜; 🚌22) The boutique Lincoln, opened in 2012, is all about kitschy fun, as the lobby's 'wall of bad art' and front desk patched together from flea market dresser drawers attest. Standard rooms are small, but vintage-cool and colorful; many have sweet views. Leafy Lincoln Park and the city's largest farmers market sprawl across the street.

On summer Wednesdays the Lincoln hosts a free outdoor yoga class at the rooftop lounge. A hotel pedicab provides transport to nearby North Avenue Beach. Bike rentals are also available.

🛏 Lake View & Wrigleyville

WRIGLEY HOSTEL   HOSTEL $

Map p302 (📞773 598 4471; www.wrigleyhostel.com; 3512 N Sheffield Ave; dm incl breakfast $30; P ❄ @ 🛜; MRed Line to Addison) Opened in May 2013, this hostel is practically within homerun distance of Wrigley Field, as well as the area's rowdy nightlife. It's unobtrusive, located in a small converted brick apartment block. The blue-and-green rooms have an average of four beds (not necessarily bunked). Bathrooms, some with vintage clawfoot tubs, are down the hall on each floor. Free, strong-signaled wi-fi permeates throughout.

The common room rocks a pool table, leather couches, bar stools and a sound system into which you can hook your iPod. The hostel also organizes trips to local blues and honky-tonk clubs. Bike rental costs $20 per day; it's about a mile to the lakefront trail. At press time, Wrigley was in the midst of expanding into the building next door to double its current 55-bed capacity.

WILLOWS HOTEL BOUTIQUE HOTEL $$

Map p302 (☑773-528-8400; www.willowshotel-chicago.com; 555 W Surf St; r incl breakfast $149-265; P❋☏; ☐22) Small and stylish, the Italianate Willows wins an architectural gold star. The chic little lobby provides a swell refuge of overstuffed chairs by the fireplace. The 55 rooms, done up in shades of peach, cream and soft green, evoke a 19th-century French countryside feel. There's free wi-fi throughout. The hotel's owners also run the City Suites and Majestic hotels.

Of the three accommodations, Willows is the furthest south, at Lake View's edge, so you're near the zoo and lakefront parklands.

MAJESTIC HOTEL BOUTIQUE HOTEL $$

Map p302 (☑773-404-3499; www.majestic-chicago.com; 528 W Brompton Ave; r incl breakfast $149-265; P❋☏; ☐151) Nestled into a row of residential housing, the Majestic is walking distance to Wrigley Field, Boystown and the lakefront. From the lobby fireplace and dark-wood furnishings to the handsome, paisley-swirled decor, the interior has the cozy feel of an English manor. Rooms are slightly larger than those at sibling hotels City Suites and Willows, and the location is more remote and quieter. Wi-fi is free.

CITY SUITES HOTEL BOUTIQUE HOTEL $$

Map p302 (☑773-404-3400; www.chicagocity-suites.com; 933 W Belmont Ave; r incl breakfast $149-265; P❋☏; Ⓜ Brown, Purple, Red Line to Belmont) The mod, art-deco-tinged rooms and lobby buzzing just off Belmont Ave are vaguely reminiscent of a European city ho-

tel. The El races right by the building, so light sleepers should ask for a room away from the tracks. Compared with the Majestic and Willows, the owners' other two properties, the City Suites skews towards a bit of a younger and livelier crowd. As with the others, there's free wi-fi throughout and a pass to a nearby fitness club.

BEST WESTERN HAWTHORNE TERRACE HOTEL $$

Map p302 (☑888-860-3400, 773-244-3434; www.hawthorneterrace.com; 3434 N Broadway; r incl breakfast $159-209; P❋@☏; ☐36) The earthy Hawthorne Terrace attracts the most mixed crowd of the neighborhood's hotels. Sporty Cubs fans check in next to gay groups, with everyone primed to go out and have some fun. Standard-issue furnishings fill the rooms, but the free wi-fi, microwaves and minifridges are nice perks, along with the continental breakfast and a small fitness room. The 1920s Federal-style apartment building may not be the newest place around, but it retains a classic appeal inside and out.

OLD CHICAGO INN B&B $$

Map p302 (☑773-472-2278; www.oldchicago-inn.com; 3222 N Sheffield Ave; r incl breakfast $100-175; ❋☏; Ⓜ Brown, Purple, Red Line to Belmont) Sure, the street din may seep into this century-old, 10-room graystone building, but that's the price you pay for being in a high-energy nightlife hub. Most of the chambers have wood floors and vintage accents; a few rooms share a bathroom. In addition to continental breakfast, you get a free dinner at the owner's pub, Trader Todd's, two doors down. There's free wi-fi and on-street parking (though you may have to search a bit).

VILLA TOSCANA B&B $$

Map p302 (☑800-404-2643, 773-404-2643; www.thevillatoscana.com; 3447 N Halsted St; r incl breakfast $119-159; ❋☏; ☐8) An 1890s Victorian home seems out of place, set next to Gay Mart on the busiest of Boystown streets. Wander through the leafy front garden and you're transported. Purple silks evoke Morocco in one room, toile recalls France in another. All eight diminutive lodgings (five with private bath) are often booked, so plan ahead. Enjoy breakfast pastries on the rear sundeck in nice weather. Free wi-fi.

🛏 Andersonville & Uptown

HOUSE 5863   B&B $$

(📞773-944-5555; www.house5863.com; 5863 N Glenwood Ave; r incl breakfast $100 180; P ♿ 🛜; Ⓜ Red Line to Thorndale) Hip and urban, sleek and sophisticated: House 5683 is a thoroughly modern B&B. You'll find no frilly ruffles here, just clean-lined furnishings and abstract art in an old apartment house. Lounge on the black leather sofa in the common living room and watch the plasma TV, or use the free wi-fi throughout. Adirondack chairs invite lolling about in the backyard. Garage parking available ($30).

🛏 Wicker Park, Bucktown & Ukrainian Village

⭐**URBAN HOLIDAY LOFTS**   HOSTEL $

Map p306 (📞312-532-6949; www.urbanholiday-lofts.com; 2014 W Wabansia Ave; incl breakfast dm $30-45, r from $100; ♿ @ 🛜; Ⓜ Blue Line to Damen) This building of loft condos has been converted into the neighborhood's nicest hostel. An international crowd fills the mix of dorms (with four to 10 beds) and private rooms, most of which share bathrooms. Exposed brick walls, hardwood floors and bunks with plump bedding are common to all 25 rooms. Free wi-fi, continental breakfast and El fare from the airport add to the deal.

The common room bustles with folks using the kitchen facilities, shooting pool and playing the Golden Tee arcade game. Loads of bars and cafes beckon from the surrounding blocks. Bike rentals are available for $20 per day. At press time, the owners were in the process of opening another, larger hostel in the neighborhood at 1659 W Division St, with similar prices.

IHSP CHICAGO INN AT DAMEN   HOSTEL $

Map p306 (📞312-731-4234; www.ihspusa.com; 1616 N Damen Ave; incl breakfast dm $25-40, r from $75; P ♿ @ 🛜; Ⓜ Blue Line to Damen) Set on Damen Ave, this hostel couldn't be any closer to the neighborhood's cache of hipster shops and eateries. The 50 chambers hold one to 10 beds in various dorm and private room configurations. The flimsy metal bunks and thin-walled bathrooms don't seem to deter the young global backpackers, who head up to the viewtastic rooftop deck to grill, drink and socialize.

Freebies include a DIY pancake breakfast, wi-fi, a game room with Wii and foosball, and your El transport fare from the airport. The social hostel organizes frequent outings. The slightly bigger, quieter private rooms are located in a separate building about a block from the main one.

WICKER PARK INN   B&B $$

Map p306 (📞773 486 2743; www.wickerparkinn. com; 1329 N Wicker Park Ave; r incl breakfast $149-199; ♿ 🛜; Ⓜ Blue Line to Damen) This classic brick row house is steps away from rockin' restaurants and nightlife. The sunny rooms aren't huge, but all have hardwood floors, soothing pastel color schemes, terry-cloth robes and small desk spaces where you can use the free wi-fi. Across the street, two apartments with kitchens provide a self-contained experience (sans the baked-good-rich breakfast). Rooms have varying minimum-stay requirements.

HOUSE OF TWO URNS BED & BREAKFAST   B&B $$

Map p306 (📞773-235-1408; www.twourns.com; 1239 N Greenview Ave; r incl breakfast $129-239; P ♿ 🛜; Ⓜ Blue Line to Division) Artists own these two houses at Wicker Park's edge, so it's no surprise both are fancifully furnished with old cameras, cobalt glass and other offbeat antiques, as well as original art. Rooms are more homey than luxurious. Those at the lower end of the spectrum share a bathroom, while those at the upper end have a Jacuzzi tub and include free off-street parking.

Guests all gather in the main dining room for a cooked breakfast, though you can request self-serve continental morning munchies. The helpful hosts also lend out umbrellas, provide free snacks and share their 200-plus DVDs. Children over age 10 are welcome.

RUBY ROOM   INN $$

Map p306 (📞773-235-2323; www.rubyroom.com; 1743-5 W Division St; r $115-185; ♿ 🛜; Ⓜ Blue Line to Division) Take a yoga class, go on a guided intuitive journey or get your chakra massaged. Ruby Room is primarily a spa and 'healing sanctuary.' Eight simplified rooms are boiled down to the essence of comfort. No TVs, no telephones, no elevator, no breakfast. Instead, expect 500-thread-count sheets, pristine white interiors, pillow-top mattresses and free wi-fi. No children under 12.

⌂ Logan Square & Humboldt Park

LONGMAN & EAGLE   INN **$$**
Map p310 (☏773-276-7110; www.longmanand-eagle.com; 2657 N Kedzie Ave; r $85-200; ❄☂; Ⓜ️Blue Line to Logan Square) Check in at the Michelin-starred tavern downstairs, then head to your wood-floored, vintage-stylish accommodation on the floor above. The six rooms aren't particularly soundproofed, but after using your whiskey tokens in the bar, you probably won't care. Artwork by local artists decorates each room.

⌂ Near West Side & Pilsen

CHICAGO PARTHENON HOSTEL   HOSTEL **$**
Map p312 (☏312-258-1399; www.chicagopar-thenonhostel.com; 310 S Halsted St; dm/r incl breakfast from $30/61; ❄☂; Ⓜ️Blue Line to UIC-Halsted) Guests young and old, international and American check in to this well-run hostel that sits next to the Parthenon Restaurant. It feels more like a hotel with bunk beds rather than a traditional hostel.

Tidy, brightly painted dorms and private rooms come in myriad configurations; the typical single-sex dorm has eight beds, with the bathroom down the hall. There's a small common area with a TV, games and books. The free continental breakfast is a nice start to the day. Dorm dwellers must pay $2 extra for towels. Wi-fi is free throughout.

**CHICAGO MARRIOTT AT
MEDICAL DISTRICT/UIC**   HOTEL **$$**
Map p312 (☏800-356-3641, 312-491-1234; www.marriott.com; 625 S Ashland Ave; r $119-269; Ⓟ❄@☂; Ⓜ️Blue Line to Medical District) This hotel works best if you're visiting the huge medical center complex nearby. A complimentary bus shuttles you to the hospital door, to the University of Illinois at Chicago or to Little Italy – anywhere within a mile radius. Rooms are standard with HDTVs, work-friendly desks and a minifridge. Wi-fi costs $14 per day.

⌂ South Loop & Near South Side

ESSEX INN   HOTEL **$$**
Map p316 (☏800-621-6909, 312-939-2800; www.essexinn.com; 800 S Michigan Ave; r $159-249;

AIRPORT ACCOMMODATIONS

Got an early flight to catch? Given the crazy Chicago traffic, or long El commute (45 minutes from the Loop), resting your head at one of the dozens of airport hotels may be your best bet. Most run free 24-hour airport shuttles.

O'Hare

Aloft Chicago O'Hare (☏847-671-4444; www.aloftchicagoohare.com; 9700 Balmoral Ave , Rosemont; r $109-189; Ⓟ❄@☂; Ⓜ️Blue Line to Rosemont) It offers the chain's usual petite, industrial-toned rooms and sociable, game-filled lobby. It's about 3.5 miles from the airport.

O'Hare Hilton (☏800-445-8667, 773-686-8000; www.hilton.com; O'Hare International Airport; r $149-289; Ⓟ❄@☂❄; Ⓜ️Blue Line to O'Hare) Attached to the airport via an underground tunnel. Relax in the sauna, take a refreshing dip in the indoor pool and then retire to your soundproofed contemporary room.

Midway

Hilton Garden Inn (☏800-445-8667, 708-496-2700; www.hiltongardeninn.com; 6530 S Cicero Ave, Bedford Park; r $149-219; Ⓟ❄@☂; Ⓜ️Orange Line to Midway) It's in the Midway Hotel Center complex of nine hotels.

Sleep Inn (☏877-424-6423, 708-594-0001; www.sleepinn.com; 6650 S Cicero Ave, Bedford Park; r incl breakfast $89-159; Ⓟ❄@☂; Ⓜ️Orange Line to Midway) Slightly cheaper than Hilton Garden Inn, but in the same complex. The modern modular rooms are perfectly acceptable. Free hot breakfast is a nice touch.

P ✳ @ 🛜 ⌨; M Red Line to Harrison) The Essex is a long-standing midrange hotel. The old-ish rooms are nothing fancy but are decent-sized with flat-screen TVs, free wi-fi, minifridges and desks. Sweet perks include the 4th-floor rooftop garden to soak in the sun, the giant glass-enclosed pool with lifeguards and the free shuttle that zips north to the Magnificent Mile.

The hotel often shows up on booking sites, but be wary of paying upper-end rack rates (ie more than $200 or so), since the quality doesn't match that price point. The pool and location near the Museum Campus draw lots of families.

BEST WESTERN GRANT PARK   HOTEL $$
Map p316 (☏866-516-3164, 312-922-2900; www.bwgrantparkhotel.com; 1100 S Michigan Ave; r $159-269; P ✳ @ 🛜 ⌨; M Red, Green, Or ange Line to Roosevelt) This very basic Best Western attracts for its location near the Museum Campus, free wi-fi and lower-than-usual downtown parking rate ($29 per day). Though the lobby's gone modern, rooms are standard faux oak and floral bedspread decor. Outside convention time, it can be a bargain. But if the rates ratchet up, remember you're getting a no-frills room for that price.

TRAVELODGE CHICAGO DOWNTOWN   HOTEL $$
Map p316 (☏800-211-6706, 312-427-8000; www travelodgechicago.com; 65 E Harrison St; r $129-169; P ✳ 🛜; M Red Line to Harrison) The nearby Essex and Best Western typically offer better quality with more amenities, but the Travelodge's prices are more consistently low. What do you say about lackluster motel-like rooms? Um, they're there.

RENAISSANCE BLACKSTONE HOTEL   HISTORIC HOTEL $$$
Map p316 (☏800-468-3571, 312-447-0955; www. blackstonerenaissance.com; 636 S Michigan Ave; r $199-319; P ✳ @ 🛜 ⌨; M Red Line to Harrison) This 1910 neoclassical, beaux-arts landmark is known as the 'hotel of presidents' (more than a dozen have slumbered here). The 23-story beauty now caters to a high-falutin business crowd. Rooms are urban stylish (downy bedding, white-marbled bathrooms, abstract artworks); several have lake views (for which you'll pay about $50 extra). Check out the painting-filled Art Hall. Wi-fi costs $13 per day.

HILTON CHICAGO   HISTORIC HOTEL $$$
Map p316 (☏800-445-8667, 312-922-4400; www.hilton.com; 720 S Michigan Ave; r $164-309; P ✳ @ 🛜 ⌨; M Red Line to Harrison) When built in 1927 (for $30 million), this was the world's largest hotel with close to 3000 rooms (and a hospital, and a theater...). Renovations brought that total down to a mere 1544, but the gilt grandeur and crystal-dripping class have remained. The rooms are reasonable, standard-issue Hilton types, with heavy drapes, cherrywood decor and comfy beds. A lake-view upgrade (about $30) makes a nice enhancement.

Anecdotes abound at the Hilton: in the 1940s it served as an army barracks; and at the height of the 1968 Democratic National Convention riots, police tossed protesters through the front plate-glass windows. Wi-fi costs $13 per day.

HYATT REGENCY MCCORMICK PLACE   HOTEL $$$
Map p316 (☏800-633-7313, 312-567-1234; www. mccormickplace.hyatt.com; 2233 S Martin Luther King Jr Dr; r $170-270; P ✳ @ 🛜 ⌨; ⛟ Metra to McCormick Place) If you're manning a show booth at McCormick Place, you can't beat the short walk to your bed in this attached hotel, where lobby monitors help you keep track of meeting schedules. However, if you're not a conventioneer, even the skyline views may not be reason enough to stay in this isolated behemoth, 2 miles south of the Loop. It is in the midst of a $110 million overhaul, including contruction of a new tower that will add even more rooms to the tally.

🛏 Hyde Park & South Side

BENEDICTINE B&B   B&B $$
(☏773-927-7424, ext 202, 888-539-4261, ext 202; www.chicagomonk.org; 3111 S Aberdeen St; r incl breakfast $165-255; ⌨8) Monks run this B&B that consists of two simple apartments offering loads of space and kitchen facilities. One is a two-bedroom garden apartment with a deck and self-serve breakfast; the other is a three-bedroom loft with breakfast prepared by the monks. It's in Bridgeport, about a mile and a half from US Cellular Field and about 1.5 miles south of Pilsen. You'll fare best if you have a car.

RAMADA CHICAGO MOTEL **$$**
Map p318 (☏773-288-5800; www.ramadachicagohotel.com; 4900 S Lake Shore Dr; r $129-179; P🞴🛜🞰; 🖳6) Rooms at this four-story motel may not be the freshest (frayed carpet, scuffed door jambs), but that should change as the Ramada was undergoing renovations at press time. Focus instead on the lakeside location, free parking and outdoor pool. A free shuttle takes you up to Michigan Ave, or you can hop on the bus for the 15-minute ride.

Understand Chicago

Chicago Today

Downtown is thriving, with new skyscrapers, ambitious renovation projects, burgeoning technology industries and a celebrated restaurant scene. The rest of Chicago, which got hit fairly hard by the economic recession, is struggling to catch up. New leadership after 22 years has helped freshen the city, though the old problems of corruption and segregation linger. In the meantime, Chicago continues its quest to be the nation's greenest metropolis.

Best in Film

Ferris Bueller's Day Off (1986) A teen truant discovers the joys of the city, from Wrigley Field to the Art Institute. Classic Chicago locations.

The Untouchables (1987) Native son David Mamet wrote the screenplay for this nail-biter about Eliot Ness' takedown of Al Capone.

The Blues Brothers (1980) Second City alums John Belushi and Dan Aykroyd star in the cult classic of two bluesmen on the run.

Best in Print

The Man with the Golden Arm (Nelson Algren; 1949) This tale of a drug-addicted kid on Division St won the 1950 National Book Award.

The Lazarus Project (Aleksandar Hemon; 2008) Chicago's police chief kills a poor Russian-born Jew and tries to cover up.

The Adventures of Augie March (Saul Bellow; 1953) Huck Finn–esque story of a destitute boy growing up in Depression-era Chicago.

The Jungle (Upton Sinclair; 1906) Immigrant life in Chicago's brutal South Side meatpacking plants.

Boom & Bust

Between 2000 and 2010, Chicago's downtown added residents faster than any other urban core in America. Developers built stacks of glossy condos, and despite the housing crash, vacancy rates for high-end ones currently stand near a 10-year low. Add in the new companies that have moved downtown, and you have a shining zone of affluence.

But there's a flip side. In outlying neighborhoods, especially on the south and west sides where mostly ethnic poor and working-class Chicagoans live, 62,000 properties stand vacant and the population is dwindling. Part of the decrease has to do with the demise of the troubled public housing high-rises, which have all been razed. Chicago's headline-grabbing violent crime and murder rates mostly come from these areas.

So there are two Chicagos, and the ever-present issue is how to bring the peripheral city on par with the booming core.

Changing of the Guard

After 22 years Mayor Richard M Daley left office in 2011, saying it was 'time to move on.' He had been the city's longest-reigning manager. The previous record holder? His dad, Richard J Daley, who was mayor for 21 years.

Enter Rahm Emanuel, President Obama's former chief of staff. He ran for mayor and crushed the competition, pledging change, transparency and an end to corruption. Unfortunately, he got handed a whopping budget deficit and began his term by cutting or consolidating city services like garbage collection, which irked the labor unions, traditional backers of his Democratic Party. He also ticked off the teachers' union by canceling contracted pay increases and lengthening the school day. Teachers staged a massive strike in 2012 that garnered nationwide media coverage.

As for other changes, well, it's pretty much business as usual at City Hall. Council members still rubber-stamp the mayor's plans for the most part, as they did during the Daley administration. Corruption is still an issue. One of the most prominent cases saw congressman Jesse Jackson Jr and his wife Sandi Jackson, a city council member, charged with spending $750,000 of campaign funds on a mink cape and other personal items.

New Projects

For most of the past decade, the pace of change here has been fast and grand. Development swept through downtown and spilled over its edges. Mod Millennium Park led the way, The Donald popped the top on his Trump Tower, and the Art Institute built a wing huge enough to make it the second-largest art museum in the nation. More recently, Jeanne Gang's Aqua Tower joined the skyscraper club to much fanfare. Civic projects are going full steam ahead. In 2013 Mayor Emanuel announced multi-million dollar upgrades were forthcoming for Navy Pier, McCormick Place, the Riverwalk and various West Loop zones.

The city has also been carving out a role as a technology hub. Hundreds of digital start-ups have moved into the River North and West Loop alongside Groupon's headquarters and Google's big local facility. Many companies cluster in the offices of 1871, a 50,000-sq-ft center for designers, engineers and entrepreneurs in the Merchandise Mart.

Culinary Revolution

Ten years ago no one came to Chicago for the food. Then, chef by chef, restaurant by restaurant, the city built a gastronomic scene. Suddenly international critics were dubbing Chicago one of the globe's top eating destinations, and locals such as Grant Achatz, Rick Bayless, Graham Elliot, Paul Kahan and Stephanie Izard were winning James Beard Awards. Now the foodie frenzy is in full force. Food trucks roll en masse. Craft brewers cook up hoppy suds and build tap rooms to serve them. And artisanal doughnut-makers and pie bakers abound.

Greening Chicago

Chicago has more LEED-certified (Leadership in Energy and Environmental Design) buildings than any other city in the country. Behemoths like the Merchandise Mart and the Willis Tower have been retrofitted to meet LEED standards. The city boasts more than 350 green roofs, covering 5.5 million sq ft downtown. One covers City Hall, and Millennium Park is technically a green roof since it tops an underground parking garage. Chicago also has added protected bike lanes to busy streets and expanded its bike-sharing program to 400 stations around town.

if Chicago were 100 people

33 would be Black
32 would be White
29 would be Latino
5 would be Asian
1 would be American Indian & Alaska Native

belief systems
(% of population)

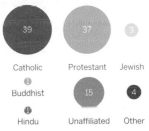

Catholic   Protestant   Jewish

Buddhist

Hindu   Unaffiliated   Other

population per sq mile

CHICAGO   USA

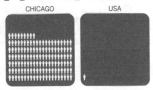

♦ ≈ 85 people

History

Much of Chicago's past is downright legendary. You've probably heard about Mrs O'Leary's cow that kicked over a lantern that started the Great Fire that torched the city. And about a gent named Al Capone who wielded a mean machine gun during an unsavory era of booze-fueled vice. And about the 'machine' that has controlled local politics for decades. Throw in the invention of the skyscraper and Ferris wheel, and you've got a whopper of a tale.

Early Days: Onions & Forts

To see where Fort Dearborn once stood downtown, look for plaques in the sidewalk marking the spot at the corner of Michigan Ave and Wacker Dr.

The Potawatomi Indians were the first folks in town, and they gave the name 'Checagou' – or wild onions - to the area around the Chicago River's mouth. Needless to say, they weren't particularly pleased when the first settlers arrived in 1803. The newcomers built Fort Dearborn on the river's south bank, on marshy ground under what is today's Michigan Ave Bridge.

The Potawatomi's resentment toward their new neighbors mounted, and bad things ensued. In 1812, the natives – in cahoots with the British (their allies in the War of 1812) – slaughtered 52 settlers fleeing the fort. The killings took place near what is today Chicago Women's Park. During the war this had been a strategy employed throughout the frontier: the British sought the allegiance of various Indian tribes through trade and other deals, and the Indians paid them back by killing American settlers.

After the war ended, everyone let bygones be bygones for the sake of the fur trade.

Real Estate Boom

Chicago was incorporated as a town in 1833, with a population of 340. Within three years land speculation rocked the local real estate market; lots that sold for $33 in 1829 now went for $100,000. Construction on the Illinois & Michigan Canal – a state project linking the Great Lakes to the Illinois River and thus to the Mississippi River and the Atlantic

TIMELINE	Late 1600s	1779	1803
	The Potawatomi Indians settle in. They paddle birchbark canoes, fish and ponder a name for the place. How about Checagou (Wild Onions), after the local plants growing here?	Jean Baptiste Pointe du Sable sails down from Québec and sets up a fur-trading post on the Chicago River. He is the city's first settler.	More settlers arrive and build Fort Dearborn at the river's mouth. The Potawatomi locals are not pleased by their new neighbors. They kill the settlers nine years later.

coast – fueled the boom. Swarms of laborers swelled the population to more than 4100 by 1837, and Chicago became a city.

Within 10 years, more than 20,000 people lived in what had become the region's dominant city. The rich Illinois soil supported thousands of farmers, and industrialist Cyrus Hall McCormick moved his reaper factory to the city to serve them.

In 1848 the canal opened. Shipping flowed through the area and had a marked economic effect on the city. A great financial institution, the Chicago Board of Trade, opened to handle the sale of grain by Illinois farmers, who now had greatly improved access to Eastern markets.

Bring on the Bacon

By the end of the 1850s, immigrants had poured into the city, drawn by jobs on the new railroads that served the ever-growing agricultural trade. Twenty million bushels of produce were shipped through Chicago annually by then. The population topped 100,000.

Like other northern cities, Chicago profited from the Civil War, which boosted business in the burgeoning steel and toolmaking industries. In 1865, the same year the war ended, the Union Stockyards opened on the South Side. Chicago's rail network and the invention of the iced refrigerator car meant that meat could be shipped for long distances, satiating hungry carnivores all the way east to New York and beyond. The stockyards soon became the major meat supplier to the nation. But besides bringing great wealth to a few and jobs to many, the yards were also a source of water pollution.

Stop the Bacon!

The stockyard effluvia polluted not only the Chicago River but also Lake Michigan. Flowing into the lake, the fouled waters spoiled the city's source of fresh water and caused cholera and other epidemics that killed thousands. In 1869 the Water Tower and Pumping Station built a 2-mile tunnel into Lake Michigan and began bringing water into the city from there; it was hoped that this set-up would skirt the contaminated areas. Alas, the idea proved resoundingly inadequate, and outbreaks of illness continued.

Two years later, engineers deepened the Illinois & Michigan Canal so they could alter the Chicago River's course and make it flow south, away from the city. Sending waste and sewage down the reversed river provided relief for Chicago residents and helped ease lake pollution, but it was not a welcome change for those living near what had become the city's drainpipe.

Historical Reads

Boss: Richard J Daley of Chicago *(Mike Royko)*

Sin in the Second City *(Karen Abbott)*

Get Capone *(Jonathan Eig)*

1837	1860	1865	1869
Chicago incorporates as a city (population: 4170). It's a happenin' place, having skyrocketed from just 340 people four years earlier. Within 10 years 16,000 folks call the city home.	The Republican Party holds its national political convention in Chicago and selects Abraham Lincoln, a lawyer from Springfield, Illinois, as its presidential candidate.	The Union Stockyards open. Thanks to new train tracks and refrigerated railcars, Chicago can send its bacon afar and becomes 'hog butcher for the world' (per poet Carl Sandburg).	The city builds the Water Tower and Pumping Station to help bring clean water in from Lake Michigan, since pollution from the stockyards was contaminating the usual supply.

Burn Baby Burn – Chicago Inferno

On October 8, 1871, the Chicago fire started just southwest of downtown. For more than 125 years, legend has had it that a cow owned by a certain Mrs O'Leary kicked over a lantern, which ignited some hay, which ignited some lumber, which ignited the whole town. The image of the hapless heifer has endured despite evidence that the fire was actually the fault of Daniel 'Peg Leg' Sullivan, who dropped by the barn on an errand, accidentally started the fire himself and then tried to blame it on the bovine.

However it started, the results were devastating. The fire burned for three days, killing 300 people, destroying 18,000 buildings and leaving 90,000 people homeless. The dry conditions and mostly wood buildings set the stage for the runaway conflagration. The primitive, horse-drawn fire-fighting equipment could do little to keep up. Almost every structure was destroyed or gutted in the area bounded by the river on the west, what's now Roosevelt Rd to the south and Fullerton Ave to the north.

Birth of the Skyscraper

Despite the human tragedy, the fire taught the city some valuable lessons – namely, don't build everything from wood. Chicago reconstructed with modern materials, and created space for new industrial and commercial buildings.

The world's best architects poured into the city during the 1880s and '90s to take advantage of the situation. They had a blank canvas to work with, a city giving them lots of dough, and pretty much the green light to use their imaginations to the fullest. The world's first skyscraper soon popped up in 1885. Several other important buildings also rose during the era, spawning the Chicago School of architecture. Daniel Burnham was one of the premier designers running the show, and he summed up the city's credo best: 'Make no little plans,' he counseled Chicago's leaders in 1909, 'for they have no magic to stir men's blood... Make big plans.'

Top History Sites

....

Graceland Cemetery

....

Water Tower

....

Haymarket Square

....

Biograph Theater

....

Nuclear Energy sculpture

Labor Riots

Labor unrest had been brewing in the city for a while. In 1876, organized strikes began in the railroad yards as workers demanded an eight-hour workday and rest breaks. The turbulence spread to the McCormick Reaper Works, which was then Chicago's largest factory. The police and federal troops broke up the strikes, killing 18 civilians and injuring hundreds more.

1871	1880s	1885	1886
The Great Fire torches the entire inner city. Mrs O'Leary's cow takes the blame, though it's eventually determined that Daniel 'Peg Leg' Sullivan kicked over the lantern that started the blaze.	People start calling Chicago the 'Windy City' – not because of its blustery weather, but because of its big-mouthed local citizenry who constantly brag about the town's greatness.	The world's first steel-frame 'skyscraper,' the Home Insurance Building, rises up. It's 10 stories (138ft) tall and paves the way for big things to come.	Workers fight for an eight-hour workday and decent pay with a rally at Haymarket Sq. The cops come, bombs explode, anarchists take the blame, and the labor movement is born.

By then, May 1 had become the official day of protest for labor groups in Chicago. On that day in 1886, around 60,000 workers went on strike, once again demanding an eight-hour workday. As usual, police attacked the strikers at locations throughout the city. Three days later, self-described anarchists staged a protest in Haymarket Sq; out of nowhere a bomb exploded, killing seven police officers. The government reacted strongly to what became known as the Haymarket Riot. Eight anarchists were convicted of 'general conspiracy to murder' and four were hanged, although only two had been present at the incident and the bomber was never identified. A sculpture marks the square today.

The White City Debuts

The 1893 World's Expo marked Chicago's showy debut on the international stage. The event centered on a grand complex of specially built structures lying just south of Hyde Park. They were painted white and were brilliantly lit by electric searchlights, which is how the 'White City' tag came to be. Designed by architectural luminaries such as Daniel Burnham, Louis Sullivan and Frederick Law Olmsted, the fairgrounds were meant to show how parks, streets and buildings could be designed in a harmonious manner that would enrich the chaotic urban environment.

Open for only five months, the exposition attracted 27 million visitors, many of whom rode the newly built El train to and from the Loop. The fair offered wonders heretofore unknown to the world: long-distance phone calls, the first moving pictures (courtesy of Thomas Alva Edison's Kinetoscope), the first Ferris wheel and the first zipper. It was at this fair that Pabst beer won the blue ribbon that has been part of its name ever since.

The entire assemblage made a huge impact worldwide, and the fair's architects were deluged with commissions to redesign cities.

The glimmering 1893 World's Expo buildings were short-lived, having been built out of a rough equivalent of plaster of Paris. Only the Fine Arts Building survived, which was revamped into today's Museum of Science & Industry (p105).

The Great Migration

Between 1910 and 1930 more than two million African Americans moved from the rural South in what came to be known as the Great Migration. Chicago played a pivotal role in this massive population shift, both as an impetus and as a destination. Articles in the black-owned and nationally circulated *Chicago Defender* proclaimed the city a workers' paradise and a place free from the horrors of Southern racism. These lures, coupled with glitzy images of thriving neighborhoods like Bronzeville, inspired thousands to relocate.

Chicago's black population zoomed from 44,103 in 1910 to 109,458 in 1920 and continued growing. The migrants, often poorly educated sharecroppers with big dreams, found a reality not as rosy as promised.

1890s	1893	1900	1908
Socialite Bertha Palmer makes trips to Paris, buying Monets, Renoirs and other impressionist works before they achieve acclaim. Her collection later forms the core of the Art Institute.	The World's Expo opens near Hyde Park, and Chicago grabs the global spotlight for the wonders it unveils, including the Ferris wheel, movies, Cracker Jack and Pabst beer.	In an engineering feat, Chicago reverses the flow of the Chicago River, forever ingratiating itself with its downstate neighbors as waste now streams in their direction.	Chicago Cubs win the World Series. But curses involving goats, fans named Bartman and general all-round crappy teams keep them winless for the next 105 years. And counting...

Employers were ready with the promised jobs, but many hoped to rid their factories of white unionized workers by replacing them with blacks, which exacerbated racial tensions. Blacks were also restricted by openly prejudicial real estate practices that kept them from buying homes anywhere except for certain South Side communities. The South Side remains predominantly black to this day.

Da Mayor No 1: Richard J Daley

In the 1930s Chicago's Democratic Party created the legendary 'machine' that would control local politics for the next 50 years. Its zenith of power began with the election of Richard J Daley in 1955. Initially thought to be a mere party functionary, Daley was reelected mayor five times before dying while still in office in 1976. With an uncanny understanding of machine politics and how to use it to halt dissent, he dominated the city in a way no mayor had before. His word was law, and the city council routinely approved all his actions, lest a dissenter find his or her ward deprived of vital city services.

Under 'the Boss's' rule, corruption was rampant. A 1957 *Life* magazine report called Chicago's cops the most corrupt in the nation. Although Daley and the machine howled with indignation over the article, further exposés by the press revealed that some cops and politicians were in cahoots with various crime rings.

CAPONE'S CHICAGO

Al Capone came to Chicago from New York in 1919. He quickly moved up the ranks and was the city's mob boss from 1924 to 1931, until Eliot Ness brought him down on tax evasion charges. Ness was the federal agent whose task force earned the name 'The Untouchables' because its members were supposedly impervious to bribes.

The success of the Chicago mob was fueled by Prohibition. Gangs made fortunes dealing in illegal beer, gin and other intoxicants. Infamous Capone sites to see include:

➜ Green Mill (p134) – the speakeasy in the basement was a Capone favorite.

➜ Holy Name Cathedral (p72) – Capone ordered a couple of hits that took place near the church.

➜ **Mt Carmel Cemetery** (cnr Roosevelt & S Wolf Rds, Hillside) – Capone is buried in this cemetery in suburban Hillside, west of Chicago. His simple gravestone reads, 'Alphonse Capone, 1899–1947, My Jesus Mercy.'

➜ St Valentine's Day Massacre Site (p103) – Capone's thugs killed seven members of Bugs Moran's gang here.

1909	1915	1929	1931
Daniel Burnham counsels Chicago's leaders on architecture: 'Make no little plans. For they have no magic to stir men's blood... Make big plans.'	The *Eastland* steamboat, filled with picnickers, capsizes in the Chicago River while still tied to the dock by LaSalle St Bridge; 844 people die, though the water is only 20ft deep.	Prohibition conflict boils over when seven people are killed in a shoot-out between gangsters Al Capone and Bugs Moran. The day becomes known as the St Valentine's Day Massacre.	After years of running the Chicago Outfit and supplying the nation with illegal booze, Capone goes to jail for tax evasion. There he's called 'the wop with the mop.'

A BOMB IS BORN

At 3:53pm on December 2, 1942, Enrico Fermi looked at a small crowd of men around him and said, 'The reaction is self-sustaining.' The scene was a dank squash court under the abandoned football stadium in the heart of the University of Chicago. With great secrecy, the gathered scientists had just achieved the world's first controlled release of nuclear energy.

The nuclear reactor was supposed to have been built in a remote corner of a forest preserve 20 miles away, but a labor strike had stopped work. The impatient scientists went ahead on campus, despite the objections of many who thought the thing might blow up and take a good part of the city with it.

Hippies & Riots Come to Town

In August 1968 Chicago hosted the Democratic National Convention, which degenerated into a fiasco of such proportions that its legacy dogged the city for decades.

With the war in Vietnam escalating and general unrest quickly spreading through the USA, the convention became a focal point for protest groups of all stripes. Enter Abbie Hoffman, Jerry Rubin, Rennie Davis, Tom Hayden, John Froines, Lee Weiner and David Dellinger – the soon-to-become 'Chicago Seven.' They called for a mobilization of 500,000 protesters to converge on Chicago. As the odds of confrontation became high, many moderate protesters decided not to attend. When the convention opened, there were just a few thousand young protesters in the city. But Daley and his allies spread rumors to the media to bolster the case for their aggressive preparations, including a claim that LSD would be dumped into the city's water supply.

The force amassed amounted to 11,900 Chicago police officers, 7500 Army troops, 7500 Illinois National Guardsmen and 1000 Secret Service agents for the August 25–30 convention. The first few nights police staged raids on protesters attempting to camp in Lincoln Park. The cops moved in with tear gas and billy clubs, singling out some individuals – including several news reporters – for savage attacks.

The action then shifted to Grant Park, across from the Conrad Hilton (now the Hilton Chicago), where the main presidential candidates were staying. Protesters attempted to march to the site, and the police again met them with tear gas and nightsticks and threw many protesters through the hotel's plate-glass windows. The media widely covered the incident, which investigators later termed a 'police riot.'

Chicago Inventions

Roller skates (1884)

Hostess Twinkies (1930)

Pinball (1930)

Spray paint (1949)

Lava Lite 'Lava Lamps' (1965)

House music (1977)

1933	1942	1955	1960
Prohibition is repealed and beer flows again. The Democratic Party come to power with a well-organized (and often corrupt) 'machine' that controls city politics for decades to come.	The first nuclear chain reaction occurs at the University of Chicago. Enrico Fermi and his Manhattan Project pals high-five each other for pulling it off – and not blowing up the city in the process.	Mayor Daley number one takes office, solidifying the Democratic Party's reign based on the unofficial motto, 'I'll scratch your back if you scratch mine.'	McCormick Place opens and is immediately hailed as the 'Mistake on the Lake.' More than 40 years later, nearby Soldier Field hones in on the title after its renovation.

Polishing the Rust

Meanwhile, the city's economy was hitting the skids. In 1971 financial pressures caused the last of the Chicago stockyards to close, marking the end of one of the city's most infamous enterprises. Factories and steel mills were also shutting down as companies moved to the suburbs or southern USA, where taxes and wages were lower. Chicago and much of the Midwest earned the moniker 'Rust Belt,' describing the area's shrunken economies and rusting factories.

But two events happened in the 1970s that were harbingers of the city's more promising future. The world's tallest building (at the time) – the Sears Tower (later renamed Willis Tower) – opened in the Loop in 1974, beginning a development trend that would spur the creation of thousands of high-paying white-collar jobs. And in 1975, the Water Tower Place shopping mall brought new life to N Michigan Ave.

The city's first and only female mayor – the colorful Jane Byrne – took the helm in 1979. Byrne's reign was followed by that of Harold Washington, Chicago's first black mayor, in 1983. His legacy was the success of the African American politicians who followed him. Democrat Carol Moseley-Braun's election to the US senate in 1992 can be credited in part to Washington's political trailblazing. Barack Obama is another name that comes to mind.

Da Mayor No 2: Richie M Daley

In 1989 Chicago elected Richard M Daley, the son of Richard J Daley, to finish the remaining two years of Harold Washington's mayoral term (Washington died in office). Like his father, Daley had an uncanny instinct for city politics. He made nice with state officials, who handed over hundreds of millions of public dollars. Among the projects that bore fruit were an O'Hare airport expansion, a huge addition to the McCormick Place Convention Center and the reconstruction of Navy Pier.

Despite falling to the third-largest US city, population-wise, in the 1990 census (behind New York and LA), Chicago enjoyed a good decade in the '90s. In 1991 the Chicago Bulls won the first of six national basketball championships. The 1994 World Cup soccer opening ceremony focused international attention on the city. And in 1996 a 28-year-old demon was exorcised when the Democratic National Convention returned to Chicago. Officials spent millions of dollars spiffing up the city, and thousands of cops underwent sensitivity training on how to deal with protestors. The convention went off like a dream and left Chicagoans believing they were on a roll.

And when you're on a roll, who else do you thank but the guy who seems to have made it all possible? Daley won his reelection bids in

1964	1968	1974	1983
The Rolling Stones come to jam with bluesman Muddy Waters at Chess Records. Keith Richards calls the place 'Mecca.'	The Democratic National Convention debacle occurs. Around 27,000 cops, army regulars and national guardsmen beat a few thousand hippie protestors.	Chicago pops the last girder into the Sears Tower, which becomes the world's tallest building at 110 stories (1454ft) and remains the record holder for the next quarter century.	Harold Washington, Chicago's first black mayor, wins election. He paves the way for black politicians down the road like Barack Obama.

1991, 1995, 1999, 2003 and 2007, pretty much by a landslide every time. That's not to say the guy didn't have issues, including the 2003 bulldozing of Meigs Field airport and the 2005 'Hired Truck scandal' in which city staff had been accepting bribes in exchange for lucrative contracts. By 2011, Daley had had enough. He chose not to run for reelection, saying it was 'time to move on.' He had been Chicago's mayor for a record-setting 22 years.

1989	2004	2008	2011
Mayor Daley number two takes office. His reign is highlighted by midnight bulldozings and shiny park unveilings. He ends up ruling the city even longer than his pa.	Millennium Park opens four years after the deadline and hundreds of millions of dollars over budget (thanks to the original contractor, who was the mayor's friend).	Local boy Barack Obama stands in the electric air of Grant Park and gives his acceptance speech as President of the United States. Chicagoans swell with pride.	Mayor Richard M Daley leaves office after 22 years, having decided not to run for reelection. Rahm Emanual, Obama's former chief of staff, takes the reigns.

Architecture

Ever since the Great Fire of 1871 reduced the city to a blank canvas, Chicago has been home to some of the nation's most exciting architecture. For residents, the skyline is more a part of daily life than just a dramatic backdrop, and the city's signature buildings from centuries past and present are both tenderly adored and vehemently hated. But whatever the verdicts of citizens and architectural critics, there's one thing these supersized buildings cannot be – and that's ignored.

First Chicago School (1872–99)

Above Rookery (p56)

Though the 1871 fire didn't seem like an opportunity at the time, it made Chicago what it is today. The chance to reshape the city's burned downtown drew young, ambitious architects including Dankmar Adler, Daniel Burnham, John Root and Louis Sullivan. These men saw the scorched Loop as a sandbox for innovation, and they rapidly built bigger, better commercial structures over the low roughshod buildings that immediately went up after the fire. These men and their colleagues made up the First Chicago School (some say they practiced the Commercial style), which stressed economy, simplicity and function. Using steel frames and elevators, their pinnacle achievement was the modern skyscraper.

The earliest buildings of the First Chicago School, such as the **Auditorium Building** (Map p290; www.roosevelt.edu; 430 S Michigan Ave), used thick bases to support towering walls above. William Le Baron Jenney, the architect who constructed the world's first iron-and-steel-framed building in the mid-1880s, had a studio in Chicago, where he trained a crop of architects who pushed the city skyward through internal frames.

In the Loop, the Monadnock Building (p56) gives you a practical sense of how quickly these innovations were catching on: the original northern half of the building consists of more traditional load-bearing walls measuring 6ft thick at ground level, while the southern half, constructed only two years later, uses the then-revolutionary metal frame for drastically thinner walls that go just as high.

No matter how pragmatic these First Chicago School architects were in their inspiration and motivation, the steel-framed boxes they erected rarely suffered from lack of adornment. Maverick firms like Adler & Sullivan and Burnham & Root used a simple, bold geometric language to rebuild downtown in style. Steel skeletons were clad in exterior masonry, often with highly decorative terra-cotta panels – which were, perhaps most importantly, fireproof – embellished with designs taken from neoclassicism or nature. When gazing up at these early skyscrapers, notice their strong vertical lines crossed gridlike by horizontal bands and topped by ledgelike ornamental cornices, contrasted with the sweeping lines of jutting bay windows, curved corners and grand entrances from the street.

Prairie School (1895–1915)

It was the protégé of Louis Sullivan – Frank Lloyd Wright – who would endow Chicago with its most distinctive style, the Prairie School. Wright, a spottily educated ladies' man from a Wisconsin farm town, was the residential designer for Adler & Sullivan until 1893, when his architectural commissions outside the firm led to his dismissal. Forced into his own practice, he eventually set up a small studio in suburban Oak Park and by 1901 had built 50 public buildings and private homes around the Chicago metro area.

Over the next 15 years, Wright's 'Prairie Houses' contrasted the grand edifices of the First Chicago School with more modest charms. His unique residential buildings emphasize low-slung structures with dominant horizon lines, hipped (shallowly sloped) roofs, overhanging eaves and unadorned open-plan spaces that mirrored the flat Midwestern landscape. To blend visually, such natural, neutral materials as brick, limestone and stucco were often used. Much in sympathy with the turn-of-the-20th-century Arts & Crafts style, Wright's 'organic architecture' was likewise anti-industrial, inspired by and aiming to exist harmoniously with nature.

Of all the Prairie Houses by Wright's hand, the Robie House (p194) is the most dramatic and successful. It's a measuring stick by which all other buildings in the style are often compared, and is alone worth the trip to Hyde Park. A bit of Wright's early work is nearer to the city center – Bronzeville's Robert W Roloson Houses (p201), which were designed in 1894 while Wright still worked for Adler & Sullivan and are his only set of row houses; and the airy atrium of the Loop's landmark Rookery (p56). Wright's notable colleagues in the Prairie style include George W Maher,

RELIANCE BUILDING

With shimmering glass walls soaring skyward, the proto-modernist skyscraper Reliance Building was restored in 1999, more than a century after it was erected. Today you can sleep inside this opulent landmark at the Hotel Burnham (p218).

Dome in the Chicago Cultural Center (p54)

Walter Burley Griffin and Marion Mahony Griffin, the latter one of the USA's first licensed female architects.

Beaux Arts (1893–1920)

While the First Chicago School and Prairie School were forward-looking inventions that grew from the marshy shores of Lake Michigan, beaux arts – named for the École des Beaux-Arts in Paris – took after a French fad that stressed antiquity. Proud local builders like Louis Sullivan hated the style, and he didn't mince words, claiming that it set the course of American architecture back 'for half a century from its date, if not longer.' Sullivan aside, these buildings are pleasing today for their eclectic mixed bag of Classical Roman and Greek elements, including stately columns, cornices and facades crowded with statuary.

The popularity of the style was spurred on by the colossal French neo-classical structures of Daniel Burnham's 'White City,' built for the 1893

FIVE CHICAGO ARCHITECTS TO KNOW

➡ **Louis Sullivan** Chicago's architectural founding father, a revolutionary of steel-frame high-rises

➡ **Frank Lloyd Wright** Sullivan's student, who took the Prairie style to global renown

➡ **Daniel Burnham** The man with the Plan that preserved Chicago's lakefront

➡ **Ludwig Mies van der Rohe** His 'less is more' motto and simple, boxy designs grounded modern skyscrapers

➡ **Jeanne Gang** Her Aqua Tower is currently the world's tallest building designed by a woman

Magnificent Mile (N Michigan Avenue; p72)

World's Fair, which also erected the Palace of Fine Arts, now housing the Museum of Science & Industry (p195). After Burnham's smash hit at the Expo, beaux arts became the city's dominant architectural paradigm for the next two decades, making a welcome contrast to the dirty, over-crowded slums that had come with Chicago's urban expansion.

Beaux arts also propelled the 'City Beautiful' urban planning movement, for which Burnham was an evangelist. Published in 1909, Burnham's own *Plan of Chicago* called for a more splendorous, scenic and well-ordered cityscape. Although much of the Burnham Plan was never actually implemented, many public parks were reclaimed along the lakeshore and a network of diagonal streets newly built, both features that still define the city today.

The impressive echoes of Burnham's White City are evidenced in some of the city's best-known civic landmarks, including downtown's Art Institute (p49) and the Chicago Cultural Center (p54). The latter began in 1897 as the Chicago Public Library, housing a donated collection of some 8000 books sent by British citizens after the Great Fire of 1871. (Many books were even autographed by the donors, including Queen Victoria, Charles Darwin and Alfred Lord Tennyson.) While the books have since been moved to the Harold Washington Library, the magnificent gilded ceilings, inlaid marble mosaics, stained-glass domes and classical details of the original beaux arts building remain.

Opposite the eclectic Wrigley Building (p72) on Chicago's Magnificent Mile, the 1923 neo-Gothic Tribune Tower (p72) is uniquely inlaid with stones from the Taj Mahal, the Great Pyramid, Notre Dame, the Great Wall of China, Lincoln's Tomb, the Alamo and more.

Art Deco (1920–39)

After the decline in popularity of beaux arts, Chicago's architects found inspiration from another French movement: art deco. The art-deco style may have been as ornamental as beaux arts, but instead of classical columns and statues, it took on sharp angles, geometric elements, reflective surfaces and a modern palette of blacks, silvers and greens.

Sadly, there are few remaining buildings in the Loop that characterize this style, which withered before WWII. An exception is the 1929 Carbide & Carbon Building, designed by Daniel Burnham's two sons, and how housing the Hard Rock Hotel Chicago (p220). Pull yourself away from the rock and roll memorabilia to check out the building's polished black granite, green terra-cotta and gold-leaf accented crown, rumored to be intended to look like a foil-wrapped champagne bottle. Another downtown deco landmark is the 1930 Chicago Board of Trade (p57), which remained the city's tallest skyscraper until 1965 when the Richard J Daley Center opened.

Second Chicago School (1946–79)

The city once again led the architectural world in the 1950s as German immigrant Ludwig Mies van der Rohe pioneered the Second Chicago School. Having previously drafted buildings in Europe alongside fellow German innovator Walter Groupius and Swiss-French modernist Le Corbusier, Mies was influenced by both the Bauhaus and International Styles. Under Mies' direction, the steel frame that once revolutionized Chicago's skyline once again became seminal, though now no longer hidden on the inside of walls.

The functional, stripped-bare style of the Second Chicago School was all about exposed metal and glass, and represents most peoples' image of the modern skyscraper. The Loop's best example of this is the **Chicago Federal Center** (Map p290; 219 & 230 S Dearborn St), Mies' masterstroke, which demonstrates both the open, universal spaces and starkly minimalist vertical I-beams he favored.

Chicago Architecture Today

In the last half of the 20th century, the Chicago architectural partnership of Skidmore, Owings & Merrill came to dominate the cityscape. Further developing Mies' ideas, they stretched the modern skyscraper even higher with the John Hancock Center (p84) in 1969, and again in 1974 with the Sears Tower, which kept its crown as the world's tallest building for almost a quarter century. Now called the Willis Tower (p51), it remained the USA's tallest building until surpassed by NYC's One World Trade Center in 2013. This same prominent architectural firm continues to hold sway on the global stage, most recently as the designer of Dubai's Burj Khalifa, the world's tallest building since it opened in 2010.

The late '90s sparked a slew of development downtown, later leading to a front-page op-ed by Mayor Daley with a headline screaming, 'No More Ugly Buildings.' The *Sun-Times* piece took local architects and developers to task for betraying Chicago with a crop of unsightly condos and townhouse developments. Blame the big, bad '80s, when downtown real estate prices were stratospheric, and largely unchecked development sprawled both north and south of the Loop.

So far, the 21st century has been marked by great architectural triumphs – including Millennium Park (p46) and Frank Gehry's sculpted steel **Jay Pritzker Pavilion** (Map p290; 201 E Randolph St) – and great controversies, such as the failed Chicago Spire (p73) and the love-it-or-hate-it Trump International Hotel & Tower (p224), now the city's second-tallest buildling. Jeanne Gang's Aqua Tower (p58), with its spectacularly undulating wavelike balconies, was named the 2010 skyscraper of the year by Emporis. Meanwhile the city almost leads the nation in ecofriendly, LEED-certified construction, helping to keep Chicago's architectural reputation sky-high.

MARINA CITY

Fans of the band Wilco or cartoon *The Jetsons* won't want to miss snapping a photo of 1960s mod Marina City (p73), with its giant corn cob–shaped towers.

Sports

Chicago is the USA's greatest sports town. There – we said it. Why? It's not because every professional sports team is winning championships these days, but because of the undying passion of the city's sports fans. Listen in at the office water cooler and the talk is all about the Bears or the Blackhawks. Eavesdrop on a conversation between neighbors as they tidy their yards, and the chatter revolves around the Cubs or the White Sox.

Many Teams, One Unified City of Fans

Almost every Chicagoan declares a firm allegiance to at least one of the city's teams, and the place goes absolutely nuts when one of them hits the big time. Take the Blackhawks' Stanley Cup win in 2013: over two million people poured into Grant Park for a raucous victory rally. When the White Sox won the World Series in 2005? Similar scene, only with a ticker-tape parade that also included F-16 fighter planes, Journey's Steve Perry and Oprah, all strangely woven together. And when the Bears went to the Super Bowl in 2007, the city couldn't talk about anything else. Businesses with coat-and-tie dress codes were suddenly requiring staff to wear blue-and-orange jerseys to the office.

Die-hard sports fandom is an accepted way of life here. This is a city that sees no conflict of interest in taking one of its most revered cultural icons – the Art Institute's lion sculptures – and plopping giant fiberglass Blackhawks helmets on them when the local team wins the Stanley Cup. The creatures also donned Bears helmets and White Sox caps when those teams played in recent championships. Even the city's staid skyscrapers get into the spirit, arranging their window lights to spell 'Go Hawks' or 'Go Cubs' when those teams make a run for the championship play-offs.

Chicago Sports Blogs

Bleed Cubbie Blue (www.bleedcubbie blue.com)

South Side Sox (www.southside sox.com)

Windy City Gridiron (www.windycity gridiron.com)

Blog-A-Bull (www. blogabull.com)

Baseball

Chicago is one of only a few US cities to boast two Major League Baseball (MLB) teams. The Cubs are the lovable losers on the North Side, with enthusiastic yuppie attendance year after year despite generally woeful

ALTERNATE WAYS TO GET CUBS TICKETS

If you can't get tickets from the Cubs directly, you can always try the frightfully named 'scalpers.' These guys stand across from the Wrigley Field entrance (on Clark St's west side and Addison St's south side). They typically charge above face value for tickets – until the third inning or so. Then tickets can be yours for a pittance. Private fans also try to unload tickets they can't use, usually at face value. Look for the sad-faced people walking around and asking, 'Anyone need tickets?'

Another option is to enquire about rooftop seats (ie those not in the park, but on the rooftops of the surrounding houses on Sheffield and Waveland Aves). They're usually booked out by groups, but not always, and they include food and drinks as part of the deal; check www.ballparkrooftops.com or www.goldstar.com (for half-price rooftop offers).

play. The White Sox are the working man's team on the South Side, and thumb their nose at all the hoopla across town.

The two ballparks are also a study in contrasts: traditional **Wrigley Field** (Map p302; ☎773-404-2827; www.cubs.com; 1060 W Addison St; tickets $16-100), aka 'The Friendly Confines,' is baseball's second-oldest park and about as charming as they get. **US Cellular Field** (333 W 35th St), or 'The Cell,' is the new breed of stadium with modern amenities like a chock-full food court and fireworks exploding if the Sox hit a home run after dark.

Basketball

The Bulls, once the stuff of legend, haven't posed much of a threat since the late 1990s, when Michael Jordan led the team. Controversial team owner Jerry Reinsdorf allowed Jordan, revered coach Phil Jackson, Scottie Pippen and other key parts of the Bulls juggernaut to leave after the 1997–98 championship year. Since then the team, which plays at **United Center** (Map p312; 1901 W Madison St), has yo-yoed from awful to stellar to just so-so.

TOP 10 CHICAGO SPORTS HEROES

Should you find yourself in a sports bar anywhere in the Windy City, a misty-eyed mention of any of the names below will help you bond with fellow drinkers. Heck, someone might even buy you an Old Style.

Mike Ditka The Chicago Bears star (and current Chicago restaurateur), Ditka is the only person to have won a Super Bowl as a player, assistant coach and head coach. His mustache is legendary.

Michael Jordan The Chicago Bulls great ended his career of 15 seasons with the highest per-game scoring average in National Basketball Association (NBA) history.

Ryne Sandberg The Cubs second baseman played a record 123 consecutive games without an error. In 2005, he became the fourth Cubs player ever to have his number (23) retired.

Dick Butkus Elected to the Pro Football Hall of Fame in 1979, the Bears' linebacker recovered a record-breaking number of fumbles during his career. *Sports Illustrated* once called him 'The Most Feared Man of the Game.'

Walter Payton This 1970s and '80s Chicago Bears great is ranked second on the National Football League (NFL) all-time rushing list, and fourth in all-time rushing touchdowns.

Ernie Banks Voted the National League's most valuable player (MVP) twice (1958 and '59) and a 14-time All-Star, 'Mr Cub' was the first player to have his number (14) retired by the Cubs. Occasionally he swings by Wrigley Field to sing 'Take Me Out to the Ball Game' during the seventh-inning stretch.

Stan Mikita The Czech-born hockey star played his entire career (1959–80) with the Chicago Blackhawks, often alongside superstar teammate Bobby Hull, aka 'The Golden Jet,' considered one of hockey's all-time greats.

Ozzie Guillén Former White Sox coach and player known for his outspoken and politically incorrect comments, Ozzie nonetheless brought the World Series trophy to Chicago in 2005 – the first big baseball win in almost a century.

Scottie Pippen Leading the Bulls through champion seasons throughout the 1990s, Pippen is known for pioneering the unofficial 'point forward' position on the basketball court.

Frank Thomas Nicknamed 'The Big Hurt' for his ability to smack balls right out of the park, this White Sox player holds the club's all-time home-run record. His number (35) was retired in 2010.

> **BEST CHICAGO SPORTS SOUVENIRS**
> ➡ Mike Ditka or Harry Caray T-shirt from Strange Cargo (p123)
> ➡ Cubs baseball cap or mini–Wrigley Field street sign from Sports World (p124)
> ➡ Ozzie Guillen bobblehead doll or a custom T-shirt from US Cellular Field (p250)
> ➡ Cubs, Bears or Hawks jersey for your pooch from Barker & Meowsky (p109)

Football

Once upon a time the Chicago Bears were one of the most revered NFL franchises. Owner and coach George Halas epitomized the team's no-nonsense, take-no-prisoners approach. The tradition continued with players such as Walter Payton, Dick Butkus and Mike Singletary and coach Mike Ditka. In 1986 the Bears won the Super Bowl with a splendid collection of misfits and characters, such as Jim McMahon and William 'the Refrigerator' Perry, who enthralled the entire city. The team has been up and down ever since, eventually making it to – and then promptly losing – Super Bowl XLI in 2007. No matter what, fans still fill the stands at sometimes snowy **Soldier Field** (Map p316; 425 E McFetridge Dr).

Hockey

What a difference a management change can make. After languishing at the bottom of Chicago's pro-sport pantheon for the past few decades, the Blackhawks have skated into prominence with a young winning team and TV and radio deals that put them back in the mainstream, largely thanks to franchise president John McDonough. Oh, and they won the National Hockey League's (NHL's) Stanley Cup in 2010, their first trophy since 1961 – and then repeated that feat in 2013. The Hawks slapshot pucks at United Center (p250).

Soccer

Thanks to support from the city's large Latino and European communities, the city's soccer team, Chicago Fire, attracts a decent-sized fan base (despite being largely ignored by the mainstream media). The team has made the Major League Soccer (MLS) play-offs several times in recent years, and last won the championship in 1998. Watch 'em kick at suburban Toyota Park (p205).

Chicago Dining

For years epicures wrote off Chicago as a culinary backwater. Then a funny thing happened: the city won a heap of James Beard awards, and foodie magazines like *Saveur* ranked it among the nation's top restaurant scenes. So get ready: from 24-course meals of 'molecular gastronomy' to deep-dish pizza slices, from porterhouse steaks to locavore salads, this town serves up a plateful. An unapologetically rich clash of high gastronomy and comfort food, at once traditional and visionary – that's Chicago dining.

Top Chicago Cookbooks

Mexican Everyday *(Rick Bayless)*

Alinea *(Grant Achatz)*

Girl in the Kitchen *(Stephanie Izard)*

Soup & Bread Cookbook *(Martha Bayne)*

Sweetness *(Sarah Levy)*

From Heartland Farms to Urban Kitchens

Plenty of meat gets carved in this city, a lasting legacy from when Chicago was 'hog butcher for the world.' Steakhouses are a dime a dozen downtown, and new gastropubs and taverns with artisanal charcuterie menus seem to open weekly. That's not to say vegetarians and vegans don't get their due, with an increasing number of upscale dining options including Green Zebra (p146).

A dynamic vanguard of Chicago chefs led by Grant Achatz and Homaru Canto has helmed the foodie trend of molecular gastronomy – a catch-all term for meal preparation that's more like a science experiment. (What exactly does a 'pillow of lavender air' taste like?) Less haute, locavore fare has come into its own as many restaurants and star chefs now source from nearby Midwestern farms and Lincoln Park's seasonal outdoor Green City Market (p103).

If getting an authentic taste of the city ranks high on your agenda, break out of the Loop. Restaurant-rich neighborhoods in the West Loop, Near North, Gold Coast, Wicker Park and Bucktown neighborhoods have a concentration of all-too-tempting eateries at their cores. Logan Square and the Ukranian Village are more off the beaten path, but deliver perhaps the most inventive fare of all – and usually at more affordable prices, too.

If you're willing to trek further still, immigrant enclaves dish out Vietnamese *banh mi* (baguette sandwiches) and Thai noodles (Uptown), Mexican tacos and tortas (Pilsen), Swedish pastries (Andersonville), Indian and Pakistani curries (Far North Side's Devon Ave) and much more of the least expensive, most genuine dishes Chicago has to offer.

For street food that breaks all the rules – c'mon, you know you're craving a meatloaf cupcake or a chicken tikka masala taco, right? – track down Chicago's newly legal food trucks online at **Roaming Hunger** (http://roaminghunger.com/chi) or by following *Chicago Magazine's* food truck list on Twitter (@ChicagoMag/chicago-food-trucks).

Chicago's Best-Loved Specialties

Deep-dish pizza is Chicago's most famous concoction. These behemoths are nothing like the flat circular disks known as pizza in the rest of the world. Here pies are made in a special cast-iron pan – kind of like a skillet without a handle – so the dough, stuffed with molten American-style mozzarella cheese, chunky tomato sauce and other typical ingredients like

---

FIVE CHICAGO CHEFS TO KNOW

➡ **Rick Bayless** He's everywhere: on TV, cooking at the White House, tending the organic garden where he grows the restaurants' herbs, and tending Xoco (p75) and Topolobampo/Frontera Grill (p76).

➡ **Grant Achatz** Made 'molecular gastronomy' a culinary catchphrase at stratospherically priced Alinea (p104) and Next (p172).

➡ **Graham Elliot** The tattooed contrarian of the group, turning the usual rules upside down at his River North restaurant Graham Elliot (p77) and the West Loop's Graham Elliot Bistro (p77).

➡ **Stephanie Izard** Gaining fame as the first woman to win *Top Chef*, this sustainable farm-to-table fan's Girl & the Goat (p172) and Little Goat (p171) are West Loop landmarks.

➡ **Paul Kahan** The son of a Chicago smokehouse and deli owner, this classically influenced chef makes waves at Avec (p172), Blackbird (p172), Publican (p172) and Big Star (p142).

---

sausage, is oven baked. The flagship Pizzeria Uno (p76) claims to have invented deep-dish pizza in the 1940s, but this, like many other fanatical conversations about food (and sports) in the Windy City, will inspire debate.

No less iconic is the Chicago-style hot dog, a wiener that's been 'dragged through the garden.' A real-deal Chicago dog (preferably a local Vienna Beef brand) requires a poppy-seed bun, a litany of toppings (you can't miss the neon-green relish) and a sophisticated construction that seems perfectly designed to defy easy consumption. And remember rule numero uno: no ketchup! For gourmet versions (chipotle-smoked chicken sausage with mole sauce, anyone?) and stalwart classics (beer-soaked brats), swing by Hot Doug's (p155), whose owner's eponymous book amusingly covers the history of both the hot dog and his innovative restaurant.

Another renowned Chicago specialty is the Italian beef sandwich, and it stacks up like this: thin-sliced, slow-cooked roast beef that's sopped in natural gravy and giardiniera (spicy pickled vegetables), then heaped on a hoagie roll. Local Italian immigrants on the South Side invented it as a low-budget way to feed factory workers during the Depression era. Try it while you're here – Mr Beef (p75) makes a winner – because you'll be hard-pressed to find one elsewhere on the planet.

Less well known, but equally messy and delicious, is the *jibarito* sandwich, developed at local Puerto Rican eatery Borinquen Restaurant (p160). It consists of steak covered in garlicky mayo and served between thick, crispy-fried plantain slices, which form the 'bread.' Many Latin American eateries in the Humboldt Park neighborhood have it on the menu.

And who could leave the Midwest without trying some pie, maybe Amish Country–style 'shoofly' molasses, juicy strawberry-rhubarb or Dutch apple layered with sour-cream custard and nutty streusel? Take a sugar-loaded tasting flight at Hoosier Mama Pie Company (p145) in the Ukranian Village – you might just devour an entire pie. Don't worry, we won't tell.

Food Media

Chicago is rarely impressed by snooty food trends, so it follows that Chicagoans are a self-reliant bunch when it comes to picking where to eat.

Chicago Foodie Websites

....

Eater Chicago (http://chicago. eater.com)

....

Gapers Block (www.gapers block.com)

....

Chicago Gluttons (www.chicago gluttons.com)

....

Local Beet (www. thelocalbeet.com)

....

LTH Forum (www. lthforum.com)

Case in point? The oft-discussed **Check, Please!** (http://checkplease. wttw.com), a local TV program airing on Public Broadcasting Service (PBS) affiliate WTTW (channel 11), which sends dining citizens to restaurants across the spectrum to get their straightforward critiques. The show has been flooded with applications from would-be food critics by the tens of thousands – not shocking in a city where a discussion about pizza can end in fisticuffs. See for yourself what locals have to say in the show's entertaining video archives online. A 'lost' episode from 2001 features a young state senator named Barack Obama enthusiastically recommending Hyde Park's now-defunct Dixie Kitchen & Bait Shop, which still dishes up Southern specialties in downtown Evanston.

The City of Chains

It's strangely fitting that Ray Kroc opened the first McDonald's franchise restaurant in a Chicago suburb, because today top-flight Chicago restaurateurs love to expand their turf to multiple locations. Sometimes – as is the case with Giordano's (p75) pizzeria and high-class pasta kitchen Rosebud (p174) – it's a good thing. In general, though, secondary outlets of local franchises such as the Billy Goat Tavern (p74) are more like the unfortunate sequel to a great movie. When possible, stick with the original location.

Music & the Arts

Juxtapositions of class, convention and perspective are what make Chicago's artistic landscape so deeply, vitally stimulating. Contrasts fuel the city's creative engine: high-concept installations occupy erstwhile warehouses, while poetry readings are nearly a contact sport. The city's dedication to populist ideals – most visible at free summer music festivals and in ubiquitous public art – lets artists push boundaries in front of unusually broad audiences. Few US cities can boast such engaging, affordable options for art lovers, and none can do so with such little pretension.

Visual Arts

Nowhere is it easier to see the great chasms and curious bridges of the city's artistic ethos than in the visual arts. Take the recent work of painter and sculptor Kerry James Marshall, who plays with comics and superheroes, or cartoonist Chris Ware, who draws graphic novels with architectural perfectionism. Photographer Rashid Johnson evokes 19th-century photographic techniques and elements of hip hop, while Dzine (pronounced 'design') draws inspiration from Chicago's graffiti movement, lowrider cars and urban street fashion to create outdoor sculptural works, large-scale paintings and art installations and performance art pieces that fuse high/low culture.

Such transgressive boundary crossings may well have rankled the fat-cat industrialists who raised marble halls and funded collections of old and new European art over a century ago, but Chicago's public has long embraced pioneering forms. Consider society matron Bertha Palmer, who fostered the city's artistic edge in the late 1800s when she collected impressionist paintings in Europe that later became the Art Institute's core. Since then, Chicago's artists have contributed to every major international

CHICAGO'S MONUMENTAL PUBLIC ART

Chicago has a standard-setting public policy that made it an international center for public art: in 1978, the city council approved an ordinance stipulating that more than one percent of costs for constructing or renovating municipal buildings be set aside for the commission or purchase of original artworks. The result? A public art collection that's as much a part of the city's character as its groundbreaking architecture.

The most prominent public artworks go well beyond the staring eyes of the Picasso at Daley Plaza or Millennium Park's *Cloud Gate* (aka 'The Bean'). Sculptor Alexander Calder has three major works in the city, all completed in 1974. The most visible is the arching red *Flamingo* at Federal Plaza. *The Universe* is hardly out of the way for most visitors – its colorful kinetic shapes grace the lobby of Willis Tower. *Flying Dragon* floats in the Art Institute's North Stanley McCormick Memorial Garden. Joan Miró's *Chicago* sculpture – originally titled *The Sun, The Moon and One Star* – is also conveniently in the Loop, as is Jean Dubuffet's *Monument with Standing Beast* sculpture and an expansive mosaic by Chagall outside Chase Tower.

To find more free public artwork locations all around town, visit www.cityofchicago.org online and search for 'Public Art.'

movement – from Archibald Motley Jr's portraits of roaring South Side jazz clubs in the 1920s to today's big-name locals such as Juan Chavez, a renegade muralist and mosaic artist, and multimedia provocateurs Matthew Hoffman and Sabrina Raaf.

Works by Chicago's younger artists demonstrate that the modern art community has few discernible commonalities. If there is such a thing as a 'Chicago style,' the man with the best idea of its definition might be former gallery owner and curator Paul Klein, whose website **Art Letter** (www.artletter.com) provides an illuminating look at the current scene.

The city's largest concentration of galleries has outgrown the River North district, migrating to the West Loop and south to the gentrifying neighborhoods of Pilsen and Bridgeport. In 2009 the Art Institute of Chicago upped the local ante by opening its Modern Wing, allowing long-hidden works by masters like Picasso to shine and providing new viewing opportunities for cutting-edge multimedia art.

Music

It's hard to tell who sounds more sincere – Frank Sinatra swinging about 'one town that won't let you down' or Wilco ruing being 'far, far away from those city lights,' hip-hop chart-topper Kanye West rhyming about watching the 'fireworks at Lake Michigan' or Magic Sam wanting to get back to his 'sweet home Chicago.' No foolin': every facet of American music has the grubby fingerprints of Chicago music makers all over it.

The birthplace of electric blues and house music, Chicago also fosters a vibrant independent rock scene, boundary-leaping jazz cats and world-class orchestras and chamber groups. From top to bottom, local musicians embody the best characteristics of the city itself: they're resourceful and hard-working, sweating it out in muggy blues clubs, sunny outdoor amphitheaters, DIY punk bars and everyplace in between.

Chicago Blues

The most famous of Chicago's musical styles comes in one color: blue. After the Great Migration of African Americans out of the rural South, Delta bluesmen set up on Chicago's street corners and in the open-air markets of Maxwell St during the 1930s, when Robert Johnson first recorded 'Sweet Home Chicago.'

What distinguishes Chicago's regional blues style from Johnson's original ode is simple: volume. Chicago blues is defined by the plugged-in electric guitars typified by genre fathers Muddy Waters and Howlin' Wolf. Bluesmen from the 1950s and '60s, such as Willie Dixon, Junior Wells and Elmore James, and later champions such as Buddy Guy, Koko Taylor and Otis Rush, became national stars.

These days, Chicago's blues clubs are still playing much the same song they were decades ago, but it's a proud one – synonymous with screaming guitars, rolling bass and R&B-inflected rhythms.

House Music

Chicago's other big taste-making musical export took root in the early '80s at a now-defunct West Loop nightclub called the Warehouse, where DJ Frankie Knuckles got tired of spinning disco and added samples of European electronic music and beats from that new-fangled invention, the stand-alone drum machine. Uninterested in appealing to commercial radio, the tracks used deep, pounding bass beats and instrumental samples made for dancing.

Top Chicago Blues Tracks

'Sweet Home Chicago' (Robert Johnson)

'Red Rooster' (Howlin' Wolf)

'Wang Dang Doodle' (Koko Taylor)

'Mannish Boy' (Muddy Waters)

'We're Ready' (Junior Wells & Buddy Guy)

ESSENTIAL CHICAGO RECORD LABELS

Chicago record labels have long been trailblazing leaders in new musical sounds, from the 1950s through to today.

➡ **Chess Records** When the blues left the Delta and migrated north, its sweet Chicago home became Chess Records, founded by Polish immigrant brothers Leonard and Phil Chess. The label also served as a catalyst for early rock 'n' roll stars. You can visit Chess' original studios at Willie Dixon's Blues Heaven (p186).

➡ **Delmark Records** (www.delmark.com) The oldest independent jazz and blues label in the country was founded in 1953 by Bob Koester after selling out-of-print blues and jazz records from his college dorm room. Today Koester also owns Chicago's Jazz Record Mart (p79).

➡ **Wax Trax!** It's hard to say what would have happened to 1980s punk, new-wave and industrial music without this local label, which tirelessly worked to import European giants and issue fledgling domestic acts such as Ministry.

➡ **Thrill Jockey** (www.thrilljockey.com) Started by NYC transplant Bettina Richards, this label is a celebrated nexus for indie bands. But it isn't limited to the 'postrock' sounds that made it famous, having signed genre-bending jazz greats to experimental electronica artists.

➡ **Bloodshot** (www.bloodshotrecords.com) Left-of-center American roots music label fuses indie and punk rock with old-school country, alt-country or (the label's preferred moniker) insurgent country.

House music DJs such as Derrick Carter and Larry Heard revolutionized the form, and huge second-wave stars like Felix Da Housecat, DJ Sneak and acid-house artist Armando took Chicago's thump worldwide. The club scene was all about big beats, wild parties and drugged-out dancing until the late '90s, when police cracked down. In recent years, the house-music scene has matured – no more rave kids with glow sticks, sorry – while still continuing to innovate.

Jazz, Folk, Rock, Hip-Hop & Gospel

For innovative, cutting-edge and avante-garde jazz, the name to know is **AACM** (AACM; http://aacmchicago.org), a Chicago-based nonprofit organization formed in 1965 that has been a big inspiration for African American musicians. Contemporary jazz scenemakers include saxophonist Ken Vandermark (a MacArthur 'genius' grant recipient) and Grammy-winning 'vocalese' singer Kurt Elling, who got his first big break at Uptown's Green Mill.

Chicago's underground rock community has filled an important niche in recent decades with established indie labels such as Drag City and Touch & Go, and younger feisty upstarts like Flameshovel Records. The reigning kings of Chicago rock are (arguably) still Wilco.

For hip-hop, the heavyweight champ is Kanye West, son of the former head of Chicago State University's English department. West put Chicago on the hip-hop map, opening the door for fresh underground names like Lupe Fiasco, Twista and Kid Sister.

Folk troubadours hold down open-mic nights and play at the North Side's Old Town School of Folk Music, while gospel choirs raise the roof at South Side churches. A worthy destination for old-school Sunday morning gospel is Greater Salem Baptist Church, where famed gospel singer Mahalia Jackson was a faithful member until her death in 1972.

Winter Garden, Harold Washington Library Center (p55)

Literature & Spoken Word

'Yet once you've come to be part of this particular patch, you'll never love another,' wrote 20th-century Chicago literary star Nelson Algren about his hometown. 'Like loving a woman with a broken nose, you may well find lovelier lovelies. But never a lovely so real.'

And Chicago writers have started to love that woman with a broken nose a whole lot. It might not be evident at the often scrappy literary events that are just as likely to take place in a bar as a bookstore, but the activity within – and the attention paid to – the written and spoken word community has dramatically flourished in recent years.

Chicago is home to the nation's gold standard of poetic journals, *Poetry*. Long a bellwether for the academic establishment, the journal got a financial boost in 2003 when pharmaceutical heiress and philanthropist Ruth Lilly bequeathed almost $200 million to its publisher, renamed the Poetry Foundation (p73). Since then, former Wall St investment banker and poet John Barr has taken over as president of the organization, creating a number of lucrative poetry prizes and the 'American Life in Poetry' project (www.americanlifeinpoetry.org).

Smaller independent book publisher **Featherproof** (www.featherproof. com) showcases local urban authors by printing idiosyncratic fiction books, many with a humorous slant. You can also check out emerging writers in **Another Chicago Magazine** (www.anotherchicagomagazine. net), whose self-effacing title perfectly exemplifies the literary scene's underdog spirit. And, of course, nothing could be more unlike the scholarly verse of *Poetry* than spending a night at the venerated Uptown Poetry Slam (p135).

For author readings and other literary events around the city, browse the websites of the **Poetry Center of Chicago** (www.poetrycenter.org),

Best Chicago Non-Fiction Books

One More Time
(Mike Royko)

Working *(Studs Terkel)*

Devil in the White City *(Eric Larson)*

Third Coast
(Thomas Dyja)

Sign on the Chicago Theatre (p57)

Chicago Reader (p268) and **Time Out Chicago** (www.timeoutchicago. com), or turn up for the **Printers Row Lit Fest** (☑312-222-3986; www. printersrowlitfest.org) and **Printers' Ball** (www.printersball.org) in summer or the **Chicago Humanities Festival** (☑312-661-1028; www.chicago humanities.org) in November.

By golly, the whole city reads together as part of the Chicago Public Library's 'One Book, One Chicago' book club program. Even the mayor turns the pages of books by Chicago-born writers, such as Saul Bellow's *The Adventures of Augie March* and Sandra Cisneros' *The House on Mango Street*, or whatever else is the current selection.

Theater & Comedy

No area of Chicago arts has seen a greater recent explosion than the theater scene. City stages have drawn international attention, with twinkling marquees advertising Broadway blockbusters at the Loop's gilded palaces.

More intimate dramatic performances happen at Steppenwolf Theatre, Lincoln Park's landmark stage, cultivating stunning talent and groundbreaking programming since 1976. Known heavyweights Joan Allen, John Malkovich and Gary Sinise are Steppenwolf alumnae, and they exemplify Chicago's bare-knuckled, physical style of acting.

Among the city's newer cultural landmarks are the award-winning Goodman Theatre and Lookingglass Theatre. Many smaller theater companies are transient, setting up DIY productions in whatever space they can get their hands on – and their sheer volume of makeshift productions defies every convention.

Along with Wonder Bread, spray paint and house music, add improvised ('Improv') comedy to the heap of Chicago's wide-reaching cultural contributions. Were it not for Chicago's Second City comedy troupe – which evolved from intentionally unstructured skits by the Compass Players, a mid-1950s group of University of Chicago undergrads – the proverbial chicken might still be crossing the road of American comedy.

The Compass Players' original gag of incorporating audience suggestions into quick-witted comedy became standard fare after 1959 at Second City Theatre. Its tongue-in-cheek name adopted from *New Yorker* articles mocking Chicago, Second City has produced some of the country's most capable funny-bone ticklers including John Belushi, Stephen Colbert, Tina Fey and Steve Carell.

Dance

Like many of the city's other expressive hallmarks, jazz dance is an art form based on jarring contradictions. At its core, it relies on exceedingly controlled yet fluidly expressive motion, a style whose invention is credited to legendary Chicago dance teacher Gus Giordano. Exhilarating performances by his namesake company, Giordano Dance Chicago, these days overseen by his daughter Nan, will quickly annihilate any associations with campy 'jazz hands' or 'razzle dazzle.'

Chicago's cultural landscape is crowded with A-list dance companies. At the forefront is the Joffrey Ballet, which relocated here from NYC in 1995. The renowned Hubbard Street Dance Chicago keeps the attention of the international community with its modern moves.

In the Loop, Columbia College supplies dancers and choreographers to innovative fledgling companies that set up shop in performance spaces around the city. Aside from calendar listings in the *Chicago Reader* (p268) and *Time Out Chicago* (p259), the best online resource covering the scene is **See Chicago Dance** (www.seechicagodance.com).

Survival Guide

Transportation

ARRIVING IN CHICAGO

Most visitors arrive by air. The city has two airports: O'Hare International Airport and Chicago Midway Airport. O'Hare is larger and handles most of the international flights, as well as domestic flights. It is one of the world's busiest airports, with delays galore should the weather go awry. Chicago Midway Airport handles domestic services plus some flights to Canada and Mexico, and is a bit closer to the Loop.

Bus services are a popular means of getting to Chicago from nearby cities such Minneapolis, Indianapolis and Detroit. Tickets are cheap, the routes are direct to the city center, and the buses usually have free wi-fi and power outlets.

It's also easy to reach Chicago by train from major cities across the country. Union Station is a hub for regional and national Amtrak services.

Flights, cars and tours can be booked online at lonelyplanet.com.

O'Hare International Airport

O'Hare International Airport (ORD; www.flychicago. com) is 17 miles northwest of the Loop. It's the headquarters for United Airlines and a hub for American. Most non-US airlines and international flights use Terminal 5 (except Lufthansa and flights from Canada). The domestic terminals are 1, 2 and 3. ATMs and currency exchanges are available throughout. Wi-fi costs $8 per day.

CTA (CTA; www.transitchicago. com) The Blue Line runs to the Loop 24/7. During peak hours it's is the quickest way to go. The underground station is a long walk from the flight terminals. Follow the signs to baggage claim, then ones that are variously marked as 'Trains to City' and 'CTA.' It takes about 40 minutes to reach the downtown and costs $5. Unless you are staying right in the Loop, you will likely have to transfer (or hail a taxi) to complete your journey.

Airport Express (☑888-284-3826; www.airportexpress. com; ◷4am-11:30pm) Shared van service goes downtown for $32 per person. Vans leave every 15 minutes. Look for ticket counters by baggage claim. It takes 60 minutes or so, depending on traffic and where your hotel is in the drop-off order.

Taxi A taxi to the Loop takes 30 to 50 minutes (depending on traffic) and costs around $50. Taxis queue outside the baggage claim area at each terminal.

CLIMATE CHANGE & TRAVEL

Every form of transport that relies on carbon-based fuel generates CO_2, the main cause of human-induced climate change. Modern travel is dependent on airplanes, which might use less fuel per mile per person than most cars but travel much greater distances. The altitude at which aircraft emit gases (including CO_2) and particles also contributes to their climate change impact. Many websites offer 'carbon calculators' that allow people to estimate the carbon emissions generated by their journey and, for those who wish to do so, to offset the impact of the greenhouse gases emitted with contributions to portfolios of climate-friendly initiatives throughout the world. Lonely Planet offsets the carbon footprint of all staff and author travel.

Chicago Midway Airport

Chicago Midway Airport (MDW; www.flychicago.com) is 11 miles southwest of the Loop. It has three concourses: A, B and C. Southwest Airlines uses B; most other airlines go out of A. There's a currency exchange in A and ATMs throughout. Wi-fi costs $8 per day.

CTA (CTA; www.transit-chicago.com) The Orange Line runs to the Loop between 4am and 1am. The station is a fairly long haul from the concourses. Follow the signs for 'Trains to City' and 'CTA.' It takes about 30 minutes to reach the downtown and costs $3.

Airport Express (☏888-284-3826; www.airportexpress. com; ⊙4am-11:30pm) Shared van service goes downtown for $27 per person. Vans leave every 15 minutes. Look for ticket counters by baggage claim. It takes approximately 50 minutes.

Taxi A taxi to the Loop takes 20 to 30 minutes (depending on traffic) and costs $30 to $40. Taxis queue outside the main entrace; follow the 'Ground Transportation' signs.

Union Station

Grand, Doric-columned **Union Station** (www.chicagounionstation.com; 225 S Canal St) is the city's rail hub.

CTA (CTA; www.transitchicago. com) For public transportation onward, the Blue Line Clinton stop is a few blocks south. The Brown, Orange, Purple and Pink Line station at Quincy is about a half-mile to the east.

Taxi Several queue along Canal St outside the station entrance.

Amtrak (☏800-872-7245; www.amtrak.com) It has more connections here than

anywhere else in the country. Three to seven trains run daily to Midwestern cities such as Milwaukee, St Louis and Detroit. One train runs daily to both New York City and San Francisco (Emeryville).

Bus Stations

Megabus (Map p290; www. megabus.com/us; Canal St & Jackson Blvd; ☏; Ⓜ Blue Line to Clinton) travels to and from major Midwestern cities. Prices are often less, and quality and efficiency better, than Greyhound on these routes. Buses arrive/depart near Union Station, on Canal St (east side) between Jackson Blvd and Van Buren St. There are no terminals: drop-offs and pickups are streetside. All purchases must be made online in advance (you cannot buy a ticket from the driver).

Greyhound (Map p312; ☏312-408-5800; www.greyhound.com; 630 W Harrison St; Ⓜ Blue Line to Clinton) travels nationwide. The main station is two blocks southwest from the CTA Blue Line Clinton stop. The station is open 24 hours, but it's pretty desolate late at night.

GETTING AROUND CHICAGO

The **Chicago Transit Authority** (CTA; www.transit-chicago.com) runs the public transportation system. It's a mix of elevated (El) and subway trains, as well as buses. Visitors will find the trains the most useful option.

To plan routes, use the website's 'trip planner.' It basically harnesses Google, as well as provides links to apps that track buses and trains. We also like Next Transit by Jamus LLC for iPhone and Ride Chicago by Dattan Labs for Android.

Train

Elevated/Subway

CTA (CTA; www.transit-chicago.com) operates the elevated/subway train system (aka the El). It will get you to most sights, hotels and business districts with ease. The network has eight color-coded lines. Two of them – the Blue Line from O'Hare to the Loop, and the Red Line from Howard to 95th/Dan Ryan – operate 24 hours a day. The other lines run from about 4am to 1am daily, every five to 15 minutes.

You can buy a Ventra Ticket or a Ventra Card – a rechargeable fare card – at train stations. The standard fare is $3 (except from O'Hare, where it costs $5) and includes two transfers. The Ventra Card has a one-time $5 fee that gets refunded once you register the card. It knocks 50¢ off the cost of each ride.

Unlimited ride passes (one-/three-/seven-day $10/20/28) are also available. Get them at rail stations and various retail locations (ie drug stores, currency exchanges).

You use your ticket/card to enter the turnstyle; you don't need it to exit.

The Ventra system is new, and may not be fully operational until 2015. Staff at rail stations can clue you in as to what you'll need in the interim.

Metra

Metra (www.metrarail.com; fares $2.75-$9.25, all-weekend pass $7) commuter trains traverse 12 routes serving the suburbs from four terminals ringing the Loop: LaSalle St Station, Millennium Station, Union Station and Richard B Ogilvie Transportation Center (a few blocks north of Union Station). Some train lines run daily, while others operate only during weekday rush hours. Buy tickets from agents and machines at major stations.

Bus

CTA buses (CTA; www.transitchicago.com) follow major arterial roads, and most operate from early morning until late evening. They roll into the furthest reaches of the city. The standard fare is $2.25. You'll need exact change. Or you can use a Ventra card.

PACE (www.pacebus.com) runs the suburban bus system that connects with city transport.

Taxi

Taxis are plentiful in the Loop, north to Andersonville and northwest to Wicker Park/Bucktown. Hail them with a wave of the hand. Fares start at $3.25 when you get into the cab, then it's $1.80 per mile. The first extra passenger costs $1; extra passengers after that are 50¢ apiece. Add 10% to 15% for a tip. All major companies accept credit cards. Venture outside the city limits and the per-mile fare goes up by 50%.

Reliable companies:

Flash Cab (☑773-561-1444; www.flashcab.com)

Yellow Cab (☑312-829-4222; www.yellowcabchicago. com)

Hailo (www.hailocab.com/chicago) Lets you book cabs and pay electronically via your smartphone for a small surcharge ($1.50 to $3).

Boat

Two different water taxi companies provides an interesting alternative to walking or busing between major sights.

Shoreline Water Taxi (www.shorelinesightseeing. com; one way adult/child $8/5; ⏱10am-6:30pm late May-early Sep) transports you on its Lake Taxi from Navy Pier (at the southwestern corner) to the South Loop's Shedd Aquarium. The River Taxi connects Gateway Park (just west of Navy Pier) to Willis Tower (via the Adams St bridge's southeast side).

Chicago Water Taxi (☑312-337-1446; www.chicagowatertaxi.com; one way $3-7, weekday/weekend all-day pass $8/10) plies the river from the Michigan Ave bridge

(northwest side, by the Wrigley Building) to Madison St (near the Metra Ogilvie Transportation Center), stopping at LaSalle/Clark en route. In summer it continues on to Chinatown.

Bicycle

Chicago has become a cycling-savvy city with its own bike-share program. A fair number of locals commute by bicycle. Riders can take bikes free of charge onto CTA trains, except during rush hour (7am to 9am and 4pm to 6pm Monday to Friday). Most CTA buses are equipped with a bike rack on the front that accommodates two bikes at a time. The city's Complete Streets (www.chicagocompletestreets.org) program has free maps showing bike lanes and other useful information for cyclists.

Rental

The first two options below include helmets and locks in the price, and they give discounts if you reserve online. They also rent child seats and tandem bikes.

Bike Chicago (Map p290; ☑312-729-1000; www.bikechicago.com; 239 E Randolph St; bikes per hr/day from $10/35, tour adult/child from $39/25; ⏱6:30am-8pm Mon-Fri, from 8am Sat & Sun, closed Sat & Sun Nov-Mar; Ⓜ Brown, Orange, Green, Purple, Pink Line to Randolph) This is part of a bigger company that rents wheels in various cities. In Chicago its main location is at Millennium Park. Other locations include the Riverwalk and Navy Pier.

Bobby's Bike Hike (Map p292; ☑312-915-0995; www.bobbysbikehike.com; 465 N McClurg Ct; half-/full day from $23/32; ⏱8am-8pm Jun-Aug, 8:30am-7pm Sep-Nov & Mar-May, closed Dec-Feb; Ⓜ Red

---

BOAT TOUR INFO

Boat tours are the most popular way to see the city. Most run May to November, several times daily. The **Chicago Architecture Foundation** (CAF; Map p290; ☑312-922-3432; www.architecture.org; 224 S Michigan Ave; tours $10-40; Ⓜ Brown, Orange, Green, Purple, Pink Line to Adams) does the best job, but several other companies offer similar tours from the docks at Michigan Ave. They cruise the river and lakefront for around 90 minutes; costs are $30/15 per adult/child on average. Check online to see what works for your schedule and budget:

Mercury Cruises (Map p290; ☑312-332-1353; www.mercurycruises.com; Ⓜ Brown, Orange, Green, Purple, Pink Line to State/Lake)

Shoreline Sightseeing (Map p295; ☑312-222-9328; www.shorelinesightseeing.com)

Wendella Boats (Map p292; ☑312-337-1446; www.wendellaboats.com; Ⓜ Red Line to Grand)

Line to Grand) Locally based Dobby's earns raves from riders. It's located at the River East Docks' Ogden Slip.

Divvy (www.divvybikes. com) Chicago's bike-sharing program launched in 2013. It's working up to a network of 4000 bicycles scattered at 400-odd stations around town. To check out a bike, select the membership (24 hours is $7), insert credit card, and off you go. The first 30 minutes are free; after that, rates rise fast ($2/$6 per extra 30/60 minutes). The system works best for point-to-point travel versus leisurely sightseeing trips.

Car & Motorcycle

Driving in Chicago is no fun. Traffic snarls not only at rush hours, but also just about every hour in between. Especially for short trips in town, use public transportation to spare yourself the headache.

Parking

➤ Meter spots and on-street parking are plentiful in outlying areas, but the Loop, Near North, Lincoln Park and Lake View neighborhoods can require serious circling before you find a spot.

➤ Note that 'meter' is a bit of a misnomer – you actually feed coins or a credit card into a pay box that serves the entire block. Decide how much time you want, then the box spits out a receipt to display on the car's dashboard. Per-hour costs range from $2 in outlying areas to $6.50 in the Loop. In many areas, you do not have to pay between 9pm and 8am. Check the pay box's instructions.

➤ Downtown garages cost about $38 per day, but will save you time and traffic tickets. **Millennium Park Garage** (www.millenniumgarages.com;

5 S Columbus Dr; per 3/24hr $23/30) is one of the cheapest.

➤ Some meter-free neighborhoods require resident parking passes, some don't. Read signs carefully.

➤ Never park in a spot or red-curbed area marked 'Tow-Away.' Your car will be towed.

Road Rules

➤ The speed limit is 30mph unless posted otherwise.

➤ You must wear your seat belt and restrain kids under eight years in child-safety seats.

➤ Driving while using a handheld cell phone is illegal.

➤ Be aware that many intersections have cameras that snap a photo if you go through a red light. A $100 ticket arrives in your mailbox not long thereafter.

Auto Association

For emergency road service and towing, members can call the **American Automobile Association** (AAA; www. aaa.com). It has reciprocal membership agreements with several international auto clubs.

Car Share

Zipcar (☎866-494-7227; www.zipcar.com) is a popular commuting tool in this town. If you're on vacation, hourly/daily rates are $8.25/74 weekdays and $9/80 weekends. That includes gas and insurance and good parking spaces around town. You need to become a member first ($60 annually plus $25 application fee).

Rental

All major car-rental agencies are in Chicago. Rates fluctuate radically. In general, it's more expensive to rent at the airport than downtown. To rent a car you typically need to be at least 25 years old, hold a valid driver's license and have a major credit card. Unless stated otherwise,

these companies have outlets at both Chicago airports and downtown.

Ace Rent a Car (☎800-323-3221; www.acerentacar. com) Off-airport independent by O'Hare, with lower than average rates. Call for airport shuttle (10 minutes to site).

Alamo (☎800-462-5266; www.alamo.com)

Avis (☎800-331-1212; www.avis.com)

Budget (☎800-527-0700; www.budget.com)

Dollar (☎800-800-4000; www.dollar.com) At the airports only.

Enterprise (☎800-867-4595; www.enterprise.com)

Hertz (☎800-654-3131; www.hertz.com)

National (☎800-227-7368; www.nationalcar.com)

Thrifty (☎800-527-7075; www.thrifty.com)

TOURS

Tours get you out on the water and into less-visited neighborhoods. Many companies offer discounts if you book online. See the Eating chapter (p26) for food-related tours, and the Sports & Activities chapter (p35) for cycling and paddling tours.

Chicago Architecture Foundation (CAF, Map p290, ☎312-922-3432; www.architecture.org; 224 S Michigan Ave; tours $10-40; MBrown, Orange, Green, Purple, Pink Line to Adams) The gold-standard boat tours ($40) sail from Michigan Ave's river dock. The popular Rise of the Skyscraper walking tours ($17) leave from the main downtown address. Weekday lunchtime tours ($10) explore individual landmark buildings and meet there. CAF sponsors bus, bike and El train tours, too. Buy tickets online or at CAF; boat tickets can also be purchased at the dock.

DIY TOURS TO DOWNLOAD

These tours are all available for free, so load 'em up on your mobile device and hit the road.

Chicago Loop Alliance (www.chicagoloopalliance.com) It offers three covering different themes downtown: Art Loop, Landmark Loop and Theater Loop.

Chicago Movie Tour (www.onscreenillinois.com) Tour sites made famous in flicks such as *The Blues Brothers, Ferris Bueller's Day Off* and *The Untouchables*.

Chicago Poetry Tour (www.downloadchicagotours. com) Famous poets give the lowdown on literary hot spots around the city; the first six stops cover the Loop.

Chicago Greeter (Map p290; ☑312-945-4231; www. chicagogreeter.com) FREE It pairs you with a local city dweller who takes you on a personal two- to four-hour tour customized by theme (architecture, history, gay and lesbian, and more) or neighborhood. Travel is by foot and/or public transportation. Reserve 10 business days in advance. Departure locations vary.

InstaGreeter (Map p290; www.chicagogreeter.com/ instagreeter; 77 E Randolph St; ☽10am-3pm Fri-Sun; Ⓜ Brown, Orange, Green, Purple, Pink Line to Randolph) FREE It's the quicker version of Chicago Greeter, offering one-hour tours on the spot from the Chicago Cultural Center visitors center. Some summers it opens neighborhood outlets on Saturdays in Old Town, Pilsen and Hyde Park for local walkabouts (it depends on funding).

Chicago History Museum (Map p298; ☑312-642-4600; www.chicagohistory.org; tours $20-55) The museum counts pub crawls, El jaunts, cycling routes and cemetery walks among its excellent tour arsenal. Departure points and times vary.

Weird Chicago Tours (Map p292; ☑888-446-7859; www. weirdchicago.com; 600 N Clark St; 3hr tours $30; ☽7pm Fri & Sat, 3pm Sat; Ⓜ Red Line to Grand) It drives by ghost, gangster and red-light sites. Departs across from the Hard Rock Cafe.

Untouchable Gangster Tours (Map p292; ☑773-881-1195; www.gangstertour. com; cnr N Clark St & W Ohio Ave; 2hr tours $28; Ⓜ Red Line to Grand) Comic, costumed actors take you by van to some of Chicago's famous gangster sights. There's usually a tour at 11am and 1pm daily, with additional offerings Friday through Sunday. Departs outside McDonald's.

Windy (Map p295; ☑312-595-5555; www.tallshipwindy.com; Navy Pier; 60-75min tours $30; Ⓜ Red Line to Grand to trolley) The four-masted schooner sets sail from Navy Pier. Trips have different themes (pirates, architecture, sailing skills etc). With only the sound of the wind in your ears, these tours are the most relaxing way to see the skyline from offshore.

Chicago Detours (☑312-350-1131; www.chicagodetours. com; tours from $26) It offers various tours (mostly walking, but also some by bus) that take in Chicago's architecture, history and culture. The Historic Bar Tour is a popular one.

Directory A-Z

Customs Regulations

For a complete list of US customs regulations, visit the official portal for **US Customs and Border Protection** (www.cbp.gov).

Duty-free allowance per person is as follows:

➡ 1L of liquor (provided you are at least 21 years old)

➡ 100 cigars and 200 cigarettes (if you are at least 18)

➡ $100 worth of gifts and purchases ($800 if a returning US citizen)

➡ If you arrive with $10,000 in US or foreign currency, it must be declared.

There are heavy penalties for attempting to import illegal drugs. Fruit, vegetables and other food must be declared.

Discount Cards

Chicago offers a couple of discount cards that also let you skip the regular queues at the main sights:

Go Chicago Card (www.gochicagocard.com) Allows you to visit an unlimited number of attractions for a flat fee; good for one, two, three, five or seven consecutive days.

CityPass (www.citypass.com) Gives access to five of the city's top draws, including Shedd Aquarium and Willis Tower, over nine days; a better option if you prefer a more leisurely sightseeing pace.

Electricity

120V/60Hz

120V/60Hz

Emergency

Police, fire, ambulance ☎911

Nonemergency police matters ☎311

Internet Access

➡ Wi-fi is common in lodgings across the price spectrum; many places also have a computer terminal for you to use. This guide uses an @ to indicate a place has a web-connected computer for public use and a 🖥 when it offers wireless internet access, whether free or fee-based.

➡ Many bars, cafes and public buildings (like the Chicago Cultural Center) offer free wi-fi.

➡ Outlets of the **Chicago Public Library** (www.chipublib.org) offer free wi-fi. There are no passwords required or time limits. Libraries also offer free computer terminals for one hour; get a 'day pass' at the counter.

➡ For a list of wi-fi hot spots (plus tech and access info), visit **Wi-Fi Alliance** (www.wi-fi.org)

PRACTICALITIES

➡ The **Chicago Tribune** (www.chicagotribune.com) is the city's conservative daily newspaper. Its competitor is the tabloid-style **Chicago Sun-Times** (www.suntimes.com).

➡ The **Chicago Reader** (www.chicagoreader.com) is a free alternative weekly that scrutinizes Chicago politics and has great entertainment coverage. It's owned by the *Sun-Times*.

➡ The main TV channels are Channel 2 (CBS), Channel 5 (NBC), Channel 7 (ABC), Channel 9 (WGN) and Channel 32 (FOX).

➡ National Public Radio (NPR) can be found on WBEZ-FM91.5.

➡ Chicago is entirely smoke-free in restaurants, bars and workplaces.

and **Wi-Fi Free Spot** (www.wififreespot.com).

Legal Matters

➡ If you are arrested, you are allowed to remain silent, though never walk away from an officer; you are entitled to have access to an attorney. The legal system presumes you're innocent until proven guilty. All arrested persons have the right to make one phone call. If you don't have a lawyer or family member to help you, call your embassy or consulate. The police will give you the number on request.

➡ The blood alcohol limit is 0.8%. Driving under the influence of alcohol or drugs is a serious offense, subject to stiff fines and even imprisonment.

➡ Possession of any illicit drug, including cocaine, ecstasy, LSD, heroin, hashish or more than an ounce of pot, is a felony potentially punishable by a lengthy jail sentence.

➡ The city recently decriminalized possession of small amounts of marijuana. If you're caught with 15g or less of pot, you can be ticketed for $250 to $500.

➡ It's against the law to have an open container of any alcoholic beverage in public. However, this is overlooked during most concerts at Millennium Park.

Medical Services

Chicago has excellent medical facilities and no unexpected health dangers; the only real concern is that a collision with the US medical system might injure your wallet. Remember to buy health insurance before you travel. Check out lonelyplanet.com/travel_services for more information. Recommended medical facilities:

Advocate Illinois Masonic Medical Center (☎773-975-1600; www.advocatehealth.com/immc; 836 W Wellington Ave; Ⓜ Brown, Purple Line to Wellington) Hospital located in Lake View.

Lurie Children's Hospital (www.luriechildrens.org; 225 E Chicago Ave; Ⓜ Red Line to Chicago) Brand-new downtown facility.

Northwestern Memorial Hospital (☎312-926-5188; www.nmh.org; 251 E Erie St) Well-respected downtown hospital.

Stroger Cook County Hospital (☎312-864-1300; www.cchil.org; 1969 W Ogden Ave) Public hospital serving low-income patients; 2.5 miles west of the Loop.

Pharmacies

Walgreens pharmacies are located all around the city. Convenient branches are located on **Michigan Ave** (☎312-664-8686; 757 N Michigan Ave; ◷ 24hr; Ⓜ Red Line to Chicago) and **W Monroe St** (☎312-346-5727; 79 W Monroe St; ◷ 7am-7pm Mon-Fri; Ⓜ Red, Blue Line to Monroe).

Money

The currency is the US dollar. Most locals do not carry large amounts of cash for everyday use, relying instead on credit and debit cards.

ATMs

ATMs are everywhere in Chicago. They are available 24/7 at most banks, and in shopping centers, airports, grocery stores and convenience shops. Most ATMs charge a service fee of $2.50 or more per transaction and your home bank may impose additional charges. For foreign visitors, ask your bank for exact information about using its cards in stateside ATMs. The exchange rate is usually as good as you'll get anywhere.

Credit Cards

Major credit cards are almost universally accepted. In fact, it's next to impossible to rent a car or make phone reservations without one. Visa and MasterCard are the most widely accepted. Contact the issuing company for lost or stolen cards.

American Express (☎800-528-4800; www.americanexpress.com)

MasterCard (☎800-627-8372; www.mastercard.com)

Visa ([☎]800-847-2911; www. visa.com)

Money Changers

Although the airports have exchange bureaus, better rates can usually be obtained in the city.

Travelex ([☎]312-807-4941; www.travelex.com; 19 S LaSalle St; ⊗8am-6pm Mon-Fri, to 1pm Sat; [M]Blue Line to Monroe)

World's Money Exchange ([☎]312-641-2151; www. wmeinc.com; 203 N LaSalle St; ⊗8:45am-4:45pm Mon-Fri; [M]Brown, Orange, Green, Purple, Pink, Blue Line to Clark/Lake)

Tipping

Tipping is not optional; only withhold tips in cases of outrageously bad service.

Airport & hotel porters $2 per bag, minimum per cart $5

Bartenders 10–15% per round, minimum per drink $1.

Hotel maids $2–5 per night.

Restaurant servers 15–20%, unless a gratuity is already charged on the bill.

Taxi drivers 10–15%, rounded up to the next dollar.

Valet parking attendants At least $2 when handed back the keys.

Opening Hours

The list below provides 'normal' opening hours for businesses. Reviews throughout this book show specific hours. Note that hours can vary a bit by season. Our listings depict peak season operating hours.

Banks & businesses 9am to 5pm Monday to Friday

Bars & pubs 11am to 2am (3am on Saturday); some bars until 4am (5am on Saturday)

Nightclubs 9pm to 2am (3am on Saturday); some clubs until 4am (5am on Saturday)

Restaurants breakfast 7am or 8am to 11am; lunch 11am or 11:30am to 2:30pm; dinner 5pm or 6pm to 10pm Sunday to Thursday, to 11pm or midnight Friday and Saturday

Shops 11am to 7pm Monday to Saturday, noon to 6pm Sunday; malls 10am to 8pm or 9pm, 11am to 6pm Sunday

---

Post

The **US Postal Service** (USPS; [☎]800-275-8777; www. usps.com) is reliable and fairly inexpensive. For 1st-class mail sent and delivered within the USA, postage rates are 46¢ for letters up to 1oz (20¢ for each additional ounce) and 33¢ for standard-size postcards. International airmail rates for postcards and letters up to 1oz are $1.10. Convenient post offices:

Fort Dearborn Station ([☎]312-644-0485; 540 N Dearborn St; ⊗8am-6:30pm Mon-Fri, 7:30am-3pm Sat, 9am-2pm Sun)

Loop Station ([☎]312-427-4225; 211 S Clark St; ⊗7am-6pm Mon-Fri)

Main Post Office ([☎]312-983-8182; 433 W Harrison St; ⊗7:30am-midnight)

Public Holidays

Banks, schools, offices and most shops close on these days:

New Year's Day January 1

Martin Luther King Jr Day Third Monday in January

President's Day Third Monday in February

Pulaski Day First Monday in March (observed mostly by city offices)

Memorial Day Last Monday in May

Independence Day July 4

Labor Day First Monday in September

Columbus Day Second Monday in October

Veteran's Day November 11

Thanksgiving Day Fourth Thursday in November

Christmas Day December 25

Safe Travel

➡ You've probably heard about Chicago's high murder rate (500 homicides in 2012 compared to 414 in New York City, which has three times the population), but know this is mostly concentrated in certain far west and far south neighborhoods.

➡ Overall, serious crime in Chicago has been dropping in recent years, and major tourist areas are all reasonably safe.

➡ That doesn't mean you shouldn't take normal, big-city precautions, especially solo at night. Many crimes involve cell phone theft, so be subtle when using yours.

Taxes & Refunds

The basic sales tax is 9.25%. The hotel tax is 16.4%; the car-rental tax is 19%. And for meals in most parts of town, there's an 11% tax added to the bill.

Telephone

The phone system mixes regional service providers, competing long-distance carriers and several cell-phone companies. Overall, the system is efficient. Calls from a regular landline or cell phone are usually cheaper than a hotel phone or pay phone. Pay phones are thin on the ground. Local calls cost 50¢. Services such as **Skype** (www.skype.com) and **Google Voice** (www.google. com/voice) can make calling home quite cheap.

Cell Phones

Most of the USA's mobile-phone systems are incompatible with the GSM 900/1800 standard used throughout Europe and Asia (though some convertible phones will work). G3 phones such as iPhones will work fine – but beware of roaming costs, especially for data. Check with your service provider about using your phone here.

It might be cheaper to buy a prepaid SIM card for the USA, like those sold by AT&T, which you can insert into your international mobile phone to get a local phone number and voicemail. **Planet Omni** (www.planetomni.com) and **Telestial** (www.telestial.com) offer these services, as well as cell phone rentals.

You can also buy inexpensive, no-contract (prepaid) phones with a local number and a set number of minutes, which can be topped up. Virgin Mobile, T-Mobile, AT&T and other providers offer phones starting at $20, with a package of minutes starting around $40 for 400 minutes. Electronics store chain **Best Buy** (Map p296; ☎312-397-2146; www.bestbuy.com; 875 N Michigan Ave; ◷10am-9pm Mon-Sat, to 7pm Sun; Ⓜ Red Line to Chicago) sells these phones, as well as international SIM cards. Another good place to poke around is on Devon Ave (p132), where several shops sell cell-phone equipment to a mostly Indian and European clientele.

Phone Codes

All phone numbers within the USA consist of a three-digit area code followed by a seven-digit local number.

➨ If you are calling from within the US to another area code, dial ☎1 + the three-digit area code + the seven-digit local number.

➨ In the city, you must dial the same way: ☎1 + the area code + seven-digit local number (even if you're calling within the same area code).

➨ Always dial ☎1 before toll-free numbers (which start with 800, 888, 877, 866). Some toll-free numbers only work within the US.

➨ Dial the international country code for the USA (☎1) if calling from abroad.

➨ To make an international call from the USA dial ☎011 followed by country code, area code and phone number. Canada is the exception, where you just dial 1 plus the area code and phone number.

➨ Dial ☎00 for assistance making international calls.

➨ Dial ☎411 directory assistance nationwide.

➨ Dial ☎800-555-1212 for directory assistance for toll-free numbers.

Phonecards

Private prepaid phonecards are available from convenience stores, supermarkets and pharmacies. AT&T sells a reliable phonecard that is widely available.

Time

Chicago is on Central Standard Time, six hours behind Greenwich Mean Time. Daylight Saving Time is observed between mid-March and early November.

Chicago is one hour behind Eastern Standard Time, which encompasses nearby Michigan and Indiana (apart from the northwestern corner of Indiana, which follows Chicago time). The border between the two zones is just east of the city.

When it's noon in Chicago, it's 1pm in New York City, 6pm in London, 3am the next day in Sydney and 5am the next day in Auckland.

Tourist Information

Choose Chicago (www.choosechicago.com) is the city's tourism bureau. The website has a 'Deals' section where hotels, restaurants, entertainment venues and shops promote their discounts. Search by date and neighborhood to narrow the list. The Twitter (@Choose Chicago) and Facebook pages list free attractions and events going on (though you'll have to scroll through a lot of ads). The free Choose Chicago app links to all of it and provides a handy events calendar.

The group also runs two visitors centers, each with a staffed information desk, CTA transit card kiosk and free wi-fi:

Chicago Cultural Center Visitors Center (Map p290; www.choosechicago.com; 77 E Randolph St; ◷9am-7pm Mon-Thu, to 6pm Fri & Sat, 10am-6pm Sun; ☏; Ⓜ Brown, Orange, Green, Purple, Pink Line to Randolph) InstaGreeter and Millennium Park tours also depart from here.

Water Works Visitors Center (Map p296; www.choosechicago.com; 163 E Pearson St; ◷9am-7pm Mon-Thu, to 6pm Fri & Sat, 10am-6pm Sun; ☏; Ⓜ Red Line to Chicago) There's a Hot Tix booth inside.

Travelers with Disabilities

Chicago is an OK destination for disabled visitors. Most museums and major sights are wheelchair accessible, as are most large hotels and restaurants.

Easy Access Chicago (www.easyaccesschicago.org) is a free resource that lists museums, tours, restaurants and lodgings, and provides mobility, vision and hearing accessibility information for each place (ie which entrances, bathrooms to use etc).

All **CTA** (CTA; www.transitchicago.com) buses are wheelchair accessible, but about one-third of El stations are not. To see a list of accessible stations, click on 'How to Ride' on the website.

The preponderance of older buildings means that doorways are narrow and stairs prevalent in many places.

The **Mayor's Office for People with Disabilities** (☑TTY 312-744-4964, 312-744-7050, www.cityofchicago.org/disabilities) can answer questions about the availability of services in the city.

Visas

Admission requirements are subject to rapid change. The **US State Department** (www.travel.state.gov/visa) has the latest information, or check with a US consulate in your home country.

➡ Under the US visa-waiver program, visas are not required for citizens of 36 countries – including most EU members, Japan, Australia, New Zealand and the UK – for visits of up to 90 days (no extensions allowed), as long as you can present a machine-readable passport and are approved under the **Electronic System for Travel Authorization** (ESTA; www.cbp.gov/esta). Note you must register at least 72 hours before arrival, and there's a $14 fee for processing and authorization.

➡ In essence, ESTA requires that you register specific information online (name, address, passport info etc) prior to entering the US. You will receive one of three responses: 'Authorization Approved' (this usually comes within minutes; most applicants can expect to receive this response); 'Authorization Pending', in which case you can go back online to check the status within roughly 72 hours; or 'Travel not Authorized.' If the latter is the case, it means your application is not approved and you will need to apply for a visa.

➡ Once approved, registration is valid for two years, but note that if you renew your passport or change your name, you will need to re-register. The entire process is stored electronically and linked to your passport, but it is recommended that you bring a printout of the ESTA approval just to be safe.

➡ Canadians are exempt from the process. They do not need visas, though they do need a passport or document approved by the **Western Hemisphere Travel Initiative** (www.getyouhome.gov).

➡ Those who need a visa should apply at the US consulate in their home country.

Behind the Scenes

SEND US YOUR FEEDBACK

We love to hear from travelers – your comments keep us on our toes and help make our books better. Our well-traveled team reads every word on what you loved or loathed about this book. Although we cannot reply individually to postal submissions, we always guarantee that your feedback goes straight to the appropriate authors, in time for the next edition. Each person who sends us information is thanked in the next edition – the most useful submissions are rewarded with a selection of digital PDF chapters.

Visit **lonelyplanet.com/contact** to submit your updates and suggestions or to ask for help. Our award-winning website also features inspirational travel stories, news and discussions.

Note: We may edit, reproduce and incorporate your comments in Lonely Planet products such as guidebooks, websites and digital products, so let us know if you don't want your comments reproduced or your name acknowledged. For a copy of our privacy policy visit lonelyplanet.com/privacy.

OUR READERS

Many thanks to the travelers who used the last edition and wrote to us with helpful hints, useful advice and interesting anecdotes:

Florian Ahrweiler, Roger Baker, Su Elliot, Jack Green, Katharine Harris, Amy Laden, Joe Lekas, Beatriz Martin, Ramin Miraftabi, Gaelle Missonnier, Paula Novo Núñez, John Potts, Martin Riley, Roberto Skinner, Anja Ziegler

AUTHOR THANKS

Karla Zimmerman

Many thanks to Neil Anderson, Lisa DiChiera, Mark Fornek, Janet Ginsburg, Jonathan Hayes, Kari Lydersen, Melissa McCarville, Betsy Riley, Diana Slickman, Bob Stockfish and Sara Zimmerman. A big round of Hoosier Mama to ace coauthor Sara Benson. Deep gratitude to all of the Lonely Planet *Chicago* writers who trod before me. Thanks most of all to Eric Markowitz, the world's best partner-for-life, who fed me, drove me and kept the house from falling apart while I wrote this book.

Sara Benson

Thanks to Jennye Garibaldi for this sweet home Chicago gig. Working with the always-amazing Karla Zimmerman was awesome – go Cubs! Thanks also to my dad, James Benson, for Chicago sports history lessons, and to Jonathan Hayes and Sara Zimmerman for being my hosts, dining-out partners and drinking buddies.

ACKNOWLEDGMENTS

Chicago Department of Cultural Affairs for *Haymarket Memorial* (p171)

Cover photograph: Chicago cityscape, Michael Bishara

THIS BOOK

This 7th edition of Lonely Planet's *Chicago* guidebook was researched and written by Karla Zimmerman and Sara Benson. Karla also wrote the previous two editions, being assisted on the 5th edition by Lisa Dunford and Nate Cavalieri. This guidebook was commissioned in Lonely Planet's Oakland office, and produced by the following:

Commissioning Editors Jennye Garibaldi, Katie O'Connell, Emily K Wolman
Coordinating Editors Carolyn Boicos, Lorna Parkes, Erin Richards
Senior Cartographer Alison Lyall
Coordinating Layout Designer Carol Jackson
Managing Editors Sasha Baskett, Brigitte Ellemor
Senior Editor Catherine Naghten
Managing Layout Designer Chris Girdler

Assisting Editors Carly Hall, Helen Koehne, Joanne Newell
Cover Research Naomi Parker
Internal Image Research Aude Vauconsant
Thanks to Elin Berglund, Ryan Evans, Justin Flynn, Larissa Frost, Paula Hardy, Jane Hart, Genesys India, Jouve India, Trent Paton, Dianne Schallmeiner, Kerrianne Southway, Gerard Walker

Index

See also separate subindexes for:

✗ EATING P278

🍷 DRINKING & NIGHTLIFE P279

☆ ENTERTAINMENT P280

🛍 SHOPPING P281

🏃 SPORTS & ACTIVITIES P281

🛏 SLEEPING P282

✕ EATING

DRINKING & NIGHTLIFE

☆ ENTERTAINMENT

Chicago Maps

Map Legend

Sights
- Beach
- Buddhist
- Castle
- Christian
- Hindu
- Islamic
- Jewish
- Monument
- Museum/Gallery
- Ruin
- Winery/Vineyard
- Zoo
- Other Sight

Eating
- Eating

Drinking & Nightlife
- Drinking & Nightlife
- Cafe

Entertainment
- Entertainment

Shopping
- Shopping

Sleeping
- Sleeping
- Camping

Sports & Activities
- Diving/Snorkelling
- Canoeing/Kayaking
- Skiing
- Surfing
- Swimming/Pool
- Walking
- Windsurfing
- Other Sports & Activities

Information
- Post Office
- Tourist Information

Transport
- Airport
- Border Crossing
- Bus
- Cable Car/Funicular
- Cycling
- Ferry
- Monorail
- Parking
- S-Bahn
- Taxi
- Train/Railway
- Tram
- Tube Station
- U-Bahn
- Underground Train Station
- Other Transport

Routes
- Tollway
- Freeway
- Primary
- Secondary
- Tertiary
- Lane
- Unsealed Road
- Plaza/Mall
- Steps
- Tunnel
- Pedestrian Overpass
- Walking Tour
- Walking Tour Detour
- Path

Boundaries
- International
- State/Province
- Disputed
- Regional/Suburb
- Marine Park
- Cliff
- Wall

Geographic
- Hut/Shelter
- Lighthouse
- Lookout
- Mountain/Volcano
- Oasis
- Park
- Pass
- Picnic Area
- Waterfall

Hydrography
- River/Creek
- Intermittent River
- Swamp/Mangrove
- Reef
- Canal
- Water
- Dry/Salt/Intermittent Lake
- Glacier

Areas
- Beach/Desert
- Cemetery (Christian)
- Cemetery (Other)
- Park/Forest
- Sportsground
- Sight (Building)
- Top Sight (Building)

EDGEWATER
LAKEWOOD-BALMORAL
Rosehill
Cemetery

7

ANDERSONVILLE

LINCOLN
SQUARE

UPTOWN

Waveland
Park

6

WRIGLEYVILLE

Horner
Park

LAKE VIEW

Belmont
Rocks

Lake
Michigan

9

LOGAN
SQUARE

BUCKTOWN

8

5

LINCOLN
PARK

Lincoln
Park

North Ave Beach

HUMBOLDT
PARK

WICKER
PARK

OLD
TOWN

4

North Branch Chicago River

Goose
Island

UKRAINIAN
VILLAGE

NEAR
NORTH

2

3

WEST
LOOP

ILLINOIS
CENTER

THE
LOOP

1

GREEKTOWN

Grant
Park

LITTLE
ITALY

DEARBORN
PARK

MUSEUM
CAMPUS

12th St Beach

Douglas
Park

10

PILSEN

CHINATOWN

11

31st St Beach

South Branch Chicago River

Woodland
Park

BRONZEVILLE

BRIDGEPORT

McKinley
Park

KENWOOD

Sherman
Park

Washington
Park

12

HYDE
PARK

Jackson
Park

MAP INDEX

THE LOOP Map on p290

Key on 289

THE LOOP

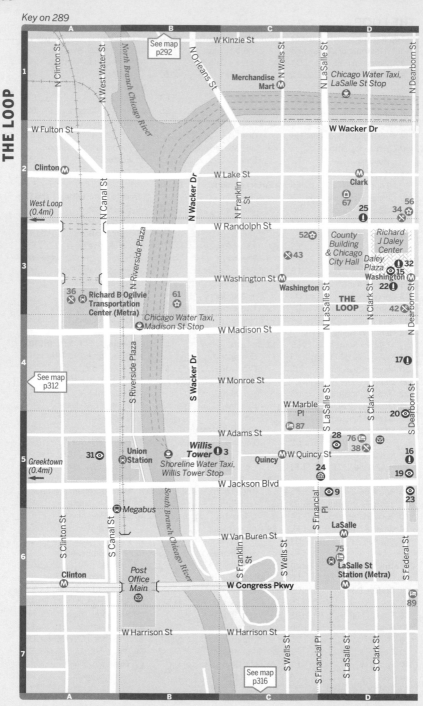

See map p292

West Loop (0.4mi)

See map p312

Greektown (0.4mi)

See map p316

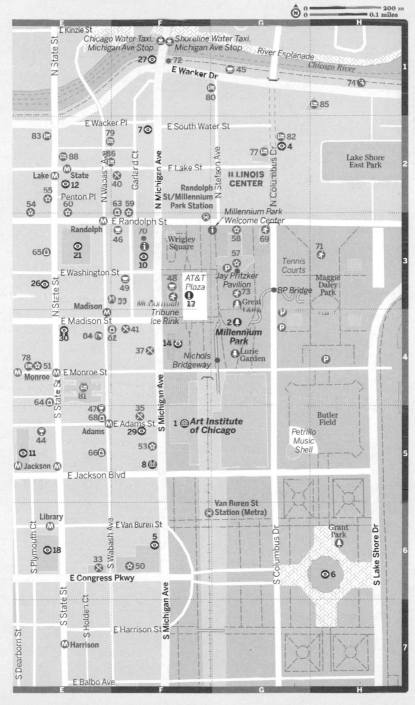

Key on p294

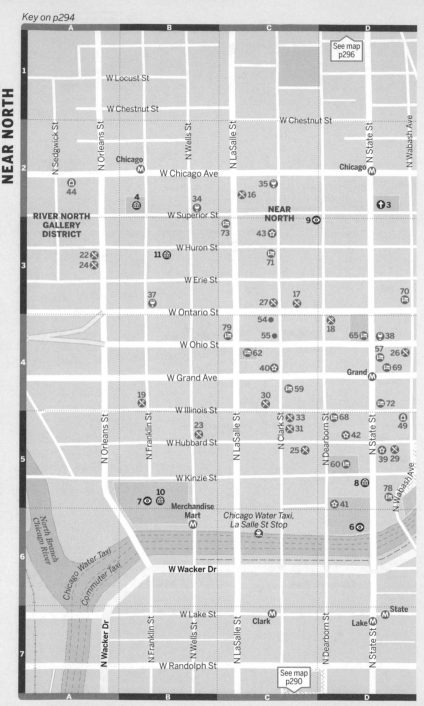

See map
p296

W Locust St

W Chestnut St

N Sedgwick St

N Orleans St

N Wells St

N LaSalle St

W Chestnut St

N State St

N Wabash Ave

Chicago

W Chicago Ave

Chicago

44

4

35

16

3

RIVER NORTH
GALLERY
DISTRICT

34

W Superior St

NEAR
NORTH

9

73

43

22

24

11

W Huron St

71

W Erie St

37

27

17

70

W Ontario St

79

54

18

55

65

38

W Ohio St

62

40

57

26

69

Grand

W Grand Ave

30

59

19

W Illinois St

72

N Orleans St

N Franklin St

23

W Hubbard St

N LaSalle St

N Clark St

33

31

68

N Dearborn St

42

N State St

49

25

39

29

W Kinzie St

60

8

78

N Wabash Ave

10

7

41

Merchandise
Mart

Chicago Water Taxi,
La Salle St Stop

6

North Branch
Chicago River

Chicago Water Taxi

Commuter Taxi

W Wacker Dr

N Wacker Dr

W Lake St

State

N Franklin St

N Wells St

N LaSalle St

Clark

Clark

N Dearborn St

Lake

N State St

W Wacker Dr

See map
p290

W Randolph St

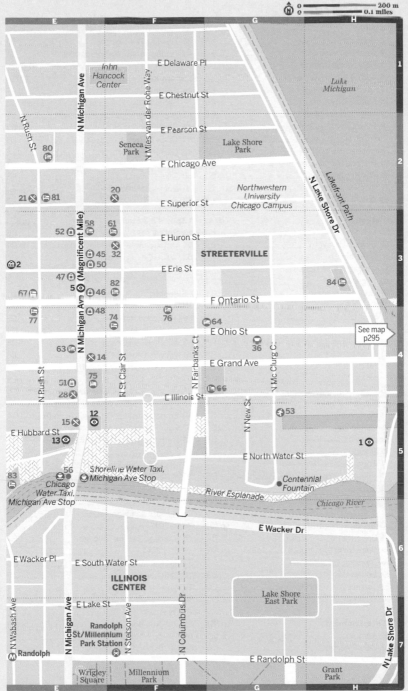

NEAR NORTH *Map on p292*

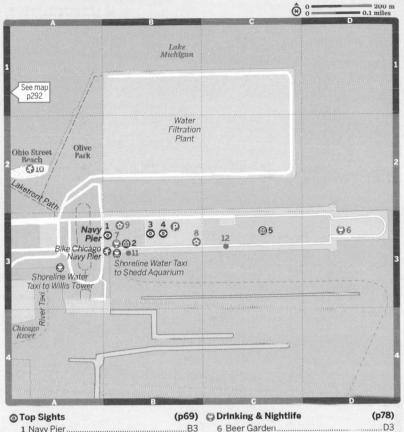

GOLD COAST

0 200 m
0 0.1 miles

See map p298

Lincoln Park

W North Ave E North Ave

W Burton Pl W Burton Pl

N North Park Ave
N Wieland St
N Wells St
N LaSalle St
N Clark St
N Dearborn St
N State Pkwy
N Astor St

W Schiller St E Schiller St

E Banks St

N Astor St

W Goethe St E Goethe St

N Lake Shore Dr
Lakefront Path

E Scott St

Clark/Division

W Division St E Division St

N Clark St
N Dearborn St

W Elm St E Elm St

Oak St Beach

E Cedar St

W Maple St E Bellevue Pl

E Oak St

W Oak St E Walton St

E Delaware Pl

Washington Square

John Hancock Center

W Chestnut St E Chestnut St

N Franklin St
N Wells St
N LaSalle St
N State St
N Rush St
N Wabash Ave
N Michigan Ave

Water Works Visitors Center

W Chestnut St

E Pearson St

W Institute Pl

Chicago

Chicago

W Chicago Ave E Chicago Ave

Water Works Pumping Station

Wateriders (1mi)

See map p292

3
7
6
4
9
22
41
25
18
21
40
29
39
37
16
42
32
12
27 14 19
8
28 13
46
10
17 20 45
48
15
26
38
47
1
36
30
35
5
31
24 23
34

GOLD COAST

Lake
Michigan

Lakefront Path

N Lake Shore Dr
E Lake Shore Dr

E Walton St
44
43
11
N Dewitt Pl
N Mies van der Rohe Way

**Museum of
Contemporary
Art**
2
Lake Shore
Park
Seneca
Park

Key on p300

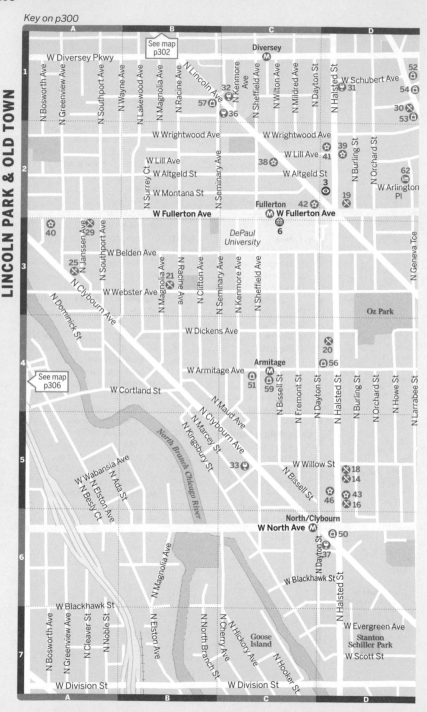

LINCOLN PARK & OLD TOWN

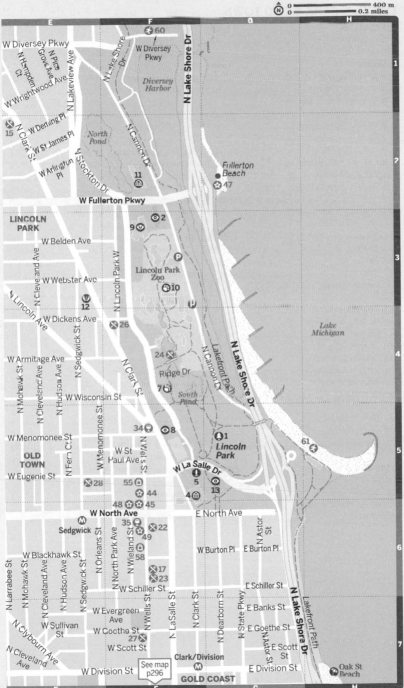

LINCOLN PARK & OLD TOWN *Map on p298*

LAKE VIEW & WRIGLEYVILLE *Map on p302*

LAKE VIEW & WRIGLEYVILLE

A **B** **C** **D**

Corn Productions (0.1mi);
Half Acre Tap Room (0.1mi);
Lincoln Square (0.4mi)

▲ Architectural
Artifacts (0.3mi)

1

W Belle Plaine Ave

W Belle Plaine Ave

22 🏠   39 ✪

W Irving Park Rd

Irving Park
Ⓜ

W Irving Park Rd

🍴 31

2

W Byron St

N Lincoln Ave

✪ 33
✪ 41

N Ravenswood Ave

W Byron St

W Grace St

W Grace St

✕ 13

N Hoyne Ave

N Damen Ave

N Hermitage Ave

N Paulina St

N Marshfield Ave

N Ashland Ave

N Southport Ave

🍴 43

3

W Waveland Ave

W Waveland Ave

Waveland
Bowl (0.3mi)
←

W Addison St

Addison
Ⓜ

W Addison St

🏠 56

4

W Cornelia Ave

W Cornelia Ave

14 ✕
W Roscoe St
✕ 15

N Lincoln Ave

Ⓜ **Paulina**

Southport
Ⓜ

W Roscoe St

W Henderson St

🍴 29

5

W School St

N Southport Ave

W School St

W Melrose St

W Melrose St

35 ✪

57 🏠

W Belmont Ave

W Belmont Ave

✪ 44

Hungry Brain (0.3mi);
Constellation (0.4mi)

51 🏠

W Fletcher St

N Ravenswood Ave

N Paulina St

N Ashland Ave

W Fletcher St

6

W Barry Ave

N Hoyne Ave

N Damen Ave

W Barry Ave

W Nelson St

W Wellington Ave

N Lincoln Ave

W Oakdale Ave

W George St

7

N Clybourn Ave

W Wolfram St

Diversey-River Bowl (0.1mi)
←
W Diversey Ave

A **B** **C** **D**

0 — 500 m
0 — 0.25 miles

Sydney R Marovitz Golf Course

Graceland Cemetery

Hebrew Cemetery

Wunders Cemetery

N Lake Shore Dr

N Recreation Dr

W Bittersweet Pl

W Irving Park Rd

N Clarendon St

N Broadway

N Kenmore Ave

N Clark St

N Lakewood Ave

W Dakin St

Sheridan Ⓜ

W Byron St

N Alta Vista Tce

W Sheridan Rd

Lincoln Park

W Grace St

N Belmont Harbor Dr

N Lake Shore Dr

Ⓢ61

WRIGLEYVILLE

21 Ⓢ
42

N Seminary Ave

N Sheffield Ave

N Fremont St

W Bradley Pl

49 Ⓢ

N Halsted St

W Waveland Ave

N Broadway

N Pine Grove Ave

65

Ⓢ26

47

W Brompton Ave

2 Ⓢ

60 Ⓢ

1
Ⓢ
Wrigley Field

28 Ⓢ

Addison Ⓜ

W Addison St

23 Ⓢ

59 Ⓢ

N Racine Ave

W Eddy St

52

38

69

53

W Cornelia Ave

24
50
67

N Elaine Pl

W Cornelia Ave

W Stratford Pl

W Hawthorne Pl

62

12 Ⓢ

W Newport Ave

10 Ⓢ Ⓢ5

W Roscoe St

27

W Roscoe St

58

11 Ⓢ

W Buckingham Pl

BOYSTOWN

19

W Aldine Ave

W Aldine Ave

16 Ⓢ

Ⓢ3

55

W Melrose St

48

66

18

45

25 30

9
32

W Belmont Ave

Belmont Ⓜ

34

40

36

63 37 46

W Briar Pl

LAKE VIEW

W Briar Pl

W Barry Ave

W Barry Ave

N Broadway

W Barry Ave

6

7

54

W Wellington Ave

8

17

Wellington Ⓜ Ⓢ4

20

W Oakdale Ave

W Surf St

68

64

N Clark St

N Sheffield Ave

N Mildred Ave

N Halsted St

N Kenmore Ave

N Seminary Ave

N Clifton Ave

N Racine Ave

N Lakewood Ave

Diversey Ⓜ

W Diversey Pkwy

See map p298

ANDERSONVILLE & UPTOWN

0 200 m
0 0.1 miles

W Bryn Mawr Ave

House 5683
(0.3mi)

Bryn Mawr

Rosehill
Cemetery
(0.2mi)

LAKEWOOD-
BALMORAL

Leonardo's Restaurant (0.1mi);
Leather Archives & Museum,
Devon Ave (1.5mi)

W Catalpa Ave

N Ashland Ave

N Clark St

N Glenwood Ave

N Wayne Ave

N Lakewood Ave

N Magnolia Ave

N Broadway

N Winthrop Ave

N Kenmore Ave

N Sheridan Rd

W Rascher Ave

W Balmoral Ave

W Summerdale Ave

Berwyn

W Berwyn Ave

W Farragut Ave

ANDERSONVILLE

W Foster Ave

W Foster Ave

W Winona St

W Winona St

W Carmen Ave

W Carmen Ave

N Glenwood Ave

W Winnemac Ave

W Winnemac Ave

W Carmen Ave

Argyle

W Argyle St

W Argyle St

W Ainslie St

St Boniface
Cemetery

W Ainslie St

N Ashland Ave

N Clark St

N Broadway

N Winthrop Ave

N Kenmore Ave

N Sheridan Rd

Lawrence

W Lawrence Ave

W Lawrence Ave

Chase
Park

UPTOWN

W Leland Ave

Lincoln Square (1mi)

N Racine Ave

N Sheridan Rd

W Wilson Ave

Wilson

W Wilson Ave

Wilson Skate
Park (0.4mi)

N Ashland Ave

N Clark St

N Dover St

N Beacon St

N Malden St

N Magnolia Ave

N Broadway

Kayak Chicago (0.8mi);
Montrose Beach (0.8mi)

W Montrose Ave

Hutchinson Street
District (0.4mi)

ANDERSONVILLE & UPTOWN

WICKER PARK, BUCKTOWN & UKRAINIAN VILLAGE

Key on p308

0   400 m
0   0.2 miles

Enlargement

See map
p298

North Branch Chicago River

WICKER
PARK

0   200 m
0   0.1 miles

N Honore St
N Wolcott Ave
W North Ave
N Elk Gve Ave
N Winchester Ave
N Milwaukee Ave
N Wicker Park Ave
Wicker
Park
N Damen Ave
Damen
W Pierce Ave
N Hoyne Ave
W Wabansia Ave

68
82
75
32
55
86
83
79
61
15
11
16
72
65
38
56
36
92
1
5
74
71
57
88
76

North/Clybourn

N Kingsbury St
W Blackhawk St

90
94
90

N Ada St
N Wabansia Ave
N Elston Ave
W North Ave
N Besly Ct

63

John F Kennedy Expwy

N Elston Ave
N Lister Ave
N Clybourn Ave
N Southport Ave
N Dominick St
N Ashland Ave

Clybourn
Station
(Metra)

94
90

66

N Marshfield Ave
N Paulina St
W Pierce Ave
N Hermitage Ave
N Wood St
W Cortland St
W Armitage Ave
W Dickens
Ave
W Webster Ave
W Shakespeare St
W Charleston St
W Dickens Ave
W McLean Ave
N Damen Ave
N Homer St
W Cortland St
W Moffat St
N Churchill St
Churchill
Field Park
W Willow St
W Wabansia Ave
N Wolcott Ave

42
89
78
43
50
84
41
22
85

BUCKTOWN

W North Ave
Damen

N Ashland Ave
W Le
Moyne St
W Beach Ave
W Le Moyne St
W Julian St
W Pierce Ave
W Blackhawk St

35
60
44
70

See Enlargement

Wicker
Park

N Wicker
Park Ave

5

See map
p298

W Leavitt St
N Leavitt St
N Caton St
W Concord Pl
W Pierce Ave
W Schiller St

N Western Ave
W Lyndale St
Holstein
Park
N Oakley Ave
Logan Square
(0.6mi)
N Wilmot Ave
N Milwaukee Ave
N Winnebago Ave
Western
N Milwaukee Ave
W Wabansia Ave
N Claremont Ave
N Oakley Ave
W Le Moyne St
N Bell Ave
W Hirsch St

20
26
28
14
23
87
61

See map
p310

N Western Ave

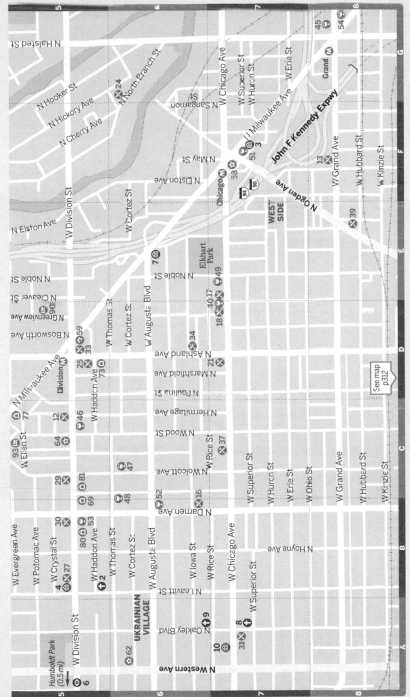

WICKER PARK, BUCKTOWN & UKRAINIAN VILLAGE

WICKER PARK, BUCKTOWN & UKRAINIAN VILLAGE

WICKER PARK, BUCKTOWN & UKRAINIAN VILLAGE Map on p306

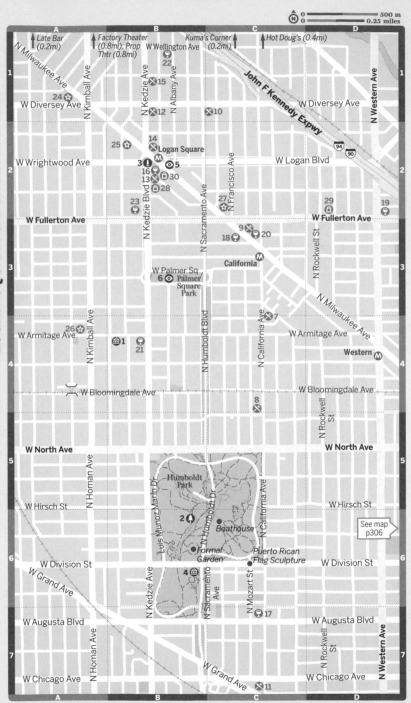

N 0 ——————— 500 m
0 ——————— 0.25 miles

Late Bar (0.2mi)
N Milwaukee Ave
N Kimball Ave
Factory Theater (0.8mi); Prop Thtr (0.8mi)
N Kedzie Ave
W Wellington Ave
N Albany Ave
Kuma's Corner (0.2mi)
Hot Doug's (0.4mi)
John F Kennedy Expwy
N Western Ave
W Diversey Ave
24
W Diversey Ave
W Diversey Ave
22
15
12
10
94
90
25
14
Logan Square
W Logan Blvd
N Francisco Ave
W Wrightwood Ave
3
5
16
30
13
28
27
29
19
W Fullerton Ave
23
W Fullerton Ave
9
18
20
N Rockwell St
California
N Sacramento Ave
W Palmer Sq
6
Palmer Square Park
7
N Humboldt Blvd
N Milwaukee Ave
W Armitage Ave
26
N Kimball Ave
W Armitage Ave
1
21
N California Ave
Western
W Bloomingdale Ave
W Bloomingdale Ave
8
N Rockwell St
W North Ave
W North Ave
N Homan Ave
Humboldt Park
N Humboldt Dr
W Hirsch St
Luis Munoz Martin Dr
2
N California Ave
W Hirsch St
Boathouse
See map p306
Puerto Rican Flag Sculpture
Formal Garden
W Division St
N Kedzie Ave
4
N Sacramento Ave
N Mozart St
W Division St
W Grand Ave
W Augusta Blvd
17
W Augusta Blvd
N Homan Ave
N Rockwell St
N Western Ave
W Chicago Ave
W Chicago Ave
W Grand Ave
11

LOGAN SQUARE & HUMBOLDT PARK

NEAR WEST SIDE & PILSEN

Key on p314

See map p306

See map p290

NEAR WEST SIDE & PILSEN

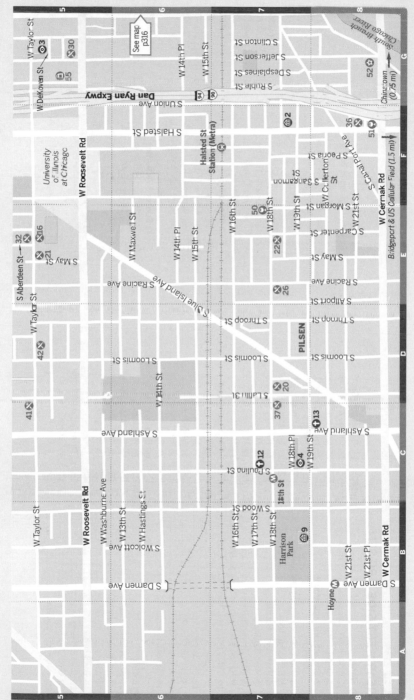

Map labels:

W Taylor St
W DeKoven St
See map p316
W 14th Pl
W 15th St
S Clinton St
S Jefferson St
S Desplaines St
S Ruble St
Dan Ryan Expwy
S Union Ave
Chinatown (0.75 mi)
South Branch Chicago River

University of Illinois at Chicago
W Roosevelt Rd
S Halsted St
Halsted St Station (Metra)
S Sangamon St
W Cullerton St
S Morgan St
S Peoria St
S Canalport Ave
W Cermak Rd
Bridgeport & US Cellular Field (1.5 mi)

S Aberdeen St
S May St
W Taylor St
W Maxwell St
W 14th Pl
W 15th St
S Racine Ave
S Blue Island Ave
W 16th St
W 18th St
W 19th St
S Carpenter St
S May St
S Racine Ave
S Allport St
W 21st St

W Taylor St
S Loomis St
S Throop St
PILSEN
S Loomis St
S Throop St

W 14th St
S Ashland Ave
S Loomis St
W 18th St
W 19th St
S Ashland Ave

W Taylor St
W Roosevelt Rd
W Washburne Ave
W 13th St
W Hastings St
S Wolcott Ave
S Paulina St
18th St
W 16th St
W 17th St
W Wood St
W 18th St

Harrison Park
Hoyne
S Damen Ave
W 21st St
W 21st Pl
W Cermak Rd

SOUTH LOOP & NEAR SOUTH SIDE Map on p316

SOUTH LOOP & NEAR SOUTH SIDE

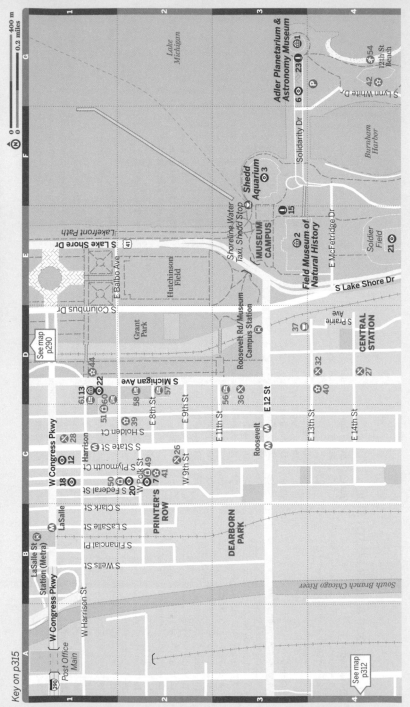

Key on p315

0 400 m
0 0.2 miles

Lake Michigan

Adler Planetarium & Astronomy Museum

12th St Beach

S Lynn White Dr

Burnham Harbor

Shedd Aquarium

Solidarity Dr

Lakefront Path

S Lake Shore Dr

Shoreline Water Taxi, Shedd Stop

MUSEUM CAMPUS

Field Museum of Natural History

E McFetridge Dr

S Lake Shore Dr

Soldier Field

Hutchinson Field

E Balbo Ave

S Columbus Dr

Grant Park

Roosevelt Rd/Museum Campus Station

S Prairie Ave

CENTRAL STATION

See map p290

S Michigan Ave

E 8th St

E 9th St

E 11th St

E 12 St

E 13th St

E 14th St

Roosevelt

S Holden Ct

S State St

W Congress Pkwy

W Harrison St

W Congress Pkwy

LaSalle St Station (Metra)

LaSalle

Post Office Main

S Plymouth Ct

S Federal St

W Polk St

W 9th St

PRINTER'S ROW

S Clark St

S LaSalle St

S Financial Pl

S Wells St

DEARBORN PARK

South Branch Chicago River

See map p312

LaSalle

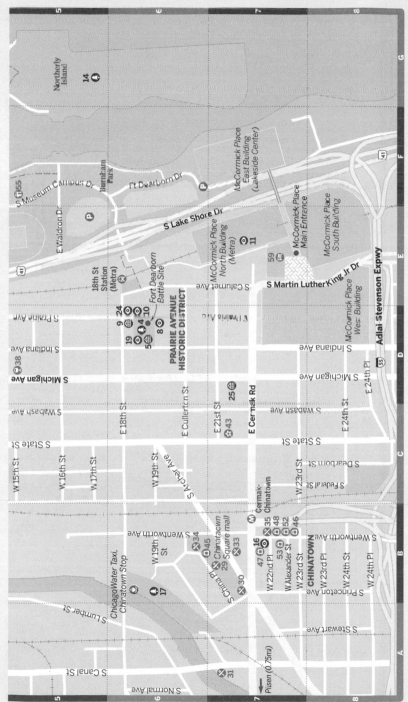

HYDE PARK & SOUTH SIDE

Scale:
0 — 400 m
0 — 0.2 miles

Grid columns: 1, 2, 3, 4

Grid rows: A, B, C, D, E, F, G

Lake Michigan

Promontory Point

Lakefront Path

S Lake Shore Dr

S Chicago Beach Dr

S Lake Shore Dr

S East End Ave

S Cornell Ave

S Lake Park Ave

S Lake Park Ave

53rd St Station (Metra)

E 53rd St

E 54th St

S Everett Ave

E 55th St

E 56th St

E 57th Dr

S Hyde Park Blvd

S Cornell Ave

S Stony Island Ave

S Cornell Ave

Museum of Science & Industry

S Harper Ave

S Harper Ave

S Blackstone Ave

S Blackstone Ave

S Dorchester Ave

S Dorchester Ave

55th-56th-57th St Station (Metra)

E 55th Pl

55th St

S Ridgewood Ct

S Kenwood Ave

S Kenwood Ave

HYDE PARK

E 49th St

E 50th St

E Hyde Park Blvd

E 52nd St

E 53rd St

E 54th St

S Kimbark Ave

S Woodlawn Ave

S Woodlawn Ave

S University Ave

S Greenwood Ave

S Greenwood Ave

S Ellis Ave

S Ellis Ave

S Ellis Ave

University of Chicago

S Woodlawn Ave

KENWOOD

S Drexel Blvd

S Cottage Gve Ave

S Cottage Grove Ave

Bronzeville (2mi)

E 50th Pl

E 51st St

E Drexel Sq

E 52nd St

E 53rd St

S Drexel Ave

S Ingleside Ave

E 55th St

E 56th St

E 57th St

S Maryland Ave

E 57th St

Payne Dr

Washington Park

S Champlain Ave

S St Lawrence Ave

Payne Dr

Our Story

A beat-up old car, a few dollars in the pocket and a sense of adventure. In 1972 that's all Tony and Maureen Wheeler needed for the trip of a lifetime – across Europe and Asia overland to Australia. It took several months, and at the end – broke but inspired – they sat at their kitchen table writing and stapling together their first travel guide, *Across Asia on the Cheap*. Within a week they'd sold 1500 copies. Lonely Planet was born.

Today, Lonely Planet has offices in Melbourne, London and Oakland, with more than 600 staff and writers. We share Tony's belief that 'a great guidebook should do three things: inform, educate and amuse'.

Our Writers

Karla Zimmerman

Coordinating Author Karla lives in Chicago, where she has been eating deep-dish pizza (Giordano's preferred) and cheering on the hopeless Cubs for 25 years. Like most Chicagoans, she's more than a little keen on her home town and will talk your ear off about its sky-high architecture, rockin' music scene, global neighborhoods and character-filled dive bars. Come wintertime, the words she uses get a bit more colorful, especially if she's just shoveled a lot of snow. Karla writes travel features for books, magazines and online outlets. She has authored or coauthored several Lonely Planet guidebooks covering the USA, Canada, the Caribbean and Europe. For more on the Windy City, see Karla's blog, www.mykindoftownandaround.blogspot.com, or follow @karlazimmerman on Twitter. Karla wrote the Plan Your Trip and Explore sections, and the Chicago Today, History, Transportation and Directory chapters.

Read more about Karla at:
lonelyplanet.com/members/karlazimmerman

Sara Benson

Born in Illinois, Sara grew up around the Windy City. She cycled beside Lake Michigan, begged her parents for money to make Mold-a-Rama models at the Museum of Science & Industry and eventually graduated from the University of Chicago. The author of 55 travel and nonfiction books, Sara toured skyscrapers in the Loop, chowed down on Midwestern charcuterie and listened to scores of Cubs games while researching and writing this guide. Follow her adventures online at www.indietraveler.blogspot.com and @indie_traveler on Twitter. Sara wrote the Architecture, Sports, Chicago Dining and Music & the Arts chapters.

Read more about Sara at:
lonelyplanet.com/members/sara_benson

Published by Lonely Planet Publications Pty Ltd
ABN 36 005 607 983
7th edition – Feb 2014
ISBN 978 1 74220 061 3
© Lonely Planet 2014   Photographs © as indicated 2014
10 9 8 7 6 5 4 3 2 1
Printed in China

E 58th St
E 59th St

S Kenwood Ave

Bond
Chapel

Robie
House

E 58th St
E 59th St

N Midway Plaisance
S Midway Plaisance

59th St
Station (Metra)

Jackson
Park

West
Lagoon

East
Lagoon

Columbia Dr

E Best Dr